Arnhem's Kaleidoscope Children

Memoir by

Graham Wilson

Book Cover designed by Nada Backovic

CONTENTS

Acknowledgements 5

Prologue...7

Introduction 11

Part 1 – Arnhem Land's Children 17

    Missionaries to the NT..17

    Oenpelli for the first time 24

    Transport – a truck and a road to Oenpelli 31

    To Darwin to live...44

    Return home to Oenpelli 60

    Away to school in Sydney 65

    Family Life at Oenpelli 78

    Teenage Adventures...94

    Living again at Oenpelli..101

    Flying and Building Outstations 108

    Buffalo and Abattoirs...125

    Oenpelli and its Aboriginal People 130

    Mining...140

Part 2 - Oenpelli and the NT as an Adult 155

    Living Far Away 155

    Crocodile..164

    Return to the NT 171

    NT Vets and Stock Inspectors 207

Part 3 – Coming to an End 217

Analysis - Seeking Understanding....................................235

Appendix 1 – NT and Oenpelli Background 243

Appendix 2 -Earliest record : Leichhardt's Journal........257

References 293

About the Author...294

ACKNOWLEDGEMENTS

I wish to thank many people who have contributed to this book.

First, thank you to those people who prompted me to write out my story telling of my distant and fading childhood memories.

It sits alongside my parents' story of coming to the remote Top End of the Northern Territory of Australia and living in a series of aboriginal communities soon after the Second World War. This was a time when there was massive development of northern Australia which changed it forever. It changed the lives of these places as a new world order of technology and modern communications came to exist, giving people undreamed of mobility and connection to the outside world.

But alongside all this change these long standing communities still continued with their own ways of living handed down over millennia.

In the mix of the old and new many painful conflicts and transitions have played out over decades and successive generations. These are the conflicts inherent when two different worlds and their systems collide and struggle to coincide

I also wish to thank the many people who have contributed to this story through lives lived in these places, particularly my extended family and the friends from these places; missionaries who worked at Oenpelli, people who worked for the Northern Territory Department of Primary Industry, many station people and people from the small towns and communities from across the NT and, most especially, the aboriginal peoples of western Arnhem Land.

Collectively you have given me the rich experiences which make this story live in my mind, and give the myriad colours to the telling.

A vital contributor to this revised edition has been Nada Backovic, the book cover designer. She took old and damaged photos taken by my father many decades ago of this place and its people, transforming these into a cover which, to me, wonderfully captures the light, colour and essence of this time and place.

THANK YOU NADA!!

PROLOGUE

Yesterday I drove to Oenpelli, my home, an aboriginal town in Arnhem Land.

It was two days after my father was buried next to my mother in Darwin.

A memorial service was held, recounting his pioneering exploits. The most beautiful part was a gathering of aboriginal women standing in a semicircle around his grave. They sang a hymn in their Kunwinjku language. It was a hauntingly lyrical melody, an expression of their private affection. Then people threw handfuls of dirt into the grave.

Other people at Oenpelli could not make the 150 mile journey to be there at the grave, but wanted to say their sorry's too. So I went and walked around the town, amongst these people, enveloped in a steamy wet season build up day. Many, who knew him, came up and murmured regrets at my Dad's passing.

Later I walked out across the town's fringing floodplains, where the first water of the wet season was spilling from the end of the billabong; just myself and a hundred squawking waterbirds feasting on natures first wet season flush.

The afternoon sky turned purple, then olive-black, above the sunlit sandstone hills, as a storm built. Flashes and rumbles increased. I walked back to Oenpelli as the sweep of rain blotted out my view of the hills. A blast of cold air at the storm's leading edge swept me with its fresh rain smell. At the church, on the edge of the plains, I took shelter. The storm lashed out its brief fury, then was gone. Rising steam and a few puddles were all that remained. I was filled with an aching familiarity for a life long gone.

I said farewell to Oenpelli: time to begin my return to Sydney. Impulse led me to drive back to Darwin another way, following the old Jim Jim Road, an early road to Oenpelli. I would camp out on the plains of the mighty South Alligator River. Here, in my childhood, buffalo by thousands and more, were seen.

Another bigger storm was brewing. I crossed the South Alligator River, driving through only a few inches of water and thought, *The big river is behind me, the road is clear ahead to Darwin.*

Soon tropical sheets of rain began to fall. I pulled onto a gravel ridge on the side of the road to sit the storm out. After half an hour, it eased to a drizzle, which continued into the night. I slept in the car, thinking morning would be a better time to travel.

Grey dawn light showed wisps of high cloud, but the rain was gone. I drove on, cautiously at first, but the gullies were dry except one or two with a trickle of water. My mind was on the events of the last few days, but all seemed well.

I swept around a bend. There was a gully with water flowing through it, *about a foot deep*, I thought. In the split second before I was into it, I had the chance to brake to a stop. But my instant decision was; *it's fine, keep going.*

Suddenly one foot of water was three. Before I knew it the current picked up the light four-wheel-drive up. I was floating in the creek, with no engine and water bubbling inside. As the car drifted downstream, away from the road, the water outside was deeper, coming up over the dash.

I thought; *Time to get out of here!* But with no engine and no electricity, the windows and doors were securely locked. I crawled into the back and tried to unlock the tail gate. No luck there either. Here I was, in a glass encased bubble, slowly flowing down an ever-increasing river towards the sea, while the car slowly settled ever deeper into the water.

After a short long time the car seemed to catch something on the bottom and movement stopped. My bubble still held me trapped. It really was time to get out, while my head was above the water. Two or three kicks at the window made no impression on the hardened glass. *Not good*, I thought.

I looked up. There was a skylight above. I couldn't open it either so it was time to kick in earnest, two hard kicks and suddenly the glass shattered.

I retrieved what I could find of my possessions, floating in the cabin, and scrambled to shore, no worse for wear, except for a few glass cuts to my feet. Two hours of trudging up the dirt road found a road train. I got a lift to Darwin. Then came the unpleasantness of dealing with destroying a rental car, expensive and embarrassing, when you have to explain your stupidity.

It was a lesson in two parts, how quickly security can turn to tragedy and that I should never have underestimated the fickle power of the Northern Territory. The rain, a moderate tropical storm where I was, had barely run water. Far upstream 84 millimetres came from this storm, focused in one narrow river channel. I tasted its power in my moment of inattention. I don't know why my hands and voice were shaking that afternoon, I was in one piece. Cars can be replaced, people can't.

Back to the first beginning: it's over six years since the fateful phone call that began the writing of this story.

My sister in New Zealand rings occasionally, at night or the weekend. So a phone call in mid-afternoon is unusual; "Have you heard what happened to Mum?"

"No!" (I think did she win a prize or something?).

"There's been a car accident and she's been killed". ... Silence!

All the urgent, routine arrangements take place; book a flight to Darwin, deal with a lot of other shocked family and friends, make funeral arrangements; it's a bit of a blur now.

The morning of the funeral I have a memory of standing and looking at Mum's face; still, peaceful, lined with seventy five years of living.

Listening to an Irish song, one line brings that image back to my mind.

'her face is a well worn page, and time all alone is the pen'

It captures a bit of my mother's passing and the rich life she lived, reflected in her final face; kind, dignified and written with its own history.

This book is my attempt to share this history and leave a record of the life of her and my father, a richness in which our whole family was part. It was a family where all five of us children grew up in this place largely forgotten by time.

As a child it did not occur to me that my parents were different from an average suburban Mum and Dad. I accepted as normal living in Arnhem Land; where the aeroplane came now and then, or sometimes a boat came up the river. Most of my playmates were black; for four or five months of each year it was a world cut off by water and, at opposite times, it was a world of smoke, fire and bulldust, punctuated by intense black thunderheads and lightning.

My earliest childhood memories, from when I was two years old, sit in that blur between babyhood and remembering.

The first is an Oenpelli visitor taking me to the back paddock behind our house, to see a new calf; walking through tall brown grass, above my head, a clear blue sky above, expecting to see a soft baby animal of the story books, small and cuddly. Instead this giant creature, taller than I, on wobbly legs, with brown and white patches on half wet skin. It jumped and frightened me when I went to touch it and we both ran opposite ways.

The next memory is crossing the river (East Alligator) with my father; sliding down a silty river bank to a huge brown-yellow channel, with green overhanging trees; being lifted into a dugout canoe, rough-carved, sculpted from one huge tree. In the bottom was grey mud, dried grass and pool of muddy water; me, looking out over sides as high as myself to the huge muddy river swirling beyond. My father with an aboriginal man of black shiny skin, push off. The current takes us and they slowly paddle across the running tide towards the green distant bank. My memory fades; no crocodiles though certainly they were there, no birds though probably screeching overhead, nothing but wonder and bright colours seen through childhood eyes.

Partial memories drift across the next two years; on a trailer behind a tractor with my mother, sisters and a tribe of aboriginal ladies and children. Past red-yellow sandstone hills, towards a billabong, gritty bulldust in our eyes and mouths. We bounce across washouts, dodge branches, pandanus prickles whip past us. We live in a tin house with ant-bed floors. Sometimes snakes and rats come in. There is a black lady my mother calls the house-girl.

My final memory is of flying to Darwin just before my fourth birthday. It is in a small plane. I look out the window and see black dots of buffalo and brown dots of ant-beds go by, interspersed amongst a mosaic of trees and floodplains. This was the end of the first great adventure of my life, as an Oenpelli child. It remains forever burnt into my mind, a child amongst children, amidst the myriad colours of Arnhem Land.

As an adult reflecting back I realise, not only was I a child of Arnhem Land, but so too were my parents; coming to this unknown land, full of strange places and unfamiliar people which they discovered for the first time. While knowing Sydney society and its ways, and with much practical common sense, they knew little of the land to which they came. This is also their story of discovery.

***

It is now ten years since I first started writing this book and over five years since the first edition was published. I am older, the age my father was when he left Oenpelli. No longer can I do all the things I tell of in this story.

I have a wonderful home in Sydney, my wife and children give me great joy, and every time I gaze out the window I marvel at the beauty of Sydney Harbour.

But a part of me will always remain in that place of bright memories, the place of a magical childhood amongst the colours and people of Arnhem Land.

INTRODUCTION

What is it about the Northern Territory that fascinates? If I mention its name in conversation people turn to listen. Why, for over 180 years, has it drawn people from all over to come, stay longer than they imagined and often never leave?

"Here I give you a history galloping wild for a century over half a million square miles, the life story of a colony in quicksand…. A nameless land, a land without flag, a vague earth bordered by the meridians of God….

Black men wandering and white men riding in a world without time where sons do not inherit, and money goes mouldy in the pocket, where ambition is wax melted in the sun, and those who sow may not reap.

I write of the Northern Territory of Australia … land of an ever-shadowed past and an ever-shining future, of eternal promise that never comes true…

From tropic seas a thousand mile south to salt lakes, between desert and desert five hundred and sixty miles wide, here is the strangest country of white men in the world, where they rode for a lifetime without a home, without a wife, safe from yesterday and tomorrow….

Here is a passionate and prolific earth never tamed and trimmed…. A sixth of Australia…. a State, and one of the greatest in its own geographical right - 523,620 square miles from under Capricorn to the Timor Sea ….

Nameless, it is still a Northern Territory, as once it was of South Australia, though it has been separated from South Australia for 40 years. Never yet has it been fully surveyed or explored. You can draw a map of England to scale in the map of the Territory without a single name in it, not even a native well….

The bad and beautiful Territory is not the youngest of the Australian family, as many believe, but third eldest. It was founded in 1824, following New South Wales and Tasmania…

Someone is always discovering the Territory, its colour and beauty, infinite resources, boundless wealth, 'forever piping songs forever new'.

What is the truth of this changeling child of ours?…

"Rich to rottenness!" cried Boyle Travers Finniss, first Administrator, in 1864, yet few save the cattle-men, remote in so many thousands of miles of wilderness, have wrested from it even a poor living. Its goldmines and its gardens are all graveyards. Until twenty years ago it was so far away from the rest of Australia that it was a land of legend – two thousand miles of desert tracks, two thousand miles by sea. Only a pilgrim could reach it….

The bagmen of today, the "old death adders Major Mitchelling around",
they were the young men of yesterday, with all the energy and dreams of youth.
Forgotten men, they failed but they believe. So hope withers away and springs
eternal in a pattern of nature too vast for human vision, a power too insensitive
to human hands."

Ernestine Hill put down these lines in the first chapter of her famous book
'*The Territory*' published in 1951. That year my parents came to Arnhem Land.

Is the Territory still the place of Ernestine Hill's imagination? Was it ever so?
Truth is rarely simple and trying to understand the multilayered dimensions of
the Territory is its own challenge: - a timeless land, wet and dry, a black and
white land, a land of opportunity and development, gateway to Asia, natural
wilderness, cattle and buffalo ranging over endless grass plains and
impenetrable scrub, land of deserts, waterfalls and sparkling ocean sunsets. It is
a place both of the exotic and quixotic!

Much has changed in the Territory over the last seven decades, since the
end of the Second World War, mostly wrought by human hands. And for
millennia before other hands too were using and slowly making their changes to
this land. Yet, as it changes, the essential essence of the Territory, '*a pattern of*
nature too vast for human vision', stays the same.

In coming to a limited understanding of my parents' lives, and the
contribution they made to these changes, I have come to realise that they came
as children to a land in which other, black hands had greater mastery, and in
which all human efforts were little more than fleabites on the vastness. As Paul
Hogan remarks in Crocodile Dundee; arguing about who owns the land is a bit
like two fleas arguing over who owns the dog.

The Northern Territory is one of the last frontiers of Australia. To this day it
is not an easy place for those from kinder climates to live. Early explorers found
it hard, as attested by the history of European settlement; more a tale of failure
than success. However many who persevered came to love it and never leave.

For Europeans the NT Top End is characterised by two seasons, wet and dry.
The wet has drenching humidity, tropical storms and mountains of water, while
the dry is the place to escape southern winter, with cool nights, bush fires, and
ever increasing aridity as everything slowly desiccates in the relentless NT sun.

Aboriginals and other long term inhabitants recognise a greater subtlety in
the seasons, the build up with towering thunderstorms, the continuous rain of

the monsoons, the final showers flattening the drying grass in March, the early dry season as humidity falls and drenched country leaks its moisture, the mid dry season of cold nights and bushfires, and the final dry blast of baked countryside, stagnant shrinking pools of water, and rising humidity, finally broken by the blessed relief of first storms.

Geography makes it a difficult place to traverse. The western wall of the Arnhem Land escarpment is an almost continuous, impenetrable barrier. It begins near Oenpelli, then runs 200 kilometres south to behind Pine Creek before curving around into Katherine Gorge and heading east. East of Oenpelli these towering sandstone ramparts continue for a couple hundred kilometres until they subside into the sandy plains and low hills of eastern Arnhem Land. Emerging from this massif are major rivers with gorges carving down through the sandstone, the Liverpool, East and South Alligator Rivers running north, the Katherine River running south then west, becoming the Daly River, the Roper River running south then east to the Gulf and the Victoria River, cutting through other rugged country west of Katherine. These rivers each discharge incredible volumes of water, flooding vast areas as monsoonal depressions and cyclones dump hundreds of millimetres of rain. Large areas become inaccessible for months, roads wash out and aquatic life on floodplains flourish.

As the country cools and dries each year, after the annual wet season ends, a period of concentrated frenetic work and travel begins about April-May to get everything done before the next rains come in November-December.

Since our family first came in the 1950s; roads have been built, rivers tamed with bridges, the population has consumer comforts. But nature remains untamed. Mighty waterfalls still crash off the escarpment after a monsoon month and show that the raw power of this world remains almost untouched.

As a child of Arnhem Land some of my strongest memories are about the capacity of the land for change and regeneration. The parched black soil plains of October, with little muddy remnants of waterholes, dust eddies and dying fish became, in January, an inland sea of water so vast that its edges were lost in a distant low horizon. In March it was a sea of waist high green grass and reeds, with the endless honking of nesting magpie geese. As the dry season broke billabongs covered in red lilies emerged, along with fruiting plants of the woodlands. Aboriginal families with digging sticks moved back onto the plains to catch buried turtles and file snakes. So the seasons continued, the people endlessly following their cues.

This is a story about the Top End of the Northern Territory and of one special place in it. To me it was called Oenpelli, now it is named Gunbalanya to approximate its aboriginal name. Oenpelli is a small town on the western edge of Arnhem Land near Kakadu National Park. Visitors remark on its natural beauty. Many hold an enduring memory of this scenery decades later.

Oenpelli is on the eastern margin of a pocket of the East Alligator floodplains. The town is about fifteen kilometres from the main river channel and five kilometres north of the sandstone escarpment of the Arnhem Land plateau. It sits on a low gravel ridge with a large billabong immediately to its south. Floodplains encircle the town on three sides, giving expansive views with abundant bird and animal life. It sits at the centre of semicircle of three hills, Arrkuluk, Injalak and Nimbabirr, each about 200 metres high and a kilometre away, arranged like wheel spokes at right angles from the town centre.

The dominant view is the towering cliffs of the Arnhem Land escarpment, seen across the billabong, rising sheer from the floodplains and woodlands to 1000 foot heights, and forming a ring around the southern side of the town. Afternoon sun reflects its myriad colours; red, brown, gold and orange hues; as the late light bounces back from these hills and forms a glowing wall.

In the wet season this is overlaid with towering black and purple storms. They form above these cliffs, then sweep across the iridescent green plains in a wall of rain, obscuring sight of the hills behind. In the centre of this escarpment sits the local waterfall, falling 100 metres. Its creek joins two other escarpment creeks to flow into the billabong before flooding out across the floodplains. In monsoon season these floodplains form a sea of water reaching towards the horizon, an expanse of thirty kilometres across before the next high ground rises on the western side of the East Alligator River.

This is also a story about aboriginal society's adaptation to and co-existence with western civilisation in the second half of the 20th century. Living within this time and place gave me insights into this process, often painful, with difficulties on both sides. However, as an ongoing, albeit occasional, visitor to this place, I never cease to be amazed by the warmth and generosity of its people. They first welcomed our family to their land more than 60 years ago and continue to welcome us as the years go by. In 2002, a few months after Mum died, I took my children to visit. My fondest memories are walking down the main streets of Oenpelli with my three children then aged 7-12. Many aboriginal people welcomed us with their broad smiles, and happy calls, using the skin name I had been given almost 50 years earlier, along with my new slang name, 'Ngaginga' (crocodile leg), and now assigning to each child their own new skin name. Some came to share their sorrow about Mum, others to welcome and greet my children, shaking hands, touching faces and saying a few words about some event of many years ago. Their generosity of spirit sits warmly with me to today.

As well as a story of two cultures Aboriginal and European existing alongside each other and dealing with each other in various ways, it is a story about the Christian values of my parents which motivated their life and the ways in which they communicated these.

It is also a story of our family coming to know and love this beautiful, sometimes hostile place, which still feels like home.

It was to this Arnhem Land that my parents came; just moving beyond the war, with missionary society aspirations for a new aboriginal role in their own communities' management but with few resources and little wider support. Their story is one of living inside this change over the next 50 years.

The story from here is in two parallel parts, the first is my parents' story, which is mainly described by my father but with some information from others.

The second part is my memories, growing up then living as an adult in the Northern Territory. I have called this Graham's Story and it runs alongside with detail increasing as I move from childhood to adult life. For those who want to know more about Oenpelli and NT history I have put a more complete account in Appendix 1. In Appendix 2 I have included supplementary information about Leichhardt's first European exploration of this land, based on extracts of his journal where, each day, he recorded a wealth of detail about his trip and the people, places and hardships he encountered.

My parents' story begins with them, as a newly married couple, coming to two small aboriginal missions in the Gulf of Carpentaria.

They went first at Groote Island and then Rose River. In 1953 they moved to Oenpelli, which is where my own memories begin.

They were Sydney children of the Depression and War, though my mother grew up in country NSW. It seems these times and families created resilient children with a can do attitude. Even though my father's first job at Oenpelli was to work in the garden, he soon took initiative. He saw a need for a road to transport stores. He bought a truck, found a road route and began the delivery of mission stores from Darwin.

Soon his role was to get a new central base for all the far flung missions in Darwin. This he did, land and buildings followed. As is often the case, opportunity favours the brave, he knew of heavy rock (manganese) from work at Groote Island. So he and another missionary acquired a miner's right to the prospective site. When he heard BHP was to mine there, he told them he held this right. It was passed to the missionary society for use on behalf of this community. A first aboriginal mining royalty agreement followed, a minor piece of history in his eyes, it was a model for other mines with far reaching effects.

Life continued on this pattern. At Oenpelli, when uranium was found, he sat behind aboriginal leaders in negotiations with the government and the Mine. What ultimately flowed was the formation of Kakadu National Park.

Seeing a need for air transport, he got a pilot's license then his own plane. He saw a desire of aboriginal clans to return to their own country and used this aeroplane to support and supply new outstations; the list goes on. And, wherever my father went, there was my mother, standing alongside him too.

The love of my parents for this NT place was passed on to me. Before long, as an adult, it drew me back too. For me the NT canvas was wider, I came when there was work was to be done on cattle stations across the length and breadth of the NT, from the deserts of the Alice to the vast grass plains of the Barkly Tableland and VRD, and on into the rough and broken lands of the Gulf and the buffalo country of the Top End. It was a fascinating time, a wonderful way to see it all and get to know its many peoples and places.

For us, children of these parents, 'can't do' was not in the lexicon, the question was how? We each tried to make our own contributions, driven by this example, if not on such a grand scale. But each of us carries a piece of this legacy forward. We hope it is passed on to our own children. It seems to me that doing something with whatever we are given is what life is mainly about.

PART 1 – ARNHEM LAND'S CHILDREN

Mum and Dad's Story

Missionaries to the NT

Mum's early life

How to tell my mother's story? When I started this account, I thought it would be as simple as taking excerpts from letters she wrote. However, as I read a selection I realised the letters describe many things that happened around her but tell almost nothing of her. Her experiences are conspicuously absent. The letters tell about other people, who went where or said what, but not what she thought and felt. Self-description was not her nature. So I have used other sources to construct a sense of my Mum's life; her younger sister Edith, her brother, Peter, memories from us children, and other people who knew her.

Mum was born Helen Trindall Smith, in July 1926, the oldest of three children to Peter (PA) Smith (Grandfather), and Ida Trindall (Ma). PA was the Presbyterian Minister in Warialda, a small country town in North Western NSW He was frequently on the road covering his large parish, first using a horse and buggy then a Model T Ford. Ma was a country nurse, married in her 30s with a career as a hospital matron before then. The eldest daughter of a Wee Waw grazier, with a property on the Namoi River, she took a large role in caring for seven younger brothers and sisters. As the Minsters wife she cared for her family, provided hospitality to the Parish and during the Depression fed many hungry men of the road coming to her door.

Sunday services were spread across the large parish requiring many trips where Grandfather would leave Friday morning and not return until late Sunday afternoon. In school holidays one of the children would be taken as gate opener, and receive dissertations on the way about the landforms; basalt country, granite country, what grew where, the weather, explaining things like that you would get general rain when the clouds built up in the north-west and the wind was from the west.

The children slept on the house verandah, open apart from a trellis around one corner. For a warm bed in winter they had a house brick, heated in the fire and wrapped in the Sydney Morning Herald. Ma made their clothes, except for winter things which Grandfather bought in Sydney.

When Helen was twelve she went to school in Sydney, living with two maiden aunts. Edith followed the next year. Church, even in summer, required wearing gloves, a hat, an edge to edge coat, and walking the three kilometres each way. After school was embroidery or knitting, then homework after tea.

One day the two girls found their Aunt Agnes lying in the garden, dead from a stroke. After this they went to school in Inverell, a town near Warialda, for a year and then for Helen's final year the two girls went to Presbyterian Ladies College in Croydon, Sydney.

After leaving school Mum got a job at Gillespie's Flour Mill in Pyrmont. Here she met Dad's sister Jude and her friend Amy, sister of Jude's future husband, George. The three girls got on really well. Jude remembers Mum's bubbly happiness and quoting poetry such as:

A mother was bathing her boiby one night,
the youngest of ten and a delicate white
The mother was fat and the boiby was thin,
it was nought but a skeleton covered in skin
The mother turned round for the soap of the rack,
she was only a moment but when she turned back
...... and in anguish she cried,
Oh where has my child gone and the angels replied
You're boiby has gone done the plug hole,
Your boiby has gone done the plug
The poor little thing was so skinny and thin,
It should have been washed in a jug,
IN A JUG.

One day Jude went to visit her brother Alf in hospital, and Mum went along. So she met Dad, and began the five decades of their life together.

Mum's Character from her Upbringing

Mum grew up in a family that was both moral and free thinking, and which got on with things with a minimum of fuss. Her father was a Presbyterian Minister in a conservative rural society but was also someone who rubbed shoulders with people from all walks of life on a frequent basis. He had a high regard for learning, and a strong interest in the world around. He could survive with a minimum of life's necessities, spending days on the road in the mud and dust of western NSW, but appreciated the comforts of station hospitality. He learned to be frugal living on a meagre stipend but his lifestyle was also helped by the generosity of the community with gifts like a car given to him and his new wife by a parishioner friend on his marriage.

Her mother was of a similar culture to her father but more practical. Ma was the one who milked the cows, rode the horses, treated injuries of her family and others and fed innumerable visitors. She supported her husband's moral values in a genteel manner. She had a similar level of education; boarding school in Newcastle, then nursing training in Sydney, before becoming Matron in a remote country hospital. When she and Grandfather married, both had lived lives as adults on their own for more than a decade, going about their business without fuss. It is no surprise these attitudes were seen in Mum's character; mixed parts of stoicism, practicality, gentility and interest in the wider world.

Dad's Early Life

My father's name was Alfred Forbes Wilson. He was a child of the Depression and grew up being adaptable and managing with little. He wrote his memoir about 18 months before he died in 2007, and I have used extracts to tell his story. I have made some word changes to make the story easier to read.

My father recalls his early life:
I was born on 6th May 1926 at Henderson a town out of Auckland in New Zealand. My sister was two years older. We lived with our mother and father on a five acre rural block in a rural fruit growing area called Oratea. With the onset of the Depression my father lost his job with the Colonial Sugar Refinery in Auckland. Eventually he decided to sell up everything and travel to Sydney where he was told he would find employment at CSR.

In 1935 my parents rented a house in Canterbury, Sydney, and my father got a job but the wages made it very difficult to pay rent and buy food. In 1937 I got a job selling papers at the tram terminus at Canterbury Station. I was not supposed to have this job until I turned 12, but I went ahead with it. Each week I earned twelve and a half shillings, which gave me between nine and eleven shillings to take home. My parents put this into my bank account and said I could buy school clothes from the tips I earned.

I was always looking for extra work and got a small amount answering the telephone at the taxi rank next to the station. There was only one taxi and the phone had an amplifier, so I could hear it on the other side of Canterbury Road. My job was to write the address of where the taxi was wanted on a pad. One evening the phone was ringing and a lot of traffic was on the road. I ran across the road and answered the phone then raced back to the paper stand. There was a screech of brakes as I went straight in front of a car.

19

A lot of people looked in horror at what happened. People gathered around me saying they did not see how I could walk away. One elderly man said. "There's only one reason. God has something for you to do!" It did not mean a lot to me.

I finished high school in 1943, joined the Air Force in 1944 and was discharged in April 1946. I enrolled to do Engineering at Sydney University. It was hopeless. I had missed 2 months of lectures and had been leading an idle life for two years. The following year I enrolled at Sydney Tech in Ultimo to do Engineering and persevered until the middle of 1948.

In September 1947 I met a local man, Ted Buckle, who had been in the Air Force. He was at Moore Theological College in Newtown and we often travelled to Engadine on the same train. Ted tried to interest me in joining with a group of young people going to a weekend camp. At first I wasn't interested but then I thought it would be worth going. So I went – and it was there I was converted. My whole life changed. I remember the minister of the Sutherland Church of England saying to me "Your whole face lit up". I remember that later night going into a sort of trance and dreaming I was moving above the ground over large areas of plains with water and grass and in the distance rocky hills and timbered country. It was a very vivid dream and remained with me. Even today I still remember it.

At this stage I had a girl-friend, Helen Smith, who was living with an aunt at Penshurst. I told her what had happened. Helen's father was a Presbyterian Minister and lived at Warialda. At Christmas 1947 Helen invited me to go to her home for two weeks and meet her parents, and we became engaged.

The following year, I became aware that God was calling me to do some special work and spoke to Ted Buckle about it. He offered to find out what work was available with the Church Missionary Society. A few days later he caught up with a Mr Montgomerie, whom he knew, and was greeted with, "Ha! Mr Buckle, have you a young man who can do pioneering work in North Australia" Ted replied that he did know a person who was interested in missionary work. "Send him in." was the reply.

So I went in to see Mr Montgomerie and made application to missionary work in North Australia. Helen also had to make an application. She stated that she did not wish to go to North Australia as a missionary but as a missionary's wife. She also made an application at Crown Street Women's Hospital to do an 18 month course in obstetrics from July 1949.

In 1949 I was told that I would have to spend three years at Moore College from 1950. This seemed an exceptionally long time. We could not get married over this time without permission, although we had been engaged for 18 months. Helen and I very much wanted to get married so, in the third term, I wrote to CMS seeking permission. During September I was told we could marry at the end of the year on the condition that we proceeded to North Australia in the New Year. I made a beeline to tell Helen. We were married on 5th January 1951, and were assigned to work amongst the people of Angurugu, Groote Eylandt.

Missionaries to Groote Eylandt

On the 21st February, 1951, we left Sydney flying to Adelaide. It was a big adventure and in Adelaide we were booked into a hotel. Two days later we flew to the Northern Territory on a DC3. At lunch break at Alice Springs the hostess had a palm branch, waving it around to chase the flies away. We arrived at Katherine late in the afternoon. Our accommodation was in the only hotel; we occupied a small shed at the rear. Next morning we assembled at the airstrip and met George the pilot. There was a fog and George commented this was a sign that the wet weather had finished.

We arrived at Roper River Mission about midday. We were to travel on to Groote Eylandt by boat and set out about 4 pm anchoring at the river mouth about midnight. With a spotlight, we saw a number of large crocodiles. I heard stories about how rough seas could be in the Gulf of Carpentaria, but next morning was dead calm. Joe Wurramurra, the skipper, took us by Low Rock, where we could see large fish in the rock pools.

At Groote we met two people who were a great help to me over the years. The first was Gerry Blitner who knew the aboriginal people at Groote very well. The other was Dick Harris, who had been in the North since 1929 and was deeply respected by both the staff and people. He spoke to me about the need to work with smaller groups of people. At Angurugu there were over 400 people and he pointed out the need for another centre to reduce that number. He took me to Emerald River, ten miles south, where he thought the remains of the Air Force wartime camp and parts of an old mission were a logical starting point for the new community. It had an abundance of fresh water, jungle type vegetation and remnants of an old banana plantation.

My first job was winding up miles of fencing wire used during the war as a telephone line from the Emerald RAAF base to the Flying Boat base at the other end of the island. Gerry organised this and I had a good team of men. Other work was to bring cypress logs to the sawmill. Men cut the logs with axes for carting and loaded the truck, a 1938, Maple leaf, three tonner. It had a twisted chassis which caused it to travel like a giant crab. The fuel pump didn't work so a petrol tank sat on the cab roof to gravity feed petrol to the engine. Once I backed into the jungle to collect a load of very heavy rocks. It was difficult to see the way through the overhanging branches. When I pulled up a man was carrying the fuel tank along the road, swept off the roof by a branch. This rock was for the causeway on the Angurugu River. We later found out the rock was manganese and it was a very valuable mineral.

Supplies were delivered by the "Cora" from Thursday Island twice a year. The ship would anchor off the reef and a bomb scow took the loading to shore. In 1952 the shipping service increased to three trips a year but our Sydney office requested we not use the extra service as there were insufficient funds.

There were frequent tribal fights. The men were not supposed to have fighting spears, known as shovel spears, in camp. They could have fishing spears, with wooden or wire tips fastened to the spear shaft. Towards the end of 1951 there was a tribal fight out bush. Word came that afternoon that two people had been speared. Gerry drove the Blitz to the scene. One woman had been speared in the chest. The spear penetrated below her throat and came out near her left breast. A man had a wooden pointed spear in his back near his kidneys. Both spear shafts were cut off for ease of transport on the back of the truck.

We had a doctor on the mission at that time. On examining both patients he decided that the man should be flown to Darwin next morning – a flight of 4 ½ hours in the Dragon Rapide. He attended to the woman at the mission about 8 o'clock in the evening. A large sheet was spread over the table and 4 of us, Tilley lamps on our heads, stood around the table to supply light. Eventually the spear was removed and the woman stitched up. Next morning she was running around with a large waddy trying to get even. The man was flown to Darwin Hospital and eventually recovered.

Late in 1951 I went to Emerald River with six men to commence clearing for an outstation. The men worked very well and when they knocked off each day they went hunting, mostly for fish in the saltwater part of the river. Once the wet season came we returned to Angurugu.

In February 1952 Helen went to Darwin for our first child. Our daughter, Robin, was born on the 1st March and they returned on the medical plane three weeks later.

At the beginning of April a cyclone formed in the Gulf of Carpentaria, crossed the western coast of Groote and continued to the mainland. All night, heavy squalls of rain and strong winds lashed the mission. A constant spray of rain came over the house walls into our bedroom. So we put Robin's cot under the table which at least shielded her from the spray of water.

Transfer to Numbulwar

Having worked at Groote Eylandt for 18 months, in 1952 Mum and Dad were transferred to a new mission being established on the inlet of a river called the Rose River, (now known as Numbulwar), opposite Groote Eylandt. They lived here among the sand hills in a grass and bark covered hut, in a similar manner to the aboriginal people.

This move must have been challenging with a baby of less than six months. The community was just a group of aboriginal people living in simple shelters. There was no airstrip and no regular supplies. Nearest communities were Groote

Eylandt, 100 kilometres and a several hour boat trip away across the Gulf of Carpentaria; or Roper River, a similar direct distance but a full day's drive across primitive bush tracks only accessible in the dry season, or almost twice that far by boat around the coast then up the river. They were many hours from simple nursing help, let alone medical evacuation to Darwin. In the wet season the only way out was a boat trip if the weather permitted passage. Few women with a baby would have lived like this, but Mum described it as if she was happy. They continued here over the next wet season, and it was not until the second half of 1953 that an airstrip was built.

My father describes this time as follows:

The Nunggubuyu people were scattered around Roper River and it was necessary to find another place with a good water supply. Coupled with this was a search for areas of cypress pine suitable for milling for building timber. The leader of the Nunggubuyu people was a man named Mardi. He was interested in his people settling on the country around Rose River. The cyclone brought heavy rains so there was an adequate supply of water.

Dick Harris set out in the 'Faith' from Groote Eylandt in the dry season of 1952 in search of a suitable place for another mission. Apart from Rose River there was little to support such a gathering of people. Thought was given to Bennet Bay, but Rose River was more accessible and was inside Nunggubuyu land. This confirmed Mardi's desire for his people to make this area their home.

In August 1952 many Nunggubuyu people left Roper, some by canoe and some to walk overland, with the women and children to travel by boat to Rose River. At Groote I was preparing to work at Emerald River when we were asked to transfer to Rose River to assist John Mercer to set up this new mission. So, with our six month old daughter, we made our camp in a shade house on the sand hills of Rose River.

The Nunggubuyu were marine hunters and the afternoons were set aside to hunt. Basic rations were issued to family groups each morning. The main work was the erection of temporary housing built of bush timber, binday grass walls and with paper bark rooves. A store was built in the same way. The next project was to clear land for an airstrip. Mardi had shown John a suitable area about two miles from the camp at the beginning of the gravel country. John paced out the airstrip area.

In June 1953 we returned from leave and John Mercer went off to get married. The work on the airstrip continued on until John came back in October.

I was expecting to go back to Angurugu to continue the Emerald River project, but I received a letter from Kevin Hoffman, the Groote Superintendent, advising me I would be welcome to return to Groote providing I did nothing further with the outstation at Emerald River. This was a blow and I pondered for a few days. The mission launch, Curtis, went round to Roper Mission and came back with the mail from Sydney. A letter came from Mr

Montgomerie asking me to give serious thought to being relocated to Oenpelli. Having received the letter from Groote this seemed to be the right way to go.

Oenpelli for the first time

So, after just over a year at Numbulwar, Mum and Dad packed their meagre possessions for a move to a third mission within 3years, Oenpelli. Here they found a real home and sense of belonging.

Mum was in advanced pregnancy with a second child, me. While Dad went to Oenpelli, with toddler Robin, now 18 months, Mum travelled to Darwin to have her baby. I presume she flew from Roper River to Darwin, via Katherine. There was no CMS base in Darwin, so it is not known how she got from the airport to the hospital, where she stayed before or after hospital, or how she got to the airport with a new baby. This time she had been to Darwin before and knew some people there. There was no money in a meagre missionary salary for hotels or taxis so, perhaps, kindly people in the community assisted with a bed and transport, as they did in her childhood living in country NSW.

Dad recounts their move thus:

Helen was expecting our second child in November and went ahead of me to Darwin. Robin came with me on the 'Curtis' to Roper. From there we flew to Katherine and on to Darwin. On 10th November 1953 I flew to Oenpelli with Robin in a chartered Auster aircraft. We stayed in one room of the concrete brick house while our future home at the back of the old store was being renovated. When Helen arrived at the end of November with Graham, we moved there. This became our house for the next four years. All our personal boxes, sent from Rose River, and our stores order, placed for our start at Oenpelli had arrived, except two boxes of groceries. I had heard of the difficulty getting supplies and it was not unusual for cargo to be stacked in Darwin for a year or more.

Grahams Story

When it Began

I don't remember, but I am told my Mum travelled to Darwin Hospital from Numbulwar and was there for three weeks before catching the mail plane to Oenpelli with a small me in her arms. My father meanwhile went directly to Oenpelli, with toddler, Robin, in tow. As I was born on the 22nd of November my mother's late pregnancy occurred in the build-up months in the NT Top End. To understand what this must have been like I give the insight I gained from the birth of my daughter.

My daughter, Zara, was born on November 28th, also in Darwin. The final three months of my wife, Mary's, pregnancy in the Top End were unpleasant for her. In these build up months Zara's rapidly growing body pumped out heat which added to the superheated NT. Mary often said "I don't think I will ever feel cool again". When all else failed she could retreat to an air-conditioned room, sit under a ceiling fan, go to an air-conditioned shopping centre or go for a swim in one of the many swimming pools around Darwin.

In the late September, two months before Zara's birth, we made a two day camping trip to Douglas Hot Springs, with our two boys, Darragh, five years, and Dylan, three years. Located two hours drive south of Darwin, the Hot Springs is an idyllic crystal clear river flowing under shady paperbark trees, where the hot water from the springs meets the cool water from the river, a pleasant place to relax in ordinary circumstances. In the NT Top End build up, with a growing baby generating still more heat, it rapidly became intolerable and, after one night, we beat a hasty retreat back to our air-conditioned Darwin house

Remembering this gives me an appreciation of my mother's experience; in an isolated location, heavily pregnant, an 18 month old toddler between her feet, in a house without insect screens, no electricity, fans, or air-conditioner, certainly no swimming pool or local shops. Mum never complained but she must have experienced the same heat and suffocating humidity as Mary did.

When Mum left hospital with me and flew to Oenpelli it was as new for her as it was for me. No doubt she marvelled at the mosaic of floodplains, fringing forests, ant-beds and buffalo she saw from the aeroplane window. Then the crossing of the broad snakelike South Alligator River and watching the distant sandstone pillars of Kakadu come into view, looming up as towering red-orange ramparts of the Arnhem Land escarpment. The plane would have made a sweep low over the East Alligator River, its iridescent green floodplains, muddy channels and black buffalo wallows, then done a lazy circuit above the three hills of Oenpelli, with a quick sight of a handful of tin roofed houses nestled around the billabong, before an final approach over plains covered with the countless thousands of magpie geese, ducks and myriad other waterbirds, gathered around diminishing waterholes; touching down and bouncing along a dusty grass airstrip, dodging graded ant-beds, and finally coming to rest as the propeller slowly wound down, surrounded by a cluster of people, miraculously gathered in the five minutes from when the plane was first heard until it rolled to a stop. All this I do not recall, but doubtless it happened like many other homecomings that I do remember.

There were perhaps ten white and one hundred black people gathered at the aeroplane, shy giggling black children holding the skirts of their mothers, men in loincloths, their glistening purple-black arms, with raised initiation welts, and the occasional fishing spear or digging stick. Perhaps there was a tractor and trailer to carry the luggage, mailbags and few groceries. Of course my father was there, hanging on tightly to his toddler daughter. A handful of other missionaries of the tiny white community would have been there to welcome us too.

Everyone would have been keen to see this new missionary woman and her baby, the story having run around the community like wildfire, since the new man and his daughter arrived.

To all accounts I was a cranky baby. Mum said, in her understated way, that I was a bit difficult. Dad told stories of having to take me for long walks along the Oenpelli airstrip to get me to sleep at night. Apparently I talked in profusion as a toddler, saying in a clear high voice, "Jesus wants me for a sunbeam"

My own memories take a couple years to emerge, the first baby calf, the river crossing, visits to the billabong, riding on a tractor and trailer, our coal black house-girl who helped my mother with the domestic chores, and from whom our family gained our aboriginal skin names, 'Nagamarrang' for me, derived from my mother's 'Ngalngarridj', as adopted sister to our house girl.

My first four years of memories are little more than a blur of bright images, interspersed with other memory fragments, and a pervading sense of the joy of life, which permeated my whole world. From this warmth of memory I don't doubt that my parents loved this simple life, notwithstanding its hardships.

Mixed with my first memories of Oenpelli is my first memory of being shown a kaleidoscope as a small child, it's flashing hues of coloured glass were a source of great wonder. These two images from my early mind have flowed through one another and the colours of Oenpelli have now taken, in my mind, hues of kaleidoscopic colour. So I think of my earliest childhood in Arnhem Land as akin to a child viewing life through a multi-coloured kaleidoscope.

Mum and Dad's Story continues

Oenpelli in the 1950s

During 1953 to 1957 when we lived at Oenpelli, Dad was often absent, camping in the bush, surveying routes for a road or locations for a Darwin base and then with a Blitz truck coming from Sydney and setting up a road transport system.

Did it bother Mum, I don't know, but she never complained.

I think she treated these things as challenges to be overcome and, once dealt with, confined to the dustbin of history. Mum had the assistance of an aboriginal house girl, Dorcas, who came for several hours each morning, but she still had three small children, a house to manage, guests to entertain and, in the absence of a nursing sister, medical emergencies, including delivering babies, using skills from midwifery training. Their house was at the back of a shop selling groceries, with packed earth (ant bed) floors, mosquito nets and a variety of wildlife including snakes, native cats and bush rats.

Dad describes their life at Oenpelli as follows:

There were a little under 200 people at Oenpelli when we arrived in 1953. Only about 50 proper Mengerr people were allowed to camp in Banyan or Arrkuluk villages. Others were allowed to camp on the saddle at the base of Arrkuluk or on the other side of the billabong. Most of these people stayed for a few months and moved on to Liverpool River or to Pine Creek. Helen kept a record of the people who came to Oenpelli. Her house girl, Dorcas, advised of movements. Dorcas's husband, Joshua was a working man. From them we were given our skin names; Joshua and I were Nakangila, Dorcas and Helen were Ngalngarridj. This skin name gave a relationship with other people. Over these four years we were at Oenpelli Helen recorded over 600 people, but at no time were there more than 200 people living there. All travel was done by foot and belongings were carried by the wife, often on the head.

Apart from the back of the store, which became our residence, there was a concrete block house which was poorly designed and became very hot in the wet season and an old iron house where the single ladies lived. At the side of the store there were two single men's rooms. A builder had been sent up but found it was impossible to build anything as there was no timber, so he went back south at the end of 1953. A small stack of timber had been put together for a house but was insufficient for the job. He set the stumps into the ground for the new place, but until some materials were delivered by boat from Darwin nothing further was done.

The workshop was 50 yards away. In the evening a generator was run until 9:30 pm and each house could have two lights. On the windmill stand, near our kitchen, there was a powerful light which lit up the area between our house and the single ladies place ten yards away. It was a great area for snakes. The light was a beacon to all the insects, which formed a swarming mass. When the power went off these insects gathered around other lights in the vicinity such as kerosene lamps in our house.

My work was in the garden and, in November, it was getting ready for wet season planting. The garden was between the billabong and houses. The ground was prepared by ploughing, then digging channels to take compost or manure, little other than grass. The women moved along making rows of hilled up ground ready for planting with mainly cassava, sweet potato, pawpaw and peanuts. Planting was done once good rainfall was received, in December to January. Several women worked together and Barnabas helped with the machinery. He was a really good worker. One day I asked him to put the tractor away in the shed. He eagerly sat on the tractor and started to drive in the direction of the shed. I did not find out until later that he didn't know how to stop. He went into the shed and kept on going, moving the back wall a couple feet until the tractor stopped. I gradually learned the various abilities of people.

Three sacks of peanuts were put aside for planting in the wet season. One afternoon I brought a sack out and the garden ladies sat in a circle. I emptied the sack out on the ground in the centre and asked them to shell the nuts. Later they had nearly finished with very few nuts to show for their work, but a great pile of shells and they were all well fed. Next morning, at Jim Blyth's suggestion, I filled a spray pack of Condy's Crystals dissolved in water. I invited the women to take two handfuls of nuts each as their ration. The rest of the nuts were sprayed vivid purple It was amazing the quantity of nuts we now got.

As well as the garden I inherited the goats. The women were rostered for morning and afternoon milking but supervision was essential. The morning bell went at daylight. Simultaneously there was a rattle of cans as the women set out for the goat yard. Often they brought children with empty tins who were anxious to try milking. It was necessary to keep these tins out of the goat yard. The shepherds were old women, two at a time. After the milking they took the goats out to the plains. At first nothing was in the garden, but as crops were planted it became a problem. One job was to fence the garden using wartime barbed wire, very rusty. It helped to have a boundary but did not keep the goats out.

There had been no nursing sister for several weeks. Denise Long, a school teacher looked after a daily dispensary but a few days after our arrival a lady came into labour. Helen, a trained midwife, assisted her through the childbirth. Everything went well and other pregnant women came to the hospital instead of having their babies in the bush.

In late 1953, we were awaiting our wet season supplies. Early showers had fallen and the afternoon build-up gave us the feeling that a lot more rain was on the way. At Oenpelli we were dependent on an agent in Darwin to arrange with a local boat owner, Leo Hickey, to round off the year's supply of our stores. By mid-December the road across the plains to the Top Landing was holding, but would go out with another heavy downpour. A message on the radio sked said that the "Zena" was due at the landing on Friday afternoon, the 18th December. Jim Blyth and a team of men set out for the landing with the crawler tractor and two trailers. The short wheel-base Blitz was left for me to take after work. We waited on the bank of the river as the tide was coming in, but no boat. The tide turned and Jim was sure there would be no boat until next day. Enquiries on the radio revealed Zena hadn't left Darwin. Saturday night it rained - a real big storm, over two inches across the plains. A radio message on Sunday advised Zena would be at the landing on the afternoon tide.

It was a hopeless job. The plains were flooded and the crawler tractor could not be driven across to the bank of the river. Men walked across and stacked the six tons of food in the little shed. The four tons of drums and other hardware were stacked outside where they would stay until the dry season. Everyone went back to the mission overnight and next day we returned with as many empty bags as it was possible to muster. At the river the 180 lb. sacks of wheat were divided into 3 X 60 lb. packs, 112 lb. sacks of flour into 2 X 56 lb. bags and the 70 lb. bags of sugar remained unopened. Men carried these bags across the swamp, three quarters of a mile, to the trailers. It was a mammoth task, but we managed to save everything.

Next year was almost identical. This time the tractor and trailer were cut off at the river when rain came overnight. Things were placed in the little shed and we explored the area. One man showed me a creek full of water with a thick crop of para-grass along it. By limiting the load to half a ton a time, we gradually shifted the food and boxes to higher ground and then to the mission. Again fuel drums were stacked on their ends at the river bank for the wet season. With very heavy rain the East Alligator flooded all the plains and the 12 drums of fuel disappeared.

At the end of the 1954 wet season we took a week's holiday at the waterfall. The school boys were given a half day holiday to come with us and carry our things to the top of the falls. I made up small packages. The morning before we left Helen asked about milk for Graham, as he was on goat's milk. That was easy – I went to the goat yard and picked out two milkers. With a rope around their necks I led them to the trailer being loaded. Our house girl, Dorcas and her husband, Joshua, came with us. We pulled out to the waves of many people and headed for the waterfall. Each boy carried a parcel up the rocky hill to the top of the falls. The goats were left in the shade at the bottom where they could get grass and water. We had an enjoyable week and on Friday tractor, trailer and schoolboys arrived to take us back.

A little later Regional CMS Secretary, the Rev Montgomerie visited, so we put on a sports afternoon. People gathered at the edge of the cross strip near the mission. Efforts to get the children competing in races were hopeless. They just sat in groups under the poinciana trees. So I went back to our place and told Helen I wanted her to make me into a 'proper blackfellow.' I scraped out soot from the bottom of the fuel stove and mixed some powdered charcoal with it. She covered my back while I attended to my front. Then she patched up where I had missed. I put on my hat and walked to the goat yard where the big horned billy goat was. Straddling him I rode to the sports gathering, steering him with his horns. It had great effect and the afternoon took off.

In 1955 our food supplies were very low, but we kept everyone working. We had a gathering of people in front of the store. I told them the situation and people agreed to go on walkabout, except for essential workers who could live on garden produce. As people moved away from the store, an aircraft circled overhead and landed. The pilot was Neil Conway with passengers Harry Frith and a photographer. A seat was empty, so I went with them to Darwin to organise transport for our stores. Leo Hickey could not bring supplies on the 'Zena' for several weeks as his wife was expecting a baby. He promised as soon as he could go back to work he would do a series of trips to bring our loading. In the meantime I got Pedersen in the 'Temora' to bring 12 tons of supplies to Smith's Landing. We brought 9 tons of equipment and three tons of food. I should have taken more food but, with Leo's assurance I felt we had enough food for a couple of months.

Back at Oenpelli, Roger Gregson asked me to come by horse to the East Alligator River. After about an hour we came to the river. The tide was out and we could see a rock bar. There was a lot of silt but the rocks stood out with three channels through them. On the western side was a large, flat part of rock and the channels were on the east. Roger pointed out how a crossing could be built. The banks would have to be cut out and the channels filled in with tree trunks. These could be wired to star pickets driven into crevices in the rocks. It seemed simple and Roger was prepared to tackle the job if we were able to buy a transport truck.

A week later we had a visitor, Jimmy Wauchope on his way to Murganella, with his 'new' truck a Chev Blitz. He told me he crossed the river in Mikginj valley and drove down the east bank into Red Lily paddock. My interest centred on the Blitz. Over a cup of tea he told me they were not easy to come by but it should be possible to get one in the South.

We went on leave to Sydney in January 1956 and my plan was to buy a good, long wheel base Blitz wagon. We were expected to find our own accommodation and with three young children, this was not easy. I had facetiously commented on occasions that we should try to find a boat going from Darwin to Sydney as was the way of travel before the war. Then we could claim to be overseas missionaries and receive the benefits available to them, such as accommodation.

Transport – a truck and a road to Oenpelli

Buying the Blitz Truck in Sydney

Superintendent Ron Ash was on leave in Sydney in early 1956 so we arranged to meet and discuss transport and a crossing over the East Alligator River. After we met I set off to explore the truck market.

In Sydney there were vehicle yards which dealt in ex-Army equipment. The normal price for a long wheel base Blitz was 500 pounds, without a winch, with tyres that had barely 50% of life left in them, with no canopy and only fair paint work. A truck with a winch cost another 250 pounds. I delayed going in to CMS to appeal for money to buy a truck, based on experience of being told they had no funds. Finally at the beginning of April went to their office. On the ground floor I met Ralph Barton, who had spent a few years at Oenpelli and was seen as an authority. He had first-hand knowledge of the transport difficulties with the loss of food on the ferry boat in January1951. I outlined my plans to him but his reply went right against my thinking. "Don't waste time and money on such a project. Get your boat system working. You will never control any road through Red Lily." As I went on upstairs I held little hope getting support for a road project. However I was told by secretary, Miss Edna Louis, that Mr Montgomerie wanted to see me. In seconds I was ushered to his inner sanctum where he gave me a letter to read.

The letter, written by Ron Ash, described trying to take delivery of 5 tons of food at Smith's Landing at the end of March. With a cyclone a few miles north, Roger Gregson and John Mildenhall set out with a team of men and the crawler tractor and trailer. The crawler broke down and the small Blitz, sent to help them through, also broke down. Mr Montgomerie needed a reply to this saga as he was visiting Oenpelli at the end of April.

It seemed a fitting occasion to open the subject of road transport. I outlined our thinking and the possibility of putting a crossing over the East Alligator River. This led into purchase of a truck and equipping it for the work. The immediate question was, "How much is this going to cost?" Miss Louis was called in and I gave a run down on what I had so far found out. I said the Army had a large number of vehicles at Moorebank for disposal. Their opinion was; Yes, we could go ahead and the cost of the vehicle would be charged to our Freight Account. A letter was written to the Army seeking permission to tender for one of these trucks.

At Moorebank, where the Army had their stores, one fenced paddock held 100 vehicles. I had the liberty to select from these. After a couple of hours I had listed six vehicles and went to the office for more information. They let me look at the maintenance logs for each vehicle. It was out of two, a Chev Blitz with a straight six cylinder engine or a Ford with a V8 engine. As we had other Chev engines in the North, I chose that one. It had a good set of tyres, a canvas canopy and doors. With these details I set out for Sydney, where Miss Louis wrote a letter to the Army tendering 375 pounds for it. After a few weeks we were given the permission to collect the vehicle once the money was paid. I took the cheque to Victoria Barracks. With the receipt I drove to Moorebank with some tools, a new battery and a jerry can of petrol. Our Blitz had been placed in a separate yard and all the good things were taken away - no doors, the tyres were bald, the canvas canopy was torn and the canopy bars were bent. When I complained about its condition I was told to go to their garage and 'for twenty quid they would fit it out like a new one'. I told them "we don't work that way". So I had to take delivery of a truck which then cost several hundred pounds to put on the road. That afternoon I drove the Blitz to Engadine and then went back by train to collect my car.

I visited almost every second hand tyre yard in Sydney and managed to buy three reasonable tyres. The local garage mechanic took an interest in my project and spent time tuning the engine and checking the truck over. He made two doors out of sheet metal, fitted with simple latches and straightened the canopy bars, charging very little. My father-in-law came from Penshurst and sand-papered areas of rust for painting. Finally the truck was ready to load.

Travelling by Blitz to Oenpelli, NT

It was now well into July. It took a few days for loading and preparations for the journey. In Queensland there were reports of very wet conditions. All I could do was head there and work out there how to get to the Northern Territory. My plan was to drive to the west bank of the East Alligator River unload, then drive in to Darwin to meet Helen and the children in three weeks. I left on 24th July, by the New England Highway. The truck engine ran well pulling a load of 5 tons. In Queensland the road through Charleville was out so I went north to Charters Towers.

From Charters Towers to Cloncurry was a reasonable road except for sandy creek crossings. My first trouble was 20 miles west where I drove off the road edge to camp. The wheels sank into the wet sandy loam soil. Four wheel drive made no difference and there was nothing to winch to. The truck had to be unloaded, unbogged, driven onto the road and reloaded. This took 24 hours then I set off again. Two days later I drove into Cloncurry. I spent one day there changing tyres. It took a long time to separate the wheel rims. The best way was with wooden wedges cut from trees.

After I changed tyres and refuelled, I set out for Mt. Isa. All tyres were in bad shape and I wondered if they would last. There was a bitumen road from Mt. Isa but the next section of road was one of the worst. At Cloncurry the man at the garage said there could be four vehicles a day on the road or you may go four days without a vehicle. The first 20 miles to Mary Kathleen uranium mine were flat but very corrugated. After this it was mountainous with very steep sections of road. I had to use a lot of low gear to pull the load up the hills and the truck engine worked hard. About 30 miles from Mt. Isa one front tyre blew out. I took the wheel off and fitted a wheel with an old bald tyre. I had scarcely finished when a mail truck pulled up. The driver was glad to help so I slid the wheel into his van and went into Mt Isa. Next morning, with a new tyre and tube and almost empty bank account, I got a lift back to the truck.

With the new tyre on I continued and was soon on a bitumen road again. Being an optimist I thought my tyre problems were over, but they were only beginning. As I left Mt Isa I picked up a hitch-hiker who wanted a lift to the Three Ways, 600 kms ahead. I drove on, vaguely aware of a slight tapping noise in the engine. It wasn't there all the time, so I continued. Then there was a flapping noise. The tread on one front tyre was lifting. Surely it would see the distance! I had no money apart from what I needed to buy petrol. I drove on at a steady pace with the faint tapping noise and the flapping tyre tread. Past half way to Camooweal a second tyre started to flap, also with tread lifting. I had to buy more tyres, which meant money wired to Camooweal from Sydney. At times the tapping noise disappeared, so I dismissed that anything was wrong with the engine.

Coming into Camooweal I was surprised how small it was. There was a small garage with nothing but bare essentials, certainly not 11 X 20 tyres. I stopped almost outside the town and asked my passenger to look after things while I went back to Mount Isa. He was happy to do so. Ten minutes later a vehicle pulled up and I went off.

In Mt Isa first I sent a telegram to CMS in Sydney for money. Next morning the money arrived and I bought three tyres. They made arrangements for me to travel back to Camooweal with the mailman. We left about five o'clock visiting several properties before camping. He had a swag in his load and said the owner wouldn't mind it being used, so I even had a swag.

I arrived about ten am. My hitchhiker was looking after everything. The first job was to remove the wheels, resting the truck on whatever we could find; rocks and pieces of timber. The wheels were taken apart and new tyres fitted. Together we rolled them to the garage/workshop to pump them up. NO WAY! If I chose to go to Mt. Isa to buy tyres, I could go to Mt. Isa to pump them up. It was useless arguing that he had no tyres in that size. So we rolled the wheels back and set about pumping each one up to 90 lbs pressure with a hand pump. We took turns pumping. After a while I noticed my companion had a handkerchief around one hand. He had a blister the size of a small hen egg on his palm. He was excused and I plodded on until they were all done and wheels fitted. By four pm we were on the road.

From Camooweal to Three Ways is 450 kilometres. It took ten hours, arriving at two in the morning. I put off my passenger and headed up the Stuart Highway. I had been on the road two weeks and still had to reach the East Alligator River, unload and reach Darwin to meet Helen in six days' time.

Next day I reached Mataranka. The tapping noise was becoming more persistent. The following day I reached Katherine, then Pine Creek. The tapping noise was much louder. I wondered if the engine would hold together long enough to get to Canon Hill, let alone back into Darwin.

At Pine Creek, I sent two telegrams; one to a Miss Blaxland in Darwin, who Helen had stayed with before, and one to Helen to let her know that I wouldn't be in Darwin to meet them. (Helen didn't receive this telegram until she was on the plane flying north).

The road out of Pine Creek was graded so I made good progress to the Mary River, a beautiful place with huge bamboo clumps and a good stream of fresh water. Then the road went through steep hills and down to Goodparla Station. The tapping noise in the engine was very persistent but the truck was pulling well. It was dark so I pushed on to the South Alligator River with the head lights. After I crossed its dry sandy bed I soon pulled up for a rest.

It was dark when I continued. After half an hour the engine made a terrific clattering noise. I knew a con rod big end had gone so I sat there until there was enough light to work on the engine. When I got the sump off, sure enough, number 2 big end bearing had gone. I looked at the leatherette sides of my shoes and was inclined to cut a piece of this out big enough for the bearing cap. But I thought it may be necessary to do a lot of walking. There was a grey army blanket on the seat. Carefully I cut a piece of this, soaked it in oil and fitted the bearing together on the crankshaft. It made a tight fit so I reassembled the engine and gave it a test run. It sounded good with no tapping noise. I set out and travelled 300 yards.

Again the clattering shattered the peace so I started over to take the sump off again. This time I fitted two thicknesses of blanket. Away I went for three miles until it happened again. I pondered then decided to take the head and sump off to remove the whole piston. This was a much bigger job. When night came, I had everything in pieces.

The timber truck from Nourlangie Timber Camp, with Les Turley, came past on his way to the mill. We exchanged greetings. He was staggered at what I was doing.

Next morning, I reassembled the engine with only five pistons. By nine o'clock it was finished. It started easily but rocked with a strong vibration. Driving slowly I kept it going, crossing Jim Jim Creeks. A mile further was another creek. This time it stalled. After trying to get the engine restarted I gave it away. I had travelled 12 miles on five pistons. Timber Camp would be another 12 miles. So I walked.

Three hours later I walked into the camp and was met by the manager, Russ Jones. My first words to him were, "Would you happen to have a 20 thou. undersize con rod for a Chev Blitz?"

"Follow me", was his reply and he led the way into his workshop. Hanging on nails on the end wall were all sorts of spare parts. He reached up to one lot of con rods and looking on the side there was '20' stamped clearly. "Here are two – take them both!" He took me to the camp where three men had walked from Oenpelli to help; Timothy, Lofty and Nameredje. Russ organised something to eat. That evening the four of us went on the timber truck to the Blitz. Next morning we rebuilt the engine with six pistons. It went like a new one and we drove on to Timber Camp.

The following morning Russ offered his Ferguson tractor with a carry platform, a drum of water and a drum of petrol. He suggested I take one man and work out where to go as the road hadn't been used for a long time and there were many different tracks left by the buffalo shooters. I selected Timothy who had worked with buffalo shooters and had good knowledge of this country. We took a few odds and ends, mainly a billy can, tea and sugar and travelled to Nourlangie Creek where there were three sandy crossings over half a mile. We crossed but I wondered how the loaded Blitz would manage.

Then we drove over some gravel ridge country and across some creeks which would be difficult for the truck. Near Mudginberry the road disappeared so Timothy walked in front directing me towards the billabong. At the end of Mudginberry airstrip, we spoke to men in the camp who knew I was coming.

About three o'clock we continued to Magela creek. No one had used this road for a long time. Timothy directed me to where the road used to be. We walked through first then drove the tractor across. From here there was little sign of a road so we followed alongside Magela Creek.

Late in the afternoon we came to a large area of plains. Timothy pointed out Canon Hill and the East Alligator River. On the edge of the plain was a muddy creek, with old wheel tracks. I drove along these, only to find the tractor wouldn't move, then the engine stopped – we had run out of fuel. We gathered our things and walked to Canon Hill shed four miles away.

Our camp that night was very simple. We had a mug of tea and we slept. It was barely daylight when we moved on. The river bank was three miles across the plains. We arrived there at about eight am. The tide was out and the canoe on the other side so we had to swim. We swam side by side, alert for crocodiles.

I reckoned Helen would be coming from Darwin by plane at about ten o'clock. Oenpelli was seven miles so we would need to push on to arrive then. Near the Mission I walked ahead towards Arrkuluk village. I was coming in the back door and thought no one would notice me. But the call went out, dogs barked and people gathered on the opposite side of the airstrip. I learnt Helen and the children were delayed in Darwin for medical checks, expected to arrive Thursday. It was good to be home.

It was only then that I found out about the difficult situation for Helen when she arrived in Darwin. The telegram I sent from Pine Creek the previous Thursday was not delivered in Sydney until the Monday morning and she was already on the plane flying to Brisbane. Her father rang the airline and it was transmitted to the aircraft, so she had some inkling. On arrival in Darwin, Miss Blaxland met them at the airport and drove them to the Darwin Hotel.

In the morning she learnt that she could not go on to Oenpelli as the children had to have Mantoux tests for TB, a new requirement. She tried to extend at the hotel but was bluntly told that she had to be out by ten am but could leave her luggage at the hotel foyer temporarily. As the booking had been made by CMS, Sydney, Helen was carrying little money. There were two other hotels in Darwin, the Victoria and the Don, but these were well out of her reach financially.

In a perplexed state of mind, she walked with the children down Mitchell Street to work out what she should do. Willie Stahl, an agronomist with the Department of Agriculture, saw her and asked what she was doing in Darwin. Willie had been at Oenpelli the previous year and had stayed with us. When Helen outlined her predicament, Willie went into action and arranged to meet her in an hour's time. In less than an hour Willie was back to pick up Helen and the three children. He drove them to Coconut Grove to Kath Hinds place, a friend who Helen had stayed with in the Red Cross cottage when Graham was born. This also gave a way forward with the truck, as we could camp on adjoining land and make use of her toilet facilities.

First Road Transport Trips to Oenpelli

John Mildenhall offered to go to Nourlangie Timber Camp and bring the truck to the river. He set out next morning with a couple men and a small drum of petrol. I appreciated this very much. It gave me a chance to catch up with Helen and the children when they arrived. It took two days for John to return the tractor and to bring the truck to Canon Hill landing. Everything was taken across the river in the canoe, then by tractor and trailer to Oenpelli.

Ron Ash told me about the effort to retrieve the five tons of food in March. The Air Force was asked if they could fly out a Dakota load of food (three tons) but did not have a Dakota available. So, in June they loaded 6 X 180 lb. sacks of wheat in the bomb bay of a Lincoln bomber. Each sack had a parachute fastened to it and the aircraft flew over the mission at 7.30 in the morning. People came from all directions to see. Over the airstrip, the bomb bay was opened and out came the cargo. Five parachutes opened, the other bag plummeted down and burst on impact.

Roger Gregson did not think he could tackle the crossing until the following year. When the truck arrived at the Canon Hill in August there was just three months before the wet season would cut the road off. We had to shift the backlog of goods in Darwin plus our wet season supplies.

Our first trip started on Monday, 20th August. With me came Timothy, Yuan Yuan and their wives, Nancy and Manguway. They were left with axes to straighten a section of road. We would pick them up on the way back. Two other men came to Darwin to help with loading. The first night we camped just out of Pine Creek, a distance of 175 miles and the following morning we travelled up the bitumen Stuart Highway to Darwin, a further 155 miles, making 330 miles each way (it is about 150 miles by air). Our cargo was stored in three different yards with things forgotten over time since they had arrived by ship from the South.

By Wednesday afternoon we were loaded for the trip back. We travelled down the highway and next day headed out from Pine Creek on the dirt road. The sandy creek crossings at the Nourlangie were trouble. With a loaded truck we needed the winch and a shovel to clear around the front wheels. We arrived at the Canon Hill landing after dark and next day shifted everything across the river to Oenpelli.

The second Darwin trip was a week later. This time we had a couple of bags of crocodile skins, dingo pelts, our swags, tucker box and five men. As it all was being stacked in the canoe I called out, "Two trips". "No more – one" was the reply.

I watched anxiously as everything was loaded.   The tide was running in rapidly. I wondered how we would get across in one trip. They showed me where I was to perch, on top of the loading. Everyone was on with two inches of freeboard. They expertly directed the canoe at an angle to the bank and turned into the tidal flow. The canoe tilted upstream. From my elevated position, I tilted, a little more than the canoe.

Over we went; passengers, luggage, swags and cargo. We floundered in the water, trying to grab our possessions. The men held the canoe and pushed it to shallow water. Then they dived for bits and pieces, some things were swept upstream. I don't think we thought of crocodiles. We finally got underway, swags opened on the truck back to dry and a sodden tucker box. I felt Aboriginal people thought me a liability, particularly in the water.

Again the Nourlangie Creeks held us up, taking an hour to get through. The main problem was the middle creek. It needed a truck load of rock, but there was no rock anywhere near, just sand.

I brought Kath Hinds out with me on one of our early trips. She stayed with us over the weekend and came back to Darwin the next week. She was amazed at the number of nocturnal animals in the store, which adjoined our house. The noise of rats, bandicoots, and phascogales vying for food, was heard throughout the building. She was convinced we needed a tabby cat.

Next trip back from Darwin Kath gave me a little tabby kitten, for our nocturnal visitors. At Barramundi Creek was a fence. The gates were made from army bed-frames with two beds for the width of the road. I pulled up. One of the men unhooked the gate and pushed the two sections open. If he held one, the other mostly stayed open. On this occasion it started to creep towards the side of the truck. I saw it happening so I put my foot down to beat it. The gate caught on the side of the truck and was elongated. With nothing to straighten it, we tied it as best we could, a landmark of the road.

The Nourlangie Creek crossings were breaking up and it took an hour to cross them. Here I realised Puss was missing. Her box behind my seat was empty, looking and calling failed to produce anything. Too bad; we would have to move on without her. Stopping for supper I heard a plaintive meow under the truck. There she was, in a channel cross member of the chassis, so we left her. At the Landing we loaded things into the canoe to take home, again Puss was missing. Most loading stayed on the truck to shift when setting out on the next trip. By that time the kitten was there too.

The old iron barge was taken to the bank of the river. We called it the flying drip tray. Jim Blyth made it out of sheet steel, beautifully welded together. It had been fitted with a Gypsy Major aero engine and was used in the wet season to bring buffalo meat and sometimes goose eggs across the flooded plains. It had a speed of 20 mph and fuel consumption of eight gallons per hour, or 2.5 miles to the gallon. Nice, but very uneconomical. Then the person who lent the engine claimed it back. So the barge had sat at the edge of the billabong with no further use. It now speeded unloading at the Landing.

The rain was early that year. Heavy showers fell in the Goodparla area but the ground was dry enough to cope with these. In mid-October I set out once more for Darwin from the Canon Hill Landing. Heavy rain had fallen over the weekend and the plains were soft with boggy patches. The section of road from the South Alligator to Goodparla was breaking up. We travelled to Darwin and found wet season stores had arrived by ship from Brisbane. This was the first time we shifted our food supplies as they arrived.

Returning towards the Canon Hill plains it was obvious there was a heavy storm while we were away. I asked the men on the truck if anyone could show me the way to the rock bar on the river. Nangalbered perched on the cab roof, directing to a suitable point and then we went 'bush'. We came out at Manbiyara, where the Border Store now is, near the rocky bar. This became our crossing for the rest of the year. It was not easy to bring loading across, with three channels in the rock, but a system was worked out, so we did not bring the barge up. It would have been better if we did, as in the wet season it washed down the river, never seen again.

From August to November we made eight trips to Darwin. The Aboriginal men stayed at Bagot Reserve to see their people. Usually we were in Darwin on Wednesday nights, because the Star Theatre had a cowboy picture. The last trip in November consisted of three tons of flour, odds and ends and, from Katherine, two bulls from Nixon's farm. It was quite a trip, keeping the flour from being contaminated by the bulls.

When everything was unloaded at the crossing we had to take the truck across the river to Oenpelli. I took Timothy and a man called Bunny. Timothy directed me back 15 miles to a place known as Hades Flats where we turned and drove south through the bush. It was late when we set out and, before long, I needed headlights. Timothy and Bunny were heading for a gap in the hills. We often had to switch off the lights so they could pick the point on the sky line. About midnight we came to this gap and camped.

Next morning we crossed a number of steep sided creeks which flowed in to a large billabong. We came to the East Alligator River about midday. It was 200 yards wide.

Timothy showed me different types of sand. One type was firm, it could be driven over. Another type was soft, even to walk on. It was to be avoided, especially with a loaded vehicle.

Crossing the river went well up to its centre. But on the eastern side of the stream was some of the sand Timothy said to avoid. The wheels sank into it and we made no progress, even in four wheel drive. With nothing to winch to we needed help.

Keith Hart was in Red Lily with the crawler tractor and trailer getting logs for milling. So we walked down the east bank to get his help. It took about two hours and another hour to return with the crawler. Soon the truck was through and we started down the east bank of the river towards the gorge, as Jimmy Wauchope described the previous year. The crawler tractor made a fresh track round the edge of the ledge in the gorge and we cautiously followed. At last we came into Red Lily paddock and continued to Oenpelli.

In the wet season I asked Timothy if there was another way to take the truck to the river avoiding Red Lily. He said there was one, but 'little bit long way'. It was too wet at that time of the year so we left it until the rains stopped. At the end of March the wet season seemed to have eased. Timothy felt it was a good time to make the trip by horse. We would see how wet the country was for a road.

In early April, we set out. We rode out to the east to Gunmayinbuk, with cloudy weather, then occasional light showers and later continual light rain. We went up the bank of Birridak Creek into the top end of Mikginj valley. The country was very rough with small hills and creeks. Further down the valley there seemed to be suitable country for a road. We camped that night in a cave. Timothy hobbled the three horses and we retreated to our shelter. The rain was persistent although light. Next day we travelled down the valley to the river coming to the place of the previous November's crossing. Light rain continued all day and we were wet. On the bank of the river Timothy showed me a crocodile nest. As the mother crocodile was somewhere near, we did not spend long.

We rode down through the gorge and at dusk came to Cahill's Crossing. Wet season water was flowing rapidly through the trees to the open river. Our camp was simple. The rain eased off and Timothy soon had a fire going. We both had a small piece of canvas which we tied together on some poles driven into the sand. It rained lightly all night and the small piece of canvas kept me partly dry. Next morning Timothy made a fire with one match. He peeled paper bark off a tree, shredding it, which produced a fire in very short time. We continued through Red Lily to our road from the previous year. Much was under water. By now it was clear to me we could not use Mikginj Valley as an access road to the East Alligator River. So we would have to be content with Red Lily and to go ahead with the planned crossing.

Coming home I found Dorothy had a bad attack of gastro enteritis and had been sick all the time I was away. Helen had nursed her, trying to get her to drink some water. The nursing sister reported her condition to Darwin Hospital but they could not evacuate her with the wet weather which was the edge of a cyclone. We received word the medical aircraft would be in that morning and that one parent had to accompany her to Darwin. Helen had to look after the other children, so I had a trip to Darwin. By this stage, Dorothy was over the worst.

I sought out Leo Hickey in Darwin. He could bring out a boat load of food and this would keep us going until the truck could get through. This trip showed me afresh the difficulty of using a boat. After a good trip from Darwin overnight, Leo went into the river on a rising tide. The force of water going upstream pushed the Zena around the bends at a rapid rate, touching the bottom a number of times and then becoming stuck. I saw the concentrated expression on Leo's face as he desperately struggled with the tiller. After half a minute, which seemed like half an hour, it came loose. Once round these sharp bends it was plain sailing and before long we were at Top Landing.

By July the country was drying out rapidly. On 15th July, we set out on our first road trip of the year; Ossie Emery (a CMS photographer), his wife Cynthia, John Mildenhall, three Aboriginal men and myself. We drove through Red Lily to it's the sandy southern end near the East Alligator, going slowly through sand heading into the gorge. It took all day to get to where we crossed the river last November. We camped on the east bank and I checked the sand in the river bed to avoid the same mistake as the last time. It seemed firm with a lot less water than when I was there with Timothy.

Next morning the truck crossed the sand to the other side without faltering. The men dug the bank out to make it easier to climb and up we went. The creeks were difficult. Some were washed out and all were wet. The billabong they fed was much higher than at the end of last season, causing the creeks to be soft. But we got through them and on to Mudginberry that night.

Next morning, at Nourlangie Creeks there was water in each creek and pieces of wood from the previous year were sticking out of the sand. We drove through and continued towards the South Alligator. In the hilly country, west of Goodparla, there was a loud bang on the roof. That was the signal to pull up, so I stopped.

One man pointed to a large grey kangaroo 200 yards away. There was the noise of the action of the bolt on the .303 as a bullet was slid into the rifle. The man with the rifle moved in a stealthy manner to the trees. In a circular route he drew nearer while another man attracted the attention of the kangaroo with imitation movements of his arms and body. We lost track of the shooter until a loud bang drew our attention back. The kangaroo dropped, then tried to run. But the men were upon it and finished it. It was a large animal and they threw it onto the back of the truck.

Gerowie Creek with beautiful, clear spring fed water was an invitation to pull up. The men cut up the kangaroo and I asked if I could have the tail. They cut it off and skinned it for me. I cut each section partly through and put the whole tail in a large billy can. It was too early for afternoon tea, so we went on to the Mary River crossing. We pulled up there and I began cooking a kangaroo tail. I knew the first boiling would not be sufficient, but felt sure that the next one, or at most the one after, would be. Before we moved on I had it bubbling away. Close to Pine Creek we found a suitable place for our evening meal. The fire was lit; the large billy, warm from earlier, was placed on the coals, bubbling away for over an hour, while we sat round eating and talking. Then it was time to move on. I pressed a fork into the tail, but no way was it ready. The billy was put back on the truck.

I became aware the truck engine was running hot. John was also driving and he agreed it was warmer than normal. We pulled up and checked. The radiator was short of water so we filled it and went on our way. Every half hour we had to do this again. With a torch we could see no leaks in the radiator. The oil level was right, so where was the water going? We drove on and camped on the edge of the MacDonald wartime airstrip. The billy went on and before long was bubbling merrily away, boiling for over an hour before the fire died down.

Next morning we had a good look at the truck engine. After filling the radiator, we found the problem. At the rear end of the engine block is a metal plug, called a welsh plug, partly covered by the clutch housing. From its edge a steady stream of water was flowing out. There was not much we could do but I pushed an oily engine rag into the space, which slowed it slightly. While this was going on the billy was back on the fire, with little sign of the tail being edible.

We moved on up the Stuart Highway, topping up the radiator. At George Creek we pulled up for a cuppa and again the billy went on again. Everyone thought it was a joke, but I persevered. Lunch time camp was 30 miles south of Darwin. Guess what? The kangaroo tail was ready!

In Darwin John and I went to our Coconut Grove camp where I was glad of John's help to unbolt the truck engine, remove the radiator and front grill and move the engine forward, away from the clutch housing. Next morning I walked to Darwin to get the parts. Putting the new welsh plug in took five minutes, but the whole job took nearly two days.

Building the East Alligator Crossing

At Oenpelli Roger Gregson was making preparations for building the crossing to start in August. Using large sheets of flat iron, he built a bulldozer blade to be bolted to the front of the kerosene tractor. The crosscut saw was sharpened and some axes. Roger felt it would not be very difficult if done in simple stages.

Many people camped at the river. The men worked on the west bank with John Mildenhall and the women on the eastern side with Roger. The first task was to cut the banks back for road access. The kerosene tractor with the flat iron blade took a bit of handling, but it made a path into the bank. Women would dig up the ground and the tractor push the dirt down the slope into the river.

On the men's side things were slower. John thought he could speed things up if he had a few sticks of gelly. So he came to me as I was preparing to do a run to town asking. "Could I bring out a box of gelignite, a tin of detonators and a few yards of fuse?"

I said; "No problem, I will see Stan Kennon in town."

At the end of the week I was back there with John's request. It was illegal to carry gelignite and fuses on the same vehicle but, by burying the gelly in the centre of the load on the back and carefully packing the detonators under the passenger side seat, I could take them together. Gelignite was one of many things I had never dealt with before.

I sat on the bank and watched John 'professionally' set up five charges! The men dug five holes in the bank and we retreated to a safe area. At last everything was ready. John lit the first fuse. I commented to John that he had a wide experience of these things. He replied he had never touched gelignite before!

As the fuse burned we waited, and waited and waited. Suddenly a bump and a few handfuls of dirt were thrown into the air. We thought that was it, but he told us there were four more to come. Patiently we waited, and waited. Behold another bump with a few more handfuls of river bank dislodged. Four of the charges went off. We waited what seemed a long time for the last one but nothing. John started walking over to see what had happened. Just as he was approaching the vital point - bump, another patch of dirt flew up. The men went back to work with shovels and the gelignite was packed away in the mission store for a more appropriate use.

Word got around that we were putting a crossing over the East Alligator River so we received a visit from two Works Department men.

"Who gave you permission to interfere with the normal flow of the river by building a road crossing? There must be many other places to cross the river rather than where you are working", and so it went on. Finally they asked "What other places are there?"

I replied the only other place was in Mikginj Valley.

"Could I show them?"

I replied, "Of course, if you bring me and drive your Landrover."

I was preparing for a Darwin trip, but I decided to delay.

We set out through the gap. About mid-afternoon we came to the river and they fell in love with it. This was a far better place to cross. They had all the answers about what we could do. It seemed unwise to comment.

After we crossed the river I pointed the way down through to the gorge and asked; "What should we do about all the sand?" There was no reply. Our wheel tracks were in the sand from taking the truck out six weeks earlier. I indicated to follow these tracks. At last we came to the gorge. There was a vague query if this was the way to go. They kept on driving quietly until at last we came to the point on the river where the rock crossing was being built.

As we pulled up I received another lecture about tampering with the normal flow of a river. They were prepared to let it remain as 'temporary road work', but pointed out it would only last one season and be washed out when the river came up.

I left our visitors who drove on to Oenpelli and I set out for Darwin.

By September, the crossing channels were ready for rock. It could not be done while the tide was in so this time was used to stack sandstone four miles away, cart it to the river on the tractor and trailer and heap it for use. The west bank approach was steep so 'touching up' this was necessary.

At last the day came, Friday, 13th September, 1956. Everyone was waiting for me to arrive from Darwin with a loaded truck. I had a passenger, Sid Hodge, from Darwin. He got out and walked part way across to take a photograph of the Blitz.

This original crossing is still under all that has been built over it through the years, and at no time was there a sign of it being washed out.

With the crossing finished there was a lot of carting to be done. I spent a lot of time in town each trip and hoped for someone else to share this truck work. Wet season supplies arrived in October and had to be shifted as soon as possible. I wondered about using the railway to Pine Creek, to save 300 miles from each trip, and found that a 20 ton load could be sent in a railway truck and would be shunted into a siding for us to collect. This gave a mobile store room.

The truck was showing signs of old age. It's steering had a strong vibration, and the rear engine oil seal was leaking so we had to carry spare oil. I felt we should look around for a spare Blitz to use for parts and made enquiries about this.

A person in the Government Stores Branch advised there was a wartime Blitz tipper in very good condition on the side of the airstrip at Anthonys Lagoon. If I made a reasonable offer they would give it favourable consideration. I made an offer of 120 pounds. After a few weeks, I received word that, on payment, I could take delivery of the vehicle at Anthonys Lagoon, 1000 kilometres away."

Gradually over the years new and improved trucks were bought, full time drivers were employed and the crossing of the River was upgraded. In time the bitumen Arnhem Highway would replace the dirt tracks, heading straight east from Humpty Doo to Jabiru and Kakadu National Park, with large all weather bridges over the Adelaide, Mary and South Alligator Rivers. These reduced the distance by road to half and the time from two long days to three to four hours.

It becomes hard to remember that, when my parents first came to Oenpelli there was no road at all. As the road and river crossing came into being another issue emerged alongside it – the need for all the NT missions to have a base in Darwin. This became my parents' next challenge.

To Darwin to live

Grahams Story continued

Darwin Childhood Stories

Things move slowly in the NT, however, after three decades of separate missions at different remote locations in the NT it was apparent that somewhere was needed as a central administrative point, a place for people to come and stay, stores to be assembled for transport and contact point for external dealings and the missionary offices in southern Australia. Darwin was the obvious place.

My father got this job, and travelled to Darwin to purchase a suitable property and to establish a base there. He bought twelve acres of Darwin stringybark scrub on the road north of Darwin town centre, going to the new suburb of Nightcliff, and commenced work building a house there.

In November 1957, my mother packed our family's few belongings and moved to Darwin to join my father. Time was of the essence as the wet season was coming. She was expecting a fourth child within a month. With her came Robin, five years, me three years and Dorothy of two years. The flight into Darwin is fixed in my mind, my first clear memory of flying in an aeroplane, seeing the dark dots of ant-beds and buffalo, landing on a grass strip at Woolner Station at the edge of the Adelaide River plains. We moved into a temporary guest house while our house was being built. A week later was my fourth birthday party; my first ever taste of fizzy drinks, delicious creamy soda, disgusting, cough medicine flavoured, sarsaparilla and lollies; what more could a four year old want! A week later my mother had a new baby, Barbara.

At some indeterminate, near future time, we moved to this new house. It sat on low piers a metre above the ground. It had a roof, floor and walls but no stairs or windows yet. So a forty-four gallon drum became the front step which we climbed up, and mosquito nets were part of sleeping. The bath was a half forty four gallon drum in the garden. The rest of the construction happened over the next few months, followed by a garden to supply fruit and vegetables, and a series of other buildings; a store shed to hold supplies for the missions, a workshop to do repairs on trucks and an office with a radio to allow scheduled radio contacts, called skeds, with all the missions.

It became a hub of people coming and going, those on the way to southern states for holidays, missionaries and aboriginal people in Darwin for medical treatment, visitors and new missionaries from the south on their way out to the missions. It seemed most nights we had an extra person or two at the table for dinner. Mum adjusted her cooking accordingly. Sometimes our menu included food brought in from the missions, buffalo and goat from Oenpelli, dugong, turtle meat and turtle eggs from Groote Eylandt, and lots of bananas, pawpaws, pineapples, mangoes, guavas and other tropical produce from our garden. We had a chook yard, and for my fifth birthday ducks followed. I carried these around on the back of my tricycle on my exploration journeys.

We made friends with the children who lived on either side of us. Freddie Drysdale lived on one side. He was my age so we went exploring the bush and riding our bikes together. On the other side was the Mooring family, with a fruit orchard. Charles, their eldest son built us a cubby house out of tin sheets in a tree between our house and the main road, and his sister was Robin's friend.

Our back yard was ten acres of Darwin stringybark and woollybut scrub with an understorey of speargrass. This grew high over our heads in the wet season, then it collapsed in the dry season forming an endless series of waist high tunnels. We discovered World War Two relics, old shell cases, pieces of machinery, a dugout bomb shelter and other treasures. It was a fertile playground for imagination. My small child reality and fantasy mingled; I told Robin incredible stories of the things I discovered, mostly invented. She went along, perhaps wanting to believe in my wonderful make believe world.

At the end of January next year Robin went to school in Darwin, while I stayed at home with Mum and my two small sisters. I spent hours playing in the sandpit below the house, full of ant-lion holes to catch wayward ants. A year later I followed Robin to school. We would walk down the track to the front of the block and wait on Bagot Road for the school bus to come. Coming home, off the bus, Robin ran ahead to tell Mum the news of the day, and I meandered along, daydreaming, looking at every ant nest, caterpillar and butterfly, taking fifteen minutes to walk the hundred yards from Bagot Road to our house.

Once an older boy rubbed Tarzans grip glue in my hair, and it had to be cut out, another time older kids taught me swear words. They told me to go home and say them to my Mum and Dad. With no idea what they meant I did just that. The taste of my mouth washed out with soap has never left me.

We all loved the wet season. Heavy rains came with lightning and massive raindrops banged on the tin roof our house, sometimes so loudly you could hear nothing else. In January and February the monsoon came and it rained for days then more days on end. We did jigsaws and Mum read us stories from across the world. She had a book with pictures of wild animals, including one of a black panther. It so fascinated me that I decided to become a zoologist when I grew up. Sometimes the rain was so heavy that Bagot Road became a strip of black tar surrounded by a sea of brown water on both sides, with my pet ducks swimming along the side of the road. At the end of the wet season mosquitoes came. Always there at night, as the water dried back, often you could not go outside in the daytime without hundreds of ravenous mosquitoes covering you.

We went barefoot except for school, church and outings. Our feet hardened until we could walk on the melting bitumen of Bagot Road in the hot afternoon sun. As the years went by my tricycle was replaced with a push bike, with another bike for Robin. These bikes had belonged to our parents, brought from Sydney and fixed up. My adult bike was so big I could barely touch the ground. Brand new bikes did not come with a missionary salary, but ours seemed just as good. Each week we each got a shilling of pocket money, spent at the shop near the airport where we bought a paddle-pop and an amazing array of lollies with our money. They lasted all day.

Soon a primary school was built in Nightcliff. A corrugated dirt road, Coconut Grove, ran along the back of our block. Robin and I rode our push bikes along it to school in Nightcliff. Occasionally a vehicle passed in a cloud of dust. One day I found a rusty knife in the long grass near the road and took it to school. Spotting a hollow in a tree at the edge of the school grounds I dropped the knife into it until after school. Going to collect the knife on the way home I saw something else in the hollow, a snake had taken up residence. Perhaps it was there all along and not liked me dropping a knife on it. In my vivid way I made up at story to my friends how it struck at me, its fangs passing between my finger and thumb. In truth I think I caught a glimpse and beat a hasty retreat.

Guy Fawkes Night, each November, was special. My father, a practical joker, bought a great store of fireworks; crackers, sparklers, Catherine Wheels, rockets and other fantastic types. Our family had a big bonfire and let them off. Dad hid away a supply of penny and tuppeny bungers, which occasionally placed under the floorboards of a sleeping friend or neighbour to liven up their day. When we found his hidden store we would sneak a few to let off down the back. Once, a school friend and I decided to have our own bonfire in the bush along Coconut Grove. Within five minutes half an acre of speargrass was burning, so we jumped on our bikes and rode off before anyone caught us.

As time passed new buildings mushroomed on our block; a visitors quarters. a house for another couple to assist Mum and Dad, by now run ragged from taking people to the airport, picking them up, organising stores and travel. An office secretary followed. Often there were several missionary families staying. My father was still doing lots of road trips to Oenpelli, each of several days, taking stores to Oenpelli, returning with loads of stinking salt cured buffalo hides, crocodile skins, bark paintings and other produce. Sometimes he went to visit the other missions, again for days at a time. Mum managed all in his absence in her no fuss manner, sometimes running non-stop all day between new arrivals, the telephone, the garden, and the kitchen.

Dad's constant companions, on trips and construction work in Darwin, were a series of aboriginal men; many remained his lifelong friends. An A frame house was built for them 100 yards behind our house, surrounded by spear-grass. I would go there quietly and talk to them in simple broken English. I watched with fascination as they cooked around the camp fire, sometimes a snake or goanna which they shared with me, their purple-black bodies covered with initiation marks, talking with strange sounding words. They would show me fishing spears, woomeras and other things they were making.

An aboriginal boy, Alex, a couple years older than me, stayed with us for six weeks after being sick in Darwin Hospital with typhoid. We became playmates and firm friends, exploring the Darwin bush together, he teaching me his ways and I showing him my past discoveries like the dugout bomb shelter.

Each two years my parents had a three month holiday in Sydney. My first memory of these was staying at my Grandparents place in Penshurst. I climbed their front fence and fell on my head, on the footpath, leading to much blood and bandaging. I also remember going to Taronga Zoo on the ferry, the animals as exciting in real life as they were in Mum's picture books. I knew, even more certainly, I would be a zoologist. My sister Dorothy wanted an elephant ride, but discovered elephants were much too big. I loved my elephant ride.

Next trip to Sydney my parents decided to drive their car, an old Vanguard. They bought a mini caravan, with a cooking part at the back and a place inside for two people to sleep. My eighth birthday present, a month before, was a tent. Robin and I shared this while the others slept in the back of the car and caravan. We drove to Katherine on the first day, camping on the river at the low level bridge for two days, before heading to Tennant Creek and across the Barkly Highway, to Queensland. Near Camooweal we stopped for a picnic lunch of egg sandwiches. We spread a rug under a half shady tree. As we opened our mouths a million flies came from every grass tussock. Every bite included another fly; ugh! - I can still remember the taste. Within five minutes we were back driving down the road, windows down to get rid of the flies, as we ate. The driving seemed to go on forever and to entertain ourselves over long hours in the car we had competitions to rip Minty wrappers into the longest strips of paper.

Until we came to Mt Isa was bitumen all the way from Darwin. Then we hit the dirt road to Cloncurry. We thought we knew corrugations in the NT, but never had we experienced corrugations like these, hour upon hour of bone shuddering, teeth rattling, vibration. The road wound up and down little stony hills. Each time we got up speed to smooth them out we would round a rock strewn corner and Dad had to slow. The thumping, hammering vibrations would resume. Interspersed with this pounding were huge flocks of brilliant green and yellow wild budgerigars. They swept through the low stony hills, dazzling us with their iridescent colour. Eventually, in the late afternoon, we made the bitumen again near Cloncurry. It was heaven to be on smooth road again.

It was wet season so the relief was short lived. Next day, back on dirt, we headed across black soil plains towards Charleville. That night, camped on a small ridge surrounded by huge open plains, a torrential downpour turned the flat grassland into a huge swamp, with us in its middle. When dawn came we looked out across something like an inland sea, water, water everywhere as far as we could see. We headed off. The first half hour was not too bad, with a bit of skidding and sliding, but the road was still solid. After that the road got wetter and the plain got wider. By lunch we were hopelessly bogged, not a tree, rock or any other thing to extricate ourselves with in sight; a car and caravan sitting in the centre of a sea of liquid bottomless mud.

We were not the only ones bogged, so slowly, over the next couple of days, a group of us extricated ourselves and moved forward in convoy until we reached bitumen again. We continued our trip to the coast at Townville.

Shopping in big city Townsville was a day out, then we drove south along the coast, with beautiful beach side stops each night. Christmas was a three day stopover, camped at Tin Camp Bay, half way down the Queensland coast.

We were sad to arrive in Sydney as our camping adventure was at an end. We moved to a house in Kangaroo Valley for the rest of our holiday. It was an old weatherboard cottage in the village, sitting at the edge of farmland with acres of blackberries. Each morning we collected these, eating as we picked, for

Mum to make pies and jam. The sheer, luminous cliffs ringing the valley with its hidden waterfalls seemed both wonderful and familiar to me; perhaps it triggered fragments of buried memories of the Oenpelli hills.

The return NT trip was shorter; stopped at a flooded creek in Central Queensland for a couple days waiting for the water to fall, then being towed through behind a truck, water flowing up over the car seats, remains in my memory. Final memories are two nights out of Darwin when we camped at Green Ant Creek, near Pine Creek. I had a swim in a water hole deeper than my head. I remember my excitement at finally learning to swim without my feet touching the bottom. The last day we stopped at Robin Falls Creek, near Adelaide River. Here the stream bed was covered in rocks and pebbles of an incredible range of colours, crystal clear water cascading over them; here the intense colours of my childhood memory fade, never seen so bright again.

Back in Darwin my new swimming prowess meant we were allowed to ride our pushbikes along the dirt of McMillans Rd to Rapid Creek and swim there in the dry season pools on hot Saturday afternoons. That was freedom!

Visit to Oenpelli

In 1962, aged eight, I was deemed old enough to accompany my father on trips into the bush. That dry season my father announced I could come on a road trip to Oenpelli. The truck was loaded with 10 tons of mixed stores by Dad, Stephen and another aboriginal man, while I tried to assist. We left Darwin next morning, me in the cab, the aboriginal men with swags, perched on top of the load.

We followed the low gravel ridges of the Stuart Highway south to the 40 mile, then turned onto a dirt track heading east to the Marrakai crossing of the Adelaide river, before winding across the Marrakai plains, crossing the Mary River near Hardy's billabong on Annaburroo, then going through stringybark woodlands, drying paperbark swamps, pandanus patches and open grass plains heading towards Goodparla. Buffalo dung was everywhere, as were freshly used wallows, their black muddy water glistening in the afternoon sun. The buffalo were quick to move away, wary of buffalo shooters.

Night camp was Flying Fox Creek, just before the South Alligator River crossing. It was bitterly cold sleeping on the ground on a dry season night, next to a camp fire where my father and the aboriginal men drunk cups of black tea. Reflected in the firelight, 50 yards away, were the eyes of many curious buffalo, however they kept their distance. Next morning I got up to another cup of tea and a bowl of hot porridge in the early dawn light. Then it was back on the truck, winding though more woodlands, crossing the South Alligator followed by Jim Jim, Nourlangie and Magela Creeks, before arriving at the East Alligator River crossing late in the morning.

It was a new moon tide with more than four feet of brown water flowing sluggishly upwards over the rock crossing. So we made camp on the bank and waited for the tide to drop. I spent a long slow afternoon in the shade of massive paperbarks of the river bank, perched high, watching the water flow up the river. Then high tide, a feeding frenzy of barramundi and other large predatory fish chomping on the bait fish as they jumped out of the water. Fins of sharks cruising the surface came sweeping past, just below my feet. Slowly the water began to run back out, then faster, as late afternoon then evening came. Still waist level water remained over the crossing.

An hour after dark the water stopped running out, sat still and, with slow eddies, began to flow in again. My father decided the river was at its lowest so we packed our day camp and climbed aboard the truck. It crawled down the road, through the cut-out dirt bank into the river, still over three feet deep. In low gear we ground our way over the rock bar, bouncing over submerged rocks, as the brown water swirled around the top of the truck tires. Finally we lurched out of the water on the other side and pulled slowly up the far bank.

All the while I enjoyed the wonder of returning to Arnhem Land, its sights, sounds, smells and teeming night wildlife in the headlights. Half an hour later the lights of Oenpelli twinkled into view.

We were welcomed by Mr Harris and a small group of people gathered in the truck headlights, wondering why we had taken so long. Mrs Harris had a hot dinner on the stove, and a bed with a mosquito net waiting for me. Next day my father unloaded the stores and returned to Darwin, leaving me in the care of the Harris family, to rediscover this place of my childhood.

A week was spent exploring, remembering and making new friends with other children, both black and white. Peter Cooke had lived here for more than a year. He showed me all his favourite places. Oenpelli had lost none of its magic, its billabong, hills and plains dotted with buffalo, horses, cattle and waterbirds, groups of aboriginals hunting bush tucker and fishing. A few days later I reluctantly returned to Darwin on the aeroplane with Robin. She had flown out with her friend Anne Cooke, Peter's older sister. Anne was living with us in Darwin that year while she went to school.

Mum and Dads Story continued

Establishing a Mission Base in Darwin

By the time we moved to Darwin Mum had three children under five and was expecting a fourth very soon. This time there was a network of friends, one of whom provided us with an initial place to stay. Dad did not fly in on the plane with us as he was doing road trips and bringing in personal items on the truck. Over the weeks that followed Mum gave birth to a fourth child.

Dad recorded of this time:

"When I arrived back at Goodparla there was a telegram for me from Helen to say that Barbara Jane was born on the Friday! With all speed I moved on up the highway to Darwin and met our new daughter that evening."

Shortly after this Mum and Dad moved to a virtual bush block. There was a partly constructed house, with frames, a tin roof and floorboards but not much else. With help from Dad, friends, neighbours and the Oenpelli community, including many aboriginal members, Mum quickly set about creating order. Soon they established a fruit and vegetable garden with paw paws, bananas, snake beans and anything else edible they could grow. They also had a chook yard to supply eggs and roast chicken dinners. At an early age we learnt how to scald and pluck chooks.

Of course they did not live in splendid isolation. Darwin was a busy place, people always coming and going from the five NT missions, and lots of trades people and deliveries of stores for later delivery to remote locations. It was a rare day without several visitors. Dad was often away for several day periods, taking loads of stores to Oenpelli or visiting other missions.

At these times, along with household and family organisation, all the general business of the NT centre would be dealt with by Mum in her polite, quiet and efficient manner. Some days it seemed like the phone never stopped ringing. I am sure she was exhausted from all the demands on her time but she was rarely cross and sometimes would give all us kids a big hug. As a cheeky six to eight year old I remember tormenting her and finally getting her cross and exasperated. She would try to smack me while I laughed and ran out of range. Only once can I remember her having a serious argument with Dad. It was over, good humour restored, in an hour or two, cause unknown.

Having given my memories of moving to Darwin I retell parts of this move and life in Darwin, again using extracts of my father's memoir for parts of the story.

An aeroplane arrived unexpectedly at Oenpelli at the end of 1955. I was persuaded to travel on it to Darwin to try to organise transport for our stores. This was the first glimpse I had of the Darwin set-up, and it was not inspiring. Our food supplies went to a store in Cavenagh Street. Here local traders could 'dip' into our supplies to satisfy the local market until the next ship arrived. Hardware went into a yard in Bishop Street and boxes of goods went to Haritos' store in Daly Street. Two boxes of our personal groceries, shipped two years before, had recently been thrown out, gone bad.

We needed a permanent base in Darwin with a person living there. I knew a few people were interested in this job and I left it as someone else's work. About February 1957, a letter came from Mr Montgomerie in Sydney, asking me to seriously consider taking this position.

I set about looking for an area of land suitable for our work. It needed to be big enough for several houses and have scope for a garden. My travel was done by foot so a lot of time was spent walking. The first area I looked at was next to Kath Hind's block in Coconut Grove. It was a big block, over 20 acres, and went through to the sea. I knew the mosquitoes and sand flies would be a problem. There did not seem to be anything else without going outside the Darwin area.

I made application to Lands Branch for a Special Purposes Lease, and wrote advising our Sydney Office. A letter came from Lands Branch advising our application was rejected, due to tidal surge in the event of a cyclone. So I had to start over. I also received a letter from CMS asking me to detail plans for establishment of the Centre, including a hostel for CMS children to attend school in Darwin. I had never contemplated this.

Word of our search got around. I was told Fred Drysdale, a Member of the Legislative Council, would like to see me. Fred had a block of nearly 14 acres on the corner of Bagot Road and McMillans Road, held as an agricultural lease. He wanted to retain a 2 acre business lease, for a garage and residence, leaving about 12 acres, which was ideal. He wanted twenty pounds an acre, which was very reasonable. We needed to apply to the Lands Branch for a Special Purposes Lease. From enquiries this should be fairly straight forward. I placed the matter in the hands of a Legal Company, 'Newell and Ward', while I continued to make road trips and work at Oenpelli.

On returning I called in to Newell and Ward's Office. The Contract was made out for 22nd July 1957. After reading it, I signed it on behalf of the Church Missionary Society. Then I received advice I should make an appointment to see Mr Harry Giese, Director of the Welfare Branch, which seemed unusual. When I met him, he was concerned I was setting up a centre without consulting him. He said he could make land, ideal for our work, available to CMS on Bagot Aboriginal Reserve.

As politely as possible I declined his offer. A consideration was the flight path of aircraft landing and taking off during the night. The new Darwin airstrip was due for completion in less than a year bringing Bagot Reserve under the flight path, and with increasing air traffic it could become a real noise problem. Our land was right under the present flight path, but this would change when the new runway was completed.

While at his office, I asked Mr Giese whether we could start building while waiting for the lease to be granted. His reply was "Under no circumstances. It would be quite illegal for you to occupy or do anything to the land until the Lease is finalised." I was sorry I raised it. CMS had shipped an Eccono steel building and I wanted it delivered on site.

By mid-October nothing was finalised with the lease, preventing building before the wet. At the end of October I left Oenpelli with our few belongings in the Blitz. One of the staff was to take back the last of the loading. Helen, expecting Barbara very soon, and the children arrived by plane a few days later. Our immediate accommodation was at the Red Cross Convalescent Home at Fannie Bay.

From November to January we stayed temporarily in two houses while the owners were away. Then we had to move; this time with nowhere to go. Kath Hinds offered to share her place at Coconut Grove, a full house with the six of us and her. In early February I went to Groote with Welfare staff to sort out a polygamy problem. Keith Hart was on the plane back to Darwin. He advised me the lease had been granted for our land.

Now the urgency was to get something built to live in, well into the wet season. By the end of March I had erected the framework of the Eccono steel building, with help from the Pastor of the Aborigines Inland Mission church. Dick Harris also passed through, on his way to Umbakumba. He gave me a day of his time, so we fixed most of the iron on the roof. By the end of April, the floor was laid and the bottom half of the walls were in place.

Kath Hinds now needed her house for visitors so we moved to our partly finished house on Saturday 3rd May, 1958. The power was not connected and water was only available at a tap in the yard. To get into the house we stepped onto a wooden box, then a 44 gallon drum on its end and then onto the floor of the house. It was difficult for Helen and four children. We needed a shower, toilet and laundry. This meant digging a septic tank pit and absorption trench. I started on building steps but there was always something else. Finally, Helen came a 'cropper' on our improvised "stairs" which placed priority on installing proper steps.

Two aboriginal men, Melville Island Charlie and an Oenpelli man, Deaf Charlie, arrived and worked with us. They preferred to camp with us rather than at Bagot and help with building. I provided sheets of corrugated iron and they built a small hut. It gave Helen more work providing their meals but it speeded up work on our house.

More Road Trips to Oenpelli

In the middle of June a new truck driver, Bill, arrived in Darwin with the Blitz. He had a large pair of buffalo horns tied to the front bull bar. I organised a load and in a couple days, the truck was ready to return. None of the maintenance work needed on the truck had been done at Oenpelli. Bill left Darwin and two days later I received a telegram from Goodparla saying he was broken down with engine, gear box and rear diff. troubles. There was nothing I could do so I waited to see what would happen. I later heard he was at Oenpelli with the truck. Then I received a telegram from Ray Taylor, Oenpelli's new Superintendent, saying the truck would not return, future loading was to be sent by boat.

We had gone back two years. It was a grind, with many other things, to find someone available and willing to take loading to the East Alligator River. Through 1958 I kept up boat transport. In September the wet season food supplies were arriving. Another boat offered to take 20 tons to Smiths Landing. It took nearly two days to load the vessel. It arrived at Smiths landing on Saturday, 4th October. Ray Taylor left Oenpelli on leave about a week later.

About mid-October a telegram from CMS in Sydney advised John Mildenhall wanted another truck to cart cattle to Darwin from Oenpelli. The only vehicle suitable was a GMC. 6X6. I knew Eric Izod had two of these in his garage in Darwin. I approached Eric about selling one of them. He was interested but wanted 1200 pounds.

The only money that I had was 1130 pounds specifically for building. I approached Eric again and tried to get the price down. He was adamant that the vehicle was worth 1200 pounds. He said there were 600 pounds worth of tyres on it. I knew one vehicle was on blocks with no tyres. It occurred to me to price a set of 7.50 X 20 tyres and tubes. The price was 380 pounds so again I confronted Eric. If we fitted the wheels with new tyres and tubes, would he register the truck for 12 months and accept 600 pounds for it. He discussed the matter with his son and eventually agreed. I set about having the eleven wheels fitted with tyres.

By the end of the week it was done and the vehicle registered. I paid the 600 pounds, loaded it with fuel drums and set out by myself in it for Oenpelli on Friday, 28th October.

Before leaving I contacted VJD (the coastal radio station), to pass a message to Oenpelli that I was coming. They advised Oenpelli had not been on the air for two weeks. This meant that either their transmitter or receiver was not working. Coonawarra Naval Base supplied a replacement transmitter and receiver as we were a recognised coast watching station.

I arrived at the East Alligator Crossing on the Saturday afternoon. The tide was out but the crossing was covered in silt. Nobody had used it for a long time and the silt had dried, apart from the centre. The truck could not drive through it. After a few tries I left the truck and walked the 10 miles to the Mission, arriving late afternoon. I was told there was no truck, tractor or crawler tractor in working order to pull the truck through the silt. They would send a team of men with shovels, on horseback, next morning after church.

At midday on Sunday we arrived at the river and the men went to work with their shovels. It was hopeless. The dried out silt was like tough leather. Stephen came to me and said, "Nabba, what about you drive that truck hard into the silt and we push?" It was worth a try. The first time we penetrated six inches. Stephen came back and said, "One more" and as we moved forward his voice came through with "wernkih" and then "one more". After three goes we penetrated a couple of yards. The men became more energetic each time. Towards the centre of the crossing the silt was wet and the wheels sank in. Slowly I came out on the other side with a loud shout of approval. The men threw their shovels on the truck, left two men to bring the horses back while the rest climbed on the back to return to the Mission. Next day the real work began, to bring in supplies that the boat had left almost a month before at Smiths landing and which were still sitting there.

Next day I set out for Smiths Landing, 38 miles each way, with six men. As the plains were dry we cut across them, coming to a creek where the water teemed with large barramundi. Men grabbed pieces of drift wood and truck tools to hit the fish. We gathered about ten large fish and went on. As we approached the landing the scene was of desolation. Heaps of food were piled up, some covered with old pieces of canvas, sheets of iron or a small amount of paperbark in a desperate attempt to keep rain off the food.

We worked loading the food most at risk while a couple of men cooked damper and fish. The covering was then used to cover other heaps of food. On the return journey we stopped at each broken down vehicle. There was the short wheel base Blitz, and a utility belonging to Big Paddy. The cover was off the rear diff. displaying a crown wheel with no teeth. A little further on was a wheel tractor with a flat rear tyre and a trailer partly loaded with food. Then came our transport Blitz, an open 44 gallon drum of water on the back and hoses going through the rear window to the radiator. The engine cowl was thrown on the back of the truck. Still further was the crawler tractor with a trailer, well loaded. We assumed it was not working. It was all a dismal sight.

We made our way back to Oenpelli with as much as we could fit on the truck. There had been early showers but the weather held off. About 6 pm we arrived at the mission and everything was unloaded into the store. Next day, Tuesday, was the same and on Wednesday, we finished bringing in the loading but not the vehicles.

On Thursday Stephen and I worked on the GMC in the workshop, trying to make a cage on the back to cart cattle to Darwin. There was little material available to use. After welding some pieces of steel and bolting pieces of timber to it, we used fencing wire. I asked Stephen if he thought it would hold the bullocks. He looked a bit puzzled and said, "Mightbe, we try." So we tried.

Next morning the stockmen loaded 6 bullocks on the back and off we went. The truck rocked about as the animals explored their confined space. In Red Lily was a part where the road sloped sideways. As we drove along a venturesome animal jumped over the lower side. We pulled up and examined the 'stockyard'. I said to Stephen, "I think we should let them all off." His immediate reply was "More better." With a pair of fencing pliers, we unfastened the rear panel and away they went. And away we went to Darwin.

What stood out at Oenpelli was the general untidiness of the whole place, buffalo bones, tins and rubbish lying around, tools not put away. It was in sharp contrast to when Ron Ash was in charge. I wrote a letter to Mr. Montgomerie about the situation at Oenpelli. Reading the Station Journal years later, the last entry made by Ray Taylor, before going on leave said; "Very broken and unsettled week. Complete break-down of transport, with stores spread all over the country, and also trucks."

I don't know if he knew of the effort required to repair the damage, but at no future time was there any suggestion that we go back to boats.

We went on holidays to Sydney after Christmas. I was asked to attend an Aborigines Committee meeting and was questioned on all aspects of the work. I did not have answers to many things, especially setting up a school children's hostel. I outlined what we had done and were planning, building a second house, the need for Aboriginal accommodation and a store for Oenpelli goods in transit.

After we returned CMS shipped the parts for a Nissan hut. By changing the design we had the roof structure for our store. At Timber Camp I bought timber to finish it. We could now transfer everything to our depot. The next project was to erect two towers for a radio transmitter to give us contact with the five missions. The Methodist Missions agreed to share their frequency so we could have daily skeds with the missions.

At the end of 1958 I was persuaded to bring to Darwin from Oenpelli, some buffalo hides, salted two years earlier. Until 1953 the buffalo hide industry had been a large industry across the plains east from the Adelaide River. Leather from buffalo hides was used as textile leather in many factories throughout the world as long machinery belting. Oenpelli shared in this industry and the collapse of this market left many people without a job. It appears a shipment of hides, at the end of the 1952 season, was caught in the Suez Canal crisis and spent months in the canal on the way to Turkey. A professional buffalo shooter told me later of things done to increase the weights of loads of hides. When an operator, taking hides on a truck to Darwin, saw some buffalo around a water hole on the way, it was common to shoot two or three and skin them. These wet untreated hides were put in the centre of the other hides. At the shipping terminal they went over the weighbridge and were loaded with other hides. Another practice was, to place flat rocks inside folded hides. Plastic and textile belting was also taking over. When the vessel was released from the Suez Canal with a putrid cargo of hides, it wrote finish to the industry.

Later attempts were made to attract southern leather manufacturers. One ordered 100 hides of approximately 60 lb. weight each. At Oenpelli we attempted to fill this order, although the normal weight for a dried hide was 100 to 120 lbs. Once the order was made up the purchasing company pulled out and we were left with this stack of hides. Dick Harris was sure others would be interested, so I inherited them.

The first wet season I stacked them on poles and covered them as best I could under sheets of iron. Next year we made a permanent storehouse for them. But with no buyers they finally they had to be disposed of. This was not easy. To send them to the tip I had to provide sufficient sump oil or old tyres to burn them. I had nothing to use for this. Finally I loaded them on the tipper and took them to a remote edge of the RAAF firing range. With the hoist on the tipper I deposited them in the bush. Grass must grow tall and green there!

Developing Darwin and the Missions

Mail drew my attention to the need to produce plans for the Darwin Centre, with boarding facilities for children. I was in a quandary as to what to do. Some of this impetus was a Government offer of low interest loans for accommodation in main centres, where children had to come for schooling. Again I was asked to attend an Aborigines Committee meeting in Sydney in February, 1960, and bring my plans for the development of our land. All I had were a few plans of housing and a general layout of future buildings

Before I left for Sydney, it occurred to me that Bush Church Aid (BCA) was experienced so we should invite them to take over the school project. The more I thought, the more I was convinced it was the right way to go. In Sydney I raised BCA being invited to do this work. This received the approval of all. They agreed I should approach Bishop Tom Jones, whose office was nearby. I made an appointment to see him. He was enthusiastic and I left feeling that this was a better way forward.

Back in Darwin a BCA representative from Sydney assessed the situation. He chose separate land at Nightcliff and a loan for 60,000 pounds was negotiated with the Government, enabling the building to go ahead. Then the Bishop of Carpentaria found out about the project and refused BCA permission to operate in the Diocese. So land and loan were transferred to its headquarters at Thursday Island. Still, slowly, the project went ahead. Eventually the boarding school, Carpentaria College, could accept students.

In1961 I received a letter from Mr Montgomerie saying an order had been placed with Leyland motors for a diesel Comet truck, with an eighteen foot tray, fitted with a removable cattle yard, to carry about 10 beasts. I was to fly to Sydney and drive it to North Australia. On a Friday afternoon, at the end of April, I took delivery of the truck, in Waterloo, Sydney and set out to get the feel of the road. Everything was well, until, going around a corner, the steering became very tight. I turned back to Waterloo. Just as I was approaching the depot the steering came right. I outlined the problem to the foreman who checked the truck and could find nothing wrong. He thought my lack of experience with trucks was the problem. I drove it home to Engadine for the weekend and the steering once more went tight on the Princes Highway. It was an intermittent fault for the next three years and gave me a back complaint.

Geoff Lucas was to travel north with me. John Donald heard of it and made a request to be in the crew. John and I shared the driving while Geoff attended other details. The first night John directed us to a truckies haunt on the Pacific Highway for a good meal. Next morning, for breakfast on the side of the road, Geoff produced a tablecloth.

We arrived in Darwin then continued to Oenpelli two days later. That night we camped on a pocket of the plains north of Mudginberry. There were plenty of buffalo. The only way to keep them out of our camp was to keep two fires burning all night so we didn't get much sleep. Next morning, Dick Harris and a team of men met us with tractors and trailers near the crossing. Our load lightened, we crossed the river. Red Lily was wet and we needed help to get through, but by lunch we were at Oenpelli.

At this point we received a telegram that Mr Montgomerie had died. We did not realise how ill he was. Shortly after Bishop Kerle was made Acting Regional Secretary until the appointment of Canon George Pearson was made.

On one trip to Oenpelli in the Leyland, in October that year I did not have anyone with me. Just after the East Alligator crossing the wheels of the truck sunk into the sandy wheel tracks. I kept going for about 50 yards but on changing gear the rear wheels burrowed into the sand and the truck stalled.

As I walked around the vehicle, Big Paddy came across from the bank of the river where he was camping, with his wife Jessie and nephew Sandy. I said I would walk to the Mission and borrow a tractor to pull the truck out. Paddy's considered opinion was "more better" and then he added "be careful of those buffalo in the paperbarks, big mob." Then on further consideration he added 'you take Sandy and I give him my 30' and then, as if an afterthought 'I give him two bullets'.

It was about six in the evening and Sandy had a torch so we set off. When we came to the paperbarks it was dark. Sandy swept the torch to and fro, alert for buffalo. As we started to walk through the paperbarks Sandy became more tense in the lead. He could see many pairs of buffalo eyes and he saw a pair moving closer. He raised the rifle; there was a loud bang, then chaos. Buffalo charged towards us. I sheltered behind an eight inch paperbark trunk, horns going past within inches.

I did not know what happened to Sandy and was not greatly concerned. After a few minutes the herd had moved onto the plains, I could see a torch flickering on some rocks. It was Sandy fiddling with the 303. I clambered up to see what he was doing. The bullet case was stuck in the chamber and he was trying to extract it. I took over and got it out. I asked Sandy for the other bullet, which he gave me. I put it in my pocket, gave Sandy back the rifle and we set off for the remaining seven mile walk.

No Longer Wanted in Darwin

In November 1961 John and Ruth Schultze were transferred to Darwin, from Numbulwar. This allowed us to go south on leave. I bought a second hand caravanette which gave sleeping accommodation for three children. It had been the custom of CMS to pay the equivalent of air fares when staff used their own vehicles to travel by road. Under the new regime only the cost of fuel was paid, the first of many changes taking place, as I was to find out in the coming months.

Near the end of May 1962, Mr and Mrs Jack Langford arrived from Melbourne. They were friends of Canon Pearson and Jack was to prepare for the position of Field Superintendent. After they arrived I spent much time with Jack going through what was happening. A few weeks later Canon Pearson arrived and Jack spent most time with him.

During this period I caught up with Gordon Symons from the Methodist Missions. Gordon queried what I had done wrong. I thought he was joking at first, but he went on to say that our new Chief from Sydney said that he had no place for me. I laughed it off but, as time went by, I became aware that there really was no place for me.

A while later there was a meeting in Darwin with superintendents from our missions. The position of Deputy Field Superintendent was given to Jack Langford. My role was Administrative Assistant. I was to do all the running around with no input into any decisions. The cartage of supplies to Oenpelli kept me occupied. So the year dragged on. When I was not away I found something to do in the store and workshop. Time dragged on into 1963.

With four children we accepted the need to be in Darwin but, as time passed, we felt our unwanted presence. I was aware a letter was sent to each of the CMS missions about the Wilsons. I did not see it although some staff mentioned it to me.

I felt they wanted me to resign. Helen and I discussed the situation and agreed it would be best to request to return to Oenpelli and go back to the garden work. An application to return to Oenpelli was soon agreed to.

On August 23rd, 1963, at the beginning of the school holidays, we left Darwin. I loaded all our furniture and belongings, including an assortment of plants, on the truck. When we came to Darwin we had to buy our own furniture. This was done gradually, as we had money, mostly at auctions. I now had an argument loading our furniture; it was felt these things belonged to CMS. So, after nearly six years, we quietly slipped out of Darwin in our own car, to start a new life back working with Aboriginal people.

Our arrival at Oenpelli was greeted with much pleasure by both staff and people. We said we were happy to return to our old house at the back of the store. Instead we were ushered into the first of the new staff houses which was almost finished. To our surprise we even found our furniture had been set out in the house and one lady had unpacked some things and put them in the pantry. It was good to be back home!

Grahams Story continued
Return home to Oenpelli

Oenpelli, in my mind, was always my home. So I do not think of the decision by my parents, when I was nine, to return to Oenpelli, as a move from one place to another, but simply as returning home. I remember the sense of excitement when it was announced one day that we were going back to Oenpelli to live in a couple months' time.

Then came the anxious anticipation, waiting and wanting that time to pass, like waiting for Christmas. At last I was packing my tent for the trip. Finally, us children, wild with excitement, piled into the Holden for the trip down the Stuart Highway. Mum, her unflappable self, made sure that lunch was packed. We stopped for a picnic lunch at Manton Dam. Then the long afternoon drive south following the narrow bitumen strip, past Adelaide River, through the hills around Hayes Creek, and a mid-afternoon stop at old Mr Ah Toy's corrugated iron shop in Pine Creek, for an ice-cream.

Here the bitumen ended, as we turned east and commenced the bush trip, following the first Oenpelli road. It ran along the western edge of the Arnhem-Kakadu escarpment. We went slowly along the corrugated track through low gravel hills, winding our way up, down and around these hills, crossing creeks flowing with dry season spring fed water. Finally we reached Mary River, amidst towering bamboo, clear and fast flowing over shallow gravel and sand. We set up our camp. I put up my tent, helped by Robin, Dorothy and Barbara.

Next day, was a glorious lazy day of camping. Just after lunch while paddling in the river, I trod on something sharp. In a few minutes piercing pain spread up my leg from a small round puncture wound in the sole of my foot. It got hard to breathe; I lay down, frightened. No doubt Mum and Dad were anxious but did not show it. Over the next couple hours it subsided to just a sore foot. Mum and Dad pronounced I had most likely trodden on a catfish.

On the road again the next day the country slowly changed, the gravel hills disappeared, and we crossed pockets of floodplains and bull dust washouts, many with fresh buffalo wallows. We got an occasional glimpse of red-purple hills rising in the distance. Buffalo were scattered through the trees and across the plains. Most moved away as we approached, leaving fresh steaming dung and their lingering smell. Late morning saw us at the South Alligator River. Dad knew this crossing from truck trips, but our car did not have truck clearance so he stopped on the bank. We piled out for a break while he walked through the crossing and surveyed the best route, choosing a downstream path where the water was shallowest, avoiding deep holes. Mum kept a half eye on her brood of four, while fixing lunch. An uneventful crossing followed, and on we went, across the plains towards Jim Jim Creeks. The hills were close now, towering out of the horizon, brilliant coloured in the afternoon sun. Mid-afternoon we found a shallow sandy place, with fresh flowing water, on Nourlangie Creek, where we made camp for the day. We children played in the shallows while Mum and Dad relaxed in the shade.

Next morning we picked our way through the Magela Creek's three crossings, coming to the East Alligator for a late morning stop, swimming in shallow pools alongside the rock crossing until the tide was right for our car to cross; perhaps an hour's delay. I remember the wondrous but familiar feeling of driving through Red Lily, its sheer rock faces, alongside paperbark swamps, billabongs and open plains; like revisiting Eden, with the pungent smell of flowering paperbarks permeating everything. As the road rounded Arrkuluk, Oenpelli opened out before us; it's sunlit backdrop of the Arnhem Land escarpment; a warm south-easterly dry season wind whistling across the open plains, a combination of greens and browns with occasional smoke plumes from aboriginal hunting fires. We all knew we were back home and belonged here.

A New House, New friends and Correspondence School

A small welcoming committee, showed us to our new house, just built and needing some finishing touches. It was not only elevated, to catch the breeze, but fly screened (no more mosquito nets) and with the incredible luxury of ceiling fans, though of course the power only ran until ten o'clock at night.

I renewed my acquaintance with Peter Cooke and his younger brother David, who were to become my lifelong friends. They showed me their special places of Oenpelli, the billabong with a dug-out canoe, which we could paddle when not in use by its aboriginal owners for fishing, Arrkuluk and Injalak Hills to climb, floodplains dotted with horses and buffalo and, emerging in a great semicircle, along the horizon were the cliff faces of the hills of the Spencer Range, all yet to be explored. They introduced me to a whole new tribe of black brothers and sisters, the aboriginal children we went to Sunday school with, played football with and communicated with in a form of broken English.

Our correspondence lessons arrived a few days later. My mother found us all desks, and tried to supervise us. Generally mornings were strict and productive, as we filled out the lesson sheets, and put them in a post bag for correction in Adelaide. In the hot, sleepy afternoons, when no one was looking, I would sneak away to meet Peter and David at the billabong pump house, for fishing or just messing around along the edge of the billabong. I went from a good student to a lazy one, there was far too much else that I wanted to do.

Horses and Mr Harris

One Saturday, a couple weeks after we arrived, in the hottest part of the afternoon, there was a knock on the door. Mr Harris, Superintendent, an erect, bandy legged 63 year old man, announced he had horses outside for us to ride. There was a quick scramble to find jeans and shoes, then up onto these huge animals we climbed, under Mr Harris's tuition. He looked like he had been born and welded into a saddle. We flopped around, gradually mastering how to sit, hold the reins and make the horse respond to our directions.

My horse was Wattle, a 16 hand grey, an old stock horse and dead quiet except for when his head was turned for home, Robin's horse was Eclipse, a feisty bay pony, much loved and still worked as a nimble stock horse. We rode across the plains and around the billabong. We came behind Injalak, returning to Oenpelli along the Waterfall road. The trip out was mostly walking, learning to ride a trot and the occasional canter on placid horses who found this hot afternoon ride less than enthralling. However as we came onto the Waterfall road, with heads turned for home, suddenly horse muscles bunched up, spring sprang into step, champing at bits, like a supercharger was added. The gentle canter rapidly turned into an all-out gallop, as we thundered around the end of the billabong, mud and dust flying off hooves, and finally, as the stockyards came in into view, our horses made a sudden shuddering stop. We climbed off our blowing, sweating mounts, wildly exhilarated by our first ride.

This was the start of an ongoing love affair with the horses of Oenpelli. Saturday afternoons were spent riding ever further afield. These merged with going mustering with aboriginal stockman, and running mobs of horses on the plains for the sheer joy of the chase, each of us tuning our skill with our favourite horse.

In the late dry season of our first year back at Oenpelli a missionary picnic was announced, held at the Springs. This is the nearest permanently flowing water to Oenpelli and sits at the edge of the hills eight miles to the south east.

Horseback was the order of transport, and a tractor and trailer for those unable to ride. Dad expressed his disgust, saying that the only horses he liked using came in large multiples under a single bonnet. Mum seemed quietly pleased with the adventure. Us, kids, thought it was a fantastic idea.

So, one Saturday, about 20 horses were saddled and riders mounted up, even my reluctant father, with Mr Harris in the lead. The road was a two wheel track which stopped half a mile short of the Springs at the edge of the sandstone. Here the tractor and trailer stopped and its human cargo and the horses walked up the creek bed. The main pool is about 50 yards long and 20 yards wide. The water was said to be over 20 feet deep. We kids could only get to the bottom with great effort. Dense paperbarks overhung the main pool. At the top a creek flowed in over white and grey quartzite and granite rocks, bubbling out of a pandanus soak up a rock valley; tens of thousands of gallons of clear water each day cascading down the hillside into the big pool below

After a day of swimming and feasting we set off back home. Half way home our horses got the scent of the Oenpelli plains, the trot turned into a canter and the canter into a gallop. Robin's pony, Eclipse, surged to the front and made a sudden swerve to avoid an ant-bed. Robin did not change direction. Her wily pony was a master at holding its breath when the girth was tightened. Next thing saddle and Robin were hanging under the horses belly, as it galloped along, dragging her with one foot stuck in the stirrup. After a few strides she and the horse separated. Eclipse was caught and a dazed Robin remounted for a more sedate ride home. Dad's view that horses were not to be trusted was reinforced, the rest of us were glad of no serious injury.

The Goats

At daybreak, a few days after we arrived at Oenpelli, Dad called Robin, Dorothy and myself from bed. In the cold dry season morning we trudged 200 yards from our house to the goat yard, carrying empty billycans. 300 goats were penned in wooden yards, with a cacophony of maaing and bleating. We climbed over the wooden fence and walked among the goats on a steaming bed of fresh dung. Dad grabbed a goat by the back leg, her well-formed udder full of milk, and demonstrated the art of goat milking. Each of us then had a turn and filled our billycan. We walked home carrying the warm goat's milk for breakfast. Our regular routine of goat milking each morning was established.

Several aboriginal women were the goat shepherds. Each day they would lead the goats out from the yards, onto the plains, accompanied by their tribe of children, to spend the day in a combination of goat herding and gathering bush tucker. After a day grazing on the short grass at plain's edge they would return to be penned overnight, their shepherds laden with turtles, magpie geese and lily bulbs for supper. For us it was our early morning ritual, huddled among the heat of the steaming goats, collecting milk, some going to the large milk can for community use, some to take home. We each had favourite goats, with quiet natures and large soft teats, and learned those to avoid which kicked out at the billycan, emptying our hard work into the steaming manure. My sisters soon had goat orphans to bottle feed, which rapidly turned into garden destroyers.

One wet season morning, when the plains were flooded and buffalo meat was scarce, instead of the ladies at the goat yards, there was a group of men catching the half grown male goats. At first we watched in interest, uncertain what they were doing, then watched with dismay as club and knife came out. Amidst the bleating of their mothers, they became lifeless carcasses, hanging on hooks to await butchering. We never ate goat meat with the same relish again.

Elijah and the bent rifle barrel

Oenpelli was separated from the plains by a series of cattle fences, which also kept the buffalo on the plains, away from where the people lived. On odd occasions a buffalo would get through the fences and wander around, terrorising the town.

Most were massive old bulls with horns five feet across. When one was sighted the alert would go out around the town, along with screams, yukais and people running for trees. A aboriginal stockman, with a rifle, would be called for to deal with it.

An old buffalo hide shooter named Elijah lived in one of the camps. He was a grizzled looking, white haired man with bowed legs from many years astride a horse. He was said to have been a hide shooter in the days of Paddy Cahill, many years before. He still was occasionally seen astride a stock horse carrying his old 303 rifle. It was said he was a legend in his early years for fearlessly galloping his horse alongside large buffalo bulls, shooting a bullet into the back behind the shoulder, smashing the spine, leaving them paralysed, then coming back to finish them, skin them, and salt and cure the hides.

One day, when an extra-large buffalo bull was sighted on the old airstrip between the camps, Elijah was called for. He emerged on his favourite stock horse, an erect grey haired figure with rifle in hand. Seeing man and horse the buffalo started running along the airstrip with Elijah in chase, but much more reluctant to close the gap than in days of yore. Bang, bang, bang, bang; soon a whole magazine of 303 bullets was used.

The buffalo looked unchanged other than becoming increasingly annoyed with the harassing horse and rider. Having exhausted his ammunition on a now very cranky buffalo, Elijah announced "this rifle, no good, no more, barrel bent." With that he said he would not be shooting buffalo anymore. He rode slowly back to camp leaving the people and the buffalo to make their peace. Eventually the buffalo wandered off and people climbed down from trees.

Away to school in Sydney

My tenth birthday came in November. I was sitting in a tamarind tree on my birthday afternoon, when someone came to tell us of hearing on the short wave radio that President Kennedy had been assassinated. About this time my parents told me and Robin that we would be going off to school in Sydney the next year, staying with our grandparents. Not knowing what to expect we first thought this something of an adventure.

All too soon the end of January came. We caught the mail plane to Darwin and then the big plane to Sydney. The trip took most of the day, getting to Sydney late in the evening. We went to our grandparents' house in Penshurst, where Robin was to stay. Next day my Nana (my father's mother) collected me to come and live with her in Engadine. Nana was a kindly lady and tried hard to make me feel happy, but after the freedom of Oenpelli I hated it, particularly her reluctance to let me go off by myself, in case something bad happened.

Our sanity was for Robin and I to spend weekends together, when we would tell endless tales of life in the NT. Mum would write letters every week to us the news from Oenpelli. My letters home were less regular.

In the school holidays we went to stay with our cousins in Wedderburn, a happy time. In October I got a phone call to say I had a baby brother, a surprise as I did not know anything was expected. Our year away from home seemed to go on forever but finally came to an end. Suddenly it was early December and we were catching the plane back to Darwin. Homecoming was fantastic after almost a year away. My six year old sister Barbara welcomed me by biting my arm. Mum, Dad, Dorothy, and the Cooke family were just the same. There was a new family of slightly older kids, the Mackenzie's who were as horse mad as we were. And there was the baby brother I always wanted, after three sisters.

School holidays passed in an excited blur. At first the seven weeks at home seemed endless. We each had our own horse for the holidays, kept in a little paddock near the billabong, so we could catch them and ride them each day. Mine was Rastus, a chestnut gelding with mild manners, who I soon learned to ride bareback and without reins. The wet season came early this year with the plains flooded and the billabong flowing before we got home. We spent many hours swimming at the waterfall, climbing hills, loving being home.

All too soon it was the end of January and time for Robin and I to leave. This time the mail plane went the other way calling at all the little communities in Arnhem Land, and finally landing at Roper River Mission, in the middle of a sweltering wet season afternoon.

The pilot went on a tour of the mission while we children passengers sat under the wing, sweating and swotting flies. He returned an hour later and we flew to Mt Isa, to meet the big airline plane to Brisbane and Sydney. Half an hour out of Mt Isa we were chatting away about meeting the plane.

Our pilot sat up and said, "What? Are you supposed to be catching the Sydney plane." We nodded. A guilty look passed across his face, "the plane is taxiing along Mt Isa runway to take off, why didn't you tell me sooner!"

Well, of course, we were not the ones who played tourist. We were delighted, both for his come-uppance leaving us in the baking afternoon and because that night we stayed in motel rooms where we could order whatever we liked from the menu, while waiting for the next day's plane.

I truly hated my second year in Sydney, staying with my grandmother. A holiday of freedom made her restrictions ever more irksome, and she was sick a lot. She tried to be kind and loving but I felt smothered. One day in July, after a big argument with her, I packed my bag and decided to go bush. I walked down to the Woronora River and spent a day there in a bush hideaway. Late that day, meagre food supplies gone and with hunger and loneliness coming, I caught the train to my other Grandparents at Penshurst and slept in their shed. By the time I emerged there was serious alarm.

I was brought back to Oenpelli, under a cloud of disapproval, for the rest of the year. Nana was mortified, and never really forgave me. For me, the alternative of going to boarding school the next year was infinitely better.

The Year the Billabong Almost Dried Up

Despite my inglorious home coming Oenpelli was just the same. My absconding resulted in Robin coming home those August holidays, so I was secretly pleased about this too. Thereafter we were brought us home twice a year.

This year, 1965, was a different to the previous dry seasons. The dry season went on longer and it was much colder. Running across to milk the goats one August morning, wearing just a pair of shorts, I thought it was a bit cold, thankful for the warmth of huddling among hundreds of goats. At the 9 o'clock weather report it was the coldest ever morning at Oenpelli, the thermometer falling to 4 degrees Centigrade or 38 degrees Farenheight.

In October it got hot and it looked like storms might come at the normal time. Instead there were just a couple spits to damp the dust and the dry season returned in earnest. By the end of October it was really hot and really dry.

Almost all the waterholes on the plains were dry. Large numbers of buffalo gathered around the small amount of water at the end of Oenpelli billabong where it flowed out onto the plains. Soon this was reduced to a mud puddle. Desperate, thirsty buffalo bogged in it, others smashed through fences into the rest of the billabong. The billabong was dropping precipitously, now a bare three feet of water remained in the middle. Fish began to die. Soon its edges were dotted with thousands of dead and dying fish. The billabong was covered in untold swarms of pelicans, feasting on all the trapped fish. They would take off in the heat of the afternoon and circle upwards, ever upwards, riding thermals from the adjoining hills, like a rising whirlwind, until almost out of sight, at the top of the spiral, then peel off and fly to places unknown.

By November the billabong was one enormous mud puddle with several feet of black liquid mud, into which the buffalo sunk, and with about a foot of almost black water floating on top. Apart from a little water still in rain tanks this was Oenpelli's water supply. Teams of men were employed to shoot the bogged buffalo and drag them away from the water. In mid-November three teams, each with a tractor, were working round the clock to keep up with the buffalo. At first they used 303 bullets on the buffalo, but as the numbers increased and the ammunition ran low, shooters became expert at using a 22 bullet.

The whole of Oenpelli was suffused in the stench of rotting buffalo carcases and dead fish. Our bath water at night was two inches of black smelly soup that smelt halfway between mud and dead fish. It was rinsed off with a cup of rainwater, leaving one feeling not much cleaner. At night, before going outside, one had to check for buffalo eyes in the garden with a torch. Often there was a bang in the night as someone dispatched a buffalo standing at the foot of their stairs with a 22 bullet. The grass on the floodplains near Oenpelli was long gone, and most animals were just skin and bone.

By the end of the November the buffalo were almost all gone, the stench abated, and the water in the billabong cleared as the mud settled. Still no rain, the billabong was now reduced to a small puddle a bare two feet deep, less than one hundred yards wide and a few hundred yards long, rather than its previous dimensions of about 300 yards wide by more than a kilometre long.

In early December, when just over a foot of water remained in the billabong three aboriginal men came to our house carrying the largest barramundi anyone had ever seen. They caught it with hand-nets in this puddle and wanted to sell it to my father. He bought it for a couple pounds. It took three of us to lift and we hung it from a bearer under our elevated house, about eight feet above the ground. With its head tied to the bearer its tail almost touched the ground. The whole community inspected it and declared it the biggest fish anyone had seen. Then it was divided between the missionary families. Each family got a slab of fish, enough for about three meals. It had a muddy taste and its texture was like chewing rubber, so we were all glad when it was finished.

Just before Christmas the rains came. We all gathered to watch the creeks from the escarpment reach the billabong. Within a day its tiny remaining puddle was a vast expanse of water, back to its former size. By January the plains were again a sea of wet season water extending far into the horizon.

The Years Roll On

One year's school holidays merge into the next. Dry season holidays were times of mustering with the stockmen on the Oenpelli and Red Lily plains. I remember one mustering trip to Red Lily with head stockman, Brian Chantrell and several aboriginal stockmen. Lunch was a cup of black tea at the edge of Red Lily billabong. In the mid-afternoon we came to a waterhole in the hills. Several whistling ducks took wing so Brian whipped out his revolver and shot three mid-air, taking off from the pool. We feasted on whistling duck, singed and roasted in the fire, before riding home.

Another time, half way across the Red Lily plains, bringing about twenty bullocks back to Oenpelli. A large goanna was seen a hundred yards away, standing up on its back legs, looking over waist high grass. With a shout the four aboriginal stockmen galloped off after the goanna, with me hot on their tail, bullocks forgotten. As we closed on the fleeing goanna the lead rider pulled a stirrup off his saddle, holding a flat gallop. With a deft swing the goanna was dispatched. We pulled our blowing horses to a stop and this rider dismounted, feeling this six foot goanna across the back. He muttered in disgust 'Him no good, him not fat one.' We rode off to regather the bullocks. The goanna lay there where it died, a feast for some less discriminating hawk or dingo.

Dry seasons were fishing trips to the surrounding country side, particularly Coopers Creek which had the biggest and best barramundi. You could see them swimming in clear pools, following your lure before they struck. The master barramundi fisherman was Ian Mackenzie. He fashioned fool-proof lures from anything, bullet shell cases, pieces cut from of old thongs, bits of tin cans. He rarely returned home without a couple of ten pound plus fish.

With his departure Brian Higginbotham took over the master fisherman's mantle, almost as good; using higher quality gear, but not quite as resourceful.

One time a boy my age from Canon Hill came to town, fishhook embedded in his knee. He was taken to see the nursing sister who lived next door. The word got out and we kids snuck over and hid behind the bushes to watch.

The sister pulled out a needle of anaesthetic. The terrified lad started crying out "No, no needle, don't give me a needle" His father held him still while she prepared. Seconds later, as she plunged the needle, he screamed, banshee like, a shriek to disturb roosting birds. It cascaded into a wailing howl, heard by people hundreds of yards away. Removing the fishhook was a silent anticlimax. Even though I was braver with needles I thought he was cool; with his 22 rifle he could go shooting whenever he wanted. I never told him of our sneaked view.

Wet Seasons

Wet seasons were part of our Christmas holidays and came in two forms. The first was thunderstorms mostly in December. Across the plains we would watch clouds pile up in the late afternoon, above the orange-brown sunlit escarpment, going from white and fluffy to grey and black. Finally, as they turned an opalescent hue of purple, navy and olive-turquoise, punctuated by bursts of light and ever increasing rumbles, they swept across the plains towards us. The hills vanished behind a wall of opaque rain, the flashes and rumbles intensified into tracer like gunfire, and there came that eerie stillness in the air followed by a sudden blast of cold air as the front edge of the storm thundered across the billabong. You could see the leading edge of drops slicing the water, and hear the hiss like an approaching snake. A quick dash to shelter and we would revel in the noise of huge raindrops banging off the tin roof, increasingly punctuated by flashes and almost simultaneous bangs of thunder. Some brave soul would turn off the power and we would sit in the dark for an hour or so while the heavy rain subsided to a drizzle. As the storm moved on, the sun re-emerged to a steamy water covered landscape of pools and puddles. Someone would check the rain gauge, announce this afternoon's storm had been one inch or two, occasionally the number rose to three, four or five.

The second type of wet season mostly came after Christmas, often with cyclone warnings on the radio. They would announce the monsoon band had moved down over the Northern Territory. We emerged each morning to the pastel washed-out grey of yet another monsoon day. Grey day would follow grey day, for a week or two, as wave after wave of showers came through, sometimes light and misty, other times heavy torrents falling from the sky.

Our whole world turned into a sea of water, the billabong extended across the plains to the horizon. Waterfalls cascaded off many hill gaps. Our own local waterfall, four miles away, was clearly audible as a muted roar after the power went off at night. An all pervasive damp came; clothes that would not dry, bed sheets half damp at night and mould grew on any surface. It was a time of less people, missionaries gone on holidays, aborigines confined to their camps, and few visitors with access roads closed. With the heaviest deluges, the airstrip was closed and planes could not get in through the pea soup of low cloud. Occasionally this meant we could not get back to school. More often they skipped that week, returning in the first week of February once we were gone.

Once, when the monsoons were at a peak Peter, David and I, decided to walk to the waterfall. Crossing the bottom of the billabong was our first challenge. The normally dry road along the fringe of the plain was covered with waist deep, flowing water coming from creeks running off every hill and gully. The main billabong creeks had expanded from a few yards wide and two feet deep to channels of hundreds of metres of continuous water with a rapid current at their centre. This washed us along as we swam across. After a couple kilometres of wading through water from a few inches to chest deep we finally arrived on dry land where the sandy wheel tracks approached the base of the escarpment hills. We wondered if the waterfall would be worth these hours of effort, trudging through water. The view remained hidden in a fold of the hills.

Rounding the final turn where it came into sight we stopped, awestruck. Usually a thin white line of water dropping 300 feet to the pool below, now a massive torrent, seeming as wide as it was high, confronted us. It poured over the cliffs, its spume obscuring the surrounding hills. The roar drowned all other noise. The main pool, merged into the creek, now only the tops of the fringing pandanus trees visible. The pool's normal flat glassy surface was covered in ocean sized waves. We sat gazing, spellbound, at this demonstration of raw power.

After an hour of sitting on its rocky shoulder, at the edge of the spray, we walked back towards Oenpelli, round the bend and out of sight. Suddenly quiet, we heard bird and insect noises again, the assault on our senses faded away.

Climbing the Hills and the Cave

Oenpelli's three hill neighbours, Arrkuluk, Injalak and Nimbabirr were another dimension of discovery. Typically we would spend a day exploring one of these hills. A group of children and occasional adults would pack a picnic lunch and head off, clambering over sandstone screed around the hill's base, then up over boulders and through crevasses until we reached their flattened tops. Here we perched on large boulders gazing across to the ringing hills, to plains dotted with birds, horses, cattle and buffalo and to a town of small black and white figures.

As we explored we often discovered aboriginal burial sites. At first we did not then understand that many of these sites were sacred to their people. Once we collected a few items which we took home. Our parents were aghast. They told us what we had done was very disrespectful and we must immediately return these things to exactly where we had taken them from. We hastily made the return trip, trying to remember the exact place from which each had come.

Arrkuluk the highest hill gave commanding views. From its top, six hundred feet above the surrounding plain, one saw hills and floodplains extending in a broad circle, from Red Lily in the west to the East Alligator River in the north-west, with its dotted tree line and beyond it the canon shaped rock of Canon Hill. North the floodplain extended half way to the horizon. Ngara, a temporary buffalo abattoir, lay on its northern margin ten miles away. Further north flat woodlands continued to the side by side mounds of Twin Hills 30 miles away on the horizon. Round from here the sweep of floodplains extended beyond a full 180 degrees, ending in the south east past Nimbabirr. In the centre foreground was the town of Oenpelli, the billabong sitting on its southern margin and Injalak behind. Further south was the cliff face wall of escarpment with Oenpelli waterfall sitting in the centre, four miles distant, sometimes a thin trickle other times a white roaring monster. Going south west, completing a circle, the Springs valley merged into jumbled sandstone hills continuing to the horizon.

Under the Top Rock on Arrkuluk, lie large piles of shellfish shells that we would puzzle over, being more that 40 miles directly to the sea. I have since learned that, a couple thousand years ago, the sea was higher and covered these coastal plains. It is easy to imagine aboriginal people of that time sitting in rock shelters, on what were then rocky islands and promontories rising above a surrounding shallow sea, feasting on a wealth of sea food, as neighbouring salt water people do to this day. To sit in a cool rock shelter on a hot wet season afternoon, as a breeze wafts through the crevices, still evokes in me the timelessness of this land.

Injalak, south across the billabong, is Oenpelli's signature hill, often called Oenpelli Hill. Great blocks of fissured sandstone rise three or four hundred feet above the floodplain, framing the billabong. The way up is from the western end over a rock screed with all other sides bordered by sheer cliffs. Clambering up this slope, amongst a tangle of vines and vegetation, one comes to a fissure between two large sandstone slabs, with a third slab perched on the top. The sides of this fissure, rising up ten feet, are polished smooth from the passage of water and many, many hands and feet over thousands of years. At the top, after a short scrabble through a thicket of stunted trees and vines in thin sandy soil, one comes into a small clearing alongside a towering rock. It is blackened with soot and polished like glass underneath. As your eyes adjust to the gloom, picture upon picture is revealed, layer on layer, new over old. Paintings of x-ray barramundi, geese and goannas, stick figures of men, women and children, mimi spirits and a vivid yellow painting, which looks like an Asian monkey, perhaps from a visitor on a trepang boat. Walking around the rock every surface seems covered in red, brown, yellow and white ochre or charcoal art, some as if done yesterday with unmarked clarity, others told of vast antiquity, seen in remnants of smudges and shadows barely visible, fading into the colours of the sandstone behind, in other places a new artist has partially painted over the old, yet a fragment of the original remains. The sides of this rock form rows of terraces, rising to over four metres before the main rock shelter looms out over the sides. On these terraces the rock is polished like glass and dozens of small semi-circular pits have been ground out for mixing ochres. The mind visions to an ancient era; a black body, chewed stick paintbrush in hand, applying layers of colour and detail. In places paintings perch ten metres above the ground with no visible way up. A further leap of imagination sees a person perched on a timber scaffold working high on the side of a cliff.

Leading off from this main gallery are fissures and tunnels in the rock, going in many directions. It is easy to become lost, finding oneself suddenly on the side of a cliff which falls 50 or 100 feet, with a challenge to retrace a safe path back to a known area. I identify with the searchers of the lost girls in 'Picnic at Hanging Rock', when I remember searching for a way through these mazes.

Everywhere signs of ancient art persist, surprise and delight. One path leads to a small gallery of paintings on a lower terrace near the north side of the hill, overlooking the billabong. Part of this path is a huge polished rock, 10 metres across at a 20 degree slope; one slides across carefully to come and go. I picture thousands of years of traversing by black hands and feet that have made it so.

In our teenage years the Cooke family went camping near the Springs at a place where two giant milkwood trees grew and the valley converged on the sandy creek. One day their exploration led them up the tributary creek opposite their camp. After following the rocky creek bed for a few hundred yards they came to a place where water cascaded over a series of waterfalls dropping 50 feet into the valley below. Clambering to the top they surveyed the surrounding hills. A huge black eye in the centre of a hill looked across at them, perhaps from a kilometre away. After a scramble across the barren hillside, they emerged at the base of this hill and climbed up to find out what was there. A cave, its mouth large enough for big aircraft to fly in towered above them. Its smooth sandy floor continued in for a couple hundred yards before, framed by distant light, it opened to the other side of the hill in an entrance still large enough for a small plane to fly through. When next home the Cooke boys showed it to me. With torches we discovered more side passages and tunnels. Years later I showed it to my naturalist friend Ian Morris, a walking encyclopaedia of the NT's animals and plants. Ian noted an unusual insect which he later sketched from memory. This turned out to be a new Australian species of whip scorpion, with its closest relative living in New Guinea.

More Horses

Oenpelli for me, first and foremost, conjures images of riding horses across the open plains, knee deep in green grass. For our first couple years, Stephen Harris, the head stockman and Dick Harris's son, organised a paddock alongside the billabong for us to keep our holiday horses, and chose a stock horse for each child to ride, with a temperament suited each person's skill. With a large group of children riding, on a daily basis, there was often a shortage of saddles, so we took to riding bareback. This developed our horseback balance and coordination much faster. Soon we were so confident that we would ride across the plains, chasing each other, or other horses. at a flat gallop, using just our balance to keep us there. We fell off from time to time, landing on the soft grass of the wet season plains. With a quick brush off we swung back over and galloped off again. Saddles became something we just used for stock work or a full day's riding. For a quick ride with a known horse, we simply caught the horse with a bridle and jumped on. As our confidence grew Peter, David and I started selecting other horses to ride, choosing less well handled horses with more spirit.

Oenpelli had ever increasing numbers of stock horses on the plains. Originally quality was maintained by purchasing an outside stallion every couple years. By the time we were teenagers there were about 500 horses in total, with between 50 and 100 broken in and used on a regular basis for stock work. Early in the holidays we would run a mob of horses off the plains, and each select a horse to ride. We had known favourites, but with teenage fearlessness we tried out less well known horses. Our theory was broken in horses generally had marks on their back from old saddle sores, but sometimes the best way to guess was if a horse would stand up and let you put a bridle on it when you pulled it up with a rope, or separated it in a round yard. We could ask the opinion of an aboriginal stockman. "Bob, see that horse there, what's he like". The reply was often an expressive shrug or "maybe little bit quiet, maybe little bit wild" or, at times, "proper good horse, Stephen bin ride him might-be last year" (might be three years ago or never), or "him OK" which was usually safe.

Sometimes this backfired and we chose horses that were completely mad. One Christmas holidays, when I was 13 or 14, and fancied my riding skills, I picked out a wild looking white gelding, with a hobble strap around his neck. He stood up quietly as I put the bridle on, then only flinched slightly as I lifted the saddle over and pulled up the girth. I have a vague memory of leading him to an area of clear open ground in front of the stockyard before I tried to get on, so as to ensure that, if anything happened, I had room to move. My next recollection is waking up with a splitting headache an hour or two later, lying on my bed. Apparently all went well till my leg was halfway over his back then he exploded. A second or two later I came down headfirst. I got groggily to my feet and said I would have another go at getting on. Someone suggested I leave it for a while, so I wandered off to wake up an hour or two later lying in my bed. Meanwhile the horse was unsaddled and let go. I never tried this one again.

Most of the horses we selected were a joy to ride, even if sometimes the getting on and off was a challenge. Wilfred Harris, another of Dick's sons, and an accomplished horseman, told me "A horse is a bit like an aeroplane, safe in the air and safe on the ground but the take-off and landing are dangerous.

In my last Christmas holidays in high school I decided that it was time I moved from riding other people's horses to breaking in my own horse. I got books from the library to get the idea. I had watched the aboriginal stockmen horse-breaking. After an hour of conversation with Beswick Bob, one of the canniest stockmen, I decided that I understood the basic technique and sought his advice on what would be a good horse to pick. I finally settled on a black medium sized gelding with a long black curly mane and tail, which gave him a brumby look. I named him Curly. Over a week, spending several hours a day, I got him used to being roped and pulled up, having a bridle fitted, then teaching him to stop, turn and respond to directions on a lunging rein in a round yard. Then came periods of bagging him, teaching him to pick up his feet, and getting him used to a saddle. Finally the day came when it was time to climb on. Already I could rest my weight on him leaning over his back. With Beswick Bob in attendance for final tuition, and making sure no one else was watching, I put foot in stirrup and swung over his back. A feeling, like an electric shock running through his body, as he first felt my full weight, while I waited for the explosion, then bang, jolt, jolt, jolt, as he launched himself into a series of bucks.

The elation, when it was over and I was still sitting mid-saddle; then the first tentative steps as I dug my heels in. He stepped forward. Next thing he was walking, like any other broken horse, around the stock yard. On and off, on and off I got; soon I was feeling confident, a trap. A lazy mounting technique and my tame horse explodes again, this time with me only half on. Next thing I know I am sitting on the ground with an excruciating pain in my backside. I have managed to land on the only rock in the round yard, a golf ball sized nugget, which leaves a bruise the size of an orange in my behind, making sitting down difficult for a couple days. However I persevere, don't fall off again and, over the next few days, graduate from riding in the stockyard to out across the plains. My holidays finish soon after. Curly is now just another stock horse. My satisfaction comes from having taken this wild animal and turned him into my stock horse.

My final memory of riding as a kid at Oenpelli is the August holidays before I finished high school. There was a horse called Injalak, a mid-sized grey stock horse, perfectly proportioned. He was normally ridden by the most experienced aboriginal stockmen, and considered one of Oenpelli's best stock horses, with lots of go but highly strung, only suitable for good riders. I ran him in with a mob on a day when we were riding to Fish Creek, ten miles away, for a day's picnic.

I decided it was time I tried him. Caught with difficulty, one could feel all his muscles tense as I lifted the saddle over, then the explosive power in his bunched muscles as he took my weight when I swung my leg over. After walking around in the stockyard I got someone to open the gate which led out to the old airstrip. I walked him out onto its wide open space. I could feel his restless energy and urged him into a gentle canter. With a soft mouth but energy to burn I could feel his desire to explode into a frenetic, all out gallop. I held him in and we wheeled back towards the stockyards.

Suddenly he decided it was his turn to take over. He surged forward as we approached the gate then veered right, straight towards the five foot barb wire fence around the perimeter. I tried to pull him in but he locked his teeth on the bit and accelerated. I let him go assuming, at the last moment, he would plant his anchors and we would come to a shuddering halt. Instead he powered on, faster and faster. Just as I was starting wonder what next he gathered himself in, and jumped clean over the fence without pause. As we landed on the other side he slowed to a trot and then a walk, as if to say, 'you think you're in charge – how about that?'

For the rest of day over our 20 mile ride he was a model horse, everything done perfectly. As we returned to Oenpelli just on dusk, with house lights twinkling, I sensed he still had energy to burn and decided we would have a final run along the old airstrip together so I headed him out along it. His body stretched out into a flying gallop, magic enveloped us, this horse and I in perfect alignment, racing through the dusk with our wild joy shared.

It lives on in my mind, decades later, as the most perfect ride of the most perfect horse, ever.

Nights at Oenpelli

When we came back to Oenpelli, in 1963, there was a small generator a couple hundred yards from the houses. Most people had kerosene fridges as the power was on for only a few hours each day including in the evening until about 10 pm to run house lights and other appliances. CMS, with its limited income, could not afford to buy fuel for power beyond this. This situation was no different from most other remote communities and cattle stations. So no-one had television and keeping up with outside news was limited to the radio, mail and an occasional newspaper, which came with the mail plane twice a week.

A great step forward for all the new houses was fly screens. This freed people from sleeping under mosquito nets and made night time living much better without the need for mosquito coils, repellent or going to bed early to escape the mosquitoes. Ceiling fans were also a wonderful invention as, on warm humid evenings, the air movement made indoors pleasant. It would be a long time until there was enough power to run air-conditioners. In the tropics night fell rapidly about seven pm. Most families had dinner at that time, while listening to the ABC news on the short-wave radio.

As dusk settled the noises of the night came out, curlews making their eerie wailing noise, water rats, native cats and phascogales emerging for nightly foraging, magpie geese fed on the short grass and lawns, often large snakes were seen hunting frogs. Owls and insectivorous bats glided silently in pursuit of prey and, from many fruit trees, came the noisy squabbling of flying foxes.

After dinner many missionary families read books, played board games, along with music on their record players. Mum and Dads taste was classics and Gilbert and Sullivan, giving me an introduction to this music, other families had modern tastes. Once or twice a week pictures were shown on an outdoors screen and people, black and white, covered themselves with mosquito repellent and took cushions, chairs and blankets to settle in for the action. Anything fast and furious was loved, all the school children cheering loudly with lots of laughing, shouting and calling in Gunwingu, with snatches of English.

On quiet nights Peter, David and I would go off walking around the plains and along the airstrip, avoiding buffalo which emerged as dark shapes with little pig like grunts and, at times when they spotted us would come cantering up in a group, noses high as they sniffed the air. At other times solitary old bulls would flick their horns at us to let us know to keep our distance. Occasionally we would grab some horses for a midnight bareback gallop, trusting the horses to see their way and avoid obstacles as we clung on.

In the background would be the rhythmic sound of aboriginal tap sticks and sometimes a didgeridoo as they followed their own cultural interests. Every few months there was be a big corroboree or ceremony when lots people gathered and music, chanting and dancing continued through much of the night. A few times we quietly went close to observe; seeing ochre painted bodies, bare feet stamping and weaving patterns in the dust, as they evoked the tapestry of their history in their own operatic tradition of music and dance.

Family Life at Oenpelli

Dad Learning to Fly

Dad, not happy with trucks and other things mechanical, decided it was time to learn to fly. At night he would pore over lessons to pass his theory exams. He progressed to flying lessons on a weekly basis with a pilot who flew a Darwin Aero Club Cessna out to Oenpelli. Ray Vuillerman, the pilot, became a weekly fixture at our lunch table, often bringing two or three sightseeing visitors, who paid the flying cost to Oenpelli and back. They would take a pair of binoculars to enjoy the myriad birds on the billabong, and soak up Oenpelli's lazy dry season atmosphere, before a return to Darwin with him in the evening.

The sudden cessation of Cessna engine buzz would provoke a short burst of alarm, but the emergency training always resolved with a sudden roar as the plane engine fired again as the ground came rushing towards it. Considering Dad's meagre salary it was amazing he could find the money, a testament to his frugality and Mums inventiveness that we could survive and feed not only ourselves, but an innumerable stream of visitors, on not much more than garden produce and Oenpelli meat. It was amazing how many ways she could find to serve pawpaw and sweet potato.

Having mastered the challenge of flying, Dads next challenge was to get his own plane, within his very limited budget. After a trip to Sydney he returned with a plane with a material skin that you could almost poke your finger through when you touched it. A tail wheel and a hand starting propeller added to its character. He would lock the brakes, get out, swing the propeller till the engine fired, then jump aboard to taxi away.

He was focused on assisting the aboriginal people to move back to their own country. This entailed a group of people moving out and building an airstrip along with a couple houses wherever their clan's country was, most often 50-100 miles east of Oenpelli. Dad, after receiving a radio message to say the airstrip was now finished, would fly out, make a couple low passes and decide whether it was long enough and smooth enough to land, and more importantly to take off again. He was soon master of the ultra-short take-off and landing.

Sometimes obstacles came into contact with the plane, including at least one camp dog. I came out on a repair trip out, miles to the north-east of Oenpelli. It took a couple hours of rough bush driving to get there. We used the fabric repair kit to patch a hole in the underside of the plane's body, the cause no longer remembered, followed by a flight back home in 15 minutes. The wheels of the plane were supported by huge rubber bands called bungies. They sometimes broke on a rough landing and he was adept at fitting new ones with minimal equipment. Stretching the new ones into place felt like trying to bend car springs. We kids queued up for these trips, never doubting our Dad's ability to get there and back in one piece.

Only rarely did Mum showed visible signs of worry. She would listen for his plane. As it taxied in she would go to the tie down area, and walk back with him at a leisurely pace in the late afternoon sun. One afternoon when Dad was due back he failed to arrive and Mum was clearly worried. Afternoon merged into evening with no sign of the plane, and soon it was completely dark. We ate a less than exuberant dinner as the evening dragged on. No radio messages came as to where he might be. After a further hour and it was decided that a group of us should drive around the plains to Ngara, where he had gone for the afternoon. It was only ten miles straight across, but the plains were too wet for this route and the road around was a slow rough 20-30 miles. As we came around the back of Oenpelli Hill, a distant vehicle light hit the sky and we stopped to wait. Shortly a tractor carrying Dad and other passengers pulled up alongside us. It transpired that the plane had torn a hole in its undercarriage on landing and the radio did not work. They walked to where they could get a tractor ride home. Mum showed little visible emotion on our return but I knew his safe return was a little miracle for her.

Religion

For my parents their Christian beliefs were an integral part of their lives. Expressions of this included saying grace before meals, going to Sunday school and church, and behaving in a kind and moral way to others. However, beyond this, religion impinged little on our everyday family life. It sat at the core of what they did and why they did things but, in the way of children, we questioned little. They lived in the company of many other missionary people who also shared this ethos. It therefore seemed natural, when something went amiss, that a prayer was said and the same on occasions of celebration.

When I was ten years old, Peter and I climbed Arrkuluk hill, accompanied by our dog Terry, a fearless black and white mongrel missile. He chased horses and other dogs and jumped into the air to catch low flying magpie geese, often with success. He did not seem to fear anything. Having reached the flat ground on the hilltop, we sat in the shade of the highest boulder, a ten metre monolith we called Top Rock. A path along a narrow ledge around its side led to its very top. We decided to go there, the place of the best view. We went up and, at the top of the ledge, there was a climb of about a metre over a shoulder of rock before one emerged onto an open flat place, several metres above the ground below. Terry had bounded up alongside us and sat next to us, panting in the heat. After a while we decided to go down and explore other parts of the hill top. Terry followed us back to the edge where you had to climb down, over the shoulder of the rock, onto the ledge, next to a seven metre drop. There he stopped, whimpering. Going up was fine, coming down; no! We cajoled, we pushed, we tried to pick him up and carry him but all that resulted was a violent scrabbling, squirming dog who would escape and retreat back to the edge at the top. We tried and we tried, but it was a stalemate. So we thought, if we go to the bottom out of sight and wait quietly for five or ten minutes maybe he will come down by himself. Off we went and sat down saying nothing for several minutes; sitting, waiting; nothing. We called him. Still no Terry came.

We returned to find him waiting plaintively at the edge of the top where we had left him, as if to say, you will have to find a way to fly to get me down. More pushing and cajoling was done, equally fruitless. Finally, one of us said to the other, 'Let's go down and say a prayer, maybe God will help us get our dog down.' We sat at the bottom of the rock and mumbled our quick prayer, expecting little. As we climbed back up the ledge, who should we see trotting down towards us but our very own black and white mongrel, wagging his tail as if to say, 'so you wanted your little miracle, well here I am.' Peter's parents and mine did not say much when told them but it was important to us.

Mr Harris, previously Superintendent and now the Minister, was a simple man from who flowed a presence of kindness, humility and quiet authority, arising from an unshakeable belief in his God. He was bandy legged and weathered from years in the saddle and he went about his day to day activities with measured purpose, lit with little flashes of humour seen as a twinkle in his eye. One day, when I was eleven, he came up to me with a small brown book in his hand. "I thought you might like to read this," he said, as he presented me with my first new testament, inscribed briefly inside the front cover 'from Dick Harris, with God's blessing, 1965. No more words, or exhortations to read, he just left it, as if he knew between me and God we would figure out its purpose. My respect for him was such that that night and several other nights I read it. Even though I then put aside, it stayed with me for years, and gave me more belief than years of church.

Mum and Dad, meanwhile, continued their day to day life of doing their missionary work with little fuss and almost no religious ceremony.

Mum at Home

To get another perspective, apart from my own memories of Mum, I asked my sisters, Dorothy and Barbara, who as younger children, lived at home at Oenpelli with Mum and Dad for longer than Robin or I before they too went off to boarding school. Dorothy also returned to work as a school teacher at Oenpelli and as a result she spent more time with my parents as an adult. I have transcribed what each of them remembers of Mum and, to a lesser extent Dad, in their own words below:

Barbara's Memories

I remember Mum as someone you could count on to be calm and know what to do in the many different situations that emerged at Oenpelli. She was always busy but always had time for people, especially family. She was resourceful.

Bread making became one of Mum's fortes and was a weekly event. I often assisted with making the bread.

Nothing was wasted. This meant that clothes and the occasional toy I grew past were passed on to someone who could benefit from them. To save a doll I had made from the same fate I took it away to school with me.

Mum had very little in the way of possessions, apart from basic necessities, but did have a great love of books and reading and read a wide range of books. So her knowledge of different places and events was vast.

Her memory was amazing. I remember, when I was studying Biomedical Science, incidentally in some of the same rooms she had used 30 years earlier when she was doing Organic Chemistry at Sydney Tech, she could recite off names of the chemicals and their reactions along with the best.

As to what her thoughts and feelings were I would only be guessing. Looking back I'd say she was a very private person.

Dorothy's Memories

Mum was always at home or close by, and rarely unreachable. She often went visiting others to meet and share stories along with the produce from our garden.

She was very good at using with what was available and could always work out how to adjust a recipe to suit a different fruit or what to use if the ingredients needed were not available. I remember being asked what she does with her spare time. While I had never been aware of their being spare time that she was trying to fill, I answered by saying that she goes to the scrap bucket to look for what she can make with the scraps and at the moment she was working on banana skins and egg shells. I guess the person was not too impressed as she left not too long after.

The reality was little was thrown away and Mum was very creative when it came to using what was around to make many delicious eats. Over ripe fruit was made into fruit leather. Orange peel kept and made into marmalade, green mangoes were used for sauce, many of the fruits were made into a variety of jams, a fallen pawpaw tree of green fruit was used for chutney and maybe a green vegetable (although I always hoped not as that was not a desired option!!!). This list could continue across so much of what we had, from bread to ice cream to many other little delicacies that found their way onto our plates. Our diets were really very varied and we were blessed!

A special memory I have of Mum is that, when I was at boarding school and had to read very long and boring novels like Pride and Prejudice and Vanity Fair, she would read them for me and summarise chapter by chapter and I could use that to do the assignments. I don't think she did that for any of my other brothers or sisters, but she said later, "I thought you would never become a reader if you had to read those books!' I guess she was right!

Many of my wonderful memories of Mum and Dad and their support centre on my coming back to the Territory after I finished my training and, in particular, when I went to Oenpelli to work. Dad was always prepared to go the extra mile to cater for me in some way, like fix my car or help do something. Mum was a wonderful companion and would listen for hours and talk with me about what was important to me. She was also willing to help in any way she could. She assisted in restocking of the preschool after it had been trashed over the Christmas holidays by making countless ice blocks which were sold and the money used to replenish the broken and destroyed resources

As to my own memories, Mum was the organiser of our domestic lives and also managed a host of social interactions across the community in a similar way to what her own mother had done as wife of a country minister in NSW. She chose not to be engaged directly in Dad's work but often discussed things with him.

As wife of the superintendent at Oenpelli, she was the first point of contact for visitors in his absence, which was frequent. It fell to her to provide meals, refreshments and accommodation for visitors and new arrivals, like an ex officio motel keeper. She did this jointly with other missionary wives such as Betty Cook and Gwen Tremlett, all sharing the work around.

At the same time she supervised correspondence and School of the Air lessons for us children, and maintained contacts across the European and aboriginal communities, particularly with other women and their children.

She was often seen on her bicycle with fresh fruit in the basket which she offered around. Our pantry was usually full of jars of jams and preserves that she made from whatever was to hand, along with drums of flour and sugar, sides of bacon and an array of tinned food - powdered milk, butter, baked beans, creamed corn, tinned vegetables; enough things to be able to survive the long wet season without deliveries.

She cooked on a wood stove, making her own bread and other local creations, some universally popular, odd ones less good, swapping recipes with others who also knew how to make use of local produce.

Barbara, my sister, told me of Mum getting assistance in the kitchen from one of her school friend's from Sydney, "During my high school years a girl from my school came to stay one holiday. At her home my friend was not allowed to do any cooking so enjoyed being able to help in our kitchen. One night, as we finished tea, the supply trucks arrived. That meant there were four extra men to be fed. My friend, ever willing to help, followed my mother into the kitchen and offered help. My mother decided the quickest and easiest way to extend what she had was to cook an egg for each man so gave my friend four eggs with the instruction to pop them into the frypan. That is exactly what my friend did. There were the eggs sitting in the pan complete with the shells still on them.

"My mother, not wanting to upset someone so eager to help, did some quick thinking and suggested that the eggs would cook quicker if she cracked the shells. My friend answered she liked cracking eggs and would do that!"

Mum was interested in the natural world. A voracious reader in her limited free time, there was a continuous flow of library books in mail-plane packages from the local library and a collection of her favourite books on the shelfs.

On hot Sunday afternoons, after roast dinner, Dad would have a siesta, and Mum would collect a book. We children would gather while she read aloud for an hour, bringing to life Mowgli and the Jungle Book, King Solomon's Mines and many others. She maintained a subscription to National Geographic, even when there was little money in the house, and there was always a magazine close at hand from which I would read the animal stories.

On many a hot mid-afternoon, I would come in while she worked in the kitchen preparing dinner and tell her of things I had seen or learned at school. Unfailingly she showed interest and listened to my story meanderings, adding her own bits of information.

As a grandmother, in later years, she showed the same capacity to listen to her grandchildren, making the long and convoluted stories they told into things of interest. She once told me that Darragh (my son) could talk a lot, with a wry smile, perhaps remembering her own children doing the same 30 years before.

As the years went by she was more seen pedalling her bike around the billabong with binoculars in hand, searching for a new sighting of some little known bird or other creature, becoming a principal contributor to the Birds Australia Atlas from the Arnhem region. She also became a mature aged student and, at night or on hot afternoons, was often found at the dining table peering through her glasses at some assignment from her course. Eventually she told us she did not need to do any more assignments, which on further questioning transpired to mean that she now had her University degree.

Throughout her years at home Mum also maintained a continuing stream of letters to family and friends which circulated information between us all. Part of a letter she wrote to Robin in the aftermath of Cyclone Tracy follows:

Dear Robin,
It seems ages since I wrote and, although I've known for a few days that letters have been going through, life has been a bit disorganised for letter writing.

I don't know whether Graham has been able to contact you, but I doubt if he's been able to fit it in. He went to Darwin last Monday and spent the morning, or as long as they wanted him, in the office and the rest of the day he worked at CMS. Dad saw him yesterday and on Monday he is proceeding to Katherine. One of the fatalities in Darwin was the man who Graham had accompanied to various places before Christmas....

When Dad turned the wireless on, on Christmas morning, and could pick up no Darwin radio station, he feared that the cyclone had really struck. Not long later Len Clements picked up a broadcast saying that Darwin had been hit by a cyclone but no contact had been made. The night before, when Dad heard that the cyclone had changed direction, and knew its position and direction of movement, he had expressed concern for Darwin. A few years before he had been discussing with the Director of Meteorology the direction from which a cyclone would come to really cause severe damage to Darwin...

Next morning Dad spent quite a while on the wireless and finally picked up a radio operator at Casuarina, who had rigged up temporary aerial and who knew CMS and Methodist Overseas Missions were probably trying to contact Darwin.... Dad went back to Darwin, and also took Graham in, and on the way they gave permission for him to land in Darwin, but as he had a vehicle waiting at Bachelor he flew there and got Graham to drive the others to Darwin He then returned and did a flight to Darwin, where he again stayed the night. By then the plane was a recognised part of the program, and next day on his way here the airport manager asked Dad to fly via Cape Don and find out how things were, and if possible get them to establish communications with Darwin. They were all quite OK, but one man was quite concerned about his wife who had been evacuated south and he didn't know where. I think that evening Ted took over the flying and Dad was home till yesterday when he did a flight bringing out 5 Uni students who'd been working at CMS, and, as we didn't know about them, there were 6 extra lunches to prepare just after we had finished. Ted did the second trip bringing the office secretary from Darwin and Mr Anderson, who has done a colossal job, not only at CMS but giving other people shelter, along with Len, who had got a small generator going so they can use refrigerators, fans and lights, Don, who'd taken a truck load in, and Ray Gillham who went and oped for the police till the navy moved in.

CMS, though near the main path of the cyclone fared better, they think probably due to the belt of trees. The winds they say were over 200 knots, but apparently something jammed at 180 knots, and it blew still stronger. With the eye of the cyclone passing over they had winds from the opposite direction, the worst winds being after the eye had passed. I think the rain gauges were blown away. However, this will interest you, there was a fall of 80 mm in the course of the cyclone which only had a diameter of 40 kms. I suppose if the spread had been wider the force would have been broken by land masses.

The medical planes were in their hangar which was badly damaged and at one stage 3 planes were flying around the hangar and somehow managed not to collide. They were all damaged of course, but the least extensively damaged was again flying a few days ago. However almost all other aircraft at Darwin were a complete write off.

The chief Connair pilot was very worried about the way the barometer was dropping and when the airport opened briefly at about 10 pm he got their three DC3's out, for which the company should be really pleased. RPU, Mudginberry's plane, Dad said was in 2 pieces and others are tangled heaps.

Dad was up in Trower Road, Rapid Creek and he saw a pot plant which had once been a cactus, and all that was left were a few fibrous threads....We heard that David Cooke got his hand damaged when a door slammed out. I think he has bones broken..

However not having been in Darwin for 2-3 days Dad was staggered at the difference yesterday and all sorts of things are showing progress. Helicopters were unloading boats and carrying an average of 100 tons of roofing iron every day.

Graham's expenses in Darwin last week will be minimal as there has been no cash economy, and food has been available at certain places, just take what you need. They are hoping to start a cash economy tomorrow. Graham has now been transferred to Katherine, and tomorrow will make his way there by some means. He expects to return here before he goes south. He still has 6 days compulsory work on pigs to fit in before Uni starts. He may even be able to manage something around Katherine.

Dad got out to Table Hill and Gumadir after not having been there for 2 weeks. At Table Hill, no one had a wireless and knew nothing of the cyclone. Dad bogged the plane and stalled, with the propeller digging into the mud. Ted checked it when he got back and it's not damaged. Later in the day he bogged at Gumadir, but got the engine turned off before it sank too deeply.

The family is all well (including horses) and they are out at the Waterfall just now. Well I've just about got writer's cramp Robin, so I'll stop now.

With lots of love from us all.

Mum

PS Could you send this on to Ma and Grandfather please Robin
PPS I believe there was a photo of a service at St Peter's Nightcliff, last Sunday in the Herald. Dad and Mr Anderson were quite recognisable.

Also from Mum, as part of a letter from the 1980's, is a rhyming ditty she wrote

English they say is the language most used,
Most spoken, most written, most cruelly abused.
The plural of box, we all know is boxes
But the plural of ox is oxen, - not oxes.
A mouse and her family are mentioned as mice
But the plural of house is houses not hice.
The plural of man? The answer is men.
The plural of pan? Who'd dare to say pen.
The personal pronouns are he, his and him
But never I'm certain she, shis and shim.
The plural of that? The answer is those.
But who'd ever swear at the cats as the cose.
For more than this thing we talk about these.
And though we say kisses we never say kese.
No wonder the foreigners nearly go mad.
And speak our good English atrociously bad!

Memories of my Sisters and Brother

In revising this book I have asked my three sisters, Robin, older than me by almost two years, Dorothy, younger than me by a little over a year, and Barbara, younger than me by four years, as well as my brother, Arthur, younger than me by eleven years what they remember. I have inserted below what they sent me, largely unchanged, to give their own perspectives of our Oenpelli childhood.

Robin's Memories - Looking Back

For me the Territory has a dreamlike quality. The environment here in New Zealand where I now live is so very different, but once it was my life. As a teenager at school in Sydney separated from my beloved 'Top End' of Australia I used to dream I was on my way back to the Territory only to find that something always thwarted me from quite getting there!

My memories of the Northern Territory are many and centre around Oenpelli where I lived from around the age of two to almost six years of age. We then had a sojourn in Darwin but, at age 11 years, my excitement was hard to contain when we learnt we were to return to Oenpelli. I felt that we were returning home; possibly Graham felt the same though I think my two sisters were a little young to feel this in quite the same way, but I'm sure Mum and Dad looked forward to their return to Oenpelli.

I don't really remember the sequence of things before we went to Darwin but there are lots of snatches of events and experiences. I recall the wooden wheelbarrow my father made for me. It had a wooden front wheel which no doubt he'd painstakingly cut out of a bigger piece of wood; I guess now that he may have made from old packing cases. I remember brown sugar on my porridge, pork crackling from what I'm sure would have been wild pig and having a birthday cake in which my mother used a magpie goose egg. I'm sure much of my life was very mundane but I do recall an exciting outing to Red Lilly Billabong. I travelled on a flat decked trailer towed by a tractor my Dad drove. I don't remember exactly who else came though my memory is that there were a bunch of aboriginal people with me on the back and that Mum stayed home to look after the younger ones. Along the way we came to a deep dry ford to cross and, because I was frightened of going through the dip on the back of trailer, one of the aboriginal women walked with me through the ford. I suspect that Dorcas, who was normally our house girl, accompanied me. I was totally taken with the beautiful red lilies and I decided to bring one home to give to my Mum. I was so disappointed that by the time we arrived home it had closed up for the night and I'm guessing that, with the stress of the heat, it never opened again.

One of my most abiding memories – it may well be an amalgam of memories – is church. Back then the order of things was that the missionary folk sat at the back, either on benches or seats, and the aborigines sat in front on the floor, women and girls on the left and men and boys on the right, from my view at the back. Hymn singing, back then, was in English, and was a really important part of the service. I especially remember us singing 'All Things Bright and Beautiful'. As I remember it I feel I heard the voices of angels, such was the beauty and raw talent of the aboriginal people singing. I could see in my mind, so clearly, 'the purple headed mountain' and the 'river running by'. The early morning sun added its cheerful luminescence to the day, everything was right with the world and it was full of possibilities.

My return to Oenpelli as an eleven year old was short lived. I completed the school year doing correspondence, along with my other siblings, and then Graham and I were off to Sydney to go to school. My time back at Oenpelli before going to school was a very happy time. Morning tea time was often in the tamarind tree with Graham and a friend. Eating the succulent sweet and sour tamarinds was an extreme taste sensation as we planned adventures which included paddling in the billabong in a commandeered dug-out canoe and horse riding trips.

I was in the Territory a couple of years ago for a family wedding. After the festivities were over, we three sisters spent a day out taking in some of what the outback out of Katherine offers. We stopped at the Edith River where we walked up to the top pool for a swim. The water was cool and inviting, and, as I soaked in the sandstone pools, I was transported 'back home' to another place in another time. Yes, I'd been to the Edith River before on a family trip in my childhood, probably only once and probably we'd only swum in the bottom pool, now closed due to crocodile infestation. The reason I was 'home' wasn't to do with whether I'd been to the exact place before or not; it was the subtle smell in the water, perhaps derived from the pandanus and territory eucalypts slowly breaking down in mineralised sandstone country water. It was I smell I'd forgotten but I could have been back in many other places in the Territory. I wanted to bottle the beautifully fragranced water and take it with me!

Barbara's Memories

The high light of the year was the wet season when enough rain flushed waterways out so we could go swimming. I remember excursions to check on the progress of the creek flowing into the billabong.

Having the use of some of the older horses and making horseback trips especially to the waterfall. My horse riding started when we moved to Oenpelli in 1963. As I had never ridden before I was put on Rupert with a lead rein and Dick Harris would take it. After several outings in this manner Dick deemed I was competent enough to ride by myself. We had ridden out to the waterfall and were just heading back when Dick took the lead rein off. Rupert immediately sensed he had an inexperienced rider on board so quickened his pace and soon was in full gallop. Not knowing what else to do I sat there. Dick came in hot pursuit but Rupert didn't slow till he was back at Oenpelli. Rupert came to a stop when he got back to where we had left and, almost immediately, Dick arrived. Surviving that ride I was deemed competent enough to ride on my own but given a quieter mount.

Another recollection of Oenpelli was the amount of wildlife around. The billabong was a mecca for birdlife. Frogs were everywhere and I was often persuaded to remove them from the toilet especially by Dorothy who did not like them.

Ants were a major challenge. In the dry season you learnt fast to let the first flush of water go because the tap would be full of ants and you could easily get a mug full of them. The kitchen table had a lid with water in it for each leg to stand in to have one space ant free. We would also have to make sure nothing touched the wall as this would give the ants another access point.

Another thing that stands out was the sounds of the night. In the early days didgeridoos and tapping sticks could be heard. Also donkeys would come in close to the community in the dry season and I remember listening to them braying when I went to bed. And, of course, the curlews with their mournful cries. In the wet season the sounds of frogs was a night constant. So much for the silence of the bush!

I remember a group of us taken by tractor and trailer for a picnic. I think it was Easter Monday. Dad drove the tractor and at one point the trailer became unhitched. I think Ian and Lesley McKenzie were on horseback and one of them had to catch up with Dad to let him know the trailer was unhitched.

I remember all four of us going out with Terry (our dog) down to the billabong and mostly, with Terry's help, catching a magpie goose and taking it home for Mum to cook. She burnt the remains to get rid of all the lice that came with it.

At the end of the wet season we would go and pick rosellas from the ones that grew wild in the horse paddock. They of course were turned into desserts and jam for the rest of the year. The jam ended getting the name 'bird's feather jam' because one of many visitors that had a meal asked what the jam was. Dad replied "Rosella Jam" to which the visitor, a little surprised, said "What, bird's feathers?" and Dad, of course, simply said "Yes".

Dorothy Remembers

I have many lovely memories of Oenpelli and, in particular, the carefree life that was a child's paradise; memories of horses, swimming, hill climbing and the outdoors. Many centre around the Christmas holidays; riding horses out to swimming holes such as the waterfall, spending the day swimming and then coming home exhausted and feeling like there was an infinite distance between the paddock where the horse went and home.

I remember Christmas Days, spending these afternoons swimming with a large group of people and then coming home to a combined meal where all the staff and families had a meal together and with gifts given at the end that were practical jokes. Dad was the brunt of many, although not the only one to be singled out.

I was the annoying sister! My main memory was when Robin and I decided to carry a tyre out to the waterfall and float back along the creek. It was a dismal failure as creek miles were so much further than the three miles by road. After getting stranded in off-shoots and being ditched under an angry green ants' nest we decided to walk home along the road carrying the tyre. Needless to say, it was a one-time event!

A Baby Brother

Growing up with three sisters I always wanted a brother; there were many things only boys could do together, so I thought. It was a complete, happy surprise when I found out I had a baby brother in my first year away at school. I don't remember much of Arthur the Christmas holidays when he was a baby.

Returning to Oenpelli, after running away when I was eleven, he was a nine month old, who had mastered locomotion on four legs. Other babies crawled, but he ran on four straight legs like a dog trotting. He went at a great pace along the polished floorboards and loved picking up stray items of clothes and dropping them in the toilet in passing. He progressed to two legs, but when in a hurry reverted to four. I thought this boy toddler was great and I could not wait for him to grow up and do things with me.

A year later, when home in the holidays, he would wake me in the night to offer a drink from an empty cordial concentrate bottle he had filled with water. He thought that this bitter water was delicious when offered at midnight.

As a two and three year old I carried him miles on my shoulders on trips of exploration around Oenpelli, as he grew older he became my blond haired shadow and companion. Mum would watch on fondly as I doted on my brother and she would regale us with tales of his exploits; him talking on 'School of the Air' radio and then saying "Over" in his prayers, so God knew it was his turn, raising an orphan kangaroo, building a boat and getting his hair full of paint as he painted the inside while it was suspended upside down.

Ruth Cooke, a year older, called Splinter because of her small size, was his regular companion, two small bodies often seen together, playing, climbing trees, or traipsing around Oenpelli.

At ten he went to boarding school at Trinity, Sydney. I was mid-way through University and brought him out from school for weekends when I could. I felt for his lonely existence, a small boy away from home. I experienced similar but had a sister to visit at weekends. Once I arranged to collect him, but forgot to go. It was an awful feeling when I remembered, late in the day and long past time to get him; this little boy sitting and waiting many long hours for a day out and it never coming. When I next saw him it was quickly forgotten.

As he became a teenager I was often busy working, so we were rarely at home together. But, on occasions, we would spend days or a week or two together, enjoying fishing or other things. One memorable afternoon was fishing at Top Landing. I had a good fishing rod, and he had a handline. After a few casts I hooked and landed a five pound barramundi. We swapped and he took the rod, doing a mighty cast into the middle of the river, only a small amount of line remaining on the spool. After a couple winds there was a twang on the line as a large fish struck, 50 yards out, standing on its tail. The drag was set just tight enough to stop it stripping the last line, but light enough not break the line on a run. Arthur slowly worked it in, taking most of his teenage strength to hold it. The fish slowly came closer. It continued to rush, stripping line, showing occasional flashes and glimpses. Half way in, it made another body out, tail dance. We realised this was no ordinary large fish but a monster.

Ever so slowly it came towards the shallows, growing larger by the minute. Arthur at last pulled it onto the mud at the edge of the river, its head a foot or two out of the water. Here, with a shake of its head, the hook came loose. For a second, fish and two fishermen hung there, suspended in time. Then before it could turn and slide back into the water we both jumped on it and bodily hauled it up the bank, its four foot silver body glistening.

Back at abattoirs, cleaned, it weighed in at just over 24 kilograms. My five pound barramundi fitted totally inside its mouth.

Arthur, a budding entrepreneur, learned early the value of money and how to make it from rich kids at Trinity, the ones who got more pocket money in a week than he got in a year. He and a mate worked out that if you bought big bags of lollies you could break them into lots of little bags and sell these for a several hundred percent profit. When no one was looking they would sneak off to the local shops to buy supplies. Finally, they got caught and their productive was business shut down. I never had this sort of business brain.

Arthur was a good letter writer, with flashes of humour I did not have. Two letters he wrote follow.

Oenpelli via Darwin NT 5791
21/5/76

Dear Graham,

Hi. When we first got to Oenpelli these holidays we were living in the place on the other side of the old store. I got the horses Arab, Cyclone, Crawler and Rodger on Friday afternoon. On Saturday Ruth and I went to get them and found they were out. On Monday the stockmen went out and brought Rodger, Crawler, Cyclone and Mick, but Arab was not there. The next day we got Arab and Tiger so I was satisfied. Wednesday Dorothy and me were invited to the Springs with the Morgans until lunch. When I got there I saw there was a lot of fish jumping around so I raced back to the Dyna and got a line. After I had been fishing for a while I was twirling it around about to let go when I caught the biggest fish I had ever caught even bigger than the ones you've caught. Guess what! I caught my leg, right on the side near the nea (knee). I tugged and pulled but it had gone in past the barb by about 3 mm. I tried to track over but did not sucede, anyway they brought me back to the hospital. The sister gave me an anaesthetic and started to hack away she made another hole and pulled it out the other side.

> That's all I kan think of now.
> From Arthur

PS We lost our horse again now

PPS 22/5/76 This afternoon I went fishing with the Hariss. First we went to a little creek that runs out of Red Lily billabong. When we were there I caught a 6 and ¾ pound barramundi. After a while we went up to your fishing hole but now it is very shallow and not much good so we went back to the Red Lily billabong were there thousands of them jumping, some real big ones too. Jonathan Harris caught one a bit smaller than mine after that the fish got wise. I forgot to say they shurekan fight because as soon as I hooked it jumped and was thrashing around then I thought that it was off but the line started zigzagging and then jumped and I nearly lost it but I did land it. I dragged it right up the bank so it would not get away. Wilfrid came over and got the hook out. We are having it for lunch tomorrow.

After tea tonight dad said come and look at Argarlook because it was on fire. It looked something like this (sketch of hill with squiggles on one side)

Second letter written sometime in 1978

Picture titled "Graham" - a head with two big ears and a few scraggly hairs coming from Trinity Logo. Then "Trinity Grammar School is a hole" alongside school letter head

Dear Graham

I spose it's your turn to get a letter from me as you written to me a couple of times. On Sunday I went abb sailing with Robin and Chris down at Glen Brook National Park. It is really nice down there and Abb sailing is reall good fun. I don't know if you have tried it.

I have to go to Cadet Camp so unfortunately I will have to waste a week of my holidays.

Hope you having fun down in Melbourne. Have you been trying to learn to ski? I know you wouldn't be any good at it seen your such a "clump donkey"

At the moment I am in sick bay with a temp, chest cold and all the other garbage that goes with it. I have been here since Monday afternoon.

On Sunday night I got kicked out of Chapel by Sarge because I just about choked.

When you see the Chocolate Boys you can say hullo for me. You might as well say Hello to all of them while your at it. Have you smashed your car yet?. (Picture of car turning into a pile of rubble)

> That's all I can think of
> Arthur

PS Hope you like my drawings
PSPS Don't forget to write to me
PSPSPS Hope you enjoy the letter, bad luck if you don't.   Arthur

Picture of person with head and shoulders buried in snow and legs with skis poking into air – caption entitled "Graham Skiing"

My Aboriginal Friends

When I came to Oenpelli from Darwin as a nine year old I already had one aboriginal friend, Alec, who I soon met up with. He introduced me, along with Peter and David, to his own group of friends, particularly Moses and Donald who were a couple years older than us, though at a similar stage of their schooling.

Doing correspondence meant that we did not go to Oenpelli school and, in that way meet with other aboriginal kids of our age. Instead we met at Sunday school each week in a class with us white kids and several aboriginal kids. At other times we would meet in various places around Oenpelli.

Our interactions, limited by our different languages and customs, were mostly friendly and sometimes competitive as when they challenged us to a game of football, which they always won, while we looked slow and clumsy.

As the years went by and we went away to school, we left them behind in our advanced education, but they always welcomed us back at school holidays, mostly curious about what we had done, perhaps with faint jealously at our opportunity. It was a relationship of genuine friends on one hand, but with so many cultural gaps between our lives and theirs on the other hand that, as time went by, our ability to talk about our common interests got harder. But still the friendship persisted. As years passed and they began work and had families of their own we kept our friendship even though it was more distant.

Many went on to become community leaders, people of power and influence. Few survived the alcohol and the rest of a western lifestyle. H owever those I still know retain the genuine bond and affection I feel from those shared childhood years, when our two worlds intersected in small parts.

Teenage Adventures

Mining and the Hafflinger

Queensland Mines discovered uranium at Nabarlek when I was in mid high school. With exploration and discovery came a lot of extra people, vehicles and other equipment. Sometimes a helicopter would come in and take whoever was around for a brief joyride over the hills. Other times they left samples they had collected in the office below our house. We marvelled at the incredible weight of these small pieces of dark rock, not knowing their significance. Shortly after came an announcement of their uranium discovery.

On the evening news Queensland Mines shares climbed, day by day, to astronomical heights and then plummeted back to earth again. In the wet season when exploration was halted by water they left equipment at Oenpelli. One wet season Union Carbide's geologist left with Cam Cooke, Peter's father, a small, all terrain vehicle called a Hafflinger. Peter had got a driving license so he used it. It was just big enough for Peter, David and I to ride in. With large tyres, four wheel drive and diff locks front and back, it went practically anywhere.

We would head out across the plains until it bogged it in a muddy channel. With front and back diff locks engaged it was unstoppable. We never found a patch of mud to beat it. With four wheels locked together it would surge out of any quagmire in its irrepressible manner. It gave us access to vast areas of wet season Oenpelli. Following the tidal creeks running off the East Alligator, near Top Landing, we discovered wet season fishing holes we had only dreamt of.

We would return from fishing trips with the Hafflinger loaded down with a dozen or two big barramundi, to distribute around the mission. Gradually others also found our places, and we had to work harder to find hungry barramundi again, but there were always new places to explore and discover.

Those casts into a new billabong: Cast one, wind in two metres, twang - line explodes out of water with a ten pound spitting shaking fish trying to throw the lure. Next cast another fish, only five pounds this time, sometimes all three of us with our fish dancing on their tails above the water together. Occasionally a quiet patch when we would cast out and wind in for half an hour before we moved on, or suddenly the water exploded again. From one little billabong arm, about 50 metres long and wide and four feet deep, connected by a tidal creek to the river, in two weeks we pulled out 100 barramundi. We would watch new fish surging on the incoming tide, coming up the small silted channel, to replace their brothers and sisters who had so recently thrown themselves onto our lines.

Trips with Buffalo Shooters

Dry seasons were a time of fire and bulldust. It was also when the Oenpelli abattoirs was in action. Big buffalo bulls were the target. A cut down short wheel base Toyota, steel bars, pulsing engine, and trailer attached, would head out around the edge of the plains, following tracks winding through scrub, littered with bull dust holes and washouts. Driver, a pro shooter, some black, some white, a heavy rifle with its telescopic sight stowed alongside and one of us kids riding jockey alongside.

It would begin with a leisurely cruise around the edge of plains and billabongs, scouting out where buffalo were to be found that day, and trying not to cause too much early disturbance. Once the first big bull was sighted within a hundred yards a sudden stop, fingers in ears as the man with the gun steadied and held his aim. A reverberating blast, a puff of acrid smoke and, mostly, the bull, seen as a small dark shape amongst the trees, head up, smelling air, fell instantly to the ground.

Toyota into gear, quickly drive up, with the back of the trailer was alongside the bull's back legs, a chain attached to a winch cable put round the feet. A quick gash to the throat with a thin pointed knife, and, as blood poured from this hole in the neck of a still twitching body, it would be hauled onto the trailer, horns gouging grooves in the sand. Within a minute the Toyota would roar back to life and be off. All that remained of 1000 pounds of life was a few marks in the sand and a pool of congealing blood, surrounded by a rapidly thickening swarm of blowflies and some desolate buffalo flies wondering where their living, breathing host had gone.

Then the mad rush to find, shoot and load more buffalo before the first ones went off. The Meat Inspector, back at the abattoir, would check for bloated carcasses or rigor mortis, giving a window of about two hours to be back. As the clock ticked in the hot sun, the pace quickened, faster stopping, faster loading, and sometime ambitious shots where the buffalo was little more than a black dot, but almost always dead, just the same, on that first shot.

Once I watched as Ed Kennedy, a favourite shooter, took aim at a bull a hundred and fifty yards off, its head partially obscured by a four inch sapling. Bang, crash, dead buffalo as normal. Asking Ed how he managed this shot he said, 'The bullets I load don't mind one tree, but two in a row gets a bit tricky."

The late stages of getting a load back to the abattoirs, before the time ran out, were akin to low flying; the Toyota now chugging with several tons of dead buffalo riding behind, propelled unstoppably by its own momentum, clearing gullies and washouts, with bare pause, a huge plume of bulldust following in its wake and announcing its arrival. In the front hunter and rider living on adrenalin as they spat out the passing flies, ducked branches and shielded their faces from the grit and dust, while the mound of black bodies in the back turned steel grey under a shroud of dust.

As the abattoir came into view the pace eased, around the mission to an almost leisurely entrance, and waiting workers emerged from the shade of building. Buffalo bodies were winched in the air, hosed clean and laid out on a frame for the deft strokes of the knifeman, cutting through thick black skin like butter, opening to the white and red tissue below. Then watching as the meat inspector moved in for initial checks, throat, shoulder glands, groin, belly, lungs. Sometimes a bad patch of TB meant half the bulls had tuberculous yellow lumps in multiple places. These were consigned to the dump, hence wasted effort, other times a small celebration when all were clean. Often the biggest, fattest bulls were the rejects, and many smart shooters avoided the worst pockets.

In an hour or two and it was time for a new load. The shooter would head off to do it all over, while the men in the boning room turned these great bodies into 60 pound cardboard boxes stamped "Boneless Oenpelli Buffalo Beef".

All else that remained were piles of white guts, skeletons, black skin, heads and horns at the offal dump, descended on by a flock of hungry birds, a million blowflies and the odd mangy dog or dingo.

Little Boy Lost

One Saturday, when David Cooke was an early teenager, he went on a day's ride with a group of aboriginal stockman to Twin Hills. The hills were just visible on the northern horizon and it was a long ride of over 20 miles each way, so they left early in the morning and were not expected back until late afternoon.

As the afternoon wore on there was no returning party with David. Finally a couple of aboriginal riders straggled in. David had disappeared about lunch time and they had not been able to locate him. So a search party of white and aboriginal men assembled and headed out. I remember the quiet anxiety of people who waited back at Oenpelli, listening in on the two-way radio for any news. In my mind sits the association with Banjo Patterson's poem

> ### "Lost"
> *He ought to be back says the old man, no doubt there's something amiss*
> *He only rode to the Two Mile and he ought to be back by this*
> *He would ride that reckless filly, he would have his wilful way*
> *And yet he's not back by evening and what will his mother say*

As night wore on, with nothing, people stopped to wait for daylight when the search resumed. Dad, back from Katherine, fuelled up the Auster and headed out with a couple spotters on board to search from the air.

About midday David emerged from the plains coming towards Oenpelli. After an unsuccessful afternoon search for his companions he had spent the night on his horse in the saddle of the twin hills. Next morning had given his horse its head to find its way back to Oenpelli.

I can still feel the ripple of joy and relief that ran around the whole community on his safe return. I also remember, many years later, when we waited in Darwin, listening on the radio and hoping for the rescue of another little boy lost, even smaller. He had gone riding his trail bike near Daly Waters. Here the days ran on with nothing, as the searchers and waiters grew less hopeful. Finally the small body was found, days to late. I feel gratitude that this was not our experience.

Peter and the Waterfall

Peter was a wiry teenager of medium size who had an air of quiet determination about whatever he did. While not powerfully built, he had large strong hands and the muscles on his slender frame were like corded wire.

He was the doer, I was more the talker. Once he set his mind to do something he was rarely stopped.

In our final Christmas holidays together, before he went off to work, we decided to camp at the bottom of the waterfall for three days. The first couple of days were spent with Peter, David and me swimming and exploring the hills. On the day before we were due to pack up and go back to Oenpelli, I noticed Peter quietly eying off the face of the waterfall.

To get to the top everyone climbed around the shoulder of the hill, some preferring the less steep western side, others preferring the steeper but quicker eastern side. However we all kept well back from the edge where sheer cliffs of 200 feet fell to the rocky shoulders of the large pool below. At the face of the waterfall was an initial section, rising to about 50 feet, which sloped at a 45 degree angle. Here the water cascaded down a series of sandstone step ledges.

At the top of this cascade was a big ledge, extending under the main fall, which the water pounded after its 200 foot sheer fall. Between the water and the cliff face was an under-hang you could walk through when the flow was not great. After crossing this ledge, under the main fall, it narrowed, then turned into a crack in the rock face, which curved around and up for perhaps another 20 feet. After this it was just the beetling overhang of the sandstone rocks extending far above, with odd cracks and crevices fissured through them.

As far as I knew no one had ever climbed it. Charlie Cuff had attempted it a few years before and, luckily for him, had fallen before he got very high and had only broken a leg. I knew of no one else who had even contemplated climbing it.

Anyway, Peter sat there at the edge of the pool and quietly looked at the face for perhaps a quarter of an hour. In a companionable way we sat alongside him, not saying much.

Then he said, speaking quietly, "I am going to climb up there." He nodded his head towards the cliff face. There was nothing else to say, his mind was made up and, in his head, he had worked out his plan of attack.

A minute later he swam across the pool and was on his way. A quick measured climb saw him go up the first 50 feet to the base of the main fall, working his way across the ledge, past where the main water flow landed. As the ledge narrowed we watched him, first crawling then sliding his lying body along it until he reached the end. So far so good! From there he picked a crack in the rock which ascended.

Hand over hand we watched him pull himself up, with body and feet wedged, gripping on small ledges in the stone. Now came the really scary part. The climb went from vertical to a massive overhang, extending outwards at a 20 or 30 degree angle past the vertical. Peter now looked not much bigger than an ant. We watched him slowly move from one ledge and crack to another, once or twice suspended by one hand.

Finally we exhaled a long painful breath as he cleared the overhang and climbed the last 50 feet, nearly vertical, before he gained the gentle final slope to the top. David and I had sat mesmerised for perhaps half an hour, barely daring to breathe, in case we hexed him. Huge euphoria washed over us as he let out a shout and we climbed to the top to join him for a well-earned swim. The only thing he said of the climb was it got a bit tricky at one stage, when a rock he was using as a hand hold broke off and left him only holding on with one hand. At that stage he knew he would have to keep going forward as he needed that broken rock as a hand hold to go back. We all decided it was better not to say anything to our parents about his success. He did tell them many years later.

To Peter that was not important, he had done it for his own satisfaction, because he believed he could. I have never heard of anyone doing the climb since, perhaps a properly equipped rock climber has, certainly not a barefooted, bare handed 16 year old boy wearing just a pair of shorts.

Across the Plains to Coopers Creek

Next August I was home for a final holiday with Peter, who was working at Oenpelli for a few months before he headed off for a job in Sydney. I was in second final year of high school. Peter got his father to lend us their Kombi van to go fishing, and John Bonney, a new teacher, was keen to come as well.

On Friday evening, after Peter finished work, we headed across the plains the ten miles to Ngara, bouncing over their cracked, buffalo pocked surface in the late afternoon, before reaching the woodland on the other side at dusk.

We continued on for another hour, following a faint set of wheel tracks which we thought led to Coopers Creek, 30 miles north. There had been a big bushfire through this area a few days before and the road was increasingly difficult to follow, no flattened grass to show a path, just a covering of black ash over everything, and feeble six volt Kombi headlights to faintly light the blackness. The landscape was littered with still burning stags of previous trees, which occasionally erupted in showers of sparks, as parts collapsed or exploded.

Finally we came to a small circular billabong where the track disappeared into a mass of buffalo pads, where they came to drink. The headlights picked up perhaps 10 or 20 dark shapes of buffalo around the water, which grunted their little pig like grunts and crashed off into the woodland on the other side as we approached. We positioned ourselves on a flat area free of buffalo dung, and half ringed by several burning trees. We soon built up a fire for light and dinner. The water's edge was 50 yards away and we could see the occasional buffalo or dingo quietly come to the edge to drink. After an hour or two of dinner, cups of tea and campfire chat, under a pitch black starry Arnhem sky, we rolled out our sways, alongside the car, and fell asleep.

An hour or two later was a whispered "Graham, look!"

Ringing us, perhaps 10-20 yards away were at least 50 dark buffalo shapes in a semicircle, their eyes faintly reflected in the burning logs. Another whisper brought John awake. We quietly retreated to the safety of the Kombi, the buffalo continued their immobile watching with an occasional sniff or snuffle, curious about this strange night time visit to their drinking and camping place. Finally, Peter flicked on the headlights and, with startled snorts, they wheeled and galloped off into the bush. We returned to our swags for a more watchful rest of the night, occasionally roused by the sound of a small group coming to the waterhole. Next morning the billabong was deserted and it was like it had all been a dream except for the piles of steaming dung and fresh tracks.

With daylight we picked up our road easily and followed it on to the edge of the Coopers Creek floodplain, where we worked our way round various small overflow billabongs, eventually coming to the larger main channels. Here we settled in for an afternoon of fishing.

The evening saw us with several five to ten pound fish.

With barramundi on the dinner menu, John, as novice bushman, said, "Shall I cook the fish?"

We, lazy, said; "Yes that's a good idea".

John added as an afterthought, "How do you cook them?"

I replied, "Just throw them in the coals."

John set too with a knife and carved off two beautiful barramundi fillets. Peter and I exchanged puzzled glances. He threw these in the burning fire embers, and after a few minutes pronounced the fish cooked. Only problem, our fillets were now completely coated in sand and inedible.

Peter, in his usual low key manner, said. "It works better if you do it like this" as he picked up another whole fish and dropped it onto the embers, then with a shovel heaped more hot embers on top, aboriginal style. Fifteen minutes later we peeled off burnt skin and ate the beautiful succulent flesh underneath.

Next morning we were up at dawn and, by lunch time, we each had half a dozen fish ranging in size from five to twenty pounds. We made our way back to Oenpelli, where there were plenty of people to help with the eating. Next day Peter was back at work and before the next weekend I was back at school. This was the last time we went bush together as children of Oenpelli.

It sits in my mind as one of those perfect times, two mates, a car and fish.

The following Christmas David was there but Peter was not. David and I were good mates and spent many enjoyable hours together, riding, mustering horses off the plains, working with the stockmen, swimming and fishing, but there was a hole where Peter used to be.

Mum and Dads Story continues
Living again at Oenpelli

Mum seemed to live happily in Darwin, but shared the joy of us children to be returning to Oenpelli to live in 1963; there was an infectious delight to our whole family on this trip. I think simple country life at Oenpelli, with its abundant nature, gave her more pleasure than suburban life in Darwin,

Dad wrote of the return to Oenpelli:

"Helen had a big job with four children to go onto Correspondence lessons. This, in itself, took a lot of time. Then there were innumerable visitors to deal with, making cups of tea if they were only passing through, and for meals if they were staying. She had a lovely house girl, Carol, whom we had known in the past and had a profound knowledge of the people generally. We found it a great pleasure to be in a house well ventilated with louvers and with flywire. The fuel stove had a heater coil which circulated hot water into the storage tank. This meant we could have a hot shower at the end of the day if there was any water. Before, there were only a few early model kerosene refrigerators. We now had a new and bigger kerosene refrigerator which worked much better than any of the old ones. A small generator was run for a few hours each night which gave two lights per house. Our yard had once been part of the garden and was neatly levelled off with neither a bush nor a blade of grass. With billabong water and plants we brought from Darwin we were able to alter the landscape a little. We also brought bamboo seedlings from the Mary River and managed to get one growing in our yard.

Of Mum's need to entertain visitors Dad wrote:
"We were constantly receiving visits. One group consisted of seven members of the House of Commons in London accompanied by Mr Jack Larcombe of the Welfare Branch. Each visit of the medical plane brought an increasing number of specialists. On one visit we had 13 people for lunch and one doctor said it was a pity they didn't have the larger aircraft yet because they would then be able to bring more specialists on these visits!

It seemed to be a favourite area for politicians to find a reason to come. No doubt, they would pass on to their colleagues the need for them also to visit. Mr. W.C. Wentworth and party arrived one Saturday, without warning, and they wanted a meeting with the staff. Saturday was a free day and most staff took the opportunity to get away from the place. Dr and Mrs. Coombs also came and Peter Carroll took them up Injalak hill.

Other well-known visitors over succeeding years included Gough Whitlam, Malcolm Fraser and Bob Hawke, who wrote their names in the Visitors Book.

Shortly after return to Oenpelli Dick Harris approached Dad to take over running of the mission. He wanted to focus on being the Chaplain and spend his time out with the aboriginal men. He knew CMS would require him to retire at 65, only a couple of years off.

Dad wrote of this period:
"In 1963 there were just over 300 people and finding work for everyone was not easy. The old men were the woodcutters and sat around the wood heap. Their job was to keep the wood drums at the houses full. They were also responsible to cook up a stew for the working men for lunch. They had a large drum and buffalo meat was cut up and boiled with vegetables. This was ladled into billycans. There was a team of stockmen, builders, a road-work team, a workshop crew and hygiene workers. Most women worked in the garden or houses, a few in the hospital and as teaching assistants. The policy was everyone had a job. In addition to those around the mission, there were groups who spent most of their time away in crocodile shooters' camps. Family groups received daily rations from the store. Basic clothing was issued about four times a year. A small amount of spending money was paid to each worker at the end of the week. With this they could purchase extras on a Friday afternoon. Tobacco was sold and most men spent money on this. Garden produce was given out after work. It mainly consisted of sweet potatoes,

cassava, pumpkins and occasionally peanuts. There was a plentiful issue of buffalo meat, and a limited amount of fresh milk.

During the dry season it was fairly simple to keep up the supply of meat, but in the wet season the buffalo moved away across the plains and it became difficult. Two men would set off with pack horses, riding round the edge of the plains until they came to a group of buffalo. One animal was shot, butchered and the meat packed into the saddle bags, followed by the long trip back round the plains to Oenpelli. They usually left about 7 am and got back about 7 pm, sometimes as late as 10 pm. The same men would be away again next morning. After two weeks another crew took over, and so it went on. With no refrigeration meat had to be used straight away. Barnabas, Davis and Brolga were particularly reliable, supported by other good stockmen.

Normal dry rations were ground wheat for porridge, flour, tea and sugar mixed together and twice a week, rice. Each day an issue of golden syrup was made, mainly used with porridge. Friday afternoon wages were five shillings each for women and seven shillings for men. This money had to be earned by the mission, trading crocodile skins and dingo pelts. Earlier the sale of buffalo hides also helped to pay wages.

In 1960 Oenpelli had an outbreak of typhoid. As a result the Health Department became very active and one action was to close access to Oenpelli unless a person was inoculated. Following this a crucial need was for a better water supply. At the end of the dry season there was little water in the wells. Therefore billabong water had to be used. The 3000 gallon tank was filled at least twice a day. It needed chlorination and I inherited this job in 1963. I had to climb the wooden posts of the tank stand, secure a footing and place 40 large chlorine tablets into a bag in the top of the tank. This was swirled in the water and left for half an hour before the outlet tap was opened.

The outflow from the billabong was a creek with little water in the bottom at the end of the dry season. Some staff felt the water supply would be improved by damming this creek and raising the water level in the billabong by six feet. Albert Abel completed the dam in December. When the heavy rains came, the billabong filled with water and first there was a small flow across the dam wall. This small flow became a bigger flow. After a few weeks the dam disappeared.

In May 1964 Don Kneebone arrived to survey our future water supply. I mentioned to Don a spring, six miles out. Next day we set out on the tractor to look at it. I raised the idea of a dam to hold back water as a lot was running down through the opening in the rocks. Don estimated this was over 4,000 gallons an hour. We needed to monitor this through the dry season to see what level it would fall to, taking readings through the year. One could collect over 90% of the flow in a bucket, measure the time to fill the bucket and work out the water flow in 24 hours. By November flow was still 1,680 gallons/hour or over 40,000 gallons per day. Water Resources Branch was happy this was sufficient to develop it and pipe water to the mission It had a pH of 5 which was acidic so it would need treatment.

The chlorination of the water supply at Oenpelli was a continual grind; climbing the tank twice a day a real bugbear. So in the workshop I put together some fittings and made an insert which held the chlorine tablets and screwed this into the inlet pipe. All that had to be done was place the tablets in the recess, screw in the bung and start up the pump. It perfectly mixed the chlorine in the water. Even the Health Inspector was impressed!

For a long time we wanted to do away with the ration system but without income it was difficult to see how it could be done. One income source was sale of meat to Darwin. This was only pet food but was supposed to bring 10 pence per pound. We requested payment for the previous year's supply and for the increased amount in this present year. Finally we received a cheque. It had only one signature and when banked was rejected; The company had closed and disappeared. However, we gradually built up funds from the sale of beef to places like Elcho Island, Umbakumba, Maningrida and occasionally Groote. Much went to the building the abattoirs and it also made other funds available.

In July, 1964, following a Station Council Meeting, a special meeting was held in the camp. People were asking for a full cash economy (excepting beef) to be introduced without rationing. The Shop should open from 7 to 7.30 am for the sale of food. The following Friday there was an increased payment of 3/6d to each worker to enable them to buy extra food. The wage payment then was one pound a week to each employed man and 15 shillings for each woman. With this most people found, if they handled this money carefully, they could buy their daily food needs. However, other people complained they didn't have any money left. An organised card group was doing well from these people so, near the end of August, we reverted to the old ration system. Many people were indignant that gambling had been introduced and playing cards were banned.

In August we had a visit from the Animal Industry Branch to T.B. test the cattle. There were ten positive reactors in the beef cattle and one in the dairy herd. In a 1954 survey it was found that 50% of the cattle were positive so this was not too bad. Back in 1954 we were advised to sell the 100 'clean' cattle and butcher the other 100. We did and sold the 100 "clean ones" to Goodparla Station. In a TB survey years later, no one could work out the reason for a pocket of TB infection in the Goodparla area. It obviously came from the 100 'clean' cattle.

A few days after testing the cattle we had another visitor from the Agriculture Branch, Tom Bell, who had heard about the cashew trees we had and how well they were growing. The cashews came from Canon Hill. In early 1954 I was sent there with a few men to clean up Jimmy Doyle's camp. At the end we sat down to enjoy papaws and cashews growing there. We put the cashew seeds in a bag and took them home with 100% germination and these trees were planted out in the garden. Ten years later there wasn't much left of the first trees but we had many more which produced well in the dry season. We did not grow them for the nuts, only the fruit.

On Friday, 18th September, we received a visit from Ted Evans of the Welfare Branch who talking to communities about the Full Citizenship Legislation which became effective on 15th September. A meeting was called and people assembled in the Dining Room. Ted spoke for an hour. I don't think many people understood. His message was that Aboriginal people were no longer Wards of the State and they were free to move around. Arnhem Land aboriginal people never considered themselves Wards of the State, with no restraint where they went. However it meant they were also free to have alcohol. This did not mean anything then but in five years it would become a big issue.

By early 1965 we moved to a full cash economy and, as far as possible, rationing ceased. Certain food lines had to be rationed especially in the wet season. The following dry season I was planning to take off all rationing, including sugar. Some staff thought I was mad but I felt sure that, after an initial splurge, the sale of sugar would come back to normal. We introduced a type of supermarket in the old store, putting in a counter where the large food drums had been stored.

The rains finished early in 1965. By September the dry conditions were really starting to take their grip. The plains were rapidly drying out and the billabong at the Top Landing was reduced to a small mud hole. Buffalo were starting to push into the Oenpelli billabong in hundreds. A desperate attempt was made to fence it off, leaving the small creek at the end of the billabong as a water supply for them. Once I had to go to start the billabong pump and took a short cut through the bananas. I suddenly came face to face with a buffalo. It was about six feet away and came towards me. I put one hand on each horn and rode along on its face, finally springing off alongside the pump house, the buffalo kept going. It was a bit too close for comfort.

With no early storms in September or October the buffalo problem was at its height by the start of November and hundreds were trying to force their way into the mission billabong. Stockmen were constantly guarding this area. It was necessary to shoot many of the animals which became bogged in the creek that leads away from the billabong and to drag the carcasses out on the plains a couple of miles away. Even from there a stench permeated the whole area. The weather continued hot and dry although to the south and west we could see some rain. It was a long way away although occasionally we got a very light shower

Phillip Dirdi and Paddy came in from their crocodile camp at Murganella. They had been away for a couple of days looking at another area for hunting and had left crocodile skins salted and rolled up ready to bring in to the mission. While they were away an aircraft landed on the plains and someone had taken their skins. The matter was reported to the police and I was not hopeful of anything happening but, on Monday, 1st November, a policeman arrived on a charter to inform Phillip they had apprehended the pilot of the aircraft in Darwin. The police wanted Phillip to go to Darwin to identify his crocodile skins. He managed to get his skins back but no action was taken against the pilot.

We had a short visit from Bob Southern of the Weather Bureau on 8th November. Over a cup of coffee he outlined some features of tropical weather. One was Darwin's "Achilles Heel". Cyclones along the top of Arnhem Land mostly move west. The worst scenario is for a cyclone to become stationary out at sea north-west of Darwin. There is what weather men call a funnel which goes down into the Darwin Harbour area. If a cyclone becomes stationary out to sea here, it may start to intensify and then slide down the funnel. Nine years later this happened to cyclone Tracy.

At the end of November the weather held off in our area but there were heavy storms to the south west. After bogging on the Marrakai road at the end of October, the truck switched to the old Pine Creek road which was holding up better. On the last trip of the year we received a message that the truck was stuck 2 ½ miles east of Goodparla. It was 13th December and Ian Mackenzie set off from Oenpelli with a team of men with two tractors and trailers, heavy steel cable and a winch. By the 15th Ian had not reached the truck and was presumed held up at the South Alligator. three inches of rain at Oenpelli and a black mass of clouds southwest gave little confidence the truck would get through.

On the 16th, I went with Harold Shepherdson from Elcho in his aircraft to look at the position from the air. Ian had crossed the South Alligator and was heading for the truck, arriving that afternoon. Some men, including Dudley were to stay with the vehicle and tractors, the rest were to walk back as far as possible and get a lift to Darwin. On 23rd December, Sheppy called in for another load of meat. I took the opportunity to go on a flight with him to the South Alligator. The river was down and it was necessary to act quickly. I called Dudley on the radio and asked him to meet me at the junction of the El Sharana and Goodparla Roads late that afternoon. Grabbing a few things I went to Darwin on the mail plane. CMS drove me through Pine Creek to the junction of the roads. We arrived after dark but the men were on the tractor with the platform; Dudley, George, Jerry and Yuan Yuan; I couldn't have wished for a better team. About midnight we reached the truck near the South Alligator River.

Friday morning, Christmas Eve, I waded through the water of the South Alligator River with a couple of men. It was about three feet deep in the main channel and water was flowing fast. We decided to camp a day to let the water go down more, giving time to check the equipment and food supplies. One trailer tyre was a bit soft, but the compressor could fix it. I looked in the normal places for it then we went through everything, emptying the cab and looking among the loading; but nothing, not even a hand pump. We would have to drag the trailer with a half flat tyre as neither trailer had a spare and the truck spare wheel was too large to fit on the hub. The soft tyre was at the front of the trailer which upset it's steering. We did not even have a wheel brace to change the wheel with a back one.

Next morning, Christmas Day, the water in the river had dropped six inches. We were ready. Dudley went first crossing the main channel without difficulty. I locked the bogey diffs and drove down into the water with the truck. It gurgled along and I came out behind Dudley. Last was George, with the trailer and half flat tyre. He got through to the other side. We headed on slowly, our speed set by Dudley in the lead tractor. A few miles on Dudley's tractor slid off the road in a wet area. I tried to drive around him to pull him out. The truck ploughed into the soft area and settled on its axles. George tried to go round us and also sank. We camped for the night. The weather had been quite good but now dirty looking clouds were to the north and the east.

There was light rain overnight and the sky was very overcast. Each morning we had a radio sked with CMS Darwin. This Sunday I said to Jack Langford that it was a day of rest, all the vehicles were resting on their axles and we were lying down under them – trying to get them back up on the road. Little did I realise that this was passed to the media. We finally got all three vehicles out with the tree puller and went a few miles to a better place to camp. The trailer tyre was flatter and pulling crookedly so George was slowly bringing up the rear. Next day, Monday, 27th, we made Jim Jim Creek where Dudley and I waited for George to catch up. By now the tyre was flat and the trailer was very difficult to manage. Once more I looked for the air gun and hose, -Nothing. – it was not on the truck. I told Dudley and George I would drive to Nourlangie and wait for them there. The weather was closing in, not heavy but long showers of light rain.

At Nourlangie I crossed the first creek and moved to the second creek. This one was deeper but I confidently headed into it and started up the other side. This started a sequence of events which was to keep us bogged for three days. The front wheels of the truck started to climb the bank but, on the loamy ground, they dug in. I backed off and tried to make a run at it but the wheels only dug in further. I could do nothing until the tractors arrived. Dudley and George arrived and we went to work with the tree puller. The men fastened it to the base of a solid paper bark tree and with two men on the handle they tried to pull the truck up the bank. The front wheels just sank deeper into the bank. The weather was now continuous light rain. A tarpaulin covered the swags and food, but we were wet and we stayed so the next three days.

On the sked I asked for an aircraft to drop a tyre pump to us, but got no reply. On the Wednesday morning we heard an aircraft and it circled the area. A large package was pushed out and landed not far from us. It was the pump. One man ran to get it. We yelled out to him to take cover, more things coming. Six more bags came down then the aircraft circled and headed back to Oenpelli. It was food of different kinds, a variation in diet.

On Wednesday afternoon we had an accident. Jerry and George were working on the handle of the tree puller, with a terrific strain on the cable. Suddenly, the chain around the tree snapped. The chain whipped round the tree and gashed the back of one of George's legs open, amazingly his leg wasn't broken. I looked for the first aid kit but had not seen it when we had looked for the tyre pump. We used a shirt and bandaged his leg which stopped the bleeding. So we put the billy on and sat around summing up our situation. The remaining chain was just long enough to still go round the base of the tree, but we had to limit the strain on the cable. We concentrated on freeing one tractor, got Dudley on the road then called it a day.

Overnight the rain eased. We manoeuvred Dudley's tractor into position with the cable attached to the truck. Numerous saplings were laid along the road and with a steady pull from the tractor I was able to shift the truck. Our pace quickened and I was able to drive it along the road without the tractor. We got a message that Vic Peterson could collect us from Mudginberry and fly us back to Oenpelli on Saturday, New Year's Day.

We continued towards Mudginberry, over the next day, with lots of stopping and starting as we hauled our way across the disintegrating road. About 16 miles from Mudginberry once more the truck bogged. We were all tired. After trying to get back on the road for a while I decided to stay there. It was late afternoon so we camped. Next morning we had another go to shift it but it wouldn't budge. So we packed up and went to Mudginberry with the tractors. George did not complain about his leg, continuing to work.

Vic Pedersen took George and Jerry first, then Dudley and Yuan Yuan. I travelled with the gear on the last trip. We appreciated Vic's help. He was prepared to go the second mile. On New Year's Day, 1966, we were back at Oenpelli. The sister at the hospital attended to George's leg and it healed up very well.

It was not until March that we were able to bring everything in. I was in a helicopter and I asked the pilot to divert to the crossing. The water had fallen a lot we could bring everything across. The following day we set out. We took our one and only remaining tractor across the river. Then, with three tractors with trailers in a line we made our way to the other side of the river and on down to the mission. This concluded the trip.

Flying and Building Outstations

The Aircraft Trial

In 1964 I attended Field Council conference in Darwin when different projects were discussed. Some of us saw a need for an aircraft but it was unclear where it would be based and how it would operate. There was also strong opposition. Then Canon Pearson, stated he had already made arrangements with a pilot to bring a light aircraft to spend one month at Oenpelli. The need for an aircraft would be assessed by the amount of use, or lack of it, the aircraft got.

Two weeks later Wal Job arrived with his Auster aircraft. It was a fiasco. No preparation had been made, not even a supply of fuel so the plane sat on the ground with absolutely no use. It appeared a good way of getting rid of a problem; everything worked out in advance. Wal was a lovely fellow and fitted in well, doing stock work, riding horses and travelling around the country. On 24th September he collected Jack Langford from Darwin for a visit by many Heads of Government Departments, who he showed around, then took Jack back the following day. It was the only time the Auster was used. On 23rd October, Wal loaded his things and set out for Darwin. Before he left, he said the only way to assess the need for an aircraft was for one of the staff to get a pilot's licence and procure an aircraft. Then gradually the need could be shown by its use and work would develop with its availability. This made sense to me and I idly wondered who would be able to do this. I commented that I couldn't agree more. At that stage I couldn't see who the person would be to get a pilot's licence. We all led busy lives.

First Steps to Become a Pilot

A week or so later we received a telegram that a Darwin Aero Club aircraft would be calling in on the Sunday morning to use some of their fuel. The aircraft duly arrived as we were walking to church so I went over to give assistance. The pilot knew his way around and taxied to the fuel area. By the time I arrived he was pumping petrol from one of the Aero Club drums. He was most apologetic at arriving at such a time and assured me he did not need help but would come back in during the afternoon for more fuel to get back to Darwin.

Sure enough about four o'clock the plane landed and taxied to the fuel drums. I was a bit nettled at his attitude. As I walked over to the plane a text of scripture came forcibly into my mind. - 'Do not neglect to show hospitality to strangers, for thereby some have entertained angels unawares'. I mellowed and invited the pilot over for a cup of coffee. We talked about things then he said, "It beats me why you people don't have an aircraft here with one of you able to fly it." So the conversation went on. I asked him how a person would go about getting a pilot's licence. He gave me the address of the College of Civil Aviation and suggested that I write to enrol. He said there were 22 lessons, which I should not find too difficult. So I enrolled to obtain a Private Pilot's Licence. I did not mention this to anyone outside the family.

Once the course was paid for lessons started to arrive. I tried to do one lesson a fortnight. It took nearly a year to complete. Eventually it was finished. I put the papers in the cupboard. With no opportunity for flying I wondered what to do next.

I did not mention it to others as it was a controversial topic. Vic Pedersen once spent a quarter of an hour showing me the use of aircraft controls. Apart from that I was 'illiterate' in the technique of flying.

Becoming a Pilot

About a week later the medical plane was in with a dentist and a doctor for the day. The pilot was Ray Vuillerman. Ray was a flying instructor with TAA, on loan to the Health Department for one year and also an honorary member of the Darwin Aero Club.

As normal everyone was at our place for lunch. After the meal the doctor and dentist went to the hospital. Ray remained and asked me if I knew of a person on one of these communities who wanted to get a pilot's licence. I quietly told him that I thought the person he was looking for was me. He asked what I had done so far. I told him I had completed all the theory lessons.

He was staggered anyone would have done that without any flying. He spent an hour going through the lessons I gave him and later in the afternoon came to me with a proposition. He said he would make it a project to teach me to fly by coming out to Oenpelli in the Aero Club Cessna 172 every second week on his day off. He had worked out the ferry costs of the aircraft and wondered if he could bring out three nursing sisters from Darwin Hospital each time, for the day, to cover these costs. An arrangement was made with the hospital sisters and there seemed no end of sisters wanting a day off like this. So he would fly the Cessna out each fortnight and we would fit in as much flying training as possible.

On one visit he was teaching me the procedure for engine failure at take-off. I took off on the airstrip alongside the abattoirs and 200 feet over the abattoirs Ray pulled off the throttle. The aircraft was rapidly placed in a glide and we descended over the houses and out over the plains. Then applying a small amount of power we did a precautionary approach from over the plains to the far end of the airstrip and landed. Charlie Cuff and his men were concreting at the abattoirs. On hearing the loss of power they set out to help us. Rather sheepishly they found us still in one piece.

I also had to do training at an aerodrome which meant going to Darwin. On 27th April 1966, I went for my Restricted Licence test which meant that I could operate an aircraft within the immediate precincts of an airport. I still had to do navigation, requiring cross country flights from a main airport which I did in July and August. After this all I had to do was a navigation theory exam to have my full private pilot licence. I completed this in Sydney while on holidays.

In April 1966 Major Vic. Pedersen called in, in his Auster. I took the opportunity to fly with him to Mudginberry to bring back the battery from the Oenpelli truck to charge it. When we arrived back I offered Vic to fill his fuel tanks. He declined saying he had plenty of fuel to get home.

A few days later we found that, approaching Katherine at last light, about five miles from the airport, his fuel ran out and the engine stopped. In the failing light he made the best of a bad situation and managed to crawl away from the wreckage. He dragged himself along the ground until he came to the edge of the Stuart Highway. He put one of his shoes on the end of stick, waving it at each passing car. For a long time no one took any notice thinking he was drunk. At last someone realised it was the Salvation Army padre. He spent a few weeks in hospital but once out he went looking for another aircraft.

First Plane – An Auster

Getting a pilot's licence was only part of having an aircraft in the North. The next stage was to buy an aeroplane and fly it north. Helen and I didn't have much money, only a very small personal bank account. The most we could find was a little over $3,000 and not much was available at that price. The Methodist missions and the Salvation Army used an Auster so I made enquiries about this type of machine. Camden had an Auster for $3000. It had done a lot of flying and had a Gypsie Major engine. This seemed reasonable and I kept it in mind.

At Bankstown an elderly gentleman, with a light aircraft business, had an Auster Autocar with a Cirrus engine. It had only done 160 hours but had an accident. It was available for $3200 after being rebuilt. I pondered, seeking advice from any in the industry. My feeling was to go with this as it had seen so little use. The Manager assured me he could have it ready in November when we were due to return north. So I paid a deposit and hoped it would be ready in time.

By the end of September no work had been carried out on rebuilding the plane. I was always assured they would soon go to work on it and it would definitely be ready. Towards the end of October there was some work going ahead and the manager informed me that it would be ready in early December. This was a problem. I still had to be endorsed on the plane and would run out of time. CMS had no goodwill towards the project and it would not be received kindly if I asked for an extension of my leave. I was six months late coming on leave but didn't want to use this as a bargaining point.

Walking in Sydney, I unexpectedly caught up with Ray Vuillerman. I outlined the situation and he simply said to leave it with him. He was looking for flying experience for junior TAA pilots. One could fly it north and return on a TAA flight.

On 16th December, I received a telegram from the pilot bringing the Auster from Sydney that the aircraft was at Katherine with a tail wheel problem and he had to return south for duty. I didn't know what to do about it. It would have been very difficult to get permission to go to Katherine to fix it and I had to be endorsed on the aircraft before I could fly it.

Next morning I received another telegram from Ron Lawford, a RAAF flight instructor, to the effect that he had seen the aircraft and with my approval would fix the problem and fly it to Oenpelli. Of course he had my approval. He arrived in the Auster at Oenpelli the next day but a broken bungy prevented my endorsement. Ron returned with his wife in January and I spent the afternoon flying with him, continuing the following day. When he was confident I was able to handle any situation I took them back to Katherine

Next morning, Sunday, I returned to Oenpelli in the middle of a ground search for David Cooke. David had set out the previous day with Jacob and Beswick Bob on horseback. David became separated and lost. He moved around on his horse unable to pick up any recognisable tracks. Finally he rode to Twin Hills and stayed on the top for the night. His disappearance triggered a large search and when I arrived back at 10.30 that morning, he hadn't been found. I took off and flew in the direction of the search party. Across the plains I saw a tractor and trailer heading back to the mission with a large group of people on the trailer. Although I couldn't see David, I was confident he was there.

Early Flying, Building Airstrips and First Outstations

The creation of outstations for aboriginal communities was an idea that Dick Harris first expressed to Dad when he came to Groote Eylandt in 1953. With Dick's encouragement he started initial work on outstation of Angurugu at Emerald River. After a year assisting in the establishment of Numbulwar he had expected to continue this project as recorded in his memoir.

I was expecting to go to Angurugu where I would continue with the Emerald River project, but I received a letter from Kevin Hoffman, the Superintendent, advising me that I would be welcome to return to Groote providing I did nothing further with the outstation at Emerald River".

It was almost two decades before the establishment of outstations moved forward. Having an aircraft available on a day to day basis was a key part of allowing outstations to establish. Typically they were several hours drive from Oenpelli over rough bush roads, which were only passable for a few months in the dry season. Therefore, for year round access to these communities, an aeroplane was the best option. Building an airstrip topped the list for most early outstation communities. Both plane and pilot had to be able to take off and land on short, narrow airstrips. These communities often had no local equipment other than some axes, shovels and occasionally a vehicle, such as a tractor or Toyota four wheel drive, if in working order.

The first airstrip to be built was at Ngara on a point of the East Alligator floodplains ten miles north of Oenpelli. It took five minutes flying against a two hour drive around the floodplain margin, with this road barely trafficable in the wet. Buffalo gathered in at Ngara in large numbers in the wet season and early dry season, a time when accessing buffalo close to Oenpelli was difficult.

An airstrip was built here soon after Dad bought the Auster in early 1967, followed by a small abattoirs for initial processing of field shot buffalo (skinning and quartering), with meat flown back to Oenpelli to complete the processing.

Other airstrips followed quickly as outstation development mushroomed.

Dad's memoir continues

Another factor which precipitated the opening up of outstations was the increasing influx of mining people with permits to explore land for minerals. There are areas of land with tribal significance and clan groups wanted to be in the vicinity when mining people were wandering over their land. After the discovery of uranium in the Mount Brockman region, intense exploration took place in the escarpment country around Oenpelli. Queensland Mines operated on an Exploration Licence taken out by Mrs Stevens over the escarpment area east of the mission and Union Carbide adjoined their area to the north-west. At this stage Aboriginal Land was merely a Reserve placed over an area of land, but this did not prevent other interests, such as mining companies, entering this land. The Government was very much part of 'the rush for the spoils', and any mining company seeking an 'Exploration Licence' over vacant reserve land, would receive that Licence.

This was happening at the beginning of the outstation movement with some people wanting to move out onto their own traditional land. One man who was very keen to do this was our head gardener, Timothy. He had been with me in the early stages of the transport work. He only really knew his own country in the Gumarrirnbang and Gumarderr areas, about 100 kilometres east of Oenpelli from when he was a small boy. His mother's country was on the eastern side of the river but he had lived on the western side in the Darnek area, although he recalls that as a small boy he was taken across the river in the dry season to the 'smoke house' This was a place his father had built and was used when the mosquitoes were very bad. In the wet season, like many other people, his family found shelter in a cave. When Timothy was about a seven or eight years old he went with his older brother in to Oenpelli to go to the new school. That was in 1929 and he remembers the two white men who came out on horses looking for children to go to school. Although he returned once, after going to school for a short period, he had not been able to return to live there until he moved back in 1967.

Timothy's wife, Nancy, died in hospital at Oenpelli in June, 1967. We knew Timothy wanted to move to his country and, soon after, he put together a few things and set out by foot for the Gumarderr River. About the middle of December, 1967, I drove with Wilfred Harris and Bruce Morrow to make contact with Timothy. The previous day Timothy had been out hunting and a bush fire had swept through his camp burning everything. We spent the afternoon with him and he came with us back to Oenpelli. Late in January Timothy came with me in the Auster and we flew over the Gumarderr area looking for a site for an airstrip. We really needed a temporary landing area to give access to land while a proper airstrip was built. In an hour flying over his land he pointed out features such as water supply, timber, gardening soil, and places to hunt. The aircraft was noisy but I heard sufficient description to build up my knowledge of the area. I was looking for areas which could be used for small airstrips. Much of this development was to come later, but my understanding of the land was increasing.

In early 1967 I had also flown along Mikginj Valley looking for a suitable site for an airstrip there. One pocket of a plain could be suitable in the dry season and once the ground was dry enough I would go and inspect it. On 15th April 1967, I returned in the aircraft, taking David Namirlmirl. He recognised the area and agreed that it would be alright in the dry season. We organised a team of four men who set out by horse, with pack horses carrying tools and supplies. A few weeks later I flew out with some bags of food, the front passenger seat removed and Clancy in the back seat. We circled the area noting progress. Then, selecting an end of the strip, I slid the side window back and Clancy handed me one bag at a time. With the control with one hand, circling to the right, I pushed the bags through the opening with my other hand. It worked well until one bag was a bit larger. On forcing it through the opening the window disappeared too. We finished and headed back, wind blowing around the cabin in a very noisy aircraft. A week later I saw Lydia, from there, at the Oenpelli shop. I asked her if they saw the window which fell from the plane. Lydia smiled and said, 'We got him.' 'Where?' I asked. 'Out there in the camp.' she replied. The airstrip's first use, in June 1967, caused great excitement among those who worked on it and at last I got my window back!

A week later I used Mikginj airstrip to visit a tin deposit in the Myra Falls area. David Namirlmirl, at Mikginj with the other workers, had a horse for me. I flew across early in the morning and we set out and arrived mid-afternoon to camp near Myra Falls. David showed me the deposit, then we spent time washing samples and I drew a map of the area.

In the approach to the 1967 wet season we were pushing ahead with the abattoirs at Ngara. On 21st December I flew there to bring home Wilfred, Bill and Richard Turley, with their tools; a heavy load. Approaching Oenpelli airstrip a heavy squall cloud was coming over the mission. It was already over the airstrip but I felt confident I could get in. I attempted to fly under it, straight down onto the airstrip.

Everything started to go wrong. I started in at 1500 feet but the turbulence was so great that the next thing I knew I was at tree top level well to the north of the runway. I was in a precarious position, rapidly losing height, the plane being thrown around in the air. With full power I could barely maintain 150 ft of height. So I had to turn away from the mission airstrip and five minutes later I was flying over the trees on the far side of the plains, heading back to Ngara.

Over Ngara airstrip I reckoned the wind was coming from the North so I lined up with the north/south strip. Not on, if anything the wind was behind us, so I went to the other end to land into the south. I then realised this wasn't going to work when I saw a man holding up a shirt to show me the wind direction. Once on the ground and very happy to be on terra firma, one of my passengers pointed to the undercarriage of the Auster. Its fabric was torn open for nearly the length of the plane. We took a tractor and trailer for a two hour trip home. It was nine o'clock at night before we arrived at Oenpelli where a search and rescue exercise was being organised. Everyone was relieved we were safe. In those days I did not operate with radio to Darwin. The wireless in the aircraft was so poor it was very difficult to contact anyone.

Next morning I set out on the tractor and trailer with my son Graham, home on school holidays. I took aircraft fabric and some dope (glue). I also had paint stripper because the aircraft was sprayed with hard surface gloss paint, and area to be mended had to be stripped back. Fabric covered aircraft can be repaired using strips of the fabric and dope, which, when it dries, causes the fabric to become stiff. At Ngara, it took an hour to make the repair and then we flew back.

Need for a Stronger Plane with a Metal Skin

The Auster had a couple of weaknesses. First the undercarriage was sprung with two heavy rubber bands called bungies. They were very difficult to replace. I made a special tool for the job. With both doors open and the floor removed, this tool was hooked over a length of water pipe and with two men on each side lifting the pipe the rubber bungie was stretched to fit over a retaining flange. I manipulated the bungie over the flange knob and did the appropriate grunting while the men did the lifting. We had a bad batch of bungies and were forever replacing them.

The second weakness was that the aircraft covering was fabric. Until then I knew nothing about patching fabric but I became an expert before long. The plane was parked in the open and cattle grazed here at night. It was a great attraction for the cattle to put a horn through the fabric. Each hole required a patch and after a few months there were patches down both sides of the fuselage. I needed a hangar, but with the aircraft privately owned, I thought the hangar would be deemed a personal expense. In that case the plane would continue to be the target of the cattle's horns.

A letter was sent to CMS, Sydney, inquiring about paying for a hangar. The reply said it should be a station expense. So, in August, its purchase was approved by Station Council, using funds from the Beef Account. It arrived at the end of 1967, but it was 1968 before it was built.

By the end of 1967 I had done nearly 200 hours in the plane. Each 100 hourly required a flight to Darwin and was worked in with other business. On one trip I reached the 30 mile point, near the Adelaide River and called Darwin for a clearance to enter the Control Zone but the radio faded out. It seemed to be battery trouble. I dared not enter the Control Zone without radio so I turned and headed back to Oenpelli. Over Point Stuart I decided to land and investigate. Sure enough the battery was quite flat. A man camping there offered me the use of the battery out of his vehicle, as he wouldn't be using it for a few days. I accepted his kind gesture and headed back to Darwin.

When I called Darwin Control again at the 30 mile point I found I had started an emergency when my first call was received. On arrival in Darwin I was met by a DCA official who examined the fault in the generator. He set out an elaborate method to rectify the fault for a mechanic to carry out. I was also taken to task for landing on an unserviceable airstrip at Point Stuart. I was sure there was no such marking on this airstrip. Returning the battery, the following day, I confirmed this. There was a dumb-bell marker indicating a pilot could use his discretion as to landing.

Eddie Connellan, of Connellan Airways, called in occasionally. He showed great interest in my humble attempt to introduce an aircraft. He would come to our place for a cup of coffee and discuss the best type of plane to use. We agreed a Cessna 185 was what I should aim at. He had one in Alice Springs but was not sure he wanted to sell it. For the time being, the Auster was all we had and, financially, I could not see a changeover was possible.

On 8th July 1968, we received another visit from Eddie Connellan, this time with Sir Donald Anderson from the Department of Aviation. Around a cup of coffee we talked about aeroplanes. I outlined problems with my fabric aircraft, which was rapidly coming to the end of the engine hours and I wondered about flying it south. Eddie Connellan thought there would be no demand for an Auster in the North. They advised me to write to DCA seeking an extension of hours to fly south. I did and was granted an additional 30 hours.

A new builder, Arthur Field, arrived from Numbulwar. An early job was to build the hangar but now I was taking the Auster south. Perhaps, in the future, I may have another aircraft. A few days after Eddie's visit I flew to Katherine. Returning to Oenpelli the hangar was finished and decorated for its plane's arrival.

Taking the Auster to Sydney to Sell

On Monday, 26th August, we loaded the plane for the trip south, everything in small parcels packed in any possible space. I had trouble fitting in the muffler. I had never used it and couldn't see where to stow it. I wondered if I could install it on the engine. It fitted and the aircraft made a lot less noise. As we finished loading I received a visit from the police. A man was missing from Field Island, in the mouth of the South Alligator River. Could I do an aerial search? Everything came out of the plane and I set out with a policeman observer. We spent an hour doing a square search of the island. There were numerous tracks but no sign of people. The policeman decided an on-the-ground search was needed and made arrangements for a helicopter. Apparently, two crocodile shooters had camped there. After an argument, one left taking the boat. He returned a few days later but there was no sign of his mate. It appears the stranded man decided to swim across the channel to the mainland. Perhaps a crocodile or a shark?

We finally got away that afternoon and flew to Katherine. Next day we flew to Alice Springs and the day after on to Oodnadatta, Leigh Creek, and then to Broken Hill. There had been storms around and they were expecting further storms overnight. A man in charge of the hangar arranged for my aircraft to be kept inside overnight. He asked if we had accommodation in Broken Hill. I told him we didn't, so he phoned places for us, explaining it would be difficult with school holidays. Eventually, he found a place for the four of us and arranged transport for us to the hotel.

Next morning, when all fuelled up and ready to go, he asked where I intended to refuel. When I replied, 'Cobar', he said, "Do you know where the key is?" I looked peculiar so he said, 'It's kept in the Wilga tree.' At Cobar the key was in the Wilga tree. I went ahead, refuelled and wrote details on the sheet provided. If I didn't know the secret of the key I would have waited a long time. From Cobar I flew to Dubbo and Bathurst. For all the trip the aircraft had started with one or two swings of the propeller. At Bathurst this changed. I had to swing, prime, and swing again for the best part of half an hour. At last it started and I taxied out. Storms and rain were forecast for Sydney but the cloud base over the mountains was high enough to get under. I knew Sydney from driving but had no visual knowledge from the air. I was told to look for a large transmitter mast 10 nautical miles from Bankstown. At that point I was to call Bankstown and get clearance to land. After the mountains we were all looking for this mast. Eventually I spotted it and fell into line with other aircraft to land. It was great to be on the ground.

The following day I went to see the man who sold me the plane nearly two years earlier. To come out even over the time I owned the plane, I needed to get back $1200. I knew he had new gipsy moth engines to fit this aircraft. He made it clear $1000 was the maximum offer. He would not budge. I went home to work out what to do. That night, as I considered the short fall in the aircraft account, Helen said, "What are you going to do with the spare parts?" I didn't know, so next morning I rang the gentleman and asked about the spares. He answered – "If they haven't been used and you have invoices they will be refunded at invoice value." I said I would be right over; the invoices added up to $237. I left Bankstown airport with a cheque for $1,237. So ended my first effort to use an aircraft.

Over the next few weeks I looked around Bankstown and Camden for another aircraft. It must be metal clad and there were two makes, Piper and a Cessna. The Piper was low winged and not really suitable. The Cessna was high winged and more rugged for our airstrips. Prices started at about $15,000. There seemed to be no way forward.

Flying for Mudginberri – Temporary Non Solution
We hadn't been home long before an enquiry came, from Mudginberry Station, asking if I would fly their aircraft, a Cessna 206. They would arrange an endorsement for me and needed a load brought once a week from Darwin. We could use extra space once their cargo was loaded and use the aircraft separately at $40 per hour. The Auster cost $8 per hour, but I felt it would be useful to have access to the aircraft, with the ability to bring out some goods in the wet season. So I went ahead with it.

The first trip for Mudginberry was on 8th January 1969. The load was delivered to Darwin airport and was 100 lbs more than legal payload with no way to return the surplus. Part of the load was a keg of beer, a further dilemma. I loaded everything and took off. Crossing the South Alligator there was very black sky to the south east. To the east the way was still open but closing in. I had to go directly to Oenpelli, with a keg of beer. Next morning I delivered it to Mudginberry.

I persevered with Mudginberry as long as I could. At best, we could expect some space going to Darwin, none was ever available coming back. In April things came to a head. A telegram had said there would be two passengers next morning to Darwin from Mudginberry. So I set out with two Oenpelli passengers and some pieces of machinery. At Mudginberry were four passengers and pieces of a gyro copter. They was also a lot of freight to come back. I thought this was a ploy to get me to do two trips. I set out with five passengers leaving the gyrocopter pilot and machinery for the second trip. In Darwin, Ossie Osgood, who maintained the aircraft, approached and said the propeller is almost out of hours. It had two hours left. I did the second trip to bring the gyro copter in then walked off to book a seat back on the mail plane at their expense. It was unsatisfactory and the last trip I would do with that arrangement. I needed another aircraft but did not seek how I could get one.

At Last a Plane with a Metal Skin

I did not have long to wait. In the first week in May 1969, I received another visit from Eddie Connellan. He had morning tea with us and, as usual, we talked about aeroplanes. He had a Cessna 182 which had been a Flying Doctor plane. He had now replaced it with a Twin Baron. It had been used for a number of years but was fully overhauled and ready to go. He wondered if it would be of use to me. The first question I asked was - how much? He said he would work out a reasonable price and get his Sales Manager to contact me. After he left, Helen and I did some financial gymnastics and wondered what we could pawn. Barely a week later I received a letter from the Sales Manager saying he had been instructed by his Chief to make the Cessna 182 available to me for $6000. It was amazing, we had scraped up exactly that amount of money Its true value was in excess of $15,000.

In 23rd May 1969, Brian Peel, Sales Manager, arrived with the aircraft. After a couple of circuits with him, I flew him to Darwin so he could catch a plane back to Alice Springs, then I headed home. The plane recently had a major inspection and the engine was completely overhauled with 1,400 hours to run. It even had a radio that worked.

Outstation Work Continues

During the dry season of 1969, there was a lot of interest in outstation development. Timothy had already moved out, and Clancy Djayhgurrnga moved into the country on the eastern side of the Gumarderr River. This was Timothy's mother's country and a good relationship existed between Timothy and Clancy. Clancy's brother, George, also went across to work with him at Guborlomborlom, together with Shorty and other relations. They made their camp alongside the billabong and started to erect a large trap yard and stockyard, planning to sell bullocks or buffaloes to the abattoirs.

Mirndabbal Manakgu was also planning to move out from Oenpelli to the north-west, creating an outstation at Wulwunj and building buffalo trapping yards. I took him out in the Toyota and he showed me the area. We looked for a temporary air strip site and a water supply. There was little surface water so we found an area to put in a well.

About the same time, Phillip Dirdi, asked me to come with him to Mangulkan, just north of Wulwunj. He showed me a bore, recently drilled by the Water Resources Branch. It did not need any pump, as it was artesian. As a young lad, Phillip was looked after by Paddy Compass in the Murganella area. Paddy told him that, when he died, Phillip would take over his land. With this assurance Phillip moved to the area preparing to use this site for a mobile abattoirs.

Work on the Gumarderr outstation, led by Timothy, was continuing. We selected the edge of a plain two miles from his camp and a group of men and women set about clearing and levelling the area. In July, word came it was ready for me to land. I arranged for Bruce Morrow to drive out and check. At the set time I circled this new airstrip, which looked horribly small from the air. It was a little more than 400 yards long. It was vital to get the wheels on the ground at the threshold with minimum airspeed. Everything went well and I taxied up to where everyone was gathered.

From this point flying and outstation development went hand in hand. As individual groups moved to clan areas, their first activity, apart from building temporary shelters, was to clear land for an airstrip. That landing at Gumarderr was the encouragement they needed. In most cases I went by road with the principal members of the clan. We looked for a good water supply, a site above flood level, and of course, suitable airstrip land.

Timothy had about 20 people living at his camp - men, women and children. His next activity was to clear a second airstrip at his camp site. The first strip, two miles out, would become inaccessible in the wet season. By early December most big trees were chopped down but there was a lot of work still to do digging out stumps and levelling the ground.

In January 1970, Mirndabbal moved to his outstation at Wulwunj. His immediate intention was to build an airstrip. With a team of three other men and a few women, they asked me to fly them to Ngara. From there they would walk to Wulwunj.

An Interesting Landing

In February, 1970 I had a late night visitor. One of Timothy's men had ridden over 90 kms to Oenpelli by horse to let me know that the airstrip was finished and everyone was short of food. It seemed unbelievable they had finished already. He assured me it was so, and the people were very hungry. Next morning I loaded the aircraft with food and took off. The airstrip looked very narrow. Because it was so narrow it looked longer from the air. Men and women were working on the sides. I decided to land and approached cautiously, landing on a grassy area on the eastern end. Timothy came running over waving his arms and calling out, "Not ready yet." I told him about the message I received. It did not come from him. We walked back to the point where I had touched down and he showed me tools I had run over – a mattock, axe and shovel handles! My problem was to get back into the air. I walked with Timothy to the far end in the west. We marked off about 400 metres on the eastern end and Timothy called all his labour force to level it off as best they could. With no load on board and fuel tanks at less than half capacity, I did a text book short field take-off, and was thankful to be back in the air. It was five weeks before this airstrip was ready for use, even then only 600 metres in length.

The Aircraft Gets Lots of Use

The aeroplane was getting an increasing amount of use. In the first year, I did over 380 hours. Newly appointed Regional Secretary, Stanley Giltrap, visited. I invited him to come and see some outstation work. He accepted and I flew him to Gumarderr, introduced him to Timothy, then flew him over some areas we expected to develop in the next year. When he returned south I felt I had an ally and this proved true.

On a flight to Darwin in August, 1970, as I was climbing at 4000 feet, a severe vibration came from the engine. I advised Darwin and nominated Woolner airstrip for an emergency landing. By reducing the power setting the vibration was barely noticeable, but with this I was gradually losing height, I arrived over Woolner at 2000 feet then landed. On the radio I arranged for Dick Skinner, our mechanic, to fly out in his aircraft. Dick worked on the engine for a while and the vibration ceased as suddenly as it started. Dick was puzzled but I did a circuit in the aircraft and it went well.

There was no further sign of the problem and I did over 100 hours during the next three months. In November I was on my way to Numbulwar, cruising at 7,500 feet, when the vibration suddenly returned. There was no landing area near so I reduced power to the point where the vibration ceased. I could not maintain height with reduced power, so I slowly increased the power to the point where the vibration reappeared. This kept me occupied for a quarter of an hour and suddenly I found I could take the power back up to its normal setting. I went back to 7500 feet and landed at Numbulwar. The return flight to Oenpelli was uneventful, however, I was determined to get to the bottom of the problem.

The following day I left the aircraft with Dick Skinner in Darwin and went to do things in town. Two hours later I called back at the hangar to find out what had happened. The person in charge told me I was wasting their time and my money. He was definite there was nothing wrong with the engine. With nothing further I could do I went back to town. At four o'clock I returned to fly home. Dick told me what had happened after I left. Another mechanic working in the hangar enquired about the problem. When Dick told him, he said the trouble would be the hydraulic tappets. Sure enough, there were two faulty ones. By the time I returned it was fixed.

It was seven years since I started on a pilot's licence. Previous senior staff had left and their replacements accepted the aircraft requirement. However, one change was still to take place. The $6000 used to buy the plane was recouped and I had a good operating account. I idly thought of buying a bigger machine but it was beyond my funds.

The aircraft did more flying than I anticipated, each month around 45 hours. After a couple years I had less than 300 hrs left on the engine. I hadn't worked out what to do when the engine needed replacing.

The Mission Takes Over the Aircraft

While we were on holidays there was a letter to the Oenpelli Council from CMS, asking their advice on the future of the aircraft and whether a future aircraft should be CMS or Station owned. At a meeting, on 6th April 1971, they recommended the aircraft be CMS owned and that there be a full time pilot. I did not know anything about this.

At the end of October 1971 I received the letter from Stanley Giltrap advising he had taken the matter of an aircraft through to the Federal Council and had agreement for an aircraft to be owned by the Society, with appointment of a commercial pilot to do the flying. I was invited to travel to Sydney to select the aircraft we would need.

On 1st November, I flew the Cessna to Darwin and tied it down in the parking area. Next day I flew to Adelaide to see what planes were available. I was shown a Cessna 207, a demonstration model with very few hours flying. It seemed an attractive aircraft, priced around $24,000. There was something about the salesman that made me hesitate so I told him I would also see what was on offer in Sydney. He was sure I would come back and select his aircraft.

At Bankstown Rex Aviation had an assortment of aircraft but again I was limited to a Cessna 207. It was baroque gold in colour and available for about the same amount as the one in Adelaide. I felt this was the better machine and discussed the trade-in of the Cessna 182. I gave them the details and they offered $6,000, the amount paid 2 ½ years earlier. We accepted their offer and I rang Adelaide to advise them. The telephone nearly exploded as the Sales Manager used all sorts of names, assuring me that I would regret my decision. I was glad I didn't take his aircraft.

On 9th November, I set out with the aircraft salesman who was to fly the 182 back. We arrived in Darwin where our new pilot, Ted Robinson, was waiting so we proceeded on to Oenpelli. It was a great day.

More Outstation Development

I had been able to save a couple of positions on the new Training Allowance system for key outstation workers. People generally, were very happy to work on their own land with no thought of payment. It was at this point we established a principle which was generally agreed to by all the people.   We would give assistance where required, but we would not do the work. This became an accepted principal of outstation work for a number of years, and was only altered when the Government organised Contractors to put in housing and water supplies.

In the Monthly Report for July 1971 I recorded the increasing interest in the establishment of Outstations and that three places are well under way. Gumarderr has cleared an area of land for bananas. A pump has been ordered and at present watering is done by hand. Wulwunj temporary airstrip is nearing completion. In addition to these three groups, including Guborlomborlom, work had also commenced at Mangulkan

On Monday, 22nd November, 1971, I took Ted Robinson with me by road to both Wulwunj and Mangulkan. Ted recognised that it would be a while before Mirndabbal would be ready with his airstrip but was quite happy to make a landing at Mangulkan. There were more than 500 metres ready and the ends were well cleared back. We set a time for Wednesday morning, 23rd, for Ted to land and I would be there in the Toyota. Everything went according to schedule.

Over 1972 I was able to make a few trips by road to the outstation areas. Timothy had taken a lot of banana suckers out early in the dry season on the Handicrafts tractor and trailer. A large group of men from Maningrida had moved on but there were still over 50 people living there. I headed south from Maningurrki on the western side of the Gumarderr River and eventually came to Big Paddy's camp at Mamadawerre. A lot of work had gone into his airstrip and I marked out a length of 500 metres on the eastern end. This mainly needed levelling and a little widening. I then drove back to the road and across the river to Guborlomborlom. Clancy and his men had progressed with his stock yard with beautiful iron wood posts and rails. He was hoping to start shifting cattle in to Oenpelli before the end of the year.

There were a number of other groups of people also wanting to move out on to their own land. One of these was the Birriwardjak people headed by Nalbered. They had spent a short time at Timothy's camp at Maningurrki and then moved across to Samuel's country at Djurlka. From there they needed to put in an unusual road. This road was put together with large rocks up the side of a rocky hill. On one of my trips out I went in to look at his work. He proudly showed me what he had been doing, and explained that that was the easy part. His objective was to put the road through to the Marburrinj country. He had men and women working carrying large rocks to be fitted in to the road. So far he had completed about 300 metres. Nalbered was a very capable man but spent most of his time at the Border Store, especially following the death of his wife the previous year. Tragically, Nalbered drowned trying to swim across the East Alligator River at the Crossing in 1973. This brought an end to the construction of this road. A few years later, opening the Marburrinj area was achieved by relatives using a different access route.

In 1972 four further outstation communities were being established and on each place the first priority was to build an airstrip. The first to complete an airstrip was Mamadawerre, 10 miles south of Timothy's camp, where an old man with a group of young men, using axes and shovels, had selected a site for an airstrip and started clearing it nearly a year earlier. They cut wooden crowbars in the bush to prize out large rocks and tree stumps. When he had a length of cleared ground he asked me to see if I could land there. I went by road to check it out. It was a short, but enough to take an empty plane in.

So in August, 1972 I landed there, which encouraged them. The men kept working on the strip and each time I landed, it was a bit longer. In September, when I landed, I punctured a tyre taxying over their fresh work. It was nearly dark when I got a new tube delivered by road, so I camped there that night. Some men had been out hunting. They brought back a kangaroo, with a joey in the pouch, and proudly gave it to me for my son, Arthur. It became part of our home and was given the name, 'Jumper'

In October, 1972, I called in at Maningurrki by road and picked up two men to take out to Gurrhgurr (Table Hill). We had already flown the area and picked out the edge of a plain which looked suitable to clear for a temporary airstrip. The original road which had been used in 1958 had more recent traffic and stood out quite clearly. The men each had an axe and a shovel and we marked out the area to be cleared and I left them with some food, telling them I would be back in about a week.

When I returned at the end of the following week there were over twelve people working on the airstrip. Some women had made rakes from tree branches and the men had a couple of tomahawks. These people lived at Marrgolidjban, about 10 kms east, and were eager to be part of the action happening in their area. There was not a lot more work to finish it and on 29th November I carried out the first landing on this temporary airstrip.

The 207 was a larger aircraft than I had used. At first I found it daunting to land on a short airstrip. There is a technique for this called 'short field landings and take-offs' which I had been practising and was starting to get the hang of. Landing was the harder skill and required approaching the strip with a minimum airspeed, just above stalling speed, and with the stall warning alarm starting to go off. Touch-down aimed to be within 10 yards of the beginning of the strip, in fact I would try to touch-down about 10 yards before the strip markers. Once the aircraft was firmly on the ground I applied the brakes. I could normally

123

pull up inside 400 yards. Now, with a larger plane and new airstrips it was important to perfect this technique.

Phillip returned to Mangulkan and drove his utility in to Oenpelli periodically to get food and find out what was happening about the mobile abattoirs. He had lengthened his airstrip and was waiting for some action. About this time word came from Croker Island that Paddy Compass had died. Phillip waited a while and finally asked me to fly him to Croker to talk to the people. At Croker a large gathering of people met in the main hall and talks went on for some time. Phillip came away a defeated man. He did not speak until we arrived back at Oenpelli, then he said, "It's all finished. They don't want me near that country." He drove his utility up to Mangulkan, loaded his few possessions and went to an old buffalo shooter's camp at Rock Hole on the Cooper Creek. He made his camp there and returned to Oenpelli over the wet season.

For some time we had been trying to get permission for each outstation to be equipped with a two-way radio. It got bogged down on the issue of the language being used on the air. It had to be English and we could not expect Aboriginal people to use English. There were other reasons why the Government did not want use of transceivers in remote areas but this was the main sticking point. With the numbers of people living in these areas and with airstrips, it seemed reasonable that communication be available. On 12th February 1973, I delivered to Timothy at Maningurrki, a spare two way radio set equipped with the CMS frequency. It took a while to put up an aerial and get everything working. I told Timothy to leave it switched on and I would go back to Oenpelli and give him a call. When I called the first time he answered, then I said I would try a different aerial. After a few minutes I gave him another call and received no reply. I called a few times but still no reply. After I put the first aerial back I called again, there was still no reply. Fearing something was wrong at Timothy's end, I flew back there the following morning. There was nothing wrong, he had heard me each time but, as he had nothing to say. he did not reply, a man of few words.

One night, returning from a full day's activities in the Table Hill and Marrgolidjban areas, I planned to camp at Maningurrki. It was eight in the evening when I arrived on a cold dry season night. Timothy took me over to an empty hut and suggested I camp inside. Shortly afterwards Audrey, his wife, came over with half a freshly baked loaf of bread, such was the way they looked after me.

At the end of June 1973, we had six outstations functioning:- Maningurrki, Mamadawerre, Guborlomborlom, Gurrhgurr (Table Hill) Mangulkan, Wulwunj and now Mikginj about to start up. Our principal, generally agreed to by people involved, that we would give assistance but not do the work, slowly broke down as the government became involved in projects. Outside contractors were then given the money to do these works.

In 1975 Ted, our pilot, resigned. We considered recruiting another but, as the Missionary Aviation Fellowship was operating in the area, we invited them to take over our flying. So they took over our aircraft at a nominal price and placed a pilot at Oenpelli.

The outstation work was proceeding rapidly by now with ten0 different groups setting up their own communities. My position at Oenpelli changed from Superintendent to Area Adviser meaning a lot of my time was spent on these emerging communities. As before, their first job was to clear an airstrip, but I no longer had an aircraft.

In 1976, while on leave, I went to Victoria to visit MAF headquarters at Ballarat, allowing me to meet some of their staff. They offered me use of their old Cessna 170 for the next 12 months and arranged for a trainee pilot to fly it to the North.

So again I was able to fly around the area. There were two Cessna 170's in Australia. It was an amazing machine, the envy of all not in a position to fly it and the despair of those who did. At one stage I had to tie the doors together on the inside to stop them opening in mid-air. MAF were rebuilding a Cessna 182, which they offered to me to take over from the 170, at a cost of $19,000. CMS gave permission for me to buy it out from a Station account. So, from 1977, I was again able to keep pace with developments on these outstation communities in my own plane.

Buffalo and Abattoirs

The buffalo camps that sprang up after the war employed many Aboriginal people. After a shipment of bad hides, Turkey cancelled further orders for hides. As a result, the buffalo hide industry collapsed, contributed to by new industrial belting made from plastics coming on to the market. It took aboriginal men a long time to accept the fact that hides were no longer required. They waited around for many months expecting things to start up again. Many went to hunting crocodiles but the supply of these was limited. Without a demand for buffalo the population on the sub-coastal plains grew rapidly until an industry based on buffalo meat became established in the early 1960's. To allow Oenpelli to participate in this industry it constructed an abattoir of a standard which allowed general sale of meat.

Dad tells about the development of this in further sections of his memoir.
"While the new airstrip was being built in 1964 the abattoirs was also in the process of being built. It was placed 100 yards north of the earlier airstrip. The new strip cleared all the trees away from the south side of the abattoirs exposing the complex as a highly visible, and less than beautiful, landmark of Oenpelli, rather than being hidden behind a layer or trees. We just had to live with that.

In October 1964 I went with Dick Harris by horse across the plains to Ngara, where the buffalo retreated to when monsoonal rains came. He showed me an area suitable for an airstrip to give access to buffalo over the wet season. As we rode back we saw pockets on the plains with hundreds of buffalo. It was obvious numbers were rapidly increasing.

The Wet Season brought difficulties in maintaining the new Oenpelli airstrip. For a period it was limited to small aircraft then, in April after heavy rain at the end of March, its length was reduced by 700 feet. With few aircraft using the airstrip we laid underground cables taking electricity to the abattoirs. Charlie Cuff and his team were doing concreting and construction work and laying drainage pipes. The plans were passed by the Animal Industry Branch of the NT Administration; the correct body to deal with abattoirs.

The Health Inspector from Darwin made regular visits to the abattoirs. He said all the drains had to be underground, completely covered over. AIB plans required half pipes, exposed to the air and sunshine, allowing drains to be inspected, hosed out and swept clean. The Health Inspector would not accept this. He demanded his system of drainage be installed. We ignored him. One afternoon the medical plane called in. On the plane was the Health Inspector. I saw a figure streak across the airstrip towards the abattoirs to carry out an inspection. He saw we had not taken any notice of his directives. I waited for him at the aircraft. He soon returned and demanded an explanation. I told him I was following the requirements of the AIB. He did not like it and was furious, but was soon lost inside the aircraft. I waved to him as it taxied out, waiting to see what happened.

A week later I received a letter from Jack Langford which said he had apologised to the Health Inspector for my behaviour on his visit. I sent a note back to Jack I did not need anyone to apologise for me and what I said to the Health Inspector I would say again.

While were south on leave Cam Cooke received another visit from the Health Inspector. He laid down the law strongly on the need for closed-in drainage pipes at the abattoirs. So Cam had ordered a lot of 6 inch earthenware pipes and they were stacked up ready for use. I told Cam that we would have to find another use for them, as they were not approved by the AIB who licensed the abattoirs. It was a pity that the two Government Departments in Darwin could not get together and sort out who was responsible. Eventually, the pipes were used as an overflow line from ground tanks to the billabong and we got our $600 back from the water program.

During 1966 the abattoirs was taking shape and expected to finish in July. It was unlikely to be licensed this year but should be for next year's buffalo season. A licence enabled us to send certified meat anywhere in Australia, mainly Melbourne. During construction we sent meat to other Aboriginal communities. The men working were skilled in identifying TB carcases but, with a licence, we needed a resident meat inspector.

I planned to get a team of men to clear an airstrip at Ngara as a wet season base for buffalo. Early in 1967 I revisited in the aircraft this area which Dick Harris had shown me. Frank Gulbirbir and Barnabas were with me. I pointed out from the air where our first airstrip could be built. I then went by road with some men, showing them what I had in mind and marking out the best place for it. They were happy to tackle this. At Oenpelli they gathered Bluey and a couple of others and set out with tools and food on horseback. In ten days they made a clearing big enough to land the Auster.

Two and half weeks later a man rode in to tell me it was ready for me to land.

I flew over and looked at it from the air. It seemed OK so, returning to the mission, I put together food for the men and went ahead with the flight, returning half an hour later. I arranged to have buffalo meat available next morning, so I removed the seats from the aircraft, taking a large sheet of plastic with me. The men had butchered and quartered two buffalo. We loaded three quarters on the plastic in the plane. As I put power on to take off, the meat slid back. I had to cut power, pull up and tie sections of meat to the front seat anchor points, before I took off. From Ngara the Abattoirs now had a regular supply of carcase buffalo meat through the wet season. I did many trips right up to June. Ultimately we put a full abattoirs at Ngara.

The Oenpelli abattoirs had a cool room in operation and, with the airstrip alongside, it made unloading easy. After meat was boned out and packed I delivered it to other communities. For loads to Elcho Island, with full tanks I could lift a little over 700 lbs. With this load the Auster was very poor at climbing and took over 20 miles to get up to 1500 ft.

Soon after the first landing at Ngara, Frank and his men started on a cross strip, better for dry season winds. It was harder going than the first strip but they persevered. At the end of May it was finished. After this Frank went off crocodile shooting. He was a tireless worker and it was good for him to get away for a while. The steady hunting of crocodiles made the river and billabongs, much safer. The income from the skins helped a lot with general workers' wages at Oenpelli.

In November we began work on a full small abattoirs at Ngara. The site depended on finding a good supply of water. I invited our minister, Lin Amey, to come with his divining equipment, (a piece of bent fencing wire). Lin walked around the area holding out his wire and came to a place which gave promise. He marked a point and said there would be water 22 feet below the surface. He could not say whether it would be fresh or salt. It was in an ideal place, close to where we hoped to put the abattoirs. With two men digging the well it took three days to get down to 20 feet, and the ground was wet. At 22 feet there was cool water in the bottom and it tasted fresh. We later found that it could also be brackish, determined by where the tide was. If the tide was high in the river, it was brackish, but if the tide was out the water was fresh. With a tank installed we had a good supply of fresh water. Wilfred then made up a mobile cool room on a trailer and Bill MacGregor, our electrician, took out a small generator to provide electricity for it.

Late in 1967 I received a radio message from Jack Langford that there was to be a meeting in Darwin to decide who had the overall say over the abattoirs, the Animal Industry Branch or the Health Department. I acknowledged the message and waited, confident the Health Department role was only after meat left the abattoirs, as was set out when we started to build the meatworks. We waited and waited but no response was received. The Health Inspector no longer visited and I had little doubt of the outcome of this meeting but we still did not receive a licence for the abattoirs. We had commenced building in 1962, and over this period had produced many tons of meat for local markets. Eventually a new Health Inspector came and he did not raise the abattoirs.

Our local markets were the Methodist Missions to our north, serviced mainly by Harold Shepherdson, at Elcho Island. Maningrida and Groote Eylandt received our meat by regular Connellan Airways flights. On occasions a special flight of the Heron was needed to shift 3000 lbs at a time to Maningrida. We also sold meat locally. When Ngara abattoirs was completed early in 1968, it became our main source of wet season buffalo meat, with large amounts packed in cartons, and many trips in the Auster to shift this meat from Ngara to the main freezer.

It was 1969 before we finally got Oenpelli abattoirs licensed. On 16th May, we received a visit by Brian Andrews and Mr Glaister. The Abattoirs was passed and licensed on 27th May 1969.

The licensing of the abattoirs opened new employment at Oenpelli for most of the year. Charlie Cuff made efforts to have a quiet herd of buffalo. It could not produce enough animals to supply the abattoirs for more than a day or so. Don Tullock paid a visit in September to see the quiet buffalo and foresaw there would be a market for bulls and heifers. Wilfred Harris wanted to use a tranquilliser gun, but this would only supply 15 to 20 animals a day when we required 40 to 50 animals each day. Also an animal that was tranquillised could not be killed until the following day.

I remember a demonstration of the Paxarm tranquilliser gun in 1963, held at Koolpinyah Station. A number of renowned stockmen assembled for this. There was a strong stockyard with a post and railing fence about eight feet high. In the centre of this yard was one of the best samples of a real scrub bull. The gathering was asked to guess the approximate weight of the beast. When a final figure was accepted, the amount of tranquilliser was placed in the syringe. One stockman was asked to fire the dart into the beast's rump. When this was done the animal stood there with muscles tensed. A space of two minutes was allowed for the drug to take effect, then the man who fired the dart was asked to walk up and pull the syringe out. "Don't be afraid," the organiser said. "The bull is quite harmless now." As the nervous stockman cautiously approached the animal's rump from behind, he put his hand out to hold the syringe, and the animal took off. With only a short run to the fence it leaped clean over the eight foot rail and headed for the scrub with the syringe still stuck in its rump! It was not a successful advertisement for the equipment. Still Wilfred felt there was a use for it.

The main supply of buffalo came from 'field-shot' animals, which had to be in at the abattoirs inside an hour. This meant these buffalo had to be available no more than 20 miles out. This was an increasing problem as animals would move around and disappear into the scrub overnight. To keep up the supply of animals to the abattoirs it was necessary to have at least two vehicles pulling large trailers. If there were a number of animals around they would take two, three, or more beasts at one time, but even this method could not be counted on to produce sufficient animals at the height of the season. Preliminary work was taking place on live catching, and ultimately this became the main method of supply.

The abattoirs commenced full operation in June 1969. In that month, it produced over 4000 lbs of buffalo meat for local markets and 51,420 lbs for southern markets. The following month the amount exported rose to 77,520 lbs for southern markets. This gave employment to 13 Aboriginal men, this figure increasing as the work expanded. The demand of southern markets for buffalo meat was due to its ability to absorb water during processing. It was a very popular meat for canned meat products. However, at that stage there was no market for the meat in its raw state.

In September, 1969, Allan and Shirley Quinn came to Oenpelli. Allan was a butcher and brought excellence to the abattoirs we had not known before. He showed the men who were cutting up meat better ways of doing it and improved the packaging system. He saw a need for a separate room for the preparation of meat for packaging. I wrote in a monthly report, "Training in butchery has produced some noteworthy results and the presentation of meat has greatly improved. Alterations to the abattoirs are being done for the next buffalo season. A separate meat preparation room is also nearing completion."

The Abattoirs went back into production on Thursday, 28th May, 1970. The meat Inspector was Cam White. A special meat preparation room was built and other alterations in the skinning area. Live catching of buffalo was improving. It was possible to bring in about 10 beasts a day in this way. These were mainly caught in the Murganella area. This number was supplemented with field shot animals from the Ngara area.

When the abattoir was inspected a number of minor things were required before the new season started. Allan Quinn expected to draw live buffalo from the Murganella area until the plains dried out from the late heavy rains. At this point he was advised that that it was not now possible as the Murganella country was being made a Wildlife Sanctuary. This took us by surprise as there had been no word about it. Finally a meeting was held at Croker Island and it was decided that the buffalo on Paddy Compass Namadbarra's country would be available to Murganella Enterprises and the buffalo available on Nelson Wagbara's country would be available to Gunbalanya Meat Supply. It was resolved we could take mature animals from this area. So we were able to go ahead with a minimum of 12 animals a day but mostly with about 20 coming in. It was difficult to market all the meat being produced because of production from other abattoirs and the limited market.

Oenpelli and its Aboriginal People

Using Kunwinjku, the Oenpelli Language

Over the years we were conscious of our inability to use the local Aboriginal language. Kunwinjku, was not really the local language but had become a common local language Some staff tried to learn it but could not put enough time into it. The one person who made progress was Mrs Harris. She translated the Gospel of Mark and the First Epistle of John. With Dr Capell and the Bible Society's help it was printed in small hard covered books.

Our dealings with Aboriginal people were in English and they grew to understand us. Occasionally a person came in from the bush with little knowledge of English and conversation was difficult. A local person would stand alongside and act as interpreter. The aboriginal people were able to understand most of what the white men said. In the village they used their own language and strenuously refused to accept Kriol, which they referred to as "rubbish English" as a language. They would speak in their own language amongst themselves, even in meetings to discuss a matter and then give their decision in English. Once, an Education Branch inspector came to school and instructed children to use English in the playground during recess. The children ignored this and in playground activities in Kunwinjku still rang out loudly and clearly.

In 1967 Peter Carroll came to Oenpelli as a linguist. He spent a few months moving amongst different groups of people, spending much time with bark painters learning the stories of the paintings and many other clan stories. In 1967, the Director of Welfare, Harry Giese, wrote to communities suggesting that Aboriginal people be given surnames. Peter Carroll and Silas discussed this with groups of people. They came up with using Aboriginal surnames taken from the grandfather's personal name. This worked well. A book of family names in 1984 listed 66 names. Women took their husband's surname on marriage with children given the same surname.

In 1969, Meryl Rowe, a Home Management Instructress, came to Oenpelli. She spent time getting to know people and was able to pick up some words of their language. She realised there was little use for her work in home management and first of all she needed to learn Kunwinjku. She asked me if she could have six months off to do this and I agreed. I think she was so surprised that she asked if there was anything she could do for me. Yes, she could type my monthly reports. This was a great help to me.

Meryl Rowe's language and literacy work advanced steadily and she conducted lessons in the old Dining Room. There was a very happy atmosphere during the lessons, and even some of the older people lined up to take part.

Aboriginal Artefacts

In the 1960s there was an increasing amount of handicraft work. Women made baskets, floor mats and place mats with pandanus. The men made bark paintings and on occasions, carvings. These were assembled into large parcels and sent to our Sydney Office. While there was only a small amount of work it was sold in the CMS Office, but as it grew a shop was rented to sell these items.

I remember a small, (and I felt rather insignificant) painting brought to me by Anchor. I turned him away twice with this piece of art and finally gave him 5 shillings for it and put it on a shelf in the store. It sat for a long time until I was making up a 22 lb parcel of paintings and needed a small painting to make up the weight. Anchor's painting was ideal and was dispatched to Sydney. Three months later I saw a publication from the shop in Sydney expounding on this form of art. It featured Anchor's painting – a clutch of eggs and a goose. This painting sold for $200, a lot of money then. We paid the artist 60% of the sale price, so Anchor had a handsome payment to collect.

With profits from Handicrafts we purchased a Ford 3000 tractor and a trailer for people to get materials for their handicrafts, such as bark, pandanus, and dyes. It was also used for people to go hunting or travel to their country.

The bark painting work grew under Peter Carroll. Jacob Nayinggul did much of the work, including recording stories, spraying the barks and packing for posting. In the early dry season groups of artists went into the bush with the tractor and trailer and collected bark, which was opened out and flattened under weights for several days. Peter was aware that the standard was slipping, so he took it up with the artists who assured him they would take more care when preparing the bark. We were aware of artists taking paintings to the Border Store where the currency was beer, a carton for a good big painting and half a carton for a small one.

Mission Administration

In July, 1963, before we left Darwin, there was a Field Council meeting. I was invited and noted of the situation on each mission. Over the previous twelve months each mission had set up a Station Council to manage mission administration. In attendance was the Superintendent of each mission plus an Aboriginal member of each Station Council.

At Oenpelli, in 1958, a Village Council had been formed and met on three occasions. There was not sufficient interest to continue. The next stage was to form a Station Council, done by Dick Harris in May 1962. It was to consist of equal numbers of aboriginal people and staff. With 8 members of the staff on the council, it meant eight Aboriginal members – four were appointed by Mr Harris and four were elected. The representatives were Rachel, Priscilla and Elizabeth, Frank Ganangu, Silas, Timothy, Robbie and Joseph (snr).

With new Aboriginal houses being built the Council decided, ahead of the completion of each batch of houses, who would occupy them. At first, preference was given to local people, and then to those who came from areas of land further out. At one meeting Timothy, the head gardener, was allocated one of these new houses. His own land was Marrirn, south of Table Hill, about 100 kms east of Oenpelli. Timothy stood up and said he did not want one of the new houses. He told all the council members that there are a lot of people at Oenpelli who do not wish to remain there very long because they want to go back to their own country. This took some staff members by surprise. It highlighted the insecurity Aboriginal people felt living on land which did not belong to them in those days.

The Station Council also had the responsibility to elect the Aboriginal delegate to the Field Council and Standing Committee. Field Council normally met in Darwin about August or September and Standing Committee in March.

In the early 1970's, we decided to have a fresh look at the structure of the Station Council. It had operated reasonably since 1962 although there were times when there was a lack of Aboriginal participation. I felt there were too many white people present and decisions made were not necessarily Aboriginal ones. The structure of the council with one Aboriginal person for each non Aboriginal staff member meant that a council meeting now had about 24 members, a major increase from when it was first formed.

In May 1972 discussions were held on forming of a Progress Association. A constitution was prepared by our solicitor and efforts were made to interpret this to groups of people. We had about 20 clan groups in the region and while some groups worked very closely together, not all did. I could not see how a Progress Association could unite them. There was fairly broad agreement from the Council that this should be done. Another arrangement was needed. In a discussion with Richard Morris of KPMG, he suggested forming a Company as the trustee for a Trust. Members or shareholders could represent the various clans in the whole area. This concept was accepted by the Oenpelli people so, on the 31st May 1972, Gunbalanya Nominees Pty. Ltd. was formed, initially with four directors and two secretaries. They were Silas Maralngurra, Elizabeth Girrabul, Peter Carroll and myself as directors and Richard Morris and Alec Rorrison as secretaries. At Oenpelli Peter and I realised that we should not be directors as we were not from a clan group so we withdrew and were made secretaries. We finished with 12 shareholders drawn from the whole area who represented the various clan groups and from these we selected six Directors. Now 30 years later, we have 23 members and 12 directors.

In September 1972, I wrote in the monthly report, 'It would not be an exaggeration to say that this last month has been one of the most difficult on record. On the one hand there has been a vast amount of activity forced on the area from outside and on the other hand there has been an increasing display of disinterestedness and irresponsibility from a large section of the work force. Working in the area over the last few weeks there have been the following Government Departments:- DCA, BMR, Water Resources and Lands and Survey. There has also been a large work force from three Darwin contracting firms engaged in the Welfare School program. In all this activity not one local Aboriginal person has been employed, and from this point alone, it is not hard to see the reason for any lack of interest. Large groups of non-workers take money from working people each payday and migrate to the East Alligator River beer store.

In October 1972, Welfare Branch invited the superintendents of Aboriginal missions and settlements to a series of meetings in Darwin. These discussed the way forward so Aboriginal people took more responsibility in running local towns. It was felt we were building communities too large and difficult for this to happen. Time was spent discussing the New Guinea model and areas of modification to suit our work. It was a useful time but little did we realise the changes which would happen in the following year.

In December 1972 when Goff Whitlam was elected Prime Minister, his government brought a policy for Aboriginal people called 'self-determination'. People were now said to be free to decide where they went and what they did. I was never aware that people of Oenpelli had any restraint in these matters yet it had become a political issue. In this philosophy there did not seem to be any requirement for responsibility. It became costlier and costlier, with anyone working having to be paid the minimum wage.

The immediate consequence was a drop in the number of people working. This smaller number working had to support all their relatives who were sitting down. Card games were rife and money changed hands rapidly. It was a real problem. We had felt we were starting to come out of the alcohol problem introduced in October 1969, but with this new policy people could do whatever they wanted with no sense of responsibility. Through it there was a core of steadfast hard working people but their numbers were diminishing.

One of the early tasks of the new national government was to set up various bodies such as a Housing Association, a Pastoral Group and a Social Activities Committee. Each group required a lot of organising and it was impossible to see how they could all function. Within a short period, only the Housing Association was still going.

With this happening and a complete change of Government and policy it was obvious to me that a different type of Station Council was needed, along similar lines to the Trustees Company. My feeling was an effective Council would have an Aboriginal chairman, the superintendent and a minute secretary and about 10 or 12 Aboriginal people representing the people of the area. Six months previously I had taken outline of a constitution to the solicitors for them to draw up the necessary documents but nothing had been produced. So we decided to go ahead with a new Council at the beginning of 1973 with, or without, the paper work.

The first meeting of the new Station Council was held on 6th February 1973. A new atmosphere was evident and a sense of greater freedom of expression stood out. One of the first items was about the Border Store. People said they had enough. A decision was made to oppose the renewal of its Licence. On 15th February, two solicitors from Darwin talked to people about objections to the Border Store Licence. On 7th March, Silas and four other councillors went to the Border Store to hand Mr Robinson the Objection Notice.

At the end of June I wrote in the monthly report, ' As we review progress of the newly enunciated principle of 'self-determination', the cardinal points of 'pace' and 'nature' of development are contrasted greatly with pressure and requirements of day to day work. The Aboriginal Council is literally bombarded with requests to make many decisions on matters they have barely had time to think about. Added to this confusion is the ever present problem of drunkenness.

The Oenpelli Council met twice in December, 1973. It was decided from January, 1974, council would meet every week. A general meeting was held in the village on New Year's Eve and over 100 people attended. It was encouraging to see recognition of the Council's responsibility in the general running of the Community. By July, 1974 so many things came before the Council that people wearied of all the meetings. Decisions were required 'urgently' on many matters. Councillors barely had time to be briefed on them, let alone give thought and discuss them before they were required to give an answer. I became aware of an impending break-down of the system.

The new routine was to have a Council meeting each Monday morning for about one hour. This started at 9 o'clock and people were normally waiting for it. Meryl Rowe took minutes in Kunwinjku.

Outstation work flourished, pushed along by all the mining interest. There were also meetings on Land Rights in preparation for Justice Woodward's commission into Aboriginal Land Rights, sponsored by the newly formed Northern Land Council. The Northern Territory Aboriginal Land Rights Act was passed by both houses of the Federal Parliament in December 1976 and in force on 26th January, 1977. However from 1975 the Northern Land Council was dealing with Arnhem Land Reserve as Aboriginal Land.

In November 1974 I went to Darwin with Silas for a meeting at Aboriginal Affairs concerning the introduction of a 'Global Grant' system of funding. Oenpelli had been selected as a community to trial this new system. Oenpelli was to be funded for all adult people above 18 years of age and not eligible for a pension, from the East Alligator River to the Liverpool River, at the rate of the basic wage, taking in all Outstation groups. People did not have to work but those who did had to be paid the basic wage. In round figures we were looking at about half a million dollars for the rest of the financial year. The Council had to work out what they would do with this finance.

Council meetings centred on the use of all the extra funding. I had limited input in my role as an 'adviser'. One thing was to make them aware of the areas that this money would have to cover. I listed these on a blackboard and set basic amounts to cover each. Silas took us all by surprise and listed a number of items for each of the six Outstations. Each place was to receive a windmill, large tank and tank-stand. There was also to be a

Peterson house for three of them – Maningurrki, Guborlomborlom and Gurrhgurr. My job was to get the prices of this and then a budget was set.

This 'Global Grant' commenced at the beginning of 1975. It involved a lot of work and responsibility for council and took up a lot of my time with meetings, all the time being careful not to override their decisions. Silas managed things well and, for the most part, the budget was closely followed. I had some misgivings about it leading to pressure to get quick answers from the Council on matters they scarcely knew anything about."

Dealing with Health, Alcohol and Affluence

One of the results of the referendum which gave aboriginal citizenship was that the previous prohibition against the purchase or consumption of alcohol by aborigines ceased. Oenpelli Mission had a history of trying to limit substance abuse and the harm it caused to the local community, originally it was a tobacco free community which Dick Harris had implemented with other missionaries, and which was in place from 1939 to 1950.

During the period up to the mid-1960s a combination of Oenpelli's isolation, alcohol restriction, and limited income of Oenpelli people resulted in little community exposure to alcohol and other of western lifestyle health threats. However the citizenship change occurred with improving access between Oenpelli and Darwin and rising affluence from a combination of increased government grants, increased revenue generation at the mission and, in the 1970s, mining royalty payments from uranium. This led to a rapid transition to a consumer society. Two demonstrable measures of this were the purchase of private vehicles in the community and the consumption of alcohol. Private vehicles made for easy transport of people to locations serving alcohol and new income gave the purchasing power for increased consumption. As a result, over about a five year period from the late 1960s to the mid-1970s, there was a huge rise in the proportion of Oenpelli's population who became heavy drinkers. This was aided by opportunists who set up alcohol outlets in close proximity, to cash in on the bonanza.

For Oenpelli this was the Border Store, on the road in to Oenpelli, just across the East Alligator River, outside Arnhem Land restrictions, but accessible to aboriginal people travelling in and out of Darwin and to communities in the Kakadu area.

In Oenpelli the willingness and capacity to work diminished in proportion to the alcohol consumption. At the same time the social security payments system, commonly called 'sit down money', gave people an income sufficient to meet their basic needs, independent of a need to work. Along with alcoholism and reduced work emerged a host of new social problems including domestic violence, neglect of children, alcohol related health problems, vehicle accident caused death and injuries and petrol sniffing in the unsupervised children. All became dominant parts of community life.

For missionaries, such as my parents, who spent decades trying to build the social fabric of the community and instil religion based, moral values, this was an immensely dispiriting, even shattering experience. They watched the community disintegrate in an alcohol fuelled craze, with many of the best educated, most prominent previous aboriginal leaders its first victims. With hindsight, it was an unavoidable change. Rights could not be withheld, and with rights came opportunities to abuse those rights, with no prospect of winding back the clock.

All that could be done was to try to minimise damage and give non participants a means of escape. Some aboriginal people, particularly senior women, resisted the damage and sought to limit community access to alcohol. The desire to escape an alcohol crazed town also became an additional factor for older people, who had known a better life, to establish outstations where their young people could grow up away from this. It should be noted that the outstation movement was underway before significant alcohol problems occurred. My father's memoir gives insights into this time.

"Robbie had made a number of trips with the Reiver but these days he spent most of his time at this new Border Store on the west bank of the East Alligator. It was managed by Terry Robinson who had built a simple sand palm shelter and was going into business selling things to Aboriginal people. He started back in 1964 and gradually built up a group of people who camped in the area. He had taken out a Garden Lease and a Store Lease. Bark paintings were very popular and he did quite a business trading in these. In early August 1969 we had a lot of grass fires. The worst affected area was adjacent to the road going out to the Crossing. There were a few beer cans along the edge of the road which indicated alcohol was being brought in. Shortly afterwards we heard that Terry Robinson who ran the 'Border' store on the west side of the East Alligator was applying for a Storekeepers Licence (allowing sale of alcohol). The date set down for the Hearing in the Darwin Court was Tuesday, 16th September. The small intrusion of alcohol to date had caused us a lot of concern and we felt we should object to the Licence being issued.

On Saturday, 13th September we held a ballot in the Dining Room as to whether we should oppose the issue of a Licence to the Border Store. The answer was loud and clear, to object to the Licence. This objection was lodged with our Solicitor in Darwin and the Court Case was deferred for two weeks.

When the Hearing took place we tried to project a case for the disruption we knew would happen once the Licence was issued. It was ruled out of order because it had not happened. When a Licence was issued, it was possible to object on the grounds that major disturbances took place. However, in our case we could not prove it because it had not happened. As we were leaving the Court I was walking past a passageway leading to the Magistrate's throne. He muttered to a companion, "This could become political."

We went home and braced ourselves for what would happen. It didn't take long. Night after night there was bedlam in the village; women would come screaming to us for protection. On one occasion there was near panic because a man had a .22 rifle and a box of bullets. Every now and then he would fire a shot into the iron walls of a house.

As I walked in to the village I said, 'Surely, there is someone who can take the rifle away from him". The reply; 'Don't go near him, he'll kill you!' Finally, I walked up to the man and said, 'Nakodjok, give me that rifle'. He quietly handed it over to me, I think, glad to get out of the problem he'd started. These types of things went on constantly. It was not possible to get to sleep at night before midnight and often much later. The road to the crossing was littered with beer cans. It was not easy to keep vehicles locked in the workshop yard and periodically drunken drivers careered through the village. Women and children came to the mission to find shelter. We now had the evidence we needed against the issue of the liquor licence, but disturbance to the local community was not a relevant clause when the licence came up for renewal in a year's time.

Towards the end of December we received nearly 10 inches of rain and parts of the road were under water. It slowed things down and some men went and lived at the Border Store. Then they started a canoe service taking cartons of beer across the flooded plains to people waiting in Red Lily. The work force suffered badly and, of wages paid, at least one third disappeared across the river.

The matter was discussed at Station Council and people felt we needed police there to keep control. So far the police did not want to become involved. At Outstations people found refuge with Timothy at Maningurrki.

The hospital was no longer a safe place at night. Drunken men came to have wounds from fighting attended and were very abusive. We discussed this and decided to put in a bell system. My house and Cam's house each had a bell installed. If there was a situation the sister could not handle at the hospital, she would press a button. Week about we were on call and, in response to the bell, would go as quickly as possible to the Sister's aid.

Approaching 1970, an area of new houses was built in Banyan village and people were taking a pride in their places. People planted mango trees around their houses and these were good for shade as well as the fruit. Old houses were also being renovated in the Arrkuluk village, and mango trees also planted there. Brenda Turley encouraged a competition for the neatest and cleanest house. This included gardens and lawns. There was not a lot of interest in the first contest but the second contest had strong interest.

After these two contests, drunkenness became widespread. Night after night there were drunken fights and arguments and beer cans littered the village. In fact, there was a line of beer cans along the road for ten miles out to the crossing. Some areas of the village were worse than others and even women were drunk. It was noticeable the children from these groups did not go to school and efforts to get them to school were short lasting.

As alcohol came into the area, it was not easy to collect payment for rent or electricity. There was also increasing damage to new houses with drunken behaviour.

In September 1971 I took Professor and Mrs Ronald Berndt to the East Alligator River Crossing to observe the state of affairs around the Border Store. They were horrified at what they saw and decided to take the matter up vigorously with the Welfare Branch.

Soon we received an unexpected visit from the Pine Creek police. People were caught taking alcohol on to the Reserve. After this quietness in the village was noticed by a number of people. Follow up visits were planned.

A series of meetings were held at Oenpelli commencing on 11th October, 1971. We invited Mr Robinson to be present and were pleased he came. After an initial discussion on the problems we moved on to ways of overcoming them. All present recognised there had to be police presence, which meant that there would have to be a police station either near the Border Store or at Oenpelli. People agreed no form of alcohol should be available on the Oenpelli side of the East Alligator River. It was felt that a Storekeepers License was not the right licence. People should be able to drink in a leisurely way with no supplies taken away from the store. Some very frank discussions took place with Mr Robinson and his cooperation was promised. He agreed the success of a licence would depend on a police presence. We could see there would no more than sporadic police visits.

After these meetings there was a lull in disturbances in the village, but gradually it became as turbulent as it was before. Eventually, I wrote a paper going into the problems we had to face daily, and the frustration of being unable to control them. I delivered this to the Director of Welfare, Harry Giese, who received it sympathetically but did not see that anything could be done unless there was police presence.

Through the 71/72 wet season there was little disturbance from alcohol but, as the country started to dry out in April, groups of men went to the bank of the East Alligator five miles north of the Crossing to buy their cartons from Terry Robinson, who delivered them to that point on the west bank.

We were alerted of something which was to become a very big problem especially with children. One morning Doug Packham reported petrol had been stolen overnight from the cement mixer. Evidence suggested school children were responsible so the matter was reported to the Headmaster. A parade of all children with their parents at the school was warned of the dangers of inhaling petrol. This was the first we were aware that petrol sniffing was taking place. It became a real problem over the following years. Efforts were made to involve children in sport and other recreational activities but there remained a core of children who reverted to petrol sniffing as often as there was opportunity.

The Border Store case came before the court in April and Silas, Nathanael, Alex and Arthur Field went in for the Hearing. Nothing could be done because a local disturbance clause was not part of the consideration. It took five years before action could be taken.

I wrote in the Monthly Report in June 'The former regular police visits for four days each pay day weekend have changed to a hit and miss whirlwind tour in one day. Large quantities of alcohol have been brought into the area with impunity, making a ridiculous situation and a heavy demand of time and energy on the part of a few people, particularly the nursing staff.

In September 1974 I wrote in the Mission Report, 'the only theme which can express the situation at Oenpelli, is one of depressing drunkenness and evasion of responsibility. If we look at the position which continues, this is soon seen to be true. In the past 20 years I have never seen the village so filthy nor the population so absorbed in pursuits of drunkenness and gambling. Gone are the days when parents were concerned if their children did not go to school, and the children would hide rather than be seen. These days the children openly move about playing, or shopping, or even lying about in their homes instead of making any attempt to go to school. Their parents have ceased to be concerned and there is no discipline which would require any change in behaviour. Damage to buildings is excessive and there is hardly one house which is not requiring extensive repairs, with the exception of the old corrugated iron huts.

The drink problem extended beyond Oenpelli; Goulburn Island had a vehicle which was used to supply a group of their people staying in the village. It also gave transport for Oenpelli people to receive cartons of beer. Eventually a permanent police presence was established which improved the worst aspects a little.

On Thursday 30th June 1977 a Local Court session was held in Oenpelli. There were 35 defendants, mostly on drink related charges. I don't think it had any impact on the drink problem. The main deterrent was now a police presence.

Preparations were going ahead in July 1977 to challenge the Border Store Liquor License. The hearing was set down for Monday 1st August. A bus was chartered to take a group of people to Darwin to give evidence. The first two days were spent in legal battles over issues as to who was the responsible party and whether Oenpelli was in the neighbourhood. It became obvious that the Border Store's solicitor was pushing for a technical victory by running out of time. He knew the magistrate was retiring at the end of the year and there would be no possibility for an extension during the present year.

In the end it was decided to make representation to the Minister for Aboriginal Affairs, Ian Viner to buy out the Border Store and surrender the license. This was eventually done but we went through another wet season with much drunkenness.

In 1978 the Prime Minister, Malcolm Fraser, visited Oenpelli and dogmatically declared that the Council was to operate the Border Store. Another requirement that the Government made was that there should be an alcohol facility at Oenpelli. This was strenuously opposed and finally a requirement was made that Oenpelli Council should conduct a poll giving people the opportunity to decide whether they wanted a club. When the final vote was taken it was slightly in favour of going ahead with a club."

Mining

Dad played an important role in some of the early mining developments in this part of the NT. Again I let his memoir tell of the key part of this.

Manganese at Groote Eylandt

When I worked at Groote Eylandt in 1951 I noticed a type of very heavy rock used to patch up the causeway of the Angurugu River.

Ten years later, when I was in Darwin, in the dry season of 1961, on one of the few occasions I was in the office, I received a visit from a geologist employed by the Bureau of Mineral Resources. He had returned from a visit to Groote Eylandt. He wanted me to know Angurugu was sitting on a large deposit of manganese. He was unsure what to do about it but felt we should know. I thanked him very much for his information. After he had gone pondered what to do. A problem at Groote was the lack of employment for many men, with some men coming into Darwin and getting into trouble at Bagot Reserve. Could we do anything with the manganese to solve this problem?

Next morning I went to the Mines Branch and took out two Miners Rights, one for Jim Taylor and one for myself. Then, on behalf of the Church Missionary Society, I applied for the Authority to Prospect on the Mission Lease at Groote. Having done this I wrote to Jim Taylor to bring him into the picture. We did not want anything going over the two way radio. Jim was cooperative and employed men to dig holes through the layers of manganese. I would ask him on the radio how the septic tanks were progressing. His reply was something like, 'We are down to six feet in three holes and still the same hard rock'.

In April 1962 I received a phone call from Welfare Branch advising me of a charter to Groote Eylandt next day, and asking if I had any small freight items to send on it. This request intrigued me so I asked why a charter was going to Groote. They said BHP had found a deposit of manganese and wanted to arrange to mine it. I replied that we held the Authority to prospect and they would have to come to CMS. The outcome was they invited me to accompany them.

At Groote, with such a big thing there was a mixed reaction. It was an aboriginal decision whether they wanted a large mining venture on their land and they did not seem to have any clear view. BHP was given approval to put in a small survey team using the old mission area at Emerald River. Once back in Darwin I sent a report to Canon Pearson. After that I had nothing more to do with it, except when the first royalties were paid in 1971. While we were at Angurugu relieving the Taylors there was a Groote Eylandt Trust meeting. I suggested 50% of the royalties be invested each year which was agreed to. After several years the Trust had extensive financial reserves.

Uranium and Tin Mining around Oenpelli

David Namirlmirl's land was an area called Myra Falls with a spectacular waterfall which flowed over the escarpment. He worked as a cook in Oenpelli but by 1968 Social Security payments meant people bought their own food. So David was free. He wanted to develop a tin deposit which he knew was on his land. His first job was to put a road to his tin deposit. Each Friday I flew across the area and noted his progress on the road. It was difficult country to build a road, but he made steady progress.

David's road travelled over the lower slope of the Green Ant Hill, an area known as Kabo Djang. David considered this an Aboriginal road. There was no conflict with Aboriginal people as long as he was the only one using it. In 1970 the Queensland Mines survey team also used it. Finding a shady tree on the side of the Green Ant Hill, south of Nimbuwah, they pulled up to boil the billy. It is possible they were following an anomaly from an aerial survey. Whatever the reason, a geologist was playing with a Geiger counter, waiting for the billy to boil. It showed an unusually high reading and, as he moved the instrument the reading went higher, resulting in discovery of the Nabarlek uranium deposit. Within days, a trencher was brought in and excavation at the site led to negotiations, with numerous visits from mining and Government officials.

This discovery set in motion concern about mining companies being free to move about on areas of land. The land was full of sacred sites. To aboriginal people this was much more important than uranium. As the word spread many people became involved, particularly those from the Welfare Branch and the Lands Branch.

In July, 1970, members of Welfare Branch and Lands Branch visited Oenpelli and identified two areas, Injalak and Nimbuwah, for gazetting as areas of special significance. The following day Peter Carroll with Joseph Girrabul, Jacob Nayinggul, Jimmy Midjaumidjau, and Welfare and Lands Branch men visited Nabarlek and identified land not be touched. A follow up visit, without the Government men, a week later attempted to set boundaries for the other sites in the area.

On 3rd August, Mrs Stevens arrived at Oenpelli for discussions and agreed to the name NABARLEK for the deposit. She spoke to me about her involvement in mining. She considered the discovery of uranium very important for medical reasons and was told by a geologist friend that the best place to find uranium would be adjacent to escarpment country, particularly in the Northern Territory. Acting on this information she took out Authorities to Prospect over two areas in the Northern Territory. One area west of the East

Alligator River resulted in the 1969 discovery of a large deposit near Jabiru by Geo Peeko and, in 1970 this second deposit was found at Nabarlek by Queensland Mines.

In September, Dr Rodd of Queensland Mines came to discuss opportunities for mining work and problems in Aboriginal areas. Queensland Mines felt Aboriginal people were creating problems for a 'successful' mining operation. Soon after Mr Hudson, Queensland Mines Manager, visited Nabarlek, but without contacting Oenpelli people.

At this time in 1970 David Namirlmirl still had no Authority to Prospect for tin at the 'Tin Camp' deposit. I spent a day with him there and we worked out a plan of how best to find the tin. His problem was water to wash the soil. This limited his activity until the wet season. However, he was producing very high grade ore.

In March, 1971, Bill Gray, from the Welfare Branch, held meetings with Nabarlek people to formulate points for discussions with Queensland Mines. At this time there were also meetings in Maningrida about establishment of an Aboriginal Mining Company, to be called FAMCO, sponsored by a mining group called Ocean Resources. After discussions at Goulburn Island, this group said they wanted to start exploration work around Oenpelli. This met with stiff resistance, bruising good relations between the communities. I felt Goulburn Aboriginal delegates were being pushed by non-Aboriginal advisers.

While on leave in 1971, I attended an Aborigines Committee meeting in Sydney. Mining was brought up and I was asked to comment. I stressed the overwhelming nature of the developments that people were not equipped to deal with. Many aspects were causing confusion and bitterness with land owners, and could do a lot of harm. I had a very attentive audience. Bishop Kerle, the chairman, said the only way mining pressure could be eased would be by Government intervention. After debate it was agreed to send a delegation from Oenpelli to Canberra, to put the case to the Prime Minister. Bishop Kerle said he would go through Ian Sinclair, representative of New England, the bishop's diocese. Bishop Kerle arranged with Ian Sinclair for a meeting with the Prime Minister, Mr McMahon, in May. The delegation was to be three people; an Aboriginal, Bishop Kerle and myself. Silas Maralngurra was elected the Aboriginal delegate.

On 3rd May, I flew to Darwin with Silas and to Sydney next day. At CMS we met Bishop Kerle and went through the issues to discuss with the Prime Minister. We felt Silas should be spokesman and we would support him. Next morning we flew to Canberra and met Ian Sinclair. At the appointed time we were ushered into the Prime Minister's Office. Silas was ill at ease and found it difficult to open the conversation. So I explained the difficulties and uncertainties for Aboriginal people at Oenpelli with the recent discovery of the Nabarlek ore body. Prime Minister McMahon agreed it was a difficult situation and that it could be introduced more slowly. We all felt a space like 20 years would be better with the other changes facing people in those communities. McMahon commented that the ore has been in the ground for millions of years and a further 20 years is hardly going to alter it. It was a good meeting.

Queensland Mines wanted an agreement on the boundaries of the proposed leases to finalise dealings with Mrs Stevens. On 13th May, I flew Peter Carroll, Silas and Joseph to Darwin for talks with Mrs Stevens. People wanted to be shown other open-cut mines particularly at Rum Jungle so Peter Carroll did this. A team of stockmen were contracted by Queensland Mines, to build a fence at Nabarlek. Queensland Mines reported that they had done an excellent job.

At Oenpelli nothing changed. Day after day aircraft came with various people for meetings and discussions. Aerial surveys were carried out, mostly at low level. It wasn't just the mining companies exerting pressure, but also the government departments such as Mines and Welfare. It was clear that the Canberra visit had not eased the pressure mining interests were exerting. Further meetings were held for the Nabarlek group, with no sign of an agreement. At one meeting at Oenpelli Mr Hudson, of Queensland Mines, was present. After no progress in discussions he offered a cash payment of $5,000. Silas first continued in a negative fashion, then paused and asked, "How much did you say?" When Hudson repeated $5000, Silas replied, "We could look at it." The meeting went on, but after this it became a matter of money. It was a pity this element had come into it.

Pressure was also being exerted by the FAMCO. In June, representatives from Goulburn Island, Croker Island, Maningrida and Millingimbi gathered at Oenpelli exerting pressure on David Namirlmirl to hand over his Authority to Prospect in the Myra Falls area to FAMCO. The meeting collapsed when Maningrida and Goulburn Island walked out.

David's Namirlmirl's lease was pegged on the 7th July 1971, made possible by a special visit from Richard Morris and Alec Rorrison. The four of us drove with David from Oenpelli to his land as both Richard and Alec knew exactly what had to be done. The following day the necessary papers were lodged with the Mines Branch.

In February 1972, the Methodist Missions called for a special meeting in Darwin relating to the FAMCO and ORMAC organizations. We had a frank discussion. The main items concerning Oenpelli were that Goulburn Island and Maningrida had not realised how separate our tribal groups were on matters of land. The FAM concept was accepted but not necessarily operated by ORMAC. This caused its head, George Alcorn, to become upset, claiming that while the two were separate one was dependant on the other.

At Oenpelli, two days later, I had a meeting with the principal local land owners Donald, Joseph, Elizabeth, Silas, Nathanael, Frank Ganangu, Magdalene, Arthur Hunter and George Gamarrawu. We discussed the situation with Reserve 337 (the land immediately around Oenpelli) and whether we should apply for Exploration Licenses in that area. MacIntyre Mines had located two anomalies from an aerial survey and there was pressure to look at these more closely. It was decided that it would be best to look at areas further out.

Late in 1972 David Namirlmirl went back to his work at on his land. Esso Mining Company quietly moved alongside him and helped him set up a washing box to remove tin from the soil. David had wearied of all the interest in his area. He had no desire to become caught up with ORMAC or FAMCO, and Esso's approach seemed more helpful.

Around then we received was from Les Penhall, a Welfare Officer, who outlined the situation regarding land and mining. There were no land rights then so Aboriginal people just had to accept mining people moving over their land, although certain areas could be excluded for cultural reasons.

Negotiations with Queensland Mines went slowly. In May, 1973, I went with Peter Carroll and Silas to a meeting at Nabarlek. Queensland Mines were trying to finalise the lease details; particularly to have one lease agreed, so they could conclude dealings with Mrs Stevens. They now said that the ore body sloped to the west meaning they would need to include the Green Ant Hill (Gabo Djang) in their land. This was the second attempt to prevent the break-up of the area and this time a large part of the Green Ant Hill was included in the lease. We were not in a position to argue which way the ore body sloped so we had to take their word for it.

A few days later a geologist from Union Carbide called at our place. I commented to him about the ore body at Nabarlek sloping to the west. He said that was a load of garbage. "We all know it slopes to the east. You can ask any geologist and they will agree." I thanked him for the information and wondered what to do about it.

A short time later another group of politicians came to Oenpelli. While at our place for morning tea, I managed to get one aside and told him what happened. He said, "Please give me a letter about this and I will see that it goes to the right person." I sent this letter to Canberra. A short time later I received a reply to the effect that they took a very dim view of Queensland Mines behaviour and would act on a recommendation from the Nabarlek Committee. Queensland Mines were asked to withdraw from the area. They left their camp manager and chief geologist at Nabarlek.

A few weeks later I received a radio message from Field Superintendent, Percy Leske. He asked me to visit Nabarlek and discuss with these two staff what they had done wrong causing their dismissal. I called to Nabarlek and spent two hours going over the areas of friction and especially the deceit. It was a pleasant meeting and they appreciated my time with them. When I left I wondered what the outcome would be.

After this, on 22nd June, 1974, came a visit by Prime Minister, Goff Whitlam. A Police Escort for the visit was arranged in Darwin. Two special visit constables were sent by road from Darwin to meet the aircraft on arrival at Oenpelli. They arrived at the East Alligator River Crossing when the tide was racing in. They called Headquarters and advised them of the situation. The reply was they were to be at Oenpelli to meet the aircraft, regardless. They could not argue so they drove their vehicle onto the flooded causeway. They did not get far. One of our staff, Ray Gillham, was on the Oenpelli side of the crossing. Ray backed his vehicle into the edge of the water and waded as far as possible to give the police the end of a cable. They fastened this to their flooded truck and Ray pulled them out. Once up on the bank they were able to get the Police vehicle going again and drove to Oenpelli. Here they learnt the visit was two hours late. Ray took them home where his wife ironed their uniforms dry so they were neatly presented when the aircraft arrived.

The old dining room was used for this visit. Silas sat up the front with the official party and things started, but nobody wanted to talk. I asked Priscilla to tell the Prime Minister what she had told me a day earlier. Priscilla stood and slowly started to speak. It took her a while to get going, but after a few minutes she became at ease and spoke brilliantly in clear English about Aboriginal feelings with regard to mining. After she sat down other people were asked if they had anything to say. People repeated some of her comments and then the Prime Minister replied. His speech was short but emphatic. If Aboriginal people did not want mining, his Government would see they did not have mining. The meeting broke up and I took the official party to our place where Helen had afternoon tea prepared. They then went on to Nabarlek. Peter Carroll was asked to go with them. When he returned he told me that the general opinion of the official party was, 'if it wasn't for me, mining would go ahead.'

A short time after the Prime Minister's visit Queensland Mines made another proposal to the Aboriginal people about mining Nabarlek. Copies were circulated throughout the village and I managed to get one. It was very interesting; they had gone through all the matters I had discussed with them, including access to the area. Each matter was carefully addressed in this fresh proposal. Access to the area would be through Wunyu Beach barge landing. There would be no resident work force other than those on shifts. People would work their shift and be flown back to Darwin, being at Nabarlek for two weeks and then in Darwin for one week. Aboriginal people would be employed at the mine, as far as possible. People were given two weeks to discuss this proposal among themselves then would give their decision.

At the time for the gathering at Nabarlek, I was very aware of what Peter Carroll had told me about the assessment of the Prime Minister's party. I did not wish to influence this decision so I asked Meryl Rowe to join the group at Nabarlek and make sure that people knew what was being talked about before making their decision. Meryl phoned that evening and said people had agreed for mining to go ahead.

Discussions had continued concerning Queensland Mines' approach to develop Nabarlek and other areas in their Exploration License. It was confusing to the Aboriginal people who, having responded by saying 'NO', were then continually and more persistently asked the same question by both the Mining Company and the Australian Government. The visit of the Prime Minister, while an honour, added to the overwhelming effect on this small group of people. Over four years, consultation in its fullest sense had taken place, and the decision made was contrary to what was expected. The Prime Minister's words rang out clearly at that meeting: 'If you do not want mining my government will see that you do not have mining.' And yet, two weeks later they agreed to the Mining Company's fresh proposal.

As time moved on some Nabarlek land owners spoke to me and outlined the situation they were in. The chief land owner was Frank Nalowed. He was under a lot of pressure from the mining company, who made sure he was well housed and looked after at the site. Oenpelli Council chairman, Silas told me people really wanted the money. Other land owners like Old Joseph and Hannah Mangiru were dead against it, however they had to bow to the authority of Frank Nalowed, as Silas sided with him. Today there are many marks where the mine has been and a large hole in the ground. All the royalties have been spent and I'm not aware of anyone who is better off.

Following the Prime Minister's visit and the meeting at Nabarlek when agreement was reached for mining to go ahead, I received a request from Canberra to meet the Secretary of the Department of Aboriginal Affairs in Darwin. This was a meeting of only the two of us. I was asked to give reasons for this sudden turn-around of attitude towards mining. I had no answer for it other than what I have recorded here. There seemed a feeling I had engineered it. I tried to outline some of the pressures people faced and how their sudden change of mind could be seen as an escape and the only way ahead. But at the end of this meeting I felt that I was seen to have had some ulterior motive.

Investigation into Uranium Mining – The Fox Inquiry

An insight into some of the difficult issues raised and dealt with during the development of mining is provided in the following material taken as excerpts from the transcript of evidence given by Dad (Alf Wilson) to the Ranger Uranium Inquiry, commonly known as the Fox Inquiry. In addition to his direct quotes, I have summarised some parts of the evidence as indicated and changed or added in the occasional word/tense, including explanation of map references to facilitate understanding of the contents. However in all cases I have attempted to represent accurately the substance of what was said, in way which can be understood by readers who are less familiar with the geography of the area.

Fox Ranger Uranium Inquiry Transcript

22nd October 1975

Transcript begins on page 2227 and records that, in addition to oral evidence and a previous written submission, 2 exhibits were tendered by Alf Wilson at 3 pm on 22nd October. Exhibit 1 was 2 maps of the East Alligator Rivers region, the first showing the normal mouth of the Magela Creek and the second showing the Magela Creek entering the East Alligator River in three parts in a major flood situation. Exhibit 2 was twelve slides shown by Mr Wilson during his submission along with a detailed list of them

Oral Evidence given by Alfred Wilson

After swearing in Mr. Cummins (legal representative of the Fox Inquiry) commenced questioning.

Question - Cummins: "Where do you live?"

Answer – Alf Wilson: "Until July, Oenpelli; we are now residing temporarily in Sydney."

Question – Cummins: "Do you intend to go back to Oenpelli?"

Answer – Alf Wilson: "Oh yes."

Question - Cummins: "You are a missionary of CMS and have been since 1951, is that so?"

Answer – Alf Wilson: "That is correct."

Question - Cummins: about prior work in the NT and with aboriginals.

Answer – Alf Wilson: describes work history including the statement "my evidence is based on observations and experience obtained during the past 24 years, and in particular my lengthy contact with the aboriginal people of Western Arnhem Land."

Question - Cummins: "Do you have a university degree?"

Answer – Alf Wilson: "I have undertaken a course in community development at the Australian National University. I do not have a degree or diploma."

Question - Cummins: "You have made a statement and wish to give evidence concerning the causes of flooding of the plains and swamp lands adjacent to the East Alligator River?"

Answer – Alf Wilson: "Yes."

Question - Cummins: "Would you commence by reading your statement?"

Answer – Alf Wilson: "I commence with the thought - I accept the scope of this inquiry is the Ranger Environmental Impact Statement, but it is important to see the total picture of proposed mining in the area. This would include the Pan Continental ore body at Jabiluka, refinement of or a Queensland Mines deposit at Nabarlek and Noranda's deposit at Koongara, and further possible ore bodies on exploration licenses 12, 219, 220, 326, 582."

Question - Cummins: "Now you refer to the EIS?" (Environmental Impact Statement).

Answer – Alf Wilson: "Throughout the EIS repeated references are made to controlled release operations from the tailing dam and the retention ponds into the Magela Creek System, section 4.7.3 refers to the 'unfounded assumption' that the Magela system has no outlet to the sea. I would support that assumption and would point out that it is one of the critical points of the proposed development.

"I wish to present a series of slides and photos showing the East Alligator region and in particular the Magela Creek, and the system of flooding during monsoonal rain. ....the point I want to make is about the drainage system of the East Alligator River and Magela Creek .... (outlines process of wet season flooding in the East Alligator River in a normal wet season from about December) .... but you will see the way that the people who drew this map up (the map in the EIS), they have shown the types of country adjacent to the East Alligator. A lot is perennial swamp country, a lot is intermittent swamp country. There are low-lying areas with permanent waterholes. Now the bank of the East Alligator River, to a large extent is higher than the adjacent country. I think this is one of the important parts of the drainage system in that water feeding out of the higher country can travel past the plains along the lower section of the river and find its way out to sea, while early rains only cause local flooding of the other areas, most of the water from early rains is taken up by absorption into the ground, feeding the dried out waterholes.

"If we could go to the next slide please.

"This is a more detailed map showing the mouth of Magela Creek, it is just a very small little mark on the map there, which leads into a large area of swamp. It is very misleading to find, in the EIS, a well-defined watercourse for the Magela Creek, and I think this is probably one of the areas which can cause a lot of misunderstanding. The Magela Creek is in no way a well-defined watercourse north of Mudginberry Station (further discussion and clarification).

Question - Cummins: "Would you now indicate that again on the map?"

Answer – Alf Wilson: "The Magela Creek mouth is this point here and it feeds into this large swamp area, which moves back approximately 20 miles from the mouth to Jabiru."

(Then discussion about drainage of the East Alligator River on the Oenpelli side)

"Slide number four will show flooding. Next slide

"…. you can see here the East Alligator River. This is all water, (referring to all the land along and near the banks of the river) this is Canon Hill and the swamp next to the Canon Hill high ground. Now when flood rains come down the East Alligator River in January-February before when the monsoons come, the River at this stage is flooding but not at the high level and the water is flowing through quite well, the plains are starting to flood locally. Then the monsoon rains come, with very heavy falls, and the East Alligator River comes down in much more volume. But if the flood is timed with the high tides (king tides) around March then the tide comes in and pushes the water back and it is from that tidal action the plains flood…. the flooding which comes from the escarpment out to the coast and over the plains is minor compared to the tidal influence of the East Alligator River. Now we get a basin effect with the plains. The plains are at a lower level generally than the actual river bed, so that the water is pushed back through these small creeks (out of the river) to flood the plains and this is where your flooding takes place … with the rising and falling of the tides you are getting a see-sawing effect, twice in 24 hours … only a 1-2 foot rising and falling, until finally the water is escaping very slowly ….

"Slide 5 please

"This is a picture of the Magela Creek system taken about March 1968. It will give you some idea of the "well defined" creek shown in the EIS (obviously said with irony). These are all paperbark swamps and the path of the river is anything but well defined.

"Now coming back to Magela Creek in particular. I think you can see what I am talking about with the undefined banks of the river up to Mudginberry Station, about there (pointing to a location on the map), and beyond that it is a well-defined creek though it does burst it's banks…. I think this illustrates the point and the vast area of water which is trapped inside the bank of the River … the edge of Mudginberry is seen there and along the banks of the Creek for about 2 miles upstream from Mudginberry groups of aboriginal people at the present stage are camping, and have done so for many years and I imagine will continue to do so into the future. My comment is that from this point on that the Magela becomes a wide open area of swamp and no longer a confined creek. It's a country in which buffalo in profusion roam and also other forms of wildlife such as turtles, geese and many forms of birdlife used for hunting. The waterholes abound in barramundi .... and this is also a source of food for the people who live in the area. .... (as per the slides) with the drainage system of Magela Creek very little water which passes Jabiru could possibly find its way into the outlet into the East Alligator River, and it can find many areas of swamp land to lodge in without ever getting to the sea... (more discussion).

"There is another set of circumstances which do not appear to have been considered. There are occasions where there is insufficient water running during the wet season to cause more than local flooding and all water is retained within the swamp."

Question - Cummins: Now the next part of your statement deals with the aboriginal environment-would you continue with that.

Answer – Alf Wilson: "... re Mount Brockman area. In section 3.10.2 (of the EIS) reference is made to the fears of the Gunwingu people if the Rainbow Serpent is disturbed, yet in almost total disregard for these fears, the boundary of the mining lease has been set to overlap with these (sacred) sites, and the only recorded person to whom it was referred was Mr Balmanidbal ....it must be recognised that the boundaries of the Aboriginal Reserve are arbitrary and followed geographical or easily identified reference points. However the boundaries of aboriginal land are not so easily defined and the importance of the land and the mythological or sacred sites can easily be underestimated. ....in the Mount Brockmann case we are only told that Mr Peter Balmanidbal was consulted. There are other people in the Alligator Rivers region that should be involved in any decision regarding these sites."

Question - Cummins: "Well stopping you there who do you consider these should be?"

Answer – Alf Wilson: "I could give you the names of some people, these are the people I have recorded from my memory of this area.

"Jacob Nayingal, Elijah".... (goes on to list 15 aboriginal people)

He continues to comment on
- "the over harvesting of barramundi by many Europeans coming into the area, particularly associated with mining.
- "the diet of the local aborigines which includes much fish at the time of the proposed release of water into Magela Creek

- makes criticism of free ranging by Europeans, particularly associated with mining, across the bushland in the area desecrating sacred sites

He then makes reference to EIS S5.6.1 'the Company cannot be held responsible for the management and supervision of its staff after working hours', stating.

"In the normal European society this statement could be accepted as right and proper, but in the context of the aboriginal environment it is pregnant with problems of erosion of aboriginal cultures and traditions and the production of a mendicant society....

"It is disturbing to see that so little importance has been placed on the social environment in relation to aborigines in the Impact Statement."

Comment continues with an extensive critique of the EIS regarding employment and social impacts, highlighting the Nabarlek experience. He then discusses the impacts of alcohol of aboriginal communities regarding adverse impacts on education and potential for employment and how this proposal will make this even worse. He concludes this section with a formal summary.

Summary

"What in effect will happen is that very few aboriginal people will seek employment. Those who do will mostly fill menial tasks, that is garbage clearance, road maintenance and toilet cleaners. The odd ones able to obtain a clerical or skilled position will only hold it for a short period of time, as mentioned in the Gove situation.

"There will however be a gathering of people in the various camps along the banks of the Magela Creek, selling women to contractors and buying cheap wine and rum from the proceeds. These people will come from areas along the top of the Reserve such as Croker Island, Maningrida, Goulburn Island and Oenpelli. As alcohol in this region is already having a disastrous impact, these communities determination to meet the new challenge of the magnitude of that presented in the Impact Statement will to a large extent disappear.

"All this may sound rather negative but in reality it is no more than a repetition of what has taken place in Australia since first settlement. Wherever intrusion into aboriginal land has taken place bringing rapid development, aboriginal people have suffered. As their land has been taken over their culture has gone and they have become confused and life has lost its purpose.

"If the Australian Government sees fit that Uranium Mining should go ahead some bold efforts are required for this to be done in harmony with the total environment. In the interests of all parties concerned I suggest that an independent body be formed to look much more critically at the real issues involved, particularly that of the aboriginal environment. ...

"In my own humble opinion I don't think it's good enough for a mining company, and this is probably a bold thing to say but it needs an independent body....."

Evidence was continued on 23rd October with extensive cross examination and further questioning, with extensive discussions about aboriginal society, the role of aboriginals in decision making and managing alcohol. Evidence continues to page 2422 of the Transcript and was concluded shortly before lunch on 23rd October 1975.

As I read through the nearly 200 pages of the transcript of evidence that my father gave 35 years ago I was struck by several things. The first was how powerfully and well he argued his case. Ranged against him were a large number of highly qualified mining engineers and geologists, many with multiple degrees from well-regarded universities and supporting them a group of lawyers and senior civil servants, many of whom wanted mining to proceed with minimal interference. He, instead of a degree or diploma, had a short course certificate in community development. Yet he was the voice of many aboriginal people who did not have even his skills in presenting a case, and they relied on him and others of similar mind to speak on their behalf. In doing so he framed and presented a compelling argument that gave a lie to much of the mining industry self-serving "pro-development with no impact" propaganda. After he made his main submissions he was questioned and cross examined about the detail over several hours.

At the same time he put forward constructive ideas, which came to fruition with Kakadu National Park, (its terms of its existence being for the purpose of protecting both natural and aboriginal heritage) and with the establishment of an independent body in the Office of the Supervising Scientist for the Alligator Rivers Region, charged with ensuring long term monitoring and protection of these assets.

As a keen observer of the natural environment and aboriginal use of it, he also presented a complex hydrological and ecological picture in simple terms that all those hearing his evidence could not fail to understand. As an experienced ecologist working for many years across a range of similar fields I would struggle to present these arguments better – the water in these wetlands does not readily escape to the sea, if radioactive contamination enters these areas it will enter the food chain consumed by the local aboriginal population who source a major part of their diet from the fish in the area, if the mining company wants to get the agreement of the aboriginal people it needs to make a serious attempt to identify the full group of people who speak for the area, that we need to respect the sacred sites and dreaming stories of these people, that token jobs to a few people will not counteract the potential for wide scale destruction of a culture and that, without dealing with the threat of alcohol, all else is futile. Of course he was not the only one to say these things, others such as Peter Carroll and the aborigines said them too, but I sense that his clear decisive evidence carried a lot of weight. As the evidence accumulated over the next 2 years until a final report was made and government decisions flowed from it seems to me that his part became a powerful piece in the jigsaw of what transpired.

As I read his full submissions and absorb the complexity of the arguments and language I see not only him, but my mother standing alongside him, often late into the night, reading and polishing his drafts, helping to formulate ideas, and providing a vision for what could be.

Of course the Commission members should receive much credit for this outcome, with their willingness to listen objectively to mountains of evidence and arguments, now represented by the 50 volumes of transcripts sitting in the National Library in Canberra. So too should many other witnesses who contributed their parts.

But to me, looking back, it is as if, just as the tide turns on the East Alligator and drives the floodwaters out across the plains, so too my Dad standing there and giving his passionate statement was an important part in the turning of the tide in understanding and acting to improve the future of Arnhem's children.

PART 2 - OENPELLI AND THE NT AS AN ADULT

Grahams Story continued

Living Far Away

In the 1970s I moved from being an Oenpelli child to an adult. At the same time I moved into a changed relationship with my parents who were finding the pressures of Oenpelli starting to wear them down. This section chronicles the evolving changes in our lives, paralleled by a changing community at Oenpelli.

Visit to Groote Eylandt

The year I finished high school was 1971. We did not return to Oenpelli for our Christmas holidays. As Jim Taylor had gone on holidays from Groote Eylandt Dad was replacing him while he was away. I missed Oenpelli, but Groote was a place Mum and Dad talked about from their earliest years in the NT. Its aboriginal people of Angurugu were famous for their ferocity. This was my chance to see it.

The first thing I noticed about Angurugu was rather, than the vast vistas from Oenpelli across the plains and hills, here it was all woodland, the views were of trees, with houses and people were interspersed amongst them and the only vast views were from the coast. There were still many beautiful places and good things to do.

The Angurugu River ran just behind the mission with crystal clear spring fed water providing a great place for an extended afternoon swim, when dozens of bodies, black and white would be here together; jumping, splashing, swinging from trees. A two to three hour paddle in kayak along the river, trailing a fishing line brought one to the open ocean of the Carpentaria Gulf, with no crocodiles in evidence. A tour of the manganese mine, with huge machinery, heavy black rocks and ore piled high, was fascinating, and it was only a ten mile bike ride along bitumen to Alyangula, a white town of 1000 people, high civilisation after the isolation of Oenpelli.

I worked in the Mission shop several days a week. Here I learned a different lingo from Oenpelli. The men seemed taller and blacker than their Oenpelli cousins and their language, 'Anindilyakwa', had a very different sound. Instead of tinned Gampie (Camp Pie) and Risstoo (Irish Stew) they loved the salt water fish, freshly caught from the ocean, with barguta (barracouta) and parrot fish most preferred. The barracouta fascinated me, three foot bodies, and an evil mouth adorned by large jagged teeth. I caught a couple small ones fishing in the kayak and those teeth flapping near my bare legs were exciting enough. Dad and Mum caught up with old friends, and we made new friends at the mission.

One was Gerry Blitner, a man with a long and colourful history, who took us fishing one Saturday between Groote Eylandt and north east Arnhem Land. We stopped for lunch at low lying Bickerton Island where we quickly caught a dozen snapper off the boat, alongside the rocks in a shallow bay. We threw them whole into the coals of a campfire. Never has fish tasted so good. An afternoon of trolling around reefs and deeper channels brought us a selection of bigger fish including a 30-40 pound turrum. One time I had a large fish, perhaps of 15-20 pounds, on the line when suddenly the line went still but with a big weight attached. I hauled it in. There was a five pound fish head, a foot across. It ended in a jagged semi-circle of teeth marks. A shark had amputated its back three quarters, just behind the head, in a single bite.

Near the end of these holidays I got my higher school certificate marks, giving me the choice of what I wanted at University. At school Science was my top subject, with interests in both biology and chemistry fostered by endless conversations with Mum, where I explored her wealth of knowledge and added my own. My ambition had been a Zoologist, but I was also interested in options like Chemical Engineering. Late in final year a school friend said he wanted to be a vet and I should do the same, because a vet would be able to get a job, whereas there were few jobs for zoologists.

Knowing almost nothing about vet science, when time came to send the forms to University, on impulse I put a Number 1 in the Vet box. My friend Carl, did not make the vet cut off but instead became a dentist. He loved his chosen profession becoming a highly successful dentist, and making vastly more money than I ever contemplated.

University

I flew to Sydney, from Groote Eylandt, at the end of January for University enrolment and to find a place to stay. My grandfather, now in his late 90's, had gone to Sydney University many decades earlier, then staying at St Andrews College. As an old boy, of more than 50 years before, he suggested I stay there. In his spidery hand he wrote a reference to the College Head, an old colleague from his time as a minister and moderator.

The next five years were mostly consumed with course attendance, growing up, learning about girls, drinking and the freedoms of a University life and at the same time applying myself sufficiently to study to get acceptable marks. I had to do practical work for my veterinary degree, staying on farms around the state. I got home once or twice a year to continue my love affair with the NT.

Cyclone Tracy

Christmas 1974 I got paid work with the Animal Industry Branch of the NT Administration in Darwin, accompanying researchers to the Douglas Daly Research Farm, and other Top End research farms and stations. After working for two weeks in December it was time to go home to Oenpelli for Christmas.

I booked a flight home on Connellan Airways, Christmas Eve. It was a wet December and, two weeks earlier, there was a cyclone scare when one formed in the Arafura Sea. It headed for Darwin but broke up and dissipated before crossing the coast. A sense of anti-climax came from the false alarm.

I stayed in a hostel in Parap, enjoying the freedom of holidays in Darwin, while actually earning real money. The weekend before Christmas I spent the afternoon watching Australia play England in a test, on the Darwin TV, a novelty not available at Oenpelli. Doug Walters crashed a century in the final session of play, finishing his ton on the final ball with a towering six.

I left most of my gear at the hostel and, on Christmas Eve morning, headed for the airport. Another low pressure system was in the Arafura Sea, somewhere north of Oenpelli and Coburg peninsula and heavy rain was pouring down in Darwin. Our flight could not take off because the weather had closed in. So, with other passengers, I sat around the airport and waited, wondering if I would get home that day.

Two hours later the rain stopped, the sky cleared and the pilot announced it was clear to Oenpelli. Just over an hour later, I was having lunch with the family at home. That afternoon we did our usual Christmas preparations, catching a bit of radio news that the low pressure system in the Arafura Sea was now officially categorised as a cyclone and was headed west along the coast, north of the Tiwi Islands. It all seemed unremarkable, another cyclone tracking west along the NT Top End Coast. Still we made a point of listening to the seven o'clock news that night, when about to sit down for dinner. The newsman, in his brief weather summary at the end, said words to the effect, 'Cyclone Tracy has continued to intensify and move south-west beyond the Tiwi Islands this afternoon. It is now located 100 kms west of Melville Island and has recently changed direction and is now heading in a south easterly direction at 10 knots.' We turned off the news, crackling amidst the static, and had dinner.

It still seemed unremarkable to me. However Dad, with his detailed knowledge of NT geography and weather, thinking it through in his mind for a minute said. "It sounds like that cyclone is now heading for Darwin," but it was not something the weather man emphasised.

Christmas Eve night was a fine night at Oenpelli with not even a storm. Next morning we woke up and all enjoyed the excitement of presents. As my younger brother Arthur was ten it was still a time of great family excitement. We half noticed the morning radio news bulletin did not seem to be there, but paid it little heed. Everyone went to Christmas morning church to celebrate the day. Returning home with guests for morning tea, it seemed funny there was no radio reception, and people were beginning to wonder.

Finally, mid-afternoon, someone picked up a short wave broadcast from elsewhere in Australia, Darwin was no more, Cyclone Tracey had struck on early Christmas morning, over 90% of buildings destroyed, many people dead, boats sunk in the harbour, and so it went on.

Dad organised a flight next morning to Darwin, taking a plane load of food, and emergency equipment, along with a couple people to assist. He returned with some displaced people from CMS whose homes were damaged. A couple days later I went in with him. By now Darwin airport was closed to anyone but officials from the government, so we flew to Bachelor, 60 miles south. He returned to Oenpelli for another load while I drove a van, loaded with goods, up to CMS Darwin.

For the first 40 miles there was nothing to see, just the same old bush, with stringybark and woollybut trees. When I got to the 20 mile I started to notice some damage, bits of broken branches off trees. As I continued on the damage rapidly grew. By the time I reached Berrimah, not a tree was left with any branch less than 4 inches thick and not a leaf remained on a tree anywhere. You could now see for miles where, before, the view was a hundred yards.

The corner of Bagot Road and the Stuart Highway was a mass of debris with just enough of a space cleared for cars to drive down the road. Galvanised iron sheeting was wrapped around everything, sheets of fibro were smashed everywhere, along with a tangle of wire and branches, over-turned cars, furniture, bits of Christmas toys; who knows what half the things once were.

Someone had said the best way to find CMS was to look for a small bit of green glass on what used to be the BP sign of a service station at the corner of Bagot and McMillans Rd, then take the next entrance past there. I continued down the road marvelling at massive steel telegraph posts bent over to the ground in the wind and at what used to be houses, now mostly just piers and floorboards, sometimes with a part wall or a toilet and bathroom still sitting 10 feet in the air.

I could not find anything resembling CMS. As the road divided between Nightcliff Rd and Trower Rd I knew I had overshot. Back I went and finally glimpsed the fragment of green glass telling me where to turn in. Once you got past all the smashed trees CMS had fared pretty well. Our old house was largely intact, only some minor damage from flying debris, a testament to my father's building quality. Other houses were also largely OK, reflecting the better standard of missionary construction. I joined in the tidying, chain-sawing trees and patching houses for the rest of the day. One thing I noticed was there was not a green ant to bite me in all the tree branches. At night Oenpelli's portable generator gave a single light per house.

Next morning I got a lift into what used to be the city, to report for work. The Mitchell Street government offices were my previous work site. A handful of the former, hundred-strong, workforce were there. Initially I helped a couple of people try to rescue some work – papers and experimental results. It was futile.

While the building was intact almost all the windows had been smashed. Inside was a litter of broken glass, furniture and piles of wet and mouldering paper. We shovelled debris out the windows as we searched for what could be salvaged, precious little.

It was obvious that there was no point me staying on here. The senior person rang his work colleague in Katherine and they agreed that, if I got myself to Katherine, they would give me a job on the experimental farm there. So I went to Katherine the next day, leaving others to clean up Darwin's mess. A cursory call to the hostel where I had stayed made it clear that there was no point looking for the things I had left before Christmas. The building had largely survived but most of the contents had been trashed by the weather and a new wave of clean-up workers was now housed there. I can't remember what I lost but it seemed pretty trivial compared to the rest.

At the end of January I finished my work in Katherine. I returned to Oenpelli for a few days before going back to University, via a Darwin beginning to get order. No longer chaos, with most of the debris gone, instead, there was an eerie silence. Where once there had been a bustling town now it was mostly empty, with more military presence than real people. There was ever present wet season dankness, with the few remaining locals mostly living in makeshift houses where a tarpaulin had been used to cover the floorboards, and the rudiments of living had been assembled under the previous house.

Everyone seemed to be doing fine physically, with all the military help, but there was a pervasive air of loss with most people gone and those who remained trying to rebuild little bits of a past life. The once bustling town of 50,000 was now just a shell. It felt to me like Darwin had lost most of its soul.

My Parents as an Adult

Somewhere around the time I finished school and went off to University I had to make a transition from regarding my parents as all knowing adults to progressively moving into an adult relationship with them. This happened gradually and there was no clear point of transition. I suspect it happened more readily with my Mum, with whom I had engaged in adult conversations about the world around since my early teenage years. Mum was always accessible for hours of chat about whatever was topical, whereas my father had always been a step removed. I think I was slightly in awe of him.

He was tremendously hard working, rising early and often working late into the evening to try and manage the mountain of issues and papers that being superintendent entailed. What I do remember is that he was highly focused on trying to do things to accord with his sense of purpose. He was not very tolerant of those with other views, although he had a strong sense of fun and mischief and enjoyed practical joking with friends and colleagues.

However it was also clear that he and Mum worked together as a team and little happened that he had not discussed in detail with her. Many was the night when they would be in their bedroom talking in muted voices until late after others were in bed. Mum seemed content not to push herself or her ideas forward in any public way, but almost all his thoughts and actions were things he shared with her. While she would occasionally take a different view, in most circumstances she gave him almost unqualified support and took for herself the role of making sure that the rest of life around him functioned in a well organised way.

As someone who had strong views, limited patience and little tolerance of fools, Dad had some legendary arguments with others at Oenpelli, particularly those of similar strong will. His shouting matches with Priscilla, an aboriginal woman of similarly forthright manner which occurred under our house, could be heard a hundred yards away and still live clearly in my memory. Arguments with health inspectors and other government officials were also famous.

However these were a relatively infrequent part of daily life and, for much of the time, he could be found industriously pursuing some project or moving around the community at a rapid pace, whether on foot, in a Toyota, or some other form of transport. Seeing him sitting down and having a slow casual chat was a rare sight as it did not fit his idea of useful occupation. As time went by, and I gradually became aware of the wider dimensions of aboriginal politics, I gained an increasing respect for what he tried to do and some of the controversies which accompanied these issues. I also got a gradual insight into the bitterly felt disappointments of the increasing alcohol and community fragmentation and of his sense of trying to swim against the tide to prevent ever increasing social disintegration of a formerly simple and happy community. I do not recall him ever walking away from, or looking for an easy out from confronting difficult issues, even when he understood that this may not be the popular or easy choice. Nor did Mum ever suggest easy outs though she often used her calm good sense to smooth more troubled waters.

As the years went by the wear and tear of day to day conflicts of the community became more significant. It must have been in my mid University years when it became apparent that Dad and Mums focus had moved away from Oenpelli. I think they needed a break and some time out. They came to Sydney for several months, doing a course as part of the new Canberra approaches to NT and aboriginal policy. Gradually their focus moved to the ever increasing number of outstations, where they saw their future in supporting many much smaller communities to function effectively and build positive environments. I think they understood Oenpelli had to devolve its governance to its aboriginal leaders and, whether this functioned well or poorly, it was time to move aside for others. So, while they continued to be seen around Oenpelli, they spent ever increasing time away in remote little communities around the Liverpool and Mann Rivers or Coopers Creek. They progressively distanced themselves from Oenpelli's day to day issues and frustrations. In doing so they gradually seemed to build a new sense of purpose for their lives and an understanding that they still had an important contribution to make.

As the years passed they gradually moved from middle age to senior citizen status. A gentler and more mentoring aspect of Dad's character emerged. Mum always had this demeanour but now Dad seemed to be learning to slow his frenetic pace and tame his impatience. They were also proud grandparents of several grandchildren and started to look beyond life at Oenpelli towards a future retirement and other activities.

The outside world moved into ever increasing contact with Oenpelli, the Woodward Royal Commission into Aboriginal Land Rights and the Fox inquiry into Uranium Mining, where Dad seemed to spend endless days, listening, consulting with aboriginal community members, discussing with lawyers, giving evidence. Then decisions to grant aboriginal freehold rights, establish Kakadu National Park and a concurrent uranium mine, debates about the disposition of royalties and how some lasting benefits could accrue to the community.

With Kakadu came new and improved roads, bridges over the major rivers east of Darwin, finally taming the mighty South Alligator. Now a road trip to Darwin from Oenpelli was reduced from days to four hours. With this came the ever increasing stream of visitors and officials who wanted to do their bit, or at least to travel around and make it seem as if they were contributing. I think Dad often sensed that self-importance and self-interest were dominant motivations of much official involvement.

Finishing University and Beginning Work

My years in University passed quickly enough. By the end of fourth year I was tired of study and bought a motorbike and headed off for a year travelling around Australia, getting work where I could find it. First a job on a cattle stud in the Adelaide Hills, then a job as a railway fettler, at William Creek, near Lake Eyre, on the old Ghan railway. Then across to the west and work in a timber mill in Pemberton and as a builders labourer in Port Hedland and Dampier.

I destroyed one bike on the rough roads and bought another. As the end of the year came around I knew that I had to get on with my life. I enjoyed the freedom of good wages and no responsibility as a labourer, but could not do this for very long before dead end boredom came.

So back to NSW I rode, with a Christmas stopover at Oenpelli. I arrived in Sydney with less than $10 in my pocket and nothing in the bank. A month or two of urgent work was required to rebuild my finances. I did lots of little dead end jobs, a service station attendant, a gardener for a rich lady in Vaucluse who brought me hot chocolate for morning tea, stacking boxes in factories.

Final year at University was a grind. Having tasted freedom the discipline of study was doubly hard. Now I was much more calculating in what I did. In the final weeks of my exams, I decided for each subject what work I thought I needed to do and, once I had done this minimum, I was bored with further study. So I sat in the library and read cheap novels while my fellow students slogged away. I passed, just.

Then, as my current girlfriend lived in Melbourne, I decided to go to Melbourne to visit her. Our relationship did not last long but, as I was in Melbourne, I decided to canvass the local vets to see if one needed an assistant. The first ones didn't but pointed me to others to try. After five or six visits in a day I found myself employed as a veterinary assistant in Dandenong.

I worked there for 18 months treating cats and dogs and a few cattle and horses on the edge of the Gippsland. Melbourne was a great place to live and, even though the work only half interested me, I found a passion for Australian Rules football, becoming a North Melbourne supporter. I also learnt to ski at Mt Buller. These two passions made living in Melbourne worthwhile. But dual pulls of wanting to work with wild animals and missing the NT were never far away.

One day I was flicking through a vet journal. I saw a small advertisement, 'Vets wanted to work for the government in the NT'. A cursory telephone interview saw me heading back to Darwin a couple months later.

It was late November, and the temperature was in the scorching 40s heading across central Queensland and on to the black soil of the Barkly Tablelands. Hours of driving, with my car window open, left me heat blasted but loving the open spaces. Finally I reached Katherine one hot November afternoon, and stopped at the low level bridge for a swim. The cool clear water washed over me and the scent of the paperbarks was overpowering.

It felt so good to be back home in the NT Top End.

I spend the next year working out of Katherine, mostly in the Victoria River District doing station work on the large properties of the Victoria River District, Wave Hill one day, Camfield the next, out to Inverway and Riveren, up to Mt Sanford and VRD stations, sometimes up to Bulloo River and Timber Creek. Other times I would head east, out beyond Mataranka, along the Roper to Elsey, or down to Daly Waters and out to Borroloola. A great life, but still my interest in wild animals drew me too.

Crocodile

It was hot. It was late in the afternoon. There was sudden stillness in the air and the surface of the small waterhole shone with an unnatural, undisturbed smoothness. Fresh pig tracks at the edge of the water suggested pigs just gone. A couple bubbles popped to the surface near the edge of the pool; just decaying vegetation, said my mind. I should have smelt crocodile!

I was realising my ambition to work with wild animals. First Melbourne Zoo as a zoo keeper, then at Taronga Zoo in Sydney and Western Plains Zoo in Dubbo, learning to be a Zoo Vet. The second half of my study course was a research project. I picked studying banteng cattle, endangered in their Asian home and held by Western Plains Zoo; their largest world population was remote Coburg peninsula in northern Arnhem Land, only 100kms from home.

I came with Charlie Meader, senior keeper at Western Plains Zoo, to spend two to three weeks at Coburg learning about the behaviour and social structure of banteng cattle. First we came to Oenpelli, and organised for Dad to fly a reconnaissance in his Cessna. In an hour flying low, over Coburg, we sighted populations of banteng around large swamps on Danger Point, a peninsula east of Smiths Point and Port Essington where the original NT settlement had been. Our flight gave us a bird's eye view of the land then we flew on to Goulburn Island to meet the traditional owners of Coburg. Over an hour of polite smiles and handshakes we explained what we proposed and they gave their agreement. Back to Oenpelli where two motorbikes and a load of food and equipment was arranged and ferried to Coburg, leaving us at a camp site on a ridge overlooking where we had seen the majority of the banteng cattle groups, about five kilometres south of Danger Point.

Charlie and I set up camp. A couple of quickly built bower sheds, covered in gum leaves, provided respite from the hot sun. We set out to explore on our bikes. Large swamps to our east provided water to boil to drink, and collect in a billycan for a pour-over wash, but the edges were shallow, and we had to walk out a long way before the water was six inches deep. We kept a constant lookout for crocodiles in these swampy places, but saw no sign.

At the coast we saw many old signs of banteng; dung and tracks along the sedge plains fringing the beaches. Pockets of fringing rainforest had been a favoured site for cattle to lie up and graze the adjoining plains at dawn and dusk and we saw old tracks and signs. But it was late August, the plains and forest edges were dry and the Banteng had moved on. We found a shallow aboriginal well in a patch of forest but it was dry and full of leaves; digging it out to get fresh water could wait.

As we explored over two or three days we gradually discovered the banteng along a valley a couple kilometres west of our camp. Here semi-open glades amongst the woodland, with moisture in depressions, provided a green pick of woodland grass for groups of cows with young calves at foot, with a wary old cow in the lead, as her daughters and their offspring trailed along. The moment they smelt us they galloped off like startled deer. Young bulls stayed with the cow groups until a year or two old, but as they matured, and their colour changed from a russet brown to jet black, they moved away, sometimes in bachelor groups but mostly as large solitary bulls with territories dotted around and between the cows. The bulls were aggressive if they found us at close range, but their eyesight was poor. Staying still and downwind they rarely spotted us.

We learned how to place ourselves downwind of approaching mobs, who grazed towards us while we stood like immobile trees, sometimes completely in the open as the cows moved past. At a critical point an eddy of breeze would carry our scent, up would go their heads and off they would run. The best time to observe was late afternoon and early morning, with them lying up in shady jungle patches in the heat of the day.

Gradually we evolved a routine of cattle spotting early and late and hours of fishing or leisure in the heat of the day. Five days passed as our explorations and observations continued. We discovered this valley of cattle to the west ran north to the coast. Here it merged into a shallow paperbark swamp a mile inland from the sea, frequented by hundreds of pigs. During the morning of the crocodile day we tried and failed to run down a sucker pig for roast pig dinner. We thought it would make a good change from our tinned meat and fish diet. Late that morning we went to the coast to fish. We decided the name Danger Point probably referred to the number of sharks in the water. While we could often hook small fish for dinner, landing them was hard. Almost always the flapping fish became shark food, often just a small piece of head remaining on the line, sometimes the fish coming in on the line inside the shark.

This midday was spent fishing. We caught a shark about three feet long, full of mature babies which swam away when removed from the mother's belly. Charlie was holding the jaws of its cut-off head when they snapped shut and caught the end of his finger. Lots of blood from the jagged gash, then a covering bandage, as we laughed at the sharks final revenge. With no bath for five days we considered a quick dip off the rocks in a shallow spot where the water was only two feet deep. We abandoned this idea when an eight foot tiger shark cruised under our feet in the place we were contemplating. Later, at low tide, we found a shallow sea pool, separated from the ocean by a sand bar, a bare 18 inches deep. Here we had a sea water wash then spent an hour feasting on oysters from the rocks, huge, incredibly fresh and in unlimited profusion.

As the hot afternoon waned we decided to head off and look for cattle or perhaps a pig for dinner. We started our bikes and headed south across the dry grass plain, until we came to the forest edge where we had seen the swamp full of pigs that morning. We parked our bikes on the edge of the plain, near where a tidal creek joined the sea. Following between the grassy edge of the swamp and the creek we headed inland. The tidal creek disappeared into an indistinct watercourse in the grassy plain, with occasional small stagnant pools.

Suddenly, opening before us, was a beautiful little pool of fresh water, perhaps ten yards long and two thirds as wide. We were approaching from the grassy plain side. We noticed there were fresh pig tracks near the water's edge. We heard the pigs run away on our approach, now no sign now remained, except fresh hoof marks indented in the soft mud. They had come almost to the edge of the water for a drink before our approach frightened them away.

We were almost at the water when two bubbles popped up a few feet out from the edge, a pocket of decaying swamp grass releasing its gas, so I thought. My mind also recorded, almost in the abstract, that there were no birds here or other bush signs or noises I normally associated with a little billabong. I guess my mind also said, "Well the pigs probably scared them away". However, with the sight of this beautiful pool of fresh water that we could almost jump across, and our salt and sweat encrusted bodies, neither Charlie or I thought of anything else except a cool, clean bath.

The side we were on had a gradual entrance to the water through swampy grass. Directly opposite was a vegetation free earth bank, about six feet high, sloping steeply to the water, and a couple trees growing at water's edge.

We agreed it would be best to backtrack, come round to the opposite side, and go in there. A minute or two later we emerged from the scrub, at the top of the bank on this side of the pool, and stripped off. Another bubble of two came up, more rotting vegetation or perhaps a fish moving about?

Charlie was about to dive in. I said; "Don't, there may be tree branches under water, wait for me to check. I will go in, feel around with my feet, and tell you if it's OK" (I remembered a person had broken their neck diving into Mudginberri billabong like that).

So Charlie stood on the bank and waited. I waded in, up to my chest, feeling with my arms and legs to both sides. I swam out a couple metres from the edge where the water was well over my head. Still no obstacles, just a foot of rotting vegetation on the bottom that squelched under my feet and released more gas pockets. Happy all was clear I headed back towards the edge.

I began to climb the bank moving from chest to waist deep water as I stepped forward. The words "I've checked, it's all clear, come in," were rolling off my tongue, when, with no warning, my right leg, trailing behind me, was seized and shaken, as if in a mighty vice. The water behind me boiled.

In that instant I knew what it was and why I should have known before.

I yelled to Charlie, poised to dive. "Crocodile, stop, go back," just in time to arrest his movement. Fortunately the forward momentum of me and crocodile kept me moving up the bank. I remember looking behind at the thrashing water for perhaps two seconds, as I pulled one way and the crocodile began to pull the other way, thinking, as the adrenalin surged, "I've got to get out of here".

No time for real fear and no pain, just the sense of my leg trapped and squashed in a huge vice, while all the time being violently shaken and tugged at by some huge animal.

Suddenly I was free, running forwards up the bank, and then standing, facing a slightly perplexed Charlie, on the flat ground at the top of the bank.

The water was instantly still. Charlie said, "Well did it get you or what"?

I, with numb leg, said "I think so."

I turned my leg around so we both could see. Charlie said "Oh Jeez" and rolled his eyes. There, where the smooth skin of my calf had been, was a gaping mass of red muscle with a jagged eight inch tear, running from mid-calf to just above the ankle. A liberal coating of billabong mud and only a few small trickles of blood.

I joked weakly, "Your finger bled better with a shark bite." As we looked more closely we could see several other tooth marks and puncture wounds in various places on my ankle and foot.

Charlie said, "Can you walk or do I need to carry you?" Apart from a dull ache my leg felt fine, just a bit numb. Otherwise I was a bit light headed but felt elated at my escape.

I said, "I think I can walk OK".

"Come on then" said Charlie, so we made our way back the couple hundred yards to the motorbikes. The back of my leg seemed fine and everything worked OK. Underneath my foot was sore where a couple puncture marks were.

Five minutes later we were at the bikes. Charlie found a water bottle with clean water to wash my leg. As he poured this on, suddenly, all the numb nerves came to life. With a surge of pain, I pulled my leg away and told him to stop. Instead I puffed antibiotic powder into the holes, took a mega dose of antibiotic tablets from our first aid kit, wrapped a bandage round my calf, put on my heavy leather boots, and pulled on jeans to protect my leg.

Charlie started the bikes and loaded gear for our departure.

We knew there was a road camp about 20 miles south, at the bottom of Danger Point peninsula, where a team was working towards us upgrading the road from wheels tracks to gravel highway.

There was fading daylight for another half hour, so we headed off together. After a couple miles my leg got sorer and the riding got harder. It was obvious I could not keep up so it was up to Charlie to continue to the camp ahead while I followed along, on my bike, as best I could manage. Charlie surged forward and I struggled on for a few more miles. In the near dark the road was getting hard to see and there were now lots of obstacles where the partially formed road was littered with unearthed loose rocks and tree stumps.

When it was almost dark I ran into a fallen tree trunk lying across the road and stalled the bike. My foot was throbbing. It was beyond me to balance on my bad leg while I kicked the starter pedal with my good leg to get it going again. The other way round was even worse as every attempt to kick with my bad leg generated a stab of pain under my foot. After several unsuccessful attempts I gave up and lay down next to the bike to wait until someone came. An hour or two passed while I kept company with my throbbing leg.

My only clear memory is that the 50 odd oysters I had eaten mid-afternoon, along with the sea salt gave me a powerful thirst and kept repeating their oyster taste.

Eventually headlights, then a four wheel drive came. A cold beer that tasted so good, and Charlie telling me he had somehow negotiated another 15 miles of obstacle track in the dark and got help. A couple of burly road workers were with him. They lifted and propped me in the Toyota, my leg supported as best possible. Another hour of slow careful driving, and we were back at camp, another beer and some pain killing tablets to take the edge of the pain.

The boot was congealed onto my foot in a mass of dried blood. Eventually, with a combination of soaking and cutting, it was removed. Another attempt to clean the wounds, caked with a combination of mud, dust and dried blood. It instantly lifted my pain from moderate to excruciating. I told them I was a vet, and had already taken a dose and put antibiotics in the wounds. Now it was best left alone until I got to a doctor, my cop out to avoid further pain. So the wounds were coated with more antibiotic and bandaged up, while I took another dose of the antibiotic tablets, to keep the germs at bay.

I had a tolerable night's sleep. Next morning they radioed Darwin for the flying doctor to collect me from the airstrip at Smiths Point a couple hours' drive away. I arrived in Darwin in the aeroplane at lunchtime and was taken by ambulance to Darwin hospital. My leg was twice its normal size and beginning to get smelly, so the doctors, after a quick look sent me to theatre to open up all the holes and scrub out the muck.

I awoke, late afternoon, leg encased in white. A resident doctor told me that they had to cut away a fair bit of rotten muscle and were worried about my leg getting gangrene, but that otherwise I was fine and very lucky to be alive.

Lots of media, well-wishers, family and friends; arrived, all wanting to know what happened. Some nurses suggested I should sell my story to the papers, others said I should go and buy a lottery ticket. I thought I had well used up my quota of luck already. If the media wanted to talk to me that was fine but it wasn't much of a story. 'Idiot local, should have known better, going for a swim in a billabong where a croc was waiting for pig dinner' and 'No, I did not want someone going out there to shoot the crocodile that bit me. It was just being a crocodile, and I was heartily glad not to have been its dinner.'

Over the next few days the doctors were perplexed at some of the bugs they grew out of my leg. I asked to have a look at the lab reports, and sure enough many were the same germs we found in the mouths of snakes and other reptiles at Taronga Zoo, plus a few new ones which specialised in billabong mud. Most were not sensitive to the antibiotics being used, but with some rigorous, if painful dressing, it was getting better regardless.

It puzzled me that cleaning the big holes on the back of my leg only hurt moderately, whereas one small round hole on the top of my foot was torture. When my foot healed I realised that, beyond this tooth hole the sensation to the top of my foot ended. Whether it was the tooth, or the cleansing surgery that cut the nerve I don't know. Every time they dressed it, packing the hole with fresh gauze and tearing it out again, those cut nerves sent a message to my brain, through a laughing gas haze. That sensation is burnt there still.

There were official inquiries from officers of the Conservation Commission who examined my leg from all angles and took photos. I had a row of teeth marks down both sides of my calf and ankle with a gap of 1½ to 2½ inches between each tooth hole. They estimated this equated to a 12-14 foot crocodile. I told them I did not know, because I had not seen it, but their estimate felt about right for size, based on the power of the bite. No one doubted I would have been dinner if the crocodile had got a better grip.

The X-ray of my ankle showed that the tooth opposite the big wound on my calf had punched through my tibia leg bone. It seems while one tooth locked into bone, the opposite tooth was in muscle, which tore. When the crocodile felt my leg slipping it opened its mouth and lunged forward for a second bite. My momentum propelled me up the bank while its pulling took it backwards. Its last lunge left a second set of teeth marks which were little more than grazes on the very end of my foot, but showed how close it had come again.

The bank was too steep for it to readily come after me, so it just settled back to the bottom to wait for its next pig dinner. Being a patient crocodile it did not mind waiting. If not that day, then the next day, or the next again, a new dinner would have come along.

I think the reason for the delay in attacking me was that it had first positioned itself for a pig coming from the other side of the billabong. It waited there for a while to see whether this pig would come back before it turned around to try for the new group of 'human' pigs coming from the other side. The few bubbles were probably its tell-tale movements as it positioned itself.

A month later, after a second lot of surgery to close up all the holes, I was back in Oenpelli, hobbling around on a pair of crutches, getting some movement back into my ankle which was seized up with the scarring to the back of my calf. Aboriginal friends coined a new name as they waved and laughed about my escape. I was Ngakinga, 'crocodile leg', which they call me still.

Charlie, who scored the job of packing up our camp, had already returned to Sydney so we could not exchange yarns. I think his was the worst part, more frightening to be a watcher, than for me with no time to be frightened.

I have been left with a sense of wonder at my miraculous escape and an understanding that life is too precious to waste on things that don't matter. But I have never been haunted by bad dreams or what might have been's.

On occasions my kids say, "Bet you don't know my Dad's been bit by a crocodile! It's a conversation stopper.

For many years an offered oyster brought back the memory of waiting, thirsty, with oysters, for rescue. Now even that is gone. Oysters taste just as good, though rarely as sweet and fresh as the Coburg ones were.

Return to the NT

After my crocodile close encounter I returned to the NT to work. I loved zoo animal work but missed the NT's wide open spaces, and the odd assortment of people who gave it part of its soul. My zoo work made clear to me that, while working with wild animals would always be something that fascinated me, my strongest love was being within the broad landscapes of the NT, with its wealth of wildlife across a vast bush, rather than working in a zoo, where animals were living in a human made construct.

My taste of station life in Katherine also gave me the wish to continue to experience this life across the breadth of the NT. So I rang my old boss in Darwin, the Chief Veterinary Officer, and asked if a job was going.

He said; yes there was still a job for me, though now in Alice Springs. So Alice Springs was my new home for the next two years on the properties in and around its ranges, extending out to the eastern and western deserts. I also spent periods working across most of the other regions before moving to Darwin to work. Some of my NT work and people experiences follow, beginning when I first returned from Melbourne.

Working in Katherine

My first job as a vet in Katherine was to go to Larrimah, a place on the Stuart Highway 160 kilometres south of Katherine. The night before was spent in the Mataranka Pub where Bluey Lunn and John Kerin, the two local stock inspectors, introduced me around as the greenhorn vet.

John warned me about a savage dog that was tied up out the back. Its range on the lead allowed it to fly out into the path of unsuspecting drinkers who made their way past to the toilet and attach to a leg. He told me I should give it a wide berth. I heeded his advice. However, an hour or two later, and some beers and rums further along, John forgot his own advice.

A yelp, squeal and curse rang out. The dog had sunk its teeth into part of John's leg. Fortunately, boot and jeans minimised the damage, but not his temper. He came back in and confronted the dog owner, saying, "If your dog ever tries to bite me again, I will blow his brains out."

The rest of the drinkers shrugged and continued on with their drinking, situation normal in an NT outback bar. Three days later we returned, and had another similar round of drinks. The dog was still there, and when John went out to relieve himself there was another yelp and curse. This time, after a minute elapsed, it was followed by a loud boom. John walked in, holding his revolver, saying. "I warned you. That's one dog that won't ever bite anyone again."

Next morning we went on to Larrimah, the place where the attempt to build a railway to Alice Springs from the north had been abandoned. In the old railway yards they had assembled a mob of rangy shorthorn cattle from the local station for me to TB test. The yards were old sharp edged rusty iron, less than safe for cattle or workers but it was an easy job and we were done by lunch time and retired to the Larrimah Hotel bar to wash off the dust.

At the bar the publican asked me if I could sort out his bitch, she had just reached an age where all the male dogs were getting interested and he did not want pups. I told him I was happy to do the bush version, and would bring the gear to do it on my next visit, but if her wanted sterile surgery he should take his dog to Katherine or Darwin for a better job, like I would have done a month before in Melbourne. He replied that if she got pregnant he would shoot her anyway, so the bush way would be fine.

I returned after three days to finish the TB test. Once my cattle work was done I gave the dog some long acting anaesthetic and set to work, using the bar top as my surgery table. Every time I put down the instruments to wipe the sweat off my face a beer was pushed in front of me, which slowed progress. My helpers were half a dozen other drinkers who offered free advice.

In an hour the job was done. The dog was put in a quiet corner to recover while I finished my second beer in peace. The dog made a good recovery and lived to a ripe old age, more than can be said for its Mataranka mate.

I remember three trips I made to Bulloo River, home of the Henderson family. The first trip I made was the wet season of early 1980, pre crocodile. I got a message, over the radio telephone, that Bulloo River needed a vet to castrate some horses. I was a bit surprised, most stations did this themselves.

So I made my way to Timber Creek, 300 kilometres west of Katherine, where I was to meet Charlie Henderson, property owner and former American Airforce fighter pilot, at the airstrip. Charlie loaded me and my vet gear into his small plane and we zoomed off. We followed the course of the Victoria River north; Charlie pointing out local geography, property boundaries, scrub bulls and crocodiles. We flew just above tree top height, with occasional quick jumps and swerves to avoid low hills and follow the river's curve.

Charlie thought he had an NT rawhide on his hands. It was clear he intended to give me a few free thrills. However I told Charlie I grew up in Arnhem Land, had been in little planes all my life, and that my Dad did lots of similar flying. So with that he decided I was OK.

He even knew Dad's aeroplane call sign and told me that he too flew meat from his mobile abattoirs to aboriginal communities in the area, similar to what happened in Arnhem Land.

I spent a two days helping Charlie's three daughters, Marlee, Bonny and Danielle, do the horse work. They were competent horse women but needed some veterinary direction, after which they did it all themselves. Each evening the family and all guests would all dress for dinner and, in the manner of people of substance, sit around the dinner table exchanging polite conversation. It was such a contrast from the rest of the station, once out of the couple square miles of station homestead facilities there was barely a yard, fence, road or anything else that made up a normal station, just miles of bush full of wild cattle.

The second trip was next dry season trip when I had to TB test some cattle. Having flown to Bulloo River from Timber Creek in 20 minutes and looking on the map which showed it was about 50 miles by road from Timber Creek, I thought I was in for an easy drive. I called local stock inspector, Bluey Lewis, on the radio to check directions. His directions were something like this. "You turn north, onto the Auvergne Road, ten ks west of Timber Creek, on the highway. Go left past the Auvergne turnoff and it will take you two hours from there."

My reply, "But it is only 50 miles from Timber Creek."

His gravelly reply, "It will still take you two hours."

I covered the first ten kilometres west on the bitumen in less than ten minutes and then headed up a graded dirt road across the open plain towards Auvergne, covering the second ten kilometres in about the same time. I thought, *this is easy, only 60 kilometres to go. I am sure it won't be that bad*. Gradually I closed the gap on a red escarpment that rose sheer before me, thinking, *There must be a gorge somewhere here for the road to go through*. Closer and closer, still no gap anywhere in sight.

At last I can make out a set of wheel tracks going straight up the mountain, at what looks like a 45 degree angle; I realise that is the road!

With all four wheels of the Landcruiser spinning on the loose rock and gravel in low range four wheel drive, the vehicle finally gained the top. Down again, weaving through trees, crossing sand patches, washouts, bull dust holes and small creeks. Up, down, around, backwards, forwards, dodge washout, go bush for a fallen tree, put into low range for the tenth time for another broken up sandy creek crossing. It was hard to imagine they actually hauled scrub bulls out of here on a cattle truck.

I finally emerged from the timber for the last kilometre's drive to the station, across open paddocks, enjoying the fact I had finally got the Toyota out of second gear for more than 50 metres. As I stepped out, enjoying the absence of steering wheel twisting and vibration, I looked at my watch. Sure enough, the two hours had elapsed since I saw the jump-up 60 kilometres ago.

I did my days work. In the late afternoon I got directions to the Bulloo River, a tributary of the mighty Victoria River where, within five minutes, I pulled out a six pound barramundi. I took it back to the station for dinner. Another civilised night's conversation and a return trip where I relived every twist and turn, arriving in Timber Creek just in time for an ice cold lunchtime beer, to wash out the bulldust. I redid it all on the third day to read my TB tests.

My third trip was about 18 months later. I had just recovered from the crocodile, with the scars still bright red on my leg. I was doing a brief stint in Katherine before going to work in Alice Springs. Again the radio-phone call from Charlie, another veterinary problem, cause no longer remembered. Even though the road might have still been open despite early wet season rain, I did not argue when Charlie suggested he collect me by plane from Timber Creek.

Another day of work and another civilised dinner, over which the conversation turned to crocodile encounters. Charlie, in his broad Yankee drawl; "Well I hear a gator almost ate ya, is that the mark on your leg. Yeah, well did you go back after and blow the big lizard out of the water? What, you just let it go? Bjeez, there's no way I'd let a gator do that to me and get away".

I begged to differ, but I'd slipped a couple notches in Charlie's estimation.

Next day, as he flew me back to Timber Creek, his parting words were: "Boy, if that was my leg, I'd go find that big ol croc and give him a third eye right between the other two, so you go find it and give it one from Charlie," all said with a flashing eye and a half grin.

With that he gave he jumped back aboard his little plane, gave a wave and roared off into the sky, a wiggle of its wings as it soared out of view, the indomitable old fighter ace to the last.

I never did revisit the croc and I never saw Charlie again, but when I heard he'd died a year later I felt the world had lost a little colour in his passing. In true Charlie fashion he had lived with style and gone out in style. Many other places in the remotest NT and its characters crowd my memories of this era. The people, often larger than life, in their many shapes and sizes, lived hard and many died young, enriching memories in their passing. I still feel lucky to have grown up in this place and amongst them.

Another station visit from Katherine, around the same time, was to Mary River Station about 50 kilometres east of Pine Creek, on the old Oenpelli Rd. One quiet wet season day, when Katherine was sweltering, pushing 40 degrees centigrade and 100 percent humidity, waiting for an afternoon storm, I was sitting in the respite of an air-conditioned office when I received a message.

Mary River Station needs a vet. The owner's horse has been shot by an arrow. Graham, can you talk to them on the radio-telephone and see if you can get out there this afternoon. The station owner's mother-in-law's voice came through, amid static crackles, on the radio-telephone. I could just make out that the station owner and his wife had gone to Darwin for the day, the mother-in-law was left in charge, and now her daughter's favourite pony had been shot with an arrow, which was still stuck in it.

Could I urgently get out there and remove the arrow before the owner came back, or there would be hell to pay. So in the early afternoon I set out on the hour and a half drive to the station, following directions off the Oenpelli Rd, crossing a tributary of the Mary River with about two feet of fresh water flowing over the crossing and getting there about three pm.

I was soon told what had happened. A young ringer (stock-hand) had been to town the previous day and bought a bow and some arrows. After he had done his morning's stock work he had gone down to the back paddock with his bow. He had loosed off an arrow into the air, in a direction where there was nothing in sight. The arrow came back to ground 100 yards away, behind a patch of scrubby trees. Immediately after the arrow's descent the favourite pony of the owner's wife came galloping out from behind these trees, arrow embedded in its neck. The ringer panicked but finally managed to catch the horse. He calmed it enough to try and pull the arrow out. He could not budge it from a now fractious horse. He only succeeded in snapping off the shaft and leaving the arrow head embedded.

I anaesthetised the horse. A quick cut took the arrow head out. I packed the wound and stitched it up. Ten minutes later the pony was back on its feet, not much worse for wear. We all retired to the house veranda for a cup of tea, with a very grateful mother in law and arrow shooter.

I was long gone before the owner, Alan Fisher, and his wife, Sherrie, returned. However I met him about a year later when I was called out to TB test some buffalo a few months after my crocodile encounter. I still had a limp and Alan had his leg in a plaster cast, from a bull catching injury, though he was running around in the stock yard working as normal. We compared notes about our gammy legs. I told him about my last visit and the arrow.

He roared laughing, saying, "I don't think that ringer ever used his bow again, though it was all hushed up by the time I got home."

Alan had grown up with his brothers on Mary River. They cut their teeth learning how to tail throw buffalo bulls from horseback. Alan described, "You rode up behind one, jumped off and grabbed the tail, with a quick flick to throw the bull off balance. Then you tied up its legs – simple really". It was all a matter of timing, but you did not want to miss on the first go or you had a buffalo horn in your ribs. But he reckoned overall it was safer than using a metal bull catcher as he had never broken a leg that way.

A memorable character of the Katherine District was Bill Tapp of Killarney Station, on the VRD road down near Top Springs. Bill was a big man of legendary drinking prowess, who also had a big stutter. His station was well named after that beautiful Irish town, nestled among lakes and mountains. It was dead flat with stunted scrubby trees and barely a dried out waterhole, let alone a lake. However it had a magnificent homestead, which was reached after opening and shutting innumerable gates. Most were of the best bushman's wire design but gradually, as you moved closer to the station, the gates got flasher. In the last mile the gates were swung from white picket posts and rails.

The station was about 1000 square miles with about 20,000 cattle, mostly shorthorn scrubbers, but the home paddocks had a magnificent Brahman herd, a quarter-horse stud and an assortment of other valuable livestock.

Whenever Bill rang, to book me for work, the call would come through on the radio telephone with the staccato sound of Bill's stutter amongst the radio static. "B-B-B-Bill here. B-b-before you come c-c-c-could you c-c-call at E-E-E-E-

Elders (the stock and station agent) and g-g-g-get m-me, and Bill would proceed to read out a shopping list that often took ten or fifteen minutes to transcribe amongst the stutters and crackles. Then two or three hours was spent driving around town to collect everything before finally departing with a heavily loaded Toyota for the 300 kilometre trip out to the station.

But the hospitality was first class so I never begrudged Bill a couple hours of my time to do this. While Bill was a formidable man who could put fear into a 'useless ringer', he had a kind soul. Driving to Katherine, should he hit a bird, which happened on many trips, he would always stop to render it first aid, showing remorse for these casualties to his car.

Near Killarney was a famous visiting place, Ma Hawk's roadhouse at Top Springs. Her meanness was legendary. At first I thought these tales were merely malicious. On frequent drives from Katherine to Wave Hill and Camfield Stations for TB testing in 1980, it was the only real stopping point in the 450 km trip, so I would often stop for a cold beer or two.

After a couple of visits it emerged I was a vet. So I was booked for my next visit to treat her dog's bad ears. A quick glance showed the dog had ears full of hair, wax and untold other muck. Next visit I gave the dog, an old and snappy terrier, an anaesthetic and cleaned out its ears as requested. The bar was my surgery table, while various drinkers looked on.

Once finished, waiting for it to wake up, I announced I was ready for a beer. Ma went to the fridge and took one out. She put it before me and announced its price, no discounts despite my free service.

Norm, assistant barman, was outraged. He said "No way is the vet paying for his beer when he has cleaned out your dog's ears." She grudgingly agreed that this one was on the house.

Each time she left the bar and went out the back, Norm went to the fridge and got me a fresh beer. Finally I had to go on. I only drove a couple hundred yards to a shady tree and pulled out my swag to sleep it off.

I was always warned not to buy my fuel at Top Springs as they ripped you off. I did not really believe this, but did not generally need fuel with my Toyota's two 130 litre fuel tanks. However, one time I had spent a couple weeks in the VRD district, travelling between stations and needed to top up the tanks, one empty and the other half full. By the time I had put 150 litres into one of my 130 litre tanks it was obvious I was being had. So I wrote out the purchase order for 130 litres, not the 150 on the petrol pump meter. Another even more ferocious bout of Ma's muttering and cursing ensued. After that I worked my future trips to avoid fill ups at Top Springs.

The worst example of her behaviour was another occasion when I stopped for a beer, chatting to Norm. An aboriginal man came in to cash his cheque. He handed over a cheque for between $250 and $300 and asked to buy a carton of beer, a carton of smokes and a couple other minor things perhaps in total it was $50-60 at her then prices. She served him, placing his goods on the bar counter, then she handed him a handful of wadded up notes and coins which she told him was his change. It looked like quite a bit of money though its value was not apparent. She obviously did not expect him to challenge her counting.

However, unlike most of his uneducated or illiterate cousins, this man was different. Perhaps he had been burnt before. Without removing his handful of change from the bar he placed it down and proceeded to unroll the notes and sort out the coins, until it was all spread out, in total adding up to about $60, at least $100 short of what he might expect. He politely said, "I gave you a cheque for XXX and I bought goods for YY and you have only given me this change.

Such a look of outrage came over her face. "You dirty black, you took some money away, how dare you accuse me," and so the nasty rant went. Norm, another drinker and myself, had observed it all. We agreed he had never taken the money off the bar and yes, he was short. So with the worst grace possible she refunded the rest of the money, banging it on the bar as she mumbled away. No doubt she had done this many times before, unchallenged.

Ma Hawk died about a year later, after I had left Katherine and gone to work at Western Plains Zoo. When the police came to deal with her death, it was said they found a box full of old banknotes, to a value of many tens of thousands of dollars, hidden amongst her possessions.

The story I heard was that these policemen officially declared finding part of this money but decided to keep the balance for their own benefit. All would have been well except that one buried his stash in his back yard. His dog dug it up and there were all these notes blowing around in the wind which others found. The source emerged and his police career came to a sudden end.

Working in Katherine I had to work closely with a unique breed of public servants, the NT Stock Inspectors. Most had previously worked as ringers and head stockmen. Many had also been station managers. They were a tough breed. It was said, in the early days, that any stock inspector who could not fight enough to beat the head stockman would not last long.

Kevin Paterson was the Senior Stock Inspector for Katherine, and came from this legacy. He was a big man, though years of hard living and drinking had softened his appearance. His reputation as a very tough, ferocious boxer, who in his early days had fought in national championship fights, still survived.

I was testing a mob of young shorthorn heifers, with a splash of Brahman, on Innesvale Station, about 100 kilometres west of Katherine. In order to identify tested animals they had ear tags applied. The heifers, not much more than scrubbers until mustered, were young, and fizzy. Many had short spiky horns with sharp tips. The cattle race into which they were loaded was far from good for testing them. They were small and it was wide, allowing them to run up and down, climb over each other and otherwise fling themselves around.

My job was the easy part; I only had to get to the tail end for a TB injection. Kevin drew the job of applying tags to these slightly mad animals, right next to their pointy horns. In his big meaty hands he held a pair of ear-tagging pliers. He would grab his chance to punch through the tags in one swift movement. But some animals would duck their heads, meaning reaching down inside the rails. One of these times, when he reached in, another spiky horned heifer came crashing through, droving her sharp horn into his hand trapped against the rail.

The rest of us could not really see what happened but 'Patto' let out a small grunt, withdrew his hand and changed the pliers to the other hand. He tucked the first hand under his arm and went on working, an intense look on his face.

Asking "Are you all right?" drew a grunt. He continued on working until the race full was done.

As the cattle were let out of the race I finally got him to show me his hand. "Ah it's not much," he said. He showed me a palm with a big hole, where the horn had gone almost right through and out the other side. All he would let me do was put some antibiotic powder and a bandage on. Then he worked with his other hand for two hours until finished. Later, pulled up under a shady tree for a coldie, before driving home he admitted, 'it's a bit sore – but nothing that a drink won't fix.'

Another memory of Katherine was my first trip out to the Gulf with Geoff Beere, a stock inspector who also had his meat inspector's ticket. We needed to check out the Macarthur River meatworks for some problem, no longer remembered. When our day's work was done Geoff, who had worked here before, gave me a guided tour of the local sights. A hidden jewel was Betsy Springs, a creek that fed into the Macarthur River, with a continuous flow of dry season water bubbling out of the ground and running along the creek, atop a red hillside, until it reached a waterfall where it plunged into clear water in a large pool below. It was spectacular scenery and, after a swim at the bottom, Geoff led me up a path that brought us to the cliff edge alongside the falls above. I did not know how high it was but it looked a long way, perhaps sixty or seventy feet, certainly a good bit more than my highest dives off the ten metre platform of a swimming pool.

Geoff said to me, with a wink and a nudge, "OK off you go!"

I shook my head, "You must be joking, I am not jumping off there, it's way too high. What about you?"

He shrugged but said, "No, never again. Last year I came here with some meatworkers, after a day in the works. I said to them, 'Who is going in?'

"Next thing I knew they had all jumped off and I was up there all alone.

"I knew I had to follow them or I would never live it down, the meat inspector who turned chicken. So I jumped in and it almost killed me, the water was so hard. It felt like I was given an enema and landed on rocks. But I lived to tell the tale so don't let me stop you." Still I shook my head!

My year in Katherine passed quickly and at the end of it I went off to learn how to become a zoo vet. I had loved this place of wide spaces and different people but it was time to follow another interest and see where it led.

Working in Alice Springs

Living and working in Alice Springs after my crocodile encounter was a new experience. It shared NT culture and spirit, but was a world away from the Top End. The Alice is closer and more joined to Adelaide for its business than to distant Darwin, close to a thousand miles north.

My first impression was a landscape that looked, smelt and felt like a different planet. It was red in all its infinite hues ranging from softest pastels of pink-orange salmon gum bark and shaded gorges to iridescent glowing reds of the rocky ranges in the afternoon sun. I had not really understood the term 'red heart' but red was everywhere; red dirt, red sand, red hills, red sunset skies, extending from horizon to horizon. The red was offset by grey-green mulga, pale gold grass, white ghost gums and a myriad of other subtle shades, under the relentless blue desert sky.

Stations were generally small in NT terms, more prosperous with better, fatter cattle which thrived on the short desert grasses when rain came. With the train line to Adelaide there was a good outlet to markets. Most stations were family owned. Their hospitality was legend, along with the quality of the beef they served. Prime cuts from a fat bullock would be hung from a mulga tree, in the dry desert air for days, until a black crust formed which sealed and protected it against the birds and flies. As the days went by the meat tenderised and the flavour grew richer. After five to seven days an inch thick slab of this steak, seared on a steel plate over a stock camp fire, was to die for.

There were also desperate and hopeless blocks, with little more than sand and spinifex, where a living was hard to make. Then there were the years when almost no rain came, and instead dust darkened skies heralded false storms.

The centre of the district was the town of Alice Springs, a bustling regional centre of 20,000 plus people, nestled in the McDonnell Ranges. Moving away the landscape transitioned, ever further out, into massive ringing deserts, the Simpson to the south and east, the Tanami to the north and west, the low spinifex ridges of the Sandover system and southern Barkly's to the north east and the Great Sandy Desert of Western Australia at its western extremity.

Yuendumu is an aboriginal community about 300 kilometres north-west of Alice on the road to the Tanami Desert. It had its own cattle herd, which I tested progressively as they were mustered over several months, under a loose arrangement with the manager, Bill McKell. Dates were a bit elastic as it depended on having enough aboriginal men in the stock camp to do a bush muster and sometimes his stock camp would go on walkabout. When they had cattle in small holding paddocks they would call me to come out in a day or two, sure they would have a mob ready to test. I would drive out in the evening and camp near the cattle yards. Next morning, at a leisurely pace, the stock camp arrived to begin work. Testing days were happy community events with half the children sitting on the top rail, watching and laughing. If they started to scream too loudly an old aboriginal stockmen would shout or wave a stick at them until they settled down or ran off to play.

Testing was proceeding well and I was up to my fifth mob when the Yuendumu Sports Day came along. This time they mustered the cattle into the stockyards and, the night before, I drove out to begin work next morning. As morning dawned it was obvious that the cattle were no longer in the stockyards. Some cheeky kids had let them out in the night. Not to worry, they were only in the holding paddock, less than one kilometre square. Two or three men on horses could muster them back in half an hour, or so I thought. No one in the community shared my priority. After an hour or two of inquiry no stockmen were interested, and there were no other volunteers to assist.

It was football day, with all the aboriginal football teams from far and near gathered to compete. Everyone else was gathered to watch. By mid-morning it was obvious that there would be no mustering or testing that day. So I settled down to watch two days of ferocious football competition and other community events. On the third day the football was over and the stock team returned to work. In half an hour the cattle were mustered. By lunch time my job was done and I was on my way back to Alice Springs.

Amaroo was another station a similar distance to the north east of Alice, out along the Sandover Highway. Amaroo was a good station, having a major flood-out of the Sandover River for its bullock paddock, from which it turned off some of the best bullocks in the Alice.

It sat next to another aboriginal station, Utopia (station of hope for the hopeless), through which the Sandover also ran but from which the good cattle country was conspicuously absent. It had been sold to the local aboriginal community some years previously when, evidently, the former owners realised there was little profit to be had running cattle on spinifex sand-plain, with patches of mixed hard mulga scrub.

Amaroo was owned by the Simpson family of washing machine fame. That they were astute in business was evident. Their store serviced their own and nearby Utopia's aboriginal communities,

Billycans were an item in high demand in these communities, and a solution was to hand. The Simpson store sold large tins of fruit, of perfect billy can size to these aborigines. These people then returned the empty tins to the store. In five minutes a tin opener cut out the tops neatly, pliers smoothed any jagged edges and a piece of fencing wire for a handle created a perfect billycan. Sold back to these same communities again everyone was happy and the money kept circulating around the local community, even if primarily one way.

The Alice was a land of extremes. Some years tropical depressions would spill clouds down from the north-west Kimberley and we would get buckets of rain, other years there would be barely enough rain to settle the dust for a couple days.

The first year I was in Alice Springs it was dry with a lot of hungry cattle. Brumbies perished as waterholes in the ranges went dry for the first time in more than a decade. Seeing, first hand, these starving dehydrated horses standing around an empty waterhole, digging in vain for vanished water until too weak to stand, convinced me that shooting horses, before they died of thirst and starvation in droughts, was a kind act. Animal welfare groups wanting to protect the brumbies viewed from city TV screens did not see this.

The next year, 1983, was opposite with 20 inches of rain in February and March. The Todd River was in flood three times in two months. The Todd and other rivers begin in ranges east and west of Alice. Then they run out into low lying desert areas where they form massive swamps, which slowly dry back over ensuing months. Their lushness after this rain was incredible; waist high grasses, forbs and herbs like verbine and bluebush, prolific. Wildlife flourished; waterbirds on swamps, finches and budgies by thousands on the grass plains.

Cattle would move into these swamps, where they would just stand and eat, then eat some more and some more and grow fat. A year after the rain out they would come, at a waddle, some of the fattest bullocks I have ever seen, emerging as the areas dried out. Another year later all life would be gone. In the place of four foot high green herbage all that remained was bare ground, dust and a few stunted shrubs, waiting for more water and life to return.

In the ranges north and east of Alice Springs were some of my favourite places on Ambalindum and Garden Stations. At the edge of towering ranges and gorges were permanent springs and waterholes, frequented by cattle, many never mustered. They had grown big, fat and wild on the mountain valley pastures. A big effort was underway to bring these properties and their stock to hand, in order to eradicate TB. In these rough valleys with lots of permanent water, helicopters were required to get the wild cattle out. Once out in the open valleys controlled paddocks were built to test young heifers and cows into. Mustering was often done into coacher mobs, but the big wild bullocks and bulls were mustered in whatever way they could be and sent off to the meatworks.

As well as cattle these ranges were full of horses. Post graduate student, David Berman, camped much of the time on the Garden while he studied them. To accurately track these horses and understand about their movements and impact on the land, he needed to fit radio collars to a selection of animals. He approached me, as a vet, to assist with the capture of the wild brumbies.

We selected suitable drugs used for darting big game in Africa, and set off for the Garden, with dart gun and other darting equipment. Dave already knew of many horse mobs and where they came and went. He had studied watering points, finding locations where they drank regularly with nearby trees.

So we placed ourselves in overlooking trees and waited for mobs to come in. We wanted to dart the stallions as we believed the mares in the mob would stay near while their stallion was immobilised, allowing him to re-join his mob.

As with things new and untested we were not really sure how it would go. After an hour or two sitting in a tree a mob of horses came walking below for a drink. A quick sighting and the dart gain was discharged. The stallion ran off with a dart protruding from its rump. It had only gone 20 yards when its knees began to buckle. Next thing it was down, us sitting astride to bolt the leather strap holding the radio-collar around its neck. Minutes later it staggered back to its feet and soon ran off to join its mob, now with a slightly wobbly gait and an appendage around its neck; which emitted a clear audible beep on our tracking device every few seconds.

It seemed so easy, and quick, different from my zoo experience where it typically took ten minutes for the dart to take effect. It was too good to be true; the first dart must have gone straight into a vein in the rump, leading to an intravenous injection effect. It never worked so well again.

Many hours were spent following darted, slightly staggering horses over long distances before a chance finally came to jump on and try to restrain. Sometimes the horse jumped up and ran away on our close approach, other times the mares seemed determined to keep the stallion awake and walking, through pushes and nudges, until it got away. Sometimes there was no visible effect, perhaps the dart did not work properly and the horse disappeared with our dart in its rump, presumably it fell out over the next few days.

However Dave persevered and gradually built up a good collection of these stallions with collars. He would spend his nights out in the bitterly cold Alice Springs winter tracking his horses' movements over many hours.

Sometimes I came along and marvelled at his endurance on sub-zero nights while the rest of us froze and shivered. After one long cold night out, I crawled out of my swag next morning, well after sun up. It seemed pretty cold and the idea of a hot cup of tea was good, so I threw a couple logs on last night's smouldering campfire embers. As the fire burst to life I went to get some water in the billy can from my vehicle's water tank. Nothing came out of the tap. I had filled it before leaving Alice, so it must have sprung a leak. There was no sign of water on the ground, so I tapped the tank. It was definitely full. I realised that the water line was frozen solid. The camp thermometer was still a chilly minus six degrees. It was nearly lunch time before the line thawed and water came through the tap.

South-east of the Alice rivers petered out amid the sand-plains and the ever increasing dunes of the Simpson Desert. The desert's western margins held flood-outs and extensive areas of short, desert grass plains. Moving east, into the desert proper, these transitioned into massive north south running dunes continuing for hundreds of kilometres, huge parallel rows of sand a hundred feet high, with desert shrubs, herbs and grasses in between these endless hills.

It was an area of bad TB from early cattle movements. Over the years odd cattle had gone bush, into the desert, from the tame herds of fringe stations; particularly Andado and New Crown stations in the NT and adjoining South Australian properties. Many of these cattle were huge, old and very crafty bullocks, that eked out an existence amongst the sand dunes, coming in for an occasional drink at bores on the desert edges when the hot weather required.

With TB eradication all these wild cattle, moving in and out of the desert, had to go. Just over the border in South Australia was an incredible flowing bore at Purnie. Drilled many years earlier it had blown a gusher, initially shooting water 30 feet into the air as the deep trapped pressure was released. Now, many years and untold millions of litres later, it had subsided into a bubbling flow of a few feet, extending into a long green, oasis like, soak. In good years, for many months after winter rain, a succulent herb called parakeelya grew amidst the desert dunes. Where this grew bullocks got their water with no need to drink. However, after many hot summer days and no rains, eventually they would be forced to come in and drink, particularly at Purnie bore.

These last of these last cattle had learnt all the human tricks and were incredibly cunning. They sneaked in, in the dead of night, for a quick drink before heading out again. Just odd hoof tracks in the soft sand and earth margins revealed their presence. Days were spent camped out waiting for these last few to come in for a final drink. Waiting, hidden, at the margins of these places, finally a big body would move into the cross hairs of a marksman's sights.

Once, at the northern margin of the desert, on Marqua Station, we were picking our way through odd pockets of gidgee scrub, just above the desert edge and finding the last of the last stragglers in a big bush paddock that had been cleaned out. A big fresh hoof print was sighted, another final straggler to be tracked down. We worked our way south carefully scanning each new valley as we crossed the ridge.

Suddenly, there it was, a big black bull standing next to a patch of scrub, perhaps 500 metres away. We slowly drove forward, down into a depression. From here the bull and nearby area disappeared from sight, though we could see all the rising ground behind it. As we emerged back into view perhaps 200 metres from where we had seen it, it had vanished.

We scanned all horizons, nothing. It could not have vanished into the ground, but where? We drove slowly forward until we were only 50 metres from where it had been seen, then 30. Finally Bryan Gill, my stock inspector companion pointed to the patch of scrub just next to where it had been standing, little more than a big scrubby bush, three or four metres across, with low spreading branches. I focused my eyes. There it was, 1000+ pounds of black bull, squatting on its haunches in this oversized bush.

We inched forward until we were barely ten metres away. It did not move a muscle. It was almost too simple to shoot it, bringing the incredible survivor to an end. Who could not respect such a preservation instinct?

At the end of this trip we ran into Soul Anderson from Tobermorey, next station out, isolated on the NT Queensland border at the northern edge of the Simpson Desert, with its flood-outs continuing another 50 miles into the desert.

A story was told of Soul having exchanged a red utility and motorbike for his cousin's girlfriend. This had precedent in an earlier generation when his mother's first husband had disappeared during the first war. The brother had taken his marriage place. When the original husband returned it was decided to leave new arrangements in place in exchange for the brother's prize horse.

Soul was known as a man of many words, very many. Out in the desert there were few to hear them. He arrived mid-morning, as we were packing up camp, about to return on the 500 km drive to the Alice. After he made an initial canvass to us for rum, a cup of tea was accepted. An hour later we tried to get ourselves moving, but Soul wanted to talk. It must have been months since his last visitor. Another hour of chatting followed as we progressively loaded all our last things onto the Toyota and tried to make our excuses. "We really must go if we are to make the six hour drive to Alice before dark," (and our Friday night at the pub after a week out bush).

Still Soul talked and talked and talked, yarn after yarn, many entertaining, with perhaps one word in a hundred from us. In the end we started our Toyota, driving slowly down the road. Soul hooked his arm through the window and walked still talking, alongside, as we slowly drove along. We had to pick up the pace, or he would walk back to Alice with us. Then he was running along with us, no slowdown in the stories. Finally with a combination of winding up the window until he had to take his arm out and driving faster, beyond his running pace, so he could no longer shout through the crack, we made our escape. Poor man, God help his next visitors, he would not let them escape so easily. Perhaps we should have given the pannikin of rum we refused to offer in the first place.

Camels were part of the Alice. A local camel farm just south of the town, and a second one a hundred kilometres further south at Orange Creek, made a steady trade capturing and taming wild camels and organising camel rides. Noel Fullerton from Orange Creek occasionally called me to bleed and test a few camels for interstate or international movements.

The first time I attended he had a camel sitting on its chest, waiting for me to collect a blood sample from its neck. As I casually strolled up to it Noel grabbed me by the arm and pulled me to a halt. "Wait, not so fast young man, these creatures can kick you from sitting with all four legs, and bite you and, if they don't they will blow their guts all over you." (a massive grass covered belch). He then grabbed the camel by the lip and muttered a stream of imprecations against misbehaviour before I was allowed to come alongside to collect a blood sample. Once restrained, collection couldn't have been easier.

After a quick hour of work it was a short drive out for a picnic lunch on the clay-pan of Rainbow Valley. Here a range of low hills eroded into an incredible range of colours, orange, pink, purple and white. After rain the clay-pan filled with water, forming a double silhouette.

One cold, cold, moonlit winter's night I sat there for two long hours, with my camera shutter open, catching a whole new wash of colours in the silvered moonlight, as stars slowly arced across the crystal clear winter sky.

I was also studying bilbies and hare wallabies in captivity, at the Arid Zone Research Institute and here I too would spend long cold nights in their enclosures awaiting their emergence, with my camera and flash to capture their late night behaviour.

For many longer trips from Alice to do cattle work it was faster and more convenient to charter a plane, which could replace five or six hours of driving with an hour in an aircraft. Bad plane trips were rare, though flying over the ranges and desert sand dunes could be turbulent. However I was well used to this and to take offs and landings on bush strips from my father's piloting. Alice Springs often served as a first job for new pilots who had recently qualified and wanted to build up their flying hours before looking for better jobs with the big airlines. Their lack of experience sometimes became apparent.

On one occasion we travelled to Coniston Station in a Cessna 210, similar to the 206 and 207 my father had flown, but with a retractable undercarriage and a much faster cruising speed which was good for the long trips. However its slick, small, three blade propeller did not have the short airstrip grunt of the 206 or 207, with its large 2 blade prop, which could really bite into the air and propel the plane forward.

The Coniston strip looked OK from the air and we landed fine and did our work over a couple hours. In the late morning, much warmer now, it was time to leave and return to the Alice. We returned to the airstrip. It had a slight ridge in the middle, which obscured end to end view, and the trees at the ends of the strip were pretty close. It was not very long, but I had been off shorter strips in a well loaded 206. I assumed the pilot knew what he was doing, so at first I paid little attention. I was aware take-off would be tight on a hot day.

In such situations my father would taxi to the very furthest extremity of the strip and run the engines up towards full power before releasing the brakes, to get off to a flying start. If it got really tight he would hold the plane down and build up maximum speed, then use a sudden jerk on the flaps and control stick to almost 'bounce' the plane into the air and get it flying.

In this case the start of the take-off was relaxed, the plane gradually rolled into take-off position and then the pilot steadily dialled up the power. We had used more than 50 yards of the runway before we were on full power, and the small propeller of the 210 struggled to bite the hot, thin desert air. All too soon we crested the mid strip rise, the far end now rapidly approaching. Our speed seemed to be off what was needed by 10-20 knots. The pilot was getting an anxious strained look.

With 100 yards to go he was past the point of no return, so he eased back on the stick, almost willing the plane to fly. After a tentative lift it started to settle back towards the ground. We were all starting to sweat now, hoping for those extra few knots to get it flying. It laboured along, holding just above the ground. As the end of strip and trees came rushing up we clawed up those last few feet to come clear and suddenly we were up, up and away. It seemed the trees passed but a few feet below us, almost tipping the wheels.

An old, canny helicopter pilot once told me there are bold helicopter pilots and old helicopter pilots but there are no old, bold helicopter pilots. I decided that I would rather fly with the old pilots than the bold pilots who had yet to learn their limits.

Dennis Morgan was the Senior Stock Inspector for the Alice, having taken over from the legendary Naish Ganley. Dennis had spent innumerable years working in and travelling across the Alice District. Sometimes, when we were doing a trip together I would say to him, as we passed some little, unknown side track; "Where does that go Dennis?"

At first one would think he had not heard. Then, after his mind had ground a few gears and summoned the distant stored memory, he would say "Well it's a few years since I've been through there, but if you head down there first you cross a big flat, then you'll cross a big sandy creek with a bad crossing, then you go through mulga country for a few miles before you come to a jump up. After you climb that you'll pass a mill and a set of yards" at Jack's bore or whatever it was. Whenever I got to test him out he was invariably correct.

Dennis liked nothing better than to pull up at a bush camp, with a good piece of Alice Springs beef on the fire and a couple pannikins of rum, and tell of memories of decades past, as the stars came out on a crisp Alice Springs night.

He told me of his first bush trip as a raw recruit. An old stockie, whose name is now lost in the mists of time, was organised to take him out for a few days around the back country and show him the ropes. Dennis, eager to please, asked his mentor what he should bring. He was told, low key "A carton will be fine."

He turned up the next morning with his swag, gear and a carton of beer thrown in the back. Later when the carton was sighted his mate almost choked. "What? Beer! What in God's name made you get that? It won't last past a night. I meant a carton of OP rum!"

So they had to make a detour to find some OP rum, Bundaberg brand. The beer was gone that first night. By the trip's end Dennis said his liver was never again the same, but his taste for rum remained.

Working in Darwin

After two years of working in Alice Springs I moved to Darwin as senior vet for this district, with my main job being to organise TB eradication programs on properties across the Top End.

One of the first places I visited, and one it's most famous stations, was the former Stapleton Station. It was built around the floodplains of the Reynolds River, 120 kilometres south west of Darwin. In early days the owners of this block considered their good country was the rough hill country behind Adelaide River. This was green and lush in the wet season, but its poor dry grass had little nutritional value in the dry season. These rocky hills, now famous as Litchfield National Park, with all its waterfalls, were sold to the Government a few years after I moved to Darwin.

Stapleton's owners by then were the Townsends, originally Americans from Florida, who still spoke in their broad Yankee drawl. Hailing from the Everglades they saw these huge swamps and year round water and understood that they were the property's real value. These wetlands starting at the western edge of the escarpment extended for 30 to 40 kilometres, out to the coast. They slowly dried back, providing abundant green grass, throughout the dry season.

The Townsends divided Stapleton into two main properties; Welltree, south of the Reynolds River going to Bob Townsend and Labelle to the north, now run by Henry, son of Bob's brother. A smaller block, Wangi, still with good floodplains sat in the centre just below the escarpment near Wangi Falls.

To get across these huge, flooded, wet season plains they used Florida style airboats, which skimmed over the water and grass with aircraft propeller type propulsion. As the plains dried out they moved to teams of light four wheel drive vehicles, cut down as bull catchers, Daihatsu's or equivalent make, fitted with large tyres to cross the soft ground.

When I arrived they had developed the most productive grazing system in the whole of the NT, each running 10 to 15000 cattle on 200-300 square kilometre sized blocks of floodplain. Their most limiting resource was their upland areas for grazing in the wet season.

At the start of the wet season they moved all the cattle from the swamp to the high ground, at the end of the wet they went in the opposite direction. In addition to airboats and bull catcher four wheel drives, helicopters were used for big musters to find and move the cattle. A few horses were used for close in work. At each station homestead was a massive shed, used to do their wet season cattle work under shelter. Each shed was the size of Jumbo jet aircraft hangar, and capable of handling mobs of 2-3000 cattle at one time.

Unfortunately these properties sat next to Wagait, an aboriginal reserve with lots of buffalo. It was the new home of TB in the Top End, having taken over from Oenpelli as TB capital. At its peak there were probably more buffalo with TB on Wagait than in the rest of the Northern Territory and more TB remained here at this time than in all the cattle in the rest of Australia.

Bob and Henry were happy to sign up to the TB eradication program in their Brahman herds, which only had low levels of TB. But they needed something done about their northern neighbour, Wagait, to ensure that getting rid of TB from their herds was not a futile exercise. Henry Townsend had built a solid barb wire fence along the Wagait boundary, running the full northern boundary of Labelle. It had lots of heavy wires and steel pickets every few metres to keep the buffalo out. A drive showed this fence was being hammered by large buffalo bulls on a daily basis, and no amount of maintenance could keep them all out.

So my purpose, on a steamy wet season morning, was to visit Bob Townsend, doing a buffalo muster, along with moving his cattle to high ground at the start of the wet. He wanted to see if we could do something with 'them darn buffalo'.

That morning I rode in an airboat, whizzing across the plains, pushing cattle along and mustering buffalo towards a set of trap yards. One of the many Townsend relatives was the airboat driver while Bob explained the operation in his slow, southern Yankee drawl. Massive big black buffalo bulls came out of swamp pockets, water and black mud glistening on their smooth ebony skins in the early morning light.

Knowing wet country and buffalo from Oenpelli soon gave Bob and I a common understanding. We would do quick mental calculations about how many cartons of beef would come from each body, and what that dollar value was. However, as Bob said, "Goddamn I will lose a quarter of them with TB going on last muster, and look at the mess they are making of my country, with their wallows everywhere and the way they just smash through the fences."

Morning tea was a delicious huge glass of iced tea, then I transferred to a helicopter to get an aerial perspective of their vast watery landscape, it was generally similar to Oenpelli, but with its own features. By lunch time a mob of 2-300 fat, shiny buffalo were in the trap yards, going off that afternoon to the meatworks, 20% later found and condemned with TB, much as Bob expected.

The Townsend view was that, although they made good money from fat buffalo at the meatworks, they were not really worth the trouble, as they were hard to fence and smashed the country. The real money was in their good Brahman cattle and they wanted to be rid of the buffalo. They said they would attend to this on their own blocks if we would deal with Wagait reserve.

I said we would give it our best shot and we could assist them with the cost with a destocking subsidy. So it was agreed that they would muster what buffalo they could and shoot the rest. Once that was done they would get serious about the testing of the cattle.

They also needed a solution to Litchfield, a Tipperary property at the mouth of the Daly on their southern boundary, again with lots of buffalo. As well as having good Brahmans, a big proportion of its cattle were scrubbers. In the dry season these would break through the southern Stapleton boundary. Bob and Henry explained how, on driving this boundary, they would watch these cattle and buffalo in the distance running for safety south towards the boundary fence, through which they had smashed holes. Many would leave too late and find themselves in the cross hairs of a bull catcher driver's gun sights, dying with noses almost touching Litchfield as bullets hit and they crashed to the ground.

So Wagait became a big preoccupation of ours, to get the buffalo off. What made Wagait special and arguably the best block in the Top End was its own floodplain system south of the Finniss River. An aerial count a year prior had estimated 16-24000 buffalo on this 1000 square km block, along with about 10% more scrubber cattle.

Wagait had been contract mustered for years, both by its northern neighbours on Finniss River and by a host of other contractors. It was said that the fattest, heaviest buffalo through Darwin meatworks came from Wagait.

Each wet season, as it flooded, thousands of buffalo were forced onto small islands, where adults would spread TB to the new calves. So the beautiful fat shiny buffalo weaners of the next year would be riddled with this disease.

The year before I came to Darwin (1983) Wagait adult buffalo had a 15% condemnation rate for TB through the meatworks. Several mobs of weaners had been tested, and 30% to 50% of them had TB. If one looked hard enough one would probably find TB in almost every buffalo from there.

The buffalo catchers had worked out the worst pockets and avoided catching there. So, over the years, a collection of aged buffalo riddled with TB remained, some with huge visible TB abscesses below the jaw or on the shoulder discharging pus, and lungs so full of TB abscesses the buffalo could barely run ten yards without coughing and heaving. Most of these buffalo were still huge, fat and shiny, difficult to believe with the advanced disease inside.

A protracted round of negotiations began between contract musterers, aboriginal owners, the Northern Land Council and us, the government men. It was finally agreed that all the cattle and buffalo on Wagait had to go.

Three years was allowed, first mustering and then, at the end, shooting whatever was left behind. The contract musterers thought our estimates of numbers based on the aerial count were ridiculously large. They were convinced there were only a third to half as many animals, perhaps 7-10,000. I held my judgement and said we would see. Obviously it would be better for them if our numbers were right as they would make more money.

So for the next three years it was all go ahead, contract musterers with bull catchers and helicopters setting up their trap yards and running in the easy animals. Now nothing could be let go again, all had to go to meatworks or be shot for pet-meat in the trap yards. In the first year everyone was pleased, they had got rid of 3000 buffalo, so they were well on the way.

Contract musterer Joe Groves hated the sight of all those black shiny buffalo weaners, going to the meatworks for almost no money. He knew that, if he could only get the level of TB on the first test to less than 5%, he could find a ready market for them going to Indonesia. But they had to start with less than 5% TB to qualify. Previous weaner testing, with 30 -50% TB positives, had cost him and other contractors a lot of money, so great improvement was required, but there must be a way.

As the big storms of that first wet brought the mustering on Wagait to an end, he and our local stock inspector, Frank Blakey, came to me with a new proposal they had worked out together.

"Doc, you know them good looking Wagait weaners?"

"Ye—s!"

"Well what Joe and me reckons is the TB is so high cause all the old buffalo spread it to them weaners every wet season on the islands when it's all flooded and their all jammed up together."

"Reckon you're probably right", I said.

"Well, Joe and I reckon that if we could shoot them old ones that we can see have TB (the big external abscesses or the ones which can't run when you chase them) then maybe we can stop the TB spreading to the calves and weaners this wet. So we want you to give us some unmusterable compensation to shoot those old buffalo with TB before the big floods of this wet."

This meant to pay them sixty dollars for each buffalo they shot.

My reply: "Right, so how many buffalo like that do you think there are?"

"Well we reckon maybe 100, 200 is tops".

Having been burnt before with other people's ideas of numbers I said, "How about I give you funds to shoot up to 500," ($30,000), thinking I could find this from some other savings.

So off they went off, booked a helicopter and flew out to Wagait to cull those obvious TB buffalo.

A week later, Frank was back again. "Doc, you know how you gave us money to shoot those TB buffalo on Wagait, well we shot the 500 hundred last week and we reckon there still a few more. So could we get some more dollars to keep on going.

At this stage I saw a never ending well, so I said "Sorry can't do that Frank". He shrugged his shoulders and went off to tell Joe.

But it worked, next year Joe yarded up a mob of weaners to test and they went 3%, then another mob at 4%. Even TB in the adult buffalo dropped below 10% that year at the meatworks so it was money well spent.

The second year of mustering another 4000 buffalo came off Wagait. By the end of that dry season there were very few buffalo seen on the plains. All were confident the end was in sight, as buffalo were getting hard to find and even harder to muster. The contractors thought this validated their numbers guess, and that the job was nearly done. They even wondered whether another year's mustering would be worthwhile, as they were barely covering their helicopter costs with what they yarded.

I suspected it was the way a canny stock inspector, with many years of buffalo catching experience, had explained to me.

"Well you see, Graham, this is what happens when they decide to do a buffalo muster. First they load up a truck with panels for the trap yard and they drive across the plains looking for a good trap yard site, panels clanging and banging as they go. Buffalo hear this truck coming several kilometres away and think "Muster Coming" so they slowly begin to walk in the other direction, leisurely, eating as they go. Then the truck stops and picks its site and they spend a few hours setting up these yards. Much more clanging and banging as they drive in the pickets and join the panels, really it's just like ringing a bell to say: "Were Coming to Get You!" More buffalo hear and slowly walk away in the opposite direction, no rush – hours to go!

Next morning, early, they are ready to muster, so they start their bull catchers, each with a great roar, and rev them a couple times for good measure just to make sure they are good and ready. Then they fire up the helicopters and give them a good spin to get the engines warm and the oil pressure up, before they take off in an even bigger roar. In the still morning air you can hear it for several kilometres. So those buffalo which had started slowly walking away yesterday just keep on walking. If they happen to be out on an open plain they go and stand under a big shady tree in a paperbark swamp. Of course there are always a few stupid ones who haven't learnt, so they get caught."

So, wondering how many remained, I booked a helicopter to have a look. Sure enough, not much to see on the big open plains, just an odd solitary bull, but still a lot of tracks, perhaps from earlier in the year. There is a huge paperbark swamp on the southern side of Wagait heading towards the coast, 15-20 kilometres long and two thirds as wide. So I directed the pilot to head there and put the chopper into a slow tight weave allowing us to see down into the gaps in the trees. Everywhere we looked there were buffalo, a quick count suggested 2-3000, all standing and waiting in their safe shelter, until the pestering humans went away. Every other patch of jungle or dense swamp looked much the same. It was clear there would still be some buffalo to come out in the next year.

The next year another 3000 buffalo were caught. By mid-year the mustering was getting really hard, often two or three helicopters would spend three hours mustering for ten head, and the cheque for the helicopters exceeded the payment from the meatworks for the buffalo. So they moved to bull catching and pet meat shooting and got a steady trickle more. Now they were convinced that it was really all over.

"Well Graham, we told you there were only 7-10,000 max and we have already got more than 10,000. So really there are almost none left, 1000 max!"

My scepticism remained. I remembered back to a time in the Alice when a property manager swore black and blue he had cleaned out his big bush paddock, 30 left tops. Again he had lost money on his last 3 helicopter musters. He signed the papers which authorised us to shoot what was left behind. Within a couple hours we had shot 300, and by the end of the day the count was well over 1000 going to almost 2000 before finished.

When he realised what had happened he completely lost it. He drove the 300 kilometres to Alice in a blind rage after telling me over the radio as he left, in a whole list of unprintable names, what he thought of me, and saying he was coming to shoot me.

I ignored the bluster and he duly arrived, three hours later, froth coming from his mouth as he confronted me. After a couple hours of swearing and ranting he calmed down. We went to the pub for a post argument beer where he admitted what galled him most was he got it so wrong and felt a complete idiot. He had worked cattle for 30 years and should have known better.

So we went for another fly over Wagait in a fixed wing plane, early one morning. My logic was that aeroplanes flew over all the time, and so buffalo would take little notice of them. We did ten big transects over Wagait and estimated that we had seen 10% of the area. As we flew we sighted about 1000 buffalo. A quick multiplication suggested that meant 10,000. With the standard 1.6 correction factor for visibility this turned into 16000.

I could almost hear howls of contractor derision before I got back. When I told them I thought there were still more than 10,000 buffalo the reaction was as expected, the government was barking mad and couldn't tell the difference between a buffalo and an ant-beds.

A bit more sporadic catching ensued until first storms. As the first storms came, bringing the end of catching for the year, it was clear we had to bring this debacle to a conclusion as per our contractual agreement. The final year of getting out buffalo had probably done little to reduce the population with its annual 20% increase rate. In fact this was probably true of the whole of the three year mustering effort.

So, after a series of political and other briefings, it was time to put the shooting helicopters in. Kel, a vet who worked closely with many of these west Darwin properties, was in my chair at this stage. (I was on a buffalo boat to Tahiti). He made the arrangements.

In order to minimise buffalo escape options he decided to start with a team of six helicopters and shooters. Within a couple weeks we shot over 10,000 buffalo and odd cattle. By the time of major wet season flooding it was 13,000. The final count went over 16,000.

I can remember flying in a fixed wing aircraft working as a spotter to find buffalo for the helicopter shooters one afternoon. We would fly away from the helicopters in large sweeping circles, doing a visual search for black buffalo and brown cattle dotted on the plains below. When 5-10 kilometres away from the helicopter we would come across a mob on the edge of the plains, perhaps 200 metres from the tree line. We would go into a wide circle keeping the buffalo in sight and radio in the nearest chopper. As we circled the buffalo they would not even raise their heads from eating. But when the helicopters was between three and five kilometres away, suddenly, buffalo heads would come up, and the old lead cow would gather her mob and move at a steady pace for the trees.

By the time the helicopter came into view, at most, a disappearing tail could be seen, until we directed the helicopter on to the mob. Sometimes they would break cover as the helicopter approached, other times they just moved further into the trees so that the helicopter needed to hold a hover and shoot down through tree gaps, often needing highly specific directions to find anything.

The outcome of this Wagait shoot was much industry anger, all the wasted meat that they would have caught if only given the chance. All we could say was we had given them every chance to catch what they could and the final numbers were no surprise. These numbers tallied almost exactly with both the pre-aerial count and with our final estimates.

About the end of January, I was called to brief the then NT Chief Minister, Marshall Peron. I explained what had happened, and that in the final year, while contractors had removed 3000 buffalo, in reality there were as many buffalo remaining as at the start of the year (based on a 20% increase of 3000 buffalo calves from a 15,000 population).

Marshall questioned me in detail saying; "So if I had agreed to give them an extra year to muster we would have shot just as many buffalo?"

"Yes, that's right Chief Minister".

He replied "Well I can see I have a political problem and you have a job to do, so you get on with the job and I will deal with the politics."

"Yes Chief Minister" (and thank you for the common sense - there was never going to be a painless solution).

In defence of the musterers, right across the Top End the story was much the same. It was even harder as a contractor who only got a part of the value of the animal for catching it, as you more rapidly reached the point where your costs exceeded returns.

Of course buffalo are highly intelligent animals with avoidance hard wired into their brains since they learnt to escape tigers in the forests of Asia. This was reinforced by a long period in the NT when everyone was either trying to catch or shoot them. Coupled with this is the fact that old buffalo cows live past 20 years and teach their family group all their best tricks. Then put the animals into some really difficult topography, with a mixture of gorges, rain forest, huge swamps and lots of water. The result is that it took special people to catch any buffalo at all. But it still sat hard with them, and their business was gone.

While Wagait progressed we were also dealing with the Tipperary group of stations – Tipperary, Litchfield and Elizabeth Downs. Fred Sutton, of Sutton Motors, was then the owner. He appeared reluctant to invest the money required to achieve cattle control, as he was making a good income from a feral harvesting operation, with a minimum of costs.

So, at the end of 1984, after a season when little had happened, I wrote him a critical letter about the management of his properties. It hit a raw nerve. A few days later I got a phone call from him telling me he was on his way to Darwin to resolve this issue. He said he had an appointment with Ian Tuxworth, the NT's then Chief Minister, and would come and see me to sort this out first, at a specified time. I replied that I had another commitment out of town that day but would be back in Darwin the next day. His reply was "That's fine I will ring Ian and tell him I will come to see him a next morning after we meet."

The implication was clear that if I did not agree with what he wanted then he would find a political solution. We met the next day and agreed on a way forward to sort this. Who knows what the meeting with Ian Tuxworth discussed.

Of course, like many NT promises, it did not really happen as promised. Finally as the pressure increased an announcement was made that the Tipperary had been sold to Warren Anderson, so the result was achieved indirectly.

I found out later, that in this year of confrontation with Tipperary, in late November, a bottle of Scotch was already waiting for me as a Christmas gift on the Tipperary manager's office shelf. I never saw it, I suppose a small pay back.

That year, in mid wet season, we were flying the Litchfield coast to get an idea of what numbers of cattle and buffalo remained. We made a circuit over the Daly River, at about 200 feet, before coming back over Litchfield The pilot pointed down in front – "look at that". Below I saw the largest crocodile I have ever seen. Lots of 10-13 footers were visible swimming in and around the edges of the Daly mouth, with a steady flow of muddy brown water running. Ahead looking like a huge tree log was a giant thing slowly floating down the river. As we came over we saw it making a bow wave as it slowly waved its tail. It was at least twice the length and many times the mass of any other crocodile in sight. To this day I have never seen another crocodile approaching its size. It was well over 20 feet. My guess was something between 25 and 30 feet. It looked like it had survived since the age of the dinosaurs, slowly cruising around the Daly.

Buffalo People

Trying to compensate in part for the loss of abundant wild buffaloes, as the TB program progressed, and to establish a domestic buffalo industry, the NT government purchased a former parcel of buffalo country in the Top End, old Point Stuart Station, where an abattoir had operated for many years.

It subdivided this into four properties which became known as the Buffalo Blocks. All were great properties with a good mix of floodplains and woodlands. They were made available, on favourable terms, to members of the buffalo industry. These were acquired by four industry hopefuls, all of modest means, but who hoped to make a go of domestic buffalo. They were the Fisher family on Swim Creek Plains, the Ansell family on Melaleuca, the Stewart family on Carmor Plains and the buffalo exporters 'Britten Jones and George' on Opium Creek.

Opium Creek was already a well-established export operation where I spent repeated days testing buffalo. One particular group was a consignment of 1500 buffalo cows to Cuba. Following completion of health testing at Opium Creek they were loaded onto the boat at Darwin. The planned vet to go with them discovered his passport had expired a day before departure, so I suddenly became the Australian Vet on board along with two Cuban Vets.

I soon got to know the Cubans well. As well as offers to meet beautiful sisters or cousins, I was told Fidel Castro was expected to be there to greet our arrival. He knew both Cuban Vets personally and had told them he would be there to welcome them. So we were looking forward to our journey's end.

We headed out from Darwin with two or three days of placid sailing across the glass like waters of the Top End and the Gulf of Carpentaria, then through Torres Strait and along New Guinea's southern coast, with its high mountain spine visible on the horizon, before heading out across the vast expanses of the open Pacific. A few days out we had to divert several hundred kilometres to avoid the path of a cyclone, somewhere north of Fiji. At its extremity we spent a couple days making heavy going through ten metre seas.

Our buffalo became very quiet with daily handling. As the weather got rougher they sat down on the deck while the boat rolled away.

Eventually we made Tahiti, our one and only landfall, where we took on water and fuel, with a 12 hour stopover. After 18 days at sea the Australian stockman, Neil Ross, and I had a developed a powerful thirst. So, while the boat refuelled, we went off to sample some local pubs in Papeete. We knew the boat must leave at midnight as it had limited food for the buffalo for the next 20 plus days and it was running into consistent headwinds across the Pacific, making our progress even slower.

We had several drinks over several hours though neither of us felt very drunk. About 10:30 that evening Neil and I agreed we would have one last drink before we returned to the boat. There my memory ends until I woke up in hospital with someone stitching up my face. I had a cut below my eye and a split lip. In a slightly dazed state I realised I must get back to the boat.

I tried to communicate this to the French speaking nurses "Le bateau, le bateau departez," (the boat, the boat is leaving), one of my few remaining bits of schoolboy French. Following some perplexed looks I tried, "Quelle heure et il?" Finally someone showed me a watch; it was 2:30 in the morning.

I realised the boat was heading out across the Pacific, and I was in Tahiti.

Castro did welcome them, brief national heroes.

I made an inglorious return to Australia, flying out of Tahiti at five am Christmas morning. An hour later we crossed the date line into Boxing Day on the way back to Sydney. So much for Christmas day!

As to what happened that night, it appears someone slipped something in our drinks and, as we were leaving, Neil got a punch in the face. With his glasses broken he could see nothing. When he tried to find me I was gone.

Neil got back to the boat and they sent out a search party, but after an hour of looking, with no sign, the boat had to go.

An hour later I woke in hospital – such is life!

For a few days my face looked like an over-ripe plum that was dropped, but it healed up fine. Otherwise I was OK, just minus a few possessions.

So I have no idea what happened, whether I was robbed, hit or just ran away and fell in the street. A minor diplomatic incident resulted. I was reported missing that night, Saturday, but it was not until the Monday I could find someone who spoke enough English to advise officialdom of who I was and what had happened. By then my name was a headline in the Australian papers

"Vet Missing!" with the Australian consul in New Caledonia involved.

Other buffalo blocks owners included Alan Fisher, my friend from Mary River, who did an amazing job cleaning out the wild buffalo from his block. His property was named Swim Creek. It had open floodplains and woodland areas on its western side. Its eastern side was Swim Creek, a deep water channel of floodplain fringed by dense rainforest and floodplain. This was a late dry season buffalo refuge for the whole area, with the main channel of grass covered deep water extending to the forest margins. Buffalo would shelter under trees and move out and graze on the lush grasses within a few metres of the tree line. So when mustering danger threatened they would be back under the trees before anyone got near.

Nevertheless Alan persisted and caught almost every buffalo on this property. He fenced off the Swim Creek channel to contain what was there, then went back day after day, month on month, until nothing remained. In the end only a handful of buffalo were shot.

The buffalo block between Swim Creek and Opium Creek was called Melaleuca. It is positioned where the fresh and salt water systems of the Mary intersect, with Shady Camp nearby. It was a total bush block with no development.

Its owners were the Ansell family. Rod Ansell had a contract to catch buffalo on Bulman station in southern Arnhem Land. His idea was to completely remove the local buffalo and then restock with TB free Bulman buffalo, a good idea in theory. However he did not have the resources of Alan Fisher at Swim Creek or of the Opium Creek operation. And, even though his block had much good country, it was fast being overrun with mimosa, a prickly noxious weed that formed impenetrable thickets five metres high in which the buffalo could hide, making its mustering a challenge. With more resources it could have become a great property, but instead it was struggle street.

Rod was famous from a few years earlier when he survived in the Fitzmaurice River for many weeks after his boat capsized, before being rescued by stockmen from the Daly Reserve. His story had been published in a book and for a time he was a media personality. Some said his story had inspired the Crocodile Dundee movie. He was a small wiry man with considerable charm and wide knowledge of the NT and Queensland bush, coming from a bush childhood plus years of contract mustering. However there was a wild edge to him, it seemed to me like a reckless fearlessness from living on the edge.

Now on his buffalo block he built a simple residence, not much more than a canvass awning, and lived there with his wife, Joanne, and their small children, when not catching in the Bulman to make money. It must have been a hard life for Joanne with small children in isolated bush camps but she was friendly and delightful, and seemed not to mind. From time to time I would visit him to see his progress on building fences and paddocks, and the rest of the time he worked away at catching and removing the local buffalo. Twice I camped on his property after spending a day driving round with him, talking through his plans and operations. Dinner was typically a haunch of agile wallaby or a goanna which he had speared during our drive around the property. He and I both had a fascination and knowledge of African wildlife. He had many books on safari hunting, one where he showed me a photo of a rhino caught by the leg by a Nile crocodile which ultimately succumbed to its pull. I told my croc story and of the huge croc I had sighted in the Daly, and we discussed many stories of bush life and wildlife with shared interest.

However, it gradually became apparent that the development of the block was beyond him. Eventually he got rid of the local buffalo, but building enough paddocks and restocking with controlled clean buffalo was beyond him. In the end he seemed mostly engaged in a running battle with the NT government about whether they would allow him to retain his lease.

After I left the NT I heard about his demise in a siege at Berry Springs, where both he and an NT policeman died in a shoot-out. It must have been a hard life with the struggle to make money and pay the bills. I think in the end it all got too much. It was several years after I left the NT that I heard of his end, but I suspect the seeds of madness were growing earlier.

Joe Groves of Woolner station was another memorable Top End Pastoralist. Joe had built up a contract mustering operation, starting out as a bull catcher on Elsey, and gradually progressing to being one of the Top End's most significant operators, with his own road trains and extensive mustering plant. He finally managed to buy Woolner station, on the coast east of the Adelaide River. It was a good floodplains block, with a large area of para-grass on the coast north of the homestead which provided excellent dry season grazing. Mary, his wife, was in many ways the operation's business brains, while Joe understood the mustering operations.

Joe had the good sense or luck to acquire a block with adjoining good properties and with absentee/government landlords on all sides. To his east was a huge paperbark swamp, equal to the best of Wagait and the Daly Reserve, called Mary River Flora and Fauna Reserve , full of buffalo. Marrakai station was south of it, having the best western side floodplains of the Mary River. Here Don Hoar had operated Wild Boar abattoir for many years. Its owner Ron Withnall was a Sydney solicitor, who had formerly worked in the NT but now was just an occasional dry season visitor. To the south of Woolner was Marrakai Flora and

Fauna Reserve, with lots of buffalo hiding in mimosa, and for which the government would let occasional mustering or pet meat tenders.

Typically, Joe put in large trap yards with two or three helicopters and a lot of on ground backup, including bull catchers to pick up the stragglers. He was happy to do wide sweeps of the boundary, and to help a few of the nearby stock to run his way. His neighbours would no doubt have done this too, but Joe was usually first and his neighbours were rarely around. So, being the canny man he was, he got the benefit of stock off three adjoining properties to support his business. He also contracted in many other areas such as Wagait.

Over the years Joe caught some of the biggest and fattest buffalo across the Top End. He also gradually built up a quality Brahman herd. Finally he sold Woolner at a handsome profit and bought a cropping farm on the Douglas Daly, called Ruby Downs.

I spent many an afternoon in a bull catcher or helicopter at one of Joe's Woolner musters. We discussed mustering tactics and NT life while he organised his operations. After a typically successful muster it was time for a post muster beer, as Joe supervised the loading of stock to meatworks. The hardest thing was to get away at night, the family were great hosts, and Joe could readily drink me under the table. Joe wore a hearing aid. At times he and Mary would have fierce disagreements. Then Joe would be observed to scratch his ear, only to have Mary retort: "Joe don't you turn down your hearing aid on me".

One evening I watched from the side of the trap yards after Joe had run in a mixed mob of about 300 buffalo and cattle including some large and ornery cattle scrub bulls. They would try to draft off and separate cattle and buffalo but this took time and was not always simple. I was sitting on top of my Toyota, sipping one of Joe's beers, looking across a side trap yard holding about 50 animals mainly buffalo, while bull catchers pushed animals up the central loading ramp, onto trucks, from the main yard.

Near me was a large, bad tempered, red scrub bull who thought he was boss and intended to show the other animals. He had harassed a combination of smaller buffalo and cattle, and was now standing by himself, slightly separated, still with a mad, ground pawing demeanour.

A big buffalo bull, with massive neck and horns ending in wicked sharp points, shorter at the shoulder but more than his equal in weight, got pushed towards him as the stock eddied around. The red bull decided he did not like this. So he proceeded to display his bad temper to the buffalo bull, snorting and dummy charging. There was little reaction from the buffalo and the red bull walked alongside him.

As his chest came alongside the buffalo's head it gave its head a quick sideways flick and drove its sharp horn into the red bulls chest, punching horn shaft between ribs, almost effortless. It embedded a couple feet of horn into the startled red bull's chest. I don't think the red bull moved, it was like a slow motion silent movie. Another quick head flick back removed the horn.

The whole thing lasted perhaps five seconds. The red bull still barely moved, it had a puzzled, slightly shocked look on its face. Then it slowly sank to the ground and died. I gained a new appreciation of a buffalo bull's power.

I spent many hours flying in helicopters over the floodplain systems east of Darwin along the Adelaide, Mary and Alligator River systems. Sometimes I was getting an understanding of progress with the mustering and removal of buffalo, other times I carried a semi-automatic rifle, assisting in removing and destroying the residual buffalo that could not be mustered. My purpose was mainly to understand what was going on, from a hands-on view.

When a buffalo was spotted in the final eradication phases it had to be destroyed. If you did not have a gun it meant that someone had to come back later, and try to find it a second time, difficult and wasteful of resources. I was not the crack marksman that most stock inspectors were but was a competent shot. With TB eradication into its destruction phase, moving from Wagait to properties east and west of Darwin, our helicopter usage soared.

My close call in a helicopter was over the Marrakai plain just below Mary River Flora and Fauna Reserve. I was doing a survey, with Simon, Joe Grove's regular helicopter pilot, skimming about 50 feet above open grass plains.

Suddenly I became aware that Simon had an intense look on his face. His knuckles, holding the control column, went white with apparent effort. Otherwise the helicopter was flying straight ahead and level. As I turned my attention his way he said, quietly, almost as an aside, "hydraulics gone".

He kept staring straight ahead, both hands gripping the control. Slowly, millimetre by millimetre, he eased the control forward. The helicopters path changed from level flying to a gradual descent until we were just skimming the open grass plain. Then, with a supreme effort, he pushed the stick forward and the helicopter came onto the ground, at the same time flaring the rotors slightly to land and immediately turning off the engine. We slid along the grass for a few feet before stopping.

He radioed a mechanic for assistance, then we walked a couple kilometres up to the road to meet our help. It was a sudden pressure failure of the power assist hydraulic system, needed to control the helicopter's rotor and steering movement. So it had become like driving a huge truck without power steering. Provided he kept the controls centred he had just enough strength to hold the helicopter on a straight ahead path. If he veered we would have spun out of control and hit the ground at 60-80 knots. Keeping his calm it all turned out well. I only understood later what a close call it was.

Not everyone was so lucky. Ed Kennedy, who had taken me buffalo shooting as a kid at Oenpelli in earlier years was now mustering the Oenpelli buffalo. He died in a crash in Arnhem Land, east of Oenpelli. Fortunately his son and the pilot survived.

Noel Ross, senior stock inspector for Darwin, also died in a helicopter crash in a similar part of Arnhem Land a couple years later, this time along with the helicopter pilot.

A couple years later again, Dave Norris, another helicopter pilot I had flown with on many occasions was killed in a freak accident when he parked his helicopter on an uneven site and walked into the spinning rotor blade, invisible at speed.

Tom Barnes, a veterinarian and the vet owner of Calvert River Station who I knew from working in the Barkly also died when his helicopter hit power lines. There were also others I knew across the NT, some in helicopters, some in planes, and some in other misfortunes.

It was a poignant and bitter part of the TB program; many hard working friends who never saw the end.

The final part of the TB program used Judas animals. Buffalo were good at hiding from mustering helicopters. As shooting progressed they became equally good at hiding from shooting helicopters. We knew many areas still had a lot of buffalo; we could see their tracks as we flew around.

The pioneer was Pat Carrick in Western Arnhem Land. Pat had caught and mustered buffalo for many years before becoming a stock inspector. He had an unsurpassed understanding of buffalo behaviour. He realised, early, that if he shot everything he could find, then finding the last remaining buffalo would be extraordinarily difficult. So, before numbers fell to critically low levels, Pat started using a dart gun to immobilise old buffalo cows, and fit them with radio-collars. He came back to track them at regular intervals, each time shooting other buffalo that had joined the group.

With success this approach was quickly taken up by other stock inspectors and vets. At the peak of the final control program we had up to 200 radio-collared buffalo and cattle distributed across the Top End, VRD and Gulf.

Week by week, month by month, they steadily found the other residual animals and led us to them.

Pat had his system working like clockwork compared to my efforts with horses in Alice Springs. He could hit a cow with a dart down through a hole in the paperbark 50 feet below. Then we would find a nearby place for the helicopter to set us down and sprint into position, just in time for the buffalo to lose its balance. We would pull it onto its side, fit the collar and let it go, back in the air in ten or fifteen minutes, following the new beeping buffalo, then backing off to let it settle back into its group.

I spent magical days with Pat putting on collars and radio-tracking in the gorges, escarpment forests and floodplain margins of western Arnhem Land, places so familiar from my childhood. Sometimes we would land for lunch by a remote Arnhem Land billabong and pull in a big barra for our lunch.

Pat was incredibly good at spotting tracks and sign of remaining buffalo. He would patiently explain to me "a buffalo has four legs and each time it takes a step forward it leaves four footprints on the ground, so if it takes 1000 steps a day that is four thousand footprints a day, 28000 footprints a week."

His point was all you needed was a pair of eyes. Mine got better with practice. Occasionally I would spot new sign before he did "How about that Pat?" Our pilot was Larry Tessman, formerly manager of Tipperary, now showing his best skills in flying a Jet Ranger.

Pat and the other stock inspectors then experimented with young heifers and bulls to find those solitary animals that would not pair up with an old cow group. Gradually the tracks become less and less until the last remaining animals could be tracked up one by one. Finally there were vast tracts of land where not a single buffalo footprint remained.

Then the last cows and bulls with collars had to go, they had served their purpose. As we found the final animals we began to take our post mortem knifes to see if these animals still had TB. Occasionally a 20 year old cow, with almost no teeth, but still a calf at foot, was riddled. So we knew that the job would not be done until all were accounted for.

I still wonder at some of the last places where a few great survivors may have hidden, perhaps some tiny gorge with a few patches of shade covered grass in the headwaters of a mighty Arnhem River. I always felt a pang at the loss of this NT icon from such vast areas.

Now this program is a distant memory. New buffalo, hopefully TB free, are moving down off the Arnhem Land plateau and starting to repopulate the lush floodplains which were once black with buffalo.

Australia, as a result of this effort is now declared officially TB free. Many biologists told me it could never be done with a wild animal across such vast areas, Proof was the doing, but the cost was high.

NT Vets and Stock Inspectors

The stock inspectors have been the core of the NT animal health system since its foundation. They are the people who blend practical common sense and understanding of station operations with the technical know how to get the job done. Some of the NT's most famous stock inspectors have gone on to become property owners and managers. Peter Sherwin, once the largest landowner in the NT, is an example.

Others become vets, or moved to other successful careers. For many it was been a lifetime career. These are gradually disappearing. Dave Napier (Napes) was one such, a one armed legend. In his early years with two arms he was considered one of Australia's best boxers. Even with one arm few would pick him. A story was told of a stockie who went too far, turning up at Napes home one evening, full of beer and bad manners. He did not take Napes advice to calm down and leave. He turned up at work next day with a face that looked like an overripe tomato dropped. It was said Napes picked him up with his one arm, bounced him off the wall and gave him a back-hander on the way down.

Napes was a gentleman and a great practical joker.

Napes lost his right arm just south of Pine Creek. It was resting it on the window of his vehicle as he drove south. The back trailer of a road train came drifting across to his side of the road, taking off all but a small stump next to the shoulder. In bed in Katherine Hospital, he was brought the next day's local paper which read: "Wanted one arm, last seen holding a green stubby 10 miles south of Pine Creek". His mate, Ticky Mick, was trying to help out.

The first time I met Napes was at the Victoria River Roadhouse, 200 kilometres west of Katherine, on a pre-wet season build-up day. We all stopped for a beer about lunch time. I walked in as Patto and Napes, just arrived, were resting at the bar. The road house was owned by Don and Frances Hoar.

Don at that time was detained at Her Majesty's pleasure. I think it was over barramundi poaching and he was later released on appeal. Dave knew Don and Frances over many years, though it may have been a stretch it to call himself a mate. Calling for service, the bar girl delivered the first round of drinks. When she asked for payment Napes announced he was Don Hoar's good friend and this one was on the house because Don would be outraged for Dave to be charged for a beer. The perplexed girl was not happy and, after five minutes of back and forth with Napes on his need to pay, she finally went out back to check with Frances Hoar. Frances said, "On no account is that man to be given credit."

By the time the barmaid returned the first beer was gone and he had obtained a second one from another waiter. Again he insisted that this beer was on the house.

Now, the poor bar girl was almost in tears; "Please Mr Napier you really must pay or I will lose my job, and I can't serve you any more till you pay."

Napes – "Absolutely not, Mr Hoar is my friend. He insists I never pay. If he finds out you charged me there will be hell to pay."

Back and forth it went, but then as Napes left the bar, a $20 note magically appeared including a substantial tip. I doubt it covered the stress.

Brian Rideout (Doc) was another famous former stock inspector who went on to become a vet. He had led a hard and punishing life, and his rum consumption was the substance of many a bush story.

I only met him once, just before I went to take up my first NT job in Katherine. I was spending an initial week in Darwin, learning the basic job procedures, and was rostered as duty pathologist doing post mortems.

In front of me was a dog, reported to have been shot. Before I started on the PM I observed a puncture hole, which could have been a bullet wound, on the right side of its chest. Just then Brian strolled in, said a quick hello and left.

I continued my PM and later wrote the report. In my mind I reversed the side of the bullet wound, the clear cause of death. I was finalising this report as Doc wandered over to my desk and flicked a casual glance at what I was writing which said "bullet wound to left side of chest."

He gave a quick flick of his head, "right side," he said, walking away. He was right of course. I was amazed he picked it up in a half glance walking through the PM room. Sadly, he died the next year, so I never really got to know him.

In the years that followed stories of him drifted out, particularly down in the Barkly's where he had played a big role in both pleuro-pneumonia and early TB days. "Did you hear about the time Doc decided to camp for the night on a windmill platform out on the Barkly's, to keep away from the snakes? Up he climbed with his rifle, swag and rum bottle. Hours later he wakes to the sight of a dingo coming in to drink. Gun to shoulder, he steps forward, takes aim, bang. Problem, he's forgotten the platform is twenty feet high and over he goes."

Another responds, "What about the time at a Barkly gate, on a long night cross-black soil drive, with his rum bottle for help. He opens the gate, climbs back in and sets off to drive again. But he forgets to put the vehicle into gear. Hours pass as he steers and drives the car. It seemed a hell of a long, slow, all night drive! Next morning he wakes to find himself still there at the gate, despite having driven all night."

Such stories were told to me second hand around the stock camps of the Barkly's. I never knew their truth, but his passing was fondly remembered, from the affection and humour of the telling.

There were many other stock inspectors I worked with across different areas of the NT, tough men who had led hard lives. Many drank too much but their common sense, toughness and loyalty was what I remember.

Noel Ross (Rossy), a big part-aboriginal man, was Senior Stock Inspector with me in the Darwin region over many years, until he died in a helicopter crash. He, with Napes and Patto, had been champion boxers. Many described Rossy as one of the prettiest and most talented boxers they had ever seen. All were gentle giants of men, despite their formidable presences.

For confrontations with difficult pastoralists, I would visit with combinations of Napes, Rossy, and Patto. With two or three of them walking at my shoulder, there were few who would seriously challenge the government's authority. Napes would mutter in his gravelly voice; "I think you need to listen to what the Doc is saying". Rossy and or Patto would nod their heads. The politeness and attention would immediately come back.

Other memorable Darwin stock inspectors are many. Dave Russell was a man of mixed ancestry with some aboriginal and Chinese heritage. He had grown up during the stolen generation time at the Reta Dixon Home in Darwin, and then become a ringer on stations south of Katherine. He was a man of hard work, great inherent decency, and was the best bush cook. He was one of the courageous ones who crossed the Mudginberri picket line to do meat inspection and keep the Jay Pendarvis's abattoir running when the Union dispute was on.

Like other NT stock inspectors who did this, none seemed comfortable with the choice they had to make, probably closer to Labor then Liberal in their political beliefs. Still I suspect, in their hearts, they thought it was unfair that a southern union could shut down a local NT plant when the local workers were happy. But first and foremost they were loyal public servants of the NT who never shirked a tough job.

Ken Martin was an exuberant character, who went by the nickname "Shonkus", for sometimes sailing a bit close to the wind. His capacity for hard work was legend, along with hard living. He would load a road train of buffalo all night, then with one or two hours sleep head for the next job to test a mob of buffalo at daylight in the morning. Occasionally, when the November build-up was at its ferocious best, I would give him directions over the radio from my comfortable office. He would then turn up at my office door a day or two later and say. "Doc, it's about time you got out of here and did some real work again." So I would go and spend a day with him in the ferocious heat and humidity, just to keep my sense of perspective.

Mick Geraghty was a Vietnam Vet, who must have done things tough on occasions. What sticks in my head about Mick, apart from his hard work, was his incredible loyalty to his mates. You always knew that Mick would be there to back you up when things got tough, no matter what it cost him. Mick was also the only person I saw who could sleep in the open at Woolner, without a mosquito net, on the edge of the floodplain. Perhaps he had enough rum in his blood to anaesthetise the mosquitoes. However, any time the heat was on for a major blue, Mick was first to come and form a wall of support for his mates. At the same time he would independently work out solutions to station problems which minimised the need for Government interference and heavy handedness.

Frank Blakey was built like a jockey, about eight or nine stone wringing wet. He could be seen at a stock camp, waving his finger at men twice his size to get them to follow the rules.

There are so many more who all made their contributions, from the Top End: Cam White, with his early career at a meat inspector across the buffalo abattoirs, Jenny Purdie who broke the male mould as a first female stock inspector and more than held her own, Kevin Liddy, who worked the eastern side of Arnhem Land, for weeks on his own, and dealt with the Arafura Swamp, Jack Wheeler, who worked across the bottom of Arnhem Land in some of the most remote and inhospitable country where only the bold or crazy would go, Don Cherry big and bluff who slowly pulled Tipperary, Elizabeth Downs and the Daly Reserve into line, Rod Dixon who ferociously drove a new broom through Tipperary until they decided they had better employ him rather than fight with him, Pat Barry, another Vietnam vet who sorted out the blockies in the rural parts of Darwin, Tony Cooley, who progressed from Darwin to Killarney and had the pleasure of dealing with the Tapp family, Tony Spring who could shoot a matchbox from a helicopter at 100 metres.

I have left many out but each made their own mark, the Fox, who could ride any horse known to man, and also quietly sort out the riff raff. Then there were a host of Gulf, VRD, Barkly and Alice Stockies, each memorable in their own way, Bluey's Lunn and Lewis, John Kerin, Bryan Gill, Greg Crawford, Tony Moran, Keith Brumby, Stumpy, Keith Hill, Coley, Geoff Beere, Freddie Dayes, Keith Hill, Larry and Chrissy at Avon, Teddy Martin taming the Gulf, and of course the inimitable Bob Baker. Bob definitely deserves a book all on his own.

Other names drift by but it doesn't make sense just to write a full list as each deserves their own chapter and story along with the vets. Perhaps one day I will try to write something approaching an uncensored version of their lives. Not all can be told in a way that the general public could know or understand.

Peter Flanagan was another who did not make a ripe old age. He was the stock inspector at Wave Hill. When I worked in Katherine he would line me up for big days of testing, 2000 plus cattle bled and tested at Number 8, Wave Hill or wherever. He and Buck Buchester, head stockman of Cattle Creek, on Wave, would joke about the new green vet they had recruited, who Buck promptly named Ornithorhynchus (Duckbill Platypus). As I neared the end of one of my first big days of testing, when the exhaustion of 200 cattle races tested had slowed my feet to a shuffle, Buck exchanged with Peter, "Well that Ornithorhynchus is OK. At least he can do a day's work."

Just then I was past caring for the grudging praise, I was too knackered.

Peter loved nothing better than a bar room brawl, having within him a touch of the mad Irish scrapper. When he was feeling bored he would say. "Hit me Doc, I want a fight." I would punch him hard two of three times in the guts, and he would just smile and say "You will have to do better than that if you want to hurt me". One night, after a long day's testing at Riveren Station, he had to drive the blood samples back to the laboratory at Wave Hill. I stayed on, enjoying dinner and a beer with the Underwood family before doing a bit of horse surgery next day on a race horse with a contracted tendon.

Next morning the radio message was. "Doc, I had a bit of an accident last night, I was fine on the bendy road before the highway, but when I hit the main road I went off to sleep and flipped it. I think there may still be a few blood bottles beside the road, perhaps you should have a look."

As I drove back that day, following his tyre tracks, all was fine until the main dirt road to Halls Creek. Then it looked like a snake had crawled along the road for a few hundred yards until a table drain formed the path of least resistance. There I found a couple missing blood sample tubes along with some other rollover detritus. Peter survived this and many other close calls but could not beat the stomach cancer that finally got him. Seeing him about a month before the end he said, "C'mon Doc, I reckon I can still go a few rounds."

At the opposite end in terms of reputation was Mick "Nasty" Carpenter. When I first heard the name Nasty, for this vet in Tennant I pictured a big ferocious man who no one dared cross. It was a typical NT name of opposites, as with our two red haired stock inspectors named Bluey. Mick was a small man with mild manners and great bush knowledge. He had worked across all NT areas before settling into Tennant Creek. I finally met him on various trips across the Barkly black soil. Indefatigably polite and helpful, he always found time to assist and give a word of encouragement along with 30 plus years of bush common sense. Wherever one went with Mick there was a station welcome and genuine affection.

Then there was my first NT vet boss, Brian Radunz, in Katherine. In moments of extreme pressure Brian would stutter out something unprintable. In his conversations with Bill Tapp on the Radio Telephone, they tried to out-compete each other in this way with long staccato bursts. Brian was followed by Ross Ainsworth, who I first met working for Bill Tapp, and who then took on the Katherine office before a short turn with the Tipperary establishment and finally making a name for himself as a livestock exporter to Indonesia. Ross was followed by Kevin De Witte who did the heavy lifting in getting the TB program going at full steam across the VRD and parts of the Gulf. And who could forget Graham Calley who, almost single handed, got the BTEC program moving across the NT, even if the cost got in front of the money. He was ably supported by his master clerk Wolfie as well as others including Lorraine, Ursula and Tanya. As order was imposed he was succeeded by Mr Efficient, Geoff Neumann, who came on loan from South Australia to teach us new tricks and carved his own mark in folklore with a toe to toe with a well-known pastoralist from the Alice.

My Top End vet colleagues were all equally memorable in their own way, Dennis Thompson, long and lanky, with legs that could outwalk a buffalo on the Arnhem Plateau, Kel Small, one of whose claims to fame was preventing Paul Hogan getting horned by a big bull buffalo in the making of Crocodile Dundee. And the Barkly stations told the tale of Geoff Niethe on Wollogorang and Brunette, followed by Chubby as the first man who stared down Peter Sherwin. And of course there was Lockie and Tabrett, both larger than life characters when I came to work in Alice Springs, not to mention some well-known lab and research vets like Taffy, Lorna, Colin McCool and Gehan J.

There were many others of course, beginning with Colonel Rose who I never knew but whose name loomed large in any NT history, Goff Letts, and Peter Hooper, both who had made their mark and were household names before my time and who I met briefly in their later careers. Other names pass by. I struggle to remember them all, though most are remembered on a station out there.

In moving around the NT I not only dealt with many white station owners but also with aboriginal communities across many areas. The NT sense of priority and timelessness was a characteristic, particularly as one got further out where there was less western influence and grog. People out there lived simple lives; their dominant needs were to collect bush food, go hunting and fishing for subsistence, and do their ceremonies. Beyond that they had time to talk and laugh and watch their children play.

Arafura Swamp is a massive paperbark swamp near the mouth of the Goyder River of 'Ten Canoes' movie fame. Its lies to the east of the town called Ramingining. A cattle station had been founded here many decades earlier which had largely been abandoned, with a selection of Brahman type cattle now running free in the swamp, along with many large crocodiles. Buffalo had later come to the southern edge of the swamp and with them TB. So the buffalo had to go, and we would then work out what to do with the cattle.

I was out there with stock inspector, Kevin Liddy, in the final stages of the buffalo shootout. I had driven across from Kakadu and Oenpelli as it was now mid dry season and the roads were open. I would continue on to Nhulunbuy to discuss our program with the aboriginal elders of eastern Arnhem Land.

The town of Ramingining has an airstrip a few kilometres away. I drove past this on my way to our camp at the bottom of the swamp. Passing the airstrip I noticed a group of aboriginal people sitting on the ground near the airstrip, under the shade of a couple spindly trees. As I was in strange country I decided to drive over for a chat, as it is not polite to drive through someone else's country without a hello. "How you going?" "Good." "Where you come from?" "Oenpelli and Maningrida." "Gamuk" (good). The chat continued for a few minutes, and I asked, "What are you doing, waiting for the plane?"

Answer "Yes, plane might-be come today, maybe tomorrow".

A few minutes later, with directions about the road around the bottom of the swamp and an assurance they were fine, I headed away. Next day I drove back past the airstrip on my way up to Ramingining shop for a few things.

The people were still sitting there so I called out "What's up, where that plane?" Reply: "Him not come yesterday, might-be come today, might-be tomorrow". Next day I called past again and they were still there, with no plane but with the same reply. Time was an eternal quality and the plane would come when it was ready. Finally on the fourth day they were no longer there, the plane had come. I thought we could learn something from their way.

One of my cynical colleagues from southern Australia asked me what NT stands for? I shrugged so he proceeded to enlighten. "Not Today, Not Tomorrow, Not Tuesday, Not Thursday, you don't work Saturdays or Sundays. So what you have left that's for working is perhaps one day a week, that's the NT."

Seeing these people I wondered who was the idiot?

During the time I worked in the NT I brought occasional visitors to Oenpelli, to share this special place. The years were passing for Mum and Dad, with children all grown up and left home, just coming back for occasional visits, and now they had a new extended family of grandchildren. The relentless change at Oenpelli was taking its toll, particularly for Dad, who moved increasingly into outstation work as Oenpelli grew and its own aboriginal leaders took over community government roles.

As Oenpelli's income grew so did its alcohol consumption.

Most money, whether uranium royalties or social security payments seemed to find its way to the social club at Oenpelli, or other outlets happy to take aboriginal money for a few green cartons.

As well as the damage it was causing to the many people my parents had grown to love, I could see this malaise was slowly eating away at them, as if all their work was destined for futility.

Working in the Barkly's

The only place in the NT I had not worked, except for a few weeks, and which I wanted to experience was the Barkly Tablelands and Tennant Creek region. So I got the job as the senior vet for this region.

My work sometimes took me up to the Gulf fall properties, rocks and scrub and occasional half-starved cattle, dissected by beautiful rivers which cut their way from the Barkly plateau into the Gulf of Carpentaria, with fishing to die for and an unspoilt wilderness of nature. Then days on the Barkly black soil, with its huge, productive cattle stations. Brunette Downs, a mere 10,000 square kilometres and 60,000 cattle, Alexandria, even bigger when all the separate leases were considered with upwards of 80,000 cattle, and of course the Peter Sherwin empire, covering almost half of the northern Barkly's with about 200,000 cattle. Days out on the black soil plains testing mobs of 2000 cattle, dust and flies so thick you could eat them, other days when the rain came and you could track the huge storms that swept over the black soil from 100 miles away. The next day's drive would be around areas as large as an inland sea covered in water while the black soil turned to liquid mud.

This brought me into contact with a whole new breed of Stockies, the black soil men. They took pride in working on the vast herds on the good country, dealing with some seriously tough characters, of Sherwin ilk, along with the well run Barkly stations. Occasionally they drifted up into the Gulf for some variety.

Bob Baker was most memorable. A whole book could be written about his exploits, most unprintable. When I first met Bob he had just returned from Queensland holiday, and had a slightly beaten looking face which he explained with pride. He had been pulled up on a minor infringement by the Queensland constabulary. On getting out of his car he remarked to the two officers that he "was surprised to see them as he thought all the pigs had been locked up in the Fitzgerald Royal Commission". Of course this led to his immediate detention and a bit more besides which his face still showed. Surviving such encounters was Bob's source of satisfaction, taking pride in the telling.

It was here one Saturday night in a pub, in Tennant Creek, that I met a new group of nurses on a working holiday; one with a lovely Irish brogue, and flashing blue eyes, who had something more. Mary, travelling around Australia, with best friend Ita, had come to Tennant to experience the Australian outback, and instead met me.

After some whirlwind trips to the gulf fishing, to Kakadu and other places, it was back to Ireland to meet my soon to be new, Irish family. I discovered a second country and family that is also precious. Ita returned, Mary stayed. She stays with me still though I am sure she sometimes wonders why.

Oenpelli Revisited Many Times

I have been back to Oenpelli many times since this, though mostly for a few days only. The plains and hills look just the same, and the people are still there, although year after year more of them disappear. A different group of children play. The ones' who were children then, now have their own children like mine. Many I knew have become older and greyer.

When I first took Mary there she felt as if she was walking out of another land into Africa. She too has been assigned her skin name, as preferred wife.

When Cam Cooke died his wish was to be buried on the top of Arrkuluk. Peter came from Queensland with his ashes, and Ruth from Murganella, where she and Stuart were staying with Frank Woerle, her father in law.

On a warm dry season afternoon we gathered on the top of Arrkuluk, with the dry season wind flowing over the plains and bouncing through the hill top rocks. With a simple ceremony his friends, black and white left him to be remembered in the heart of the land he loved, forever watching morning sunrises over the plains, seeing the late afternoon sun light up the glowing walls of the escarpment and hearing the occasional call of a whistling eagle which hovers in the uplifting breeze at the edge of the mountain.

While we were there Peter showed me again how it is still possible to catch a barramundi in any waterhole, and we travelled up to Murganella, half way to Coburg, where Frank regaled us with tales of the NT bush, its characters and the best of wine to wash down a feast of turtle, ocean fish and buffalo.

It was on one of these nights that our second child commenced his journey towards life in Arnhem Land. Though now he is grown and knows it not, still his given skin name remains, a forever tie to this place.

PART 3 – COMING TO AN END

Mum and Dad as Senior Citizens -Oenpelli moving on

In 1963, when Dad and Mum moved back to Oenpelli, they were both 37 and in the prime of their lives, bursting with energy. Often, once something was decided, Dad would exclaim, 'Boing', meaning, in aboriginal, 'It's finished' (or agreed), clap his hands and head off. Most major achievements in developing the community and its facilities occurred over the next decade

In the mid-1970s' a gradual devolution of administration to the aboriginal people was underway. By 1976, with the end of the Whitlam government, the coming of aboriginal land rights and the reality of uranium mining, my parents were both moving into their 50th year, with youngest child, Arthur, in Sydney at High School. So mostly it was just the two of them again, with a much quieter life. Mum, more and more, became a grandmother figure to the community. Her hair now white, she would deliver surplus fruit and bicycle amongst the European and Aboriginal households, hearing of the activities of these families, telling news of her own and offering occasional wise advice to others. She had much more time for her bird watching passion and made many records of new species found in the woodlands, hills and wetlands of Oenpelli.

Dad's memoir ends in the early 1980's and what he records of his last years at Oenpelli is minimal. From the mid-1970s he moved out of the position of Superintendent into the role of Area Advisor, spending an ever increasing time away from Oenpelli at the different outstations. He progressively became distanced from the day to day problems and administration of the Oenpelli community, though he remained in close contact with many of its people.

His focus was on assisting aboriginal groups to achieve their aspiration to return to their own country, the early stages of which his memoir describes. With continuing Government largesse his idea of communities doing their own work was being replaced by contractors coming into them with government grants to build new facilities, usually at several times the cost of previous work. With this came a danger of outstations just becoming new places of inactivity, further out. However these early leaders stayed committed to a vision of hard work and independence, even if not all outstation members saw it that way.

Dad also developed an interest in the community's cultural development, and was a mentor for many younger people, happy to talk at length about how things could be done. Earlier he was too busy and impatient to keep moving, now he could sit and discuss in leisure, often spending half an hour chatting with one of the old men and recounting memories of decades earlier. He took on a project to collect an oral history of the early days from various aboriginal men and some women who had lived through that era, Big Bill Neiji was one.

Dad and Mum now moved into a wind down phase of their Oenpelli life, planning for their own departure and retirement.

Conclusion of Mum and Dad's work At Oenpelli

In the early 1980s Mum and Dad bought 20 acres of land, stringybark and woollybut scrub, 50 kilometres south of Darwin. It was similar to our first ten acres in Nightcliff. In 1985, they retired from Oenpelli and moved there, building a simple house: something between our first Darwin house and our Oenpelli house. A lush tropical garden followed and, for Dad, a workshop of tools to construct his favourite projects.

Dad kept his pilot's license and a four wheel drive vehicle, going to Oenpelli for a few days each month. He continued as a trustee on the Outstation Company, using his experience on a range of issues. He loved going bush, doing hands on outstation work, fixing a pump or windmill or doing whatever else the situation required.

During his 60s his health slowly deteriorated, first came a heart attack, requiring him to give up his pilot's license, then there was a bout of prostate cancer which appeared to resolve.

Dad was never a patient man who could sit inactive for extended periods. His intolerance for zealous officials and officialdom's stupidity was a thing of legend. As he aged these characteristics became more pronounced, but we all knew what he was like: that was just 'Dad'.

Mum sometimes went with Dad to Oenpelli. More she involved herself in the local community, becoming honorary grandmother to a generation of school children at Berry Springs School. Mum's other great passion was their block of land, its abundant wildlife and increasing garden. One friend described it as like a botanical garden and I watched as Mum swelled with obvious pride.

A description of their land written by her in the early 1990's follows:
We moved to our rural 8 ha block in January 1985, but apart from a small household garden, little was done to develop it until our house was completed in late 1986. Our aim, then was to combine a productive fruit and vegetable garden with pleasant surroundings,

incorporating exotics and native plants with already existing shrubs and trees…. Excluding grasses we have found more than 60 different types of plants growing on our block!

Wildlife
There is a good selection of woodland birds – butcher birds, cuckoo shrikes, parrots, doves and other less well known like the partridge pigeon. Dollar birds are seen in the wet season. Other visitors are less frequent, e.g. yellow and olive backed orioles, weebills and pardelotes. We were delighted in January to have a pair of white gaped honeyeaters take up residence, perhaps partly due to a population explosion, but also we think attracted by the growth and variety of our garden.

We also have lizards ranging in size from the sand monitor to geckoes and skinks. There are also blue tongued lizards, frill necked, spotted tree goannas, and the little dragons we call shaky paws. This last variety has become abundant near our house and we frequently see them on the concrete floor of the verandah, or on plants nearby, even at rest on a monstero deliciosa fruit. We do see the occasional bandicoot, native cat and antilopine kangaroos are quite abundant. Wallabies favour the far end of our block and are less frequently seen near our house. Because of our abundant wildlife we have had to fence in our vegetable garden area.

During the wet season our block is very green and leafy but it looks fairly bare about September when all the deciduous trees have lost their leaves. However there is some shade particularly close to the house. We feel we have a block that caters well for our needs and also meets the requirements of a number of bush creatures.

She also wrote a contribution to the local newspaper, the 'Litchfield Times' Nature Column, circa 2000

JOY OF THE BUSHLAND
A few months ago the Royal Australasian Ornithologists Union commenced a five year scheme called the Australian Bird Count to monitor populations and movements of Australian Land Birds. The participants nominate particular areas for regular surveys and one of my survey areas is the Manton Dam Recreational Reserve. I spend periods of 20 minutes counting the birds or I see or hear in three different sites – on the hillside sloping down to the dam, part of the foreshore and what I originally called the creek but have since found it to be the Manton River upstream of the dam! These visits provide me with a double interest – the birds and the plant life.

When I visited in November, many of the trees on the stony hillside were bare while others had a light covering of new leaves. The main trees in that area are woolybutts, iron woods, terminalias and owenias. There were a few zamias in the understorey but the undergrowth appeared sparse. There were some bare stalks of hyptis that had evidently survived a fire earlier in the year, a few dry tussocks of grass and stones.

What a difference in early January! The trees were all thickly covered with leaves and the variety was greater than I had previously realized. Xanthostemon paradoxus had a few bright yellow flowers in which were feeding white throated honey eaters. Grevillea docurrens shrubs which had not been noticed earlier were well covered in leaves and large numbers of pale pink flowers which were being enjoyed by a pair of white gaped honey eaters. A number of northern fantails were flitting about the trees and bushes searching for insects. Between the tussocks of grass on the slope were large numbers of wild grape plants, mostly small with inconspicuous greenish flowers on them. Interspersed among them were pachynema dilatum, easily recognized by their unusually shaped flat leaves. Perhaps they will be flowering on my next visit. There were also other vines and herbs scattered among them.

There was not a great difference in the foreshore on the second visit, but the upstream site, much of which had been bare underneath paperbarks and large wattles, had become a tangled mass of grass and vines. There were numerous hibiscus meraukensis, not yet in flower, and another type with soft furry leaves and small bright pink flowers. In the thick riverine vegetation following the watercourse, I heard the musical calls of two little shrike thrushes, saw a koel cuckoo and a pair of bower birds feeding on fruit high up in a tree.

The water itself is also interesting. The water lilies have increased and a number of lily trotters with their incredibly long feet could be seen. Other waterbirds present were cormorants, egrets, magpie and pygmy geese, sacred ibis and whistling ducks, while overhead hovered a whistling kites and an impressive sea eagle.

Because of the nature of my surveys I have limited time for looking at the flora in the Recreation Reserve. There is doubtless a much wider range than I have mentioned so visitors to the bushland there could have an interesting time seeking what is to be found.

Contributed by Helen Wilson. Many thanks!!

Mum was famous for her home baked bread; many visitors complementing her on it. She first made two batches a week in her wood stove at Oenpelli.

As children moved away it reduced to a weekly batch on Saturday; fresh bread rolls for lunch. I would take my children to visit mid-morning Saturday so they could assist Grandma making bread. On the table would be a large bowl full of rising dough covered with a tea towel. They would assist, giving the bread its final kneading, eating pieces of dough along the way. While she formed bread rolls and put bread for loaves into tins she would give each child a piece of dough and a baking tray to make their own creations, rolls and other interesting shapes, long pieces like snakes, faces with currant eyes, anything that took their fancy. Lunch was keenly anticipated as the smell of baking bread permeated. Each child had their things in pride of place.

Mums recipe, handwritten from a letter follows.

> *Bread*
> *4 cups flour*
> *1 ½ cups warm water*
> *½ teasp salt (not in packet recipe)*
> *1 sachet yeast*

Mix salt into flour. I also add grated carrot and sunflower seed, and use half high fibre flour or wholemeal flour and half white flour. According to the directions on the High Fibre Grain Bread Mix, the flour and yeast are mixed together and water added and mixed to a dough with a spoon. Then, with lightly floured hands, you knead the mixture. According to these instructions you knead the bread over a period of 5-8 minutes, roll it into a loaf shape, stand for about ½ hour then cook. You can make into bread rolls instead of a loaf.

I do not make as above but mix yeast, a desert spoon of flour and some of water in a jug, and leave it until there is a good head of froth, and then mix liquid into flour mixture and knead well until no longer sticky. I then leave it in dish in plastic bag until double size, knead it again, making it into rolls loaves etc. Let stand as above and then cook

Mum also continued her regular letter and post card writing through retirement with excerpts below

Post card to Darragh (picture : Antrim Road near Glenarm, Northern Ireland)

Dear Darragh,
You may have travelled in this area while you were living in Belfast. That's a while ago now. This year Grandpa has relocated 14 possums and two black footed tree rats. They all loved our jak fruit, and twice animals were attracted just by the smell when no jak fruit had been left in the cage. We had something on our verandah last night that got into our boxes of mangoes and chewed 3 or 4.
> *Love from Grandma X*

Letter to Dylan (dated 2nd April 2000)

Dear Dylan,
Your Dad said you have begun playing soccer and you have just had a practice match. He said you were very quick so I guess you were able to dodge in and out and quickly get away.

Annette Heriot who lives across the road from us has just started to play soccer too. She had been chosen to go to Borrooloola in a few weeks. Her sister Denise has been playing for a few years.

With love from Grandma X

Mums final letter to our family, dated 25th August was posted 2 days before she died. We received it on our return to Sydney after her funeral. It is typical of the hundreds of letters she sent over many years

Dear Graham and Mary,
We were glad to have the opportunity to talk to you on the phone last Friday night. I hope you had a good night out Mary. I was amused when Zara came back the second time. She said to me, "Do you know what?" and of course I didn't know. Then she told me she five (or maybe six) pimples, so I asked her were they sore. She said, "No, but they're pink and bumpy".

Dorothy (my sister), Phil and family will be up for a few days arriving tomorrow afternoon, so hopefully we'll get the sending of emails sorted out better. We received a delightful one a few days ago from Oliver (her grandson) done by a Speech Recognition Programme. He is teaching it to understand his voice and it has trouble with his Kiwi accent (being US produced), but its accuracy has now improved from 10% to 75% with five hours training. The message has a tremendous number of capital letters, so I imagine where Oliver's sound intensity increases it puts a capital – even occasionally part way through a word. He had a PPS. "It Is Still SlowEr Than Typing" (It doesn't always have everyone starting with a capital letter)…

I'll finish off now with lots of love to you all.
Mum

Remembering Mum at the End

In January 2001 Mum and Dad had been married 50 years, and led by Robin, the five of us children, along with our extended families decided to have a celebration to mark the occasion. My Auntie Jude has about 30 acres of land at Wedderburn, 60 kilometres southwest of Sydney. About 50 extended family members and old friends came along. One activity was for guests to take a letter of the alphabet and use it to weave a story of something about Mum and Dad's life, and over 2 hours a succession of skits, anecdotes and stories of their life emerged. Mum and Dad were keen push bike riders and Dad loved collecting discarded items from the tip and turning them into something useful. So our children's contribution, under the letter B was a collection, from kerb-side rubbish, of parts of old, rusted bikes, assembled into something resembling a push bike for Dad to repair and use. Others contributed stories of memories or other items, marking half a century of their life together.

Mum was the glue who maintained a myriad of relationships, while ensuring food on the table, visitors entertained, children and grandchildren cared for and scientific interests pursued. This provided fitting recognition, telling how she provided ongoing ideas, support and encouragement for Dad to do the many things he did.

A speech by old friend Geoff Lucas reflected on the occasion.

Celebrating Alf and Helen Wilson's Golden Wedding Anniversary

6th January 2001

I first met Alf and Helen in Darwin in March 1958

For quite some time CMS (Church Missionary Society) had felt they needed to establish a field headquarters in Darwin – which was the centre of government and health in the NT.

Alf had been paramount in recommending an 11 acre bushland site at Nightcliff – on the outskirts of Darwin, purchased from William Drysdale at 20 pounds an acre. However many thought it was too far out of Darwin, and preferred an area under the flight path of the then, small Darwin airport.

History proved the wisdom on Alf's choice, because it wasn't long before the metropolis moved out and engulfed Nightcliff and far beyond. For about 40 years the Nightcliff property was a valuable resource:
- For aboriginal people wanting a safe oasis out of the bright lights of Darwin
- For CMS personnel as it provided a servicing, accommodation and R&R centre
- For the Anglican church

When I arrived in Darwin Alf was involved in the erection of the first econo steel framed building and whilst there we were able to get up the walls of the building.

My relationship with Alf and other personnel in the north was through the Sydney office to help provide them with the means to do the job to which god had called them – the care and friendship of aboriginal people – at the same time introducing them to the saviour and hope of mankind.

There are three areas where Alf showed amazing foresight in his work in the north, and it was clear he had god's leading to make these steps possible:

Firstly – most of you are aware that Arnhem Land, where Alf & Helen spent most of their time, is a very beautiful place – the scenery enchants the visitor and captivates the residents. However part of its fascination lies in its inaccessibility.

In the wet season most of western Arnhem Land is awash and supplies have to brought in during the dry. Because of the enormous difficulty in obtaining reliable contractors to do the job – Alf decided the only way forward was for the society to purchase a truck and bring them in by road.

The first was an ex-army blitz which was procured in Sydney with an old torn canopy, bald tyres and both doors missing – this was in mid 1956. Then followed a variety of ex-army GMC vehicles purchased at base prices with all the skill used in an Arabian bazaar.

However it was not until 1961 that the society had funds available to purchase a new Leyland diesel comet truck. This was driven to Darwin by Alf and John Donald with me going along to ensure that each of these truckies had an equal share of the driving.

As a city slicker I was pleased on the trip to ensure we ate with proper decorum – so when I produced a tablecloth for breakfast Alf and John could hardly contain themselves – Alf reckons over the years he has been in many different camps – but that was the only one with a tablecloth.

The important fact in all this was that, as a result of his ingenuity - - on the smell of an oil rag – Alf had proven the reliability and economic viability of the society undertaking its own road transport.

Secondly, the same applies to his vision for the use of air transport – a very controversial subject with CMS because of previously costly experiences.

The problem of how this would be implemented seemed insurmountable especially when a pilot said to Alf – " the only way this would happen is for one of the staff to get a pilot's license and then procure an aircraft" – just like that out of the middle of nowhere in Arnhem Land.

Alf believed that if it was going to happen - he was most likely the one who was going to make it happen

It all started with an aircraft arriving on a Sunday morning requiring fuel, just as Alf was walking up to church. He was first put out by the intrusion but then he remembered the verse - "do not neglect to show hospitality to strangers, for thereby some have entertained angels unawares".

Over a cup of tea the pilot said – "it beats me why you people don't have an aircraft here with someone able to fly it. He then went on to explain how to go about getting a license.

In nothing short of remarkable circumstances, Alf obtained his pilot's license and he and Helen scraped together $3200 of their own money to buy an Auster. Working on the principle that there is no such thing as a free ride he paid off the Auster by using it on mission transport.

He had then purchased - again from their own money – a Cessna 182 which had been used on the flying doctor service from Conellan airways for $6000. Alf says that it had been completely overhauled and its value was more like $15000.

Again by transport operations Alf was able to pay off the aircraft and by this time CMS were convinced that a society aircraft should be part of their operations. Typical of Alf and Helen's generosity, was that they handed the 182 to the society as a deposit on a new Cessna 207. Furthermore flying was now occupying so much time that a commercial pilot was recruited to act as pilot.

Then thirdly was Alf's involvement with the outstation or homeland centres out of Oenpelli. By 1966 there was a need for decentralisation, because as one aboriginal person put it

"at Oenpelli there are too many people, too many whites, too many children out of control, too much alcohol and too many fights." Alf was able to combine his normal duties with the practical help of transporting people and their supplies by air.

He visited the outstations regularly, encouraged the aboriginal people and kept in touch with the families both Helen and he had got to know during their 32 years of service. Even after they resigned as CMS missionaries in 1984 they have still kept in contact with their Oenpelli aboriginal friends who love and respect them for their support.

Now I have spent a lot of time talking about Alf, what can we say of Helen.

Well I understand that whilst studying chemistry – which must have been unusual for a women in that era – she terminated the course to take up midwifery in preparation for missionary service and ended up topping the year.

She came from an illustrious family. Her father was one of the early students of Sydney Boys High and we think later a teacher – and regularly contributed to the Herald's letters to the editors page – putting straight the record in respect to the history of the school – what the school motto veritate et virtute meant and matters generally about Latin.

Enid and I understand that Helen's father, Mr Smith was to take up an early post with the Presbyterian church in Ballina. He was originally to go by boat but they wanted him earlier.

Not to be daunted by a small problem like this – he decided to catch a train to Tenterfield with his bike – then ride down the very steep decline to Ballina using a bough tied to the back of his bike as a brake.

It seemed to us that Helen was the quiet support for Alf and the family and through the years in the territory developed a remarkable knowledge of its flora and fauna.

She had an enormous interest in her fruit and vegie garden – and showed a remarkable ingenuity in preserving them for use in the off season.

May we join with you all in congratulating Helen and Alf in reaching their golden milestone of marriage. May god grant you many more years together.

Geoff Lucas
5th January 2001.

One of the final things in Mums life was she was nominated in August 2001 by Berry Springs School to receive a Certificate of Appreciation for the International Year of the Volunteer. The transcript of a letter proposing this nomination, about two weeks before Mum died, and statements of support follow.

IYV Nominations
C/- Warren Snowdon
Re Certificate of Appreciation Nomination
Dear Warren

Please find attached a Nomination for the International Year of the Volunteer, Certificate of Appreciation.

Our school wishes to nominate Mrs Helen Wilson. Mrs Wilson is an aged pensioner who lives in our rural district. Mrs Wilson has been adopted as our schools 'Grandmother'. She has volunteered her time to the school every week since 1986, and in 2001 she still comes as regular as clockwork to spend Thursdays helping out the children.

Many of our children do not have extended family in the NT and Mrs Wilson in many ways fills the gap this leaves. She is well known and very well liked by all the students and staff of the school.

Mrs Wilson epitomises the 'quiet Australian' Volunteer. She is unassuming and does not want rewards or recognition, she simply gives of her time to help others. She is a very special Australian.

Thank you
Terry Quong,
Assistant Principal

One of the highlights of my time at Berry Springs School was to meet and work with Mrs Wilson, a long term volunteer and 'adopted grandmother' of the school. Mrs Wilson's caring nature and positive outlook quickly endears her to the students, school staff and community. She is held in the highest regard by the whole school community for her willingness to assist students and teachers and her overall commitment to the school and its programs. I have been fortunate to witness first hand her work with the students and their thorough enjoyment of having her as part of the class. She has a wealth of knowledge and experience that she willingly shares. She is always keen to be involved in community school events. Of particular mention was her assistance with an Upper Primary special needs student who required emotional support and a little 'TLC' and understanding that only a caring grandmother can give. Mrs Wilson went above and beyond the call of duty to organize an interesting and successful program for this student who responded positively to her approach. A sincere thank you to Mrs Wilson for her support with this program and for her ongoing support and commitment to Berry Spring School and its students.

June Wessels
Principal, Bakewell Primary School (previously Berry Springs School)
5/8/01

Goodbye Mum

Mum was driving back from one of her school grandmother days, after a normal, happy half day with the class, when she apparently lost concentration and drove into the path of an oncoming vehicle. She died instantly. It was a huge shock to all our family and friends.

Our whole extended family assembled at our family home in Darwin a few days later, each of us travelling from our different homes scattered across Australia and New Zealand.

A simple service was held to commemorate Mum's life at St Peters Church, Nightcliff, not far from the first land they bought in Darwin many years before.

A family friend, Jenny Green, spoke briefly about Mum at her funeral service

For Helen – St Peters Church Nightcliff, Wednesday 5th September 2001

Today we say goodbye to Helen, although the reality of her going has hardly begun to sink in. She will not soon be forgotten as each one of us moves on with our lives.

Rather she will be long remembered as one of the most kind and caring people in our community.

Those memories will surely include:

- *Generosity – the sharing of produce such as limes, mangoes, pawpaws, tomatoes, cumquats, etc, etc*
- *Hospitality – "when you're down this way call in for a cuppa", "come and have lunch", "call in for a chat"*
- *Encouragement – notes and letters sent to many when sick or in other need., building friendships with newcomers, lonely people, refugee families*
- *Time and Faith – many hours of involvement with school classes teaching Religious Instruction, helping on excursions, with craft and so on. Around the shops you might hear a little voice pop up "Hallo, Mrs Wilson"*
- *Sharing – her kitchen and culinary skills with her grandchildren and others. "Let's make biscuits today", "I'll teach you how to cook a casserole" What does it matter if in their enthusiasm the biscuits aren't quite cooked through. Her skills included mending the fallen apart hymn books and sewing up and stuffing the toys knitted for Palliative Care, giving each its own huggable personality*

And so the list goes on, you surely have your own experiences to add.

Alf, you have been an integral part of this and you of course will miss her more than any of us. Our love goes to you and the family today. We want to be there for you.

The last time I saw Helen was at the Territory Wildlife Park two weeks ago. It was a Thursday and she was there with the Berry Springs students on an excursion to find out about animal behaviour at different times of the day. From the train we saw her standing in the shade of a tree, wearing her blue and white dress and a big sunhat. As she chatted with a teacher, the children scrambled over the play equipment. It was a beautiful picture that will stay with me forever. In recognition of Helen's love of nature, particularly birds, this little sparrow is being given to her as a symbol that she (and we) are worth more than many sparrows in Gods sight

...... and not one falls to the ground without our heavenly father knowing.

Jenny Green

My sister Robin wrote about Mum when deciding on a headstone

Helen Trindall Wilson
July 30th 1926 – August 30th 2001
You touched so many lives

This is the simple plaque that adorns my mother's grave. As a family we couldn't find a more fitting tribute. Each of us knows how much she touched our life and those of our family around us. But her influence extended far beyond her family.

The school community and beyond into the local high school reeled in shock as the children who had treasured her morning with them extended right through to those now in the final year of high school. Three months later Berry Springs School opened a garden and birdbath dedicated to Helen's memory filled with plants donated from the families whose children attended the school. A special dedication assembly was held at which my Dad was asked to speak. I think Mum would have been a little bemused at all the fuss but would have accepted it in the end as it was so important to those left behind.

My Children Return

Dad's life was moving in a stable path towards old age until my Mums death caused a massive disruption in 2001.

The Christmas after my Mum died I brought our three children, Darragh, Dylan and Zara to visit Dad. He was struggling to come to terms with life alone.

I asked him if he could organise for us to go out to Oenpelli to stay for a few days. So after a couple days at the house near Darwin, we drove to Jabiru. I had the children on lookout for the first glance of the Arnhem Land escarpment in Kakadu, remote and purple in the morning haze. We were met by the MAF aeroplane. I asked the pilot to do a low run across the plains from Mudginberri, over the East Alligator River crossing then around the hills to Oenpelli.

My children, for whom Oenpelli was only a word in their fathers imagination, watched entranced, as we skimmed low over floodplains, flushed with early wet season floods and dotted with lazy waterbirds which took off and flew a hundred yards before settling again. Coming over the Magela, they recognised the home of Crocodile Dundee, where he entranced a buffalo with the power of his finger. Then came the outlier hills of Arnhem Land, merging to the solid block of the main ranges, fissured with endless rainforest gullies amidst towering rocky crags. The East Alligator flashed by, the Rapid River of Dundee

229

fame, now with a couple metres of tea coloured water flowing out of the sandstone and over the crossing. A final skip across the eastern plains of the river and there, as a series of dots, with houses and people beside the billabong, set amongst the three hills, was Oenpelli. A minute of two later we were on the airstrip bouncing along the gravel to a stop.

Everyone pushed a strut to roll the plane into the hangar. Then we piled into the Toyota Land Cruiser for the trip to town where a person away on holidays lent us their house to stay in.

My kids, on push bikes, were off, riding around the town, amazed at the chatter in another language, and the friendly waves and laughs. An old man comes up to them who knows Dad and Mum. He shakes their hands and tells them each their skin name. Someone else comes up with tears and says he is very sorry about Mum.

Over the next few days I took them to visit many places of my childhood. Swimming at the little waterfall was most favoured, where clear wet season water tumbled over the rapids and low falls into a clear shallow pool. We could not swim at the bottom of the big waterfall as someone said "might-be kinga (crocodile) in there", however we climbed to the top pool, above the falls, for a lazy swim and to enjoy the view.

One morning I took the two boys fishing while Zara stayed with Dad. The billabong of 100 barramundi, took two hours to walk to in the early morning, over tracks now overgrown with thick vegetation, without the buffalo to keep it clear. The billabong was so thick with weed it was impossible to get a clear cast, you could see the fish but you just could not get them on a weed covered line.

After a couple hot frustrating hours we headed back, across the now baking country, pursued by a million march flies and ferocious morning humidity. Darragh, twelve, had a big time dummy spit at the heat and flies. His stoic nine year old brother Dylan, trudged on. Finally we got back to the comfort of an air conditioned car and house.

Not a morning of pleasure, but a reminder of the country in all of its extremes, which at times gets lost in rose coloured hindsight. The five days passed very quickly and then it was time to go.

It was not reliving my childhood, which belongs to another time, although still in the same place. But it was a small insight for my children into that life which lives on in my mind. For me it was different things happening at once, an introduction between my children and the aboriginal world they never had really known, but where they are known and remain part of a continuing story. It was also a chance to say goodbye to my Mum in my own way, in the place she lived in and loved for the biggest part of her life. For my children I hope that, in seeing the sights, smelling the scents, feeling and tasting the presence of Oenpelli, they too will form a lasting special image, alive in their memories.

A Second Family and a Final Childhood.

In the first year after Mum died Dad did it tough. While Dad revelled in social gatherings it was always Mum who organised them. She had also organised the day to day household activities, the food, cooking, cleaning. Dad helped, but many required domestic skills that were foreign to him. A few months after we came back from Oenpelli Dad came to Sydney to help my brother renovate a house. This gave him some practical purpose, but the long cold winter of NSW ground him down, and old age was taking its toll and slowing him. His shock and grief over Mum were very raw, and he seemed like a lost soul.

Finally as the Sydney winter eased he headed back to the NT, and seemed to be settling back into some normalcy in his NT life. Odd phone calls kept us informed about his goings on. On one occasion he told me that an old friend from Oenpelli, Betty Cooke, whose husband Cam had died a few years earlier, was visiting the NT and he had caught up with her.

Another couple weeks passed then suddenly, a bolt from the blue. Dad's voice was on the phone.

"I just wanted to let you know that I have been seeing Betty Cook and we have decided to get married. I will be coming to Sydney in a few weeks and we will get married there."

Peter Carroll later remarked "I think I was one of the first people your father told about his plans. He and Betty were both concerned about the reaction of their children."

Betty had been like a second Mum to us as kids, with Peter and I moving between houses, as suited, and our brothers and sisters doing the same. Cam and Dad had been partners in mischief on many occasions and Mum and Betty were frequently observed having long chats about whatever it was they talked about. I just don't think it had ever occurred to us that Dad and Betty would meet up and decide so quickly to get married. But our family we were delighted on Dads choice and just hoped that Betty could cope with our slightly cantankerous father. However he was an adult, who had made up his own mind, and it was the same for Betty, so we decided that we couldn't think a better second Mum. Not to mention that our childhood best friends would become our new extended family.

After the previous bout of prostate cancer and a heart bypass, Dad's health now seemed good, and all was fine.

The wedding proceeded as planned and then Dad and Betty went back to Darwin to begin their life together. We wondered whether he would sell the Darwin property and move to Queensland to be closer to Betty's family,

With much effort and help from Betty, Dad published his memoirs, a culmination of several years' work. As publication drew to a close, it was obvious that Dad's memory was failing and his behaviour was increasingly erratic.

The prostate cancer returned and, faced with declining health, Dad and Betty sold the Darwin property and moved to Sydney, where they bought a retirement unit in Narellan, on Sydney's outskirts.

Within three months it became obvious that Dad was in his last stages. After what appeared to be a couple of minor strokes Dad spent a few days in hospital. Now he could only walk with someone holding both arms and it was beyond Betty to manage him alone.

So we arranged for a bed in a nursing home, where he became a favourite with the nurses. He was now confined to a wheelchair and barely able to feed himself on good days. Flashes of his old lucidity occasionally returned, but little of the memory remained. When you asked him what he had for lunch he gave a vacant shrug, and then smiled vaguely. When Betty came to visit him, his face would light up, but he could no longer hold a conversation with her.

On one of his last days, I am sitting outside in the winter sunshine with him. The blanket on his knees is annoying him and he wants to fold it up. He tries to reason out how to do it. It requires bringing two ends together, but which two, he tries the diagonal's first, then a range of other haphazard combinations, it's beyond him to achieve a square fold, then finally, whether by accident or chance he gets two adjacent ends, and achieves the first fold. But, by now it's beyond him to remember what he was actually trying to do, and finally the blanket drops back upon his knees. He looks up at me and gives a vacant shrug and a half smile, as if to say. What was that all about?

The effort and frustration are gone, like small child his concentration span is now measured in minutes. His body looks like Dad, but really is just a shell, while somehow, what used to be the man of concentration, willpower and determination, has just slid away.

I understand that the Dad I knew is gone and now we wait for the body to go too. He told Betty, shortly before this, when in hospital that he was ready to move on, he had made his peace.

In the final three months of his life he can no longer feed himself and on visits there are often only brief bouts of awake between sleep. What remains is a gentle soul, who smiles and opens his mouth for the occasional mouth of food. The nurses are kind and he seems to respond to kindness with his own warmth, but it's a twilight of existence, as his soul increasingly moves across to another place. Then of course one day the phone rings to say it's over.

What moves me is not his passing, for me he had already gone, but the outpouring of affection from both his second family and many friends. To them the real Dad was the man of Oenpelli, living on in their memory as someone who had worked, walked and talked with them, sharing a love for the people and the world to which he had come.

Moving from childhood to adulthood the NT's wonder has never left me. I now mostly live in Sydney, but each NT visit is like a returning to my childhood, the bright colours and sparkling clarity. My parents have gone to another place, but their life has given something of immense value to me.

John Denver captured something of this life spirit they radiated in his song to his Uncle Mathew.

"Joy was just a thing that he was raised on
Love was just a way to live and die
Gold was just a windy Kansas wheat field
Blue was just a Kansas summer sky"

For me the nearest thing remaining of my parents essence on earth sits somewhere between the hills and sky across a Top End Escarpment. Here they are forever young as when they first came to become children of Arnhem Land.

ANALYSIS - SEEKING UNDERSTANDING

This book began as an attempt to record my mother and my father's lives.

However it has also evolved into a chronicle of social change in the Northern Territory, telling a part of the jigsaw of its aboriginal history. I have found myself making evaluations of what occurred, both in the context of the time and of latter day society views. In this way I am giving a social commentary, in part to deal with the views of others in documents I read to write this story.

What I have written here is entirely my own analysis and understanding of these events, including of the role Mum, Dad and other missionaries played, having regard for the community changes and politics which accompanied them. It is a view seen from close by, but one step removed, from many events. Others may form different views; the positive views in Missionary Society narratives and less charitable views, as in the negative story of missionary activities portrayed in 'An Intruders Guide to North East Arnhem Land'. Most likely, real truth lies in the middle, as we are all selective in what we remember or portray.

When my parents first came to Groote Eylandt, Rose River and Oenpelli, they moved into simple communities, comprising a very small number of Europeans, living within a largely traditional aboriginal society, notwithstanding the many changes arising from missions to aboriginal living patterns. At this time wider contact between members of these communities and the broader European community was extremely limited. Very few aboriginal people had visited Darwin or other towns with significant European populations; there was no media information coming to most members of these communities and almost no other means of communication with the outside world.

Over the last six decades this has been transformed; dealings between aboriginals and the rest of the world have multiplied by many orders of magnitude. The changes wrought from outside into the social fabric of their lives have been extraordinary. Peter Carroll's information on outstations (see References), shows that remote communities have access to television, phone and often internet, giving instant information about the world beyond and an ability to communicate with all corners of the world.

Some changes over the last six decades have been positive; giving people greater control over their daily lives, allowing people to earn living wages, move back to outstations in their homelands and have a say in mining and other development through land rights.

However many impacts have been very negative. Obvious harmful impacts come from alcohol and other substance abuse in communities and their impacts on physical and mental health. Less obvious, harmful impacts arise from payment of social welfare (often called sit-down money) in removing the need for many people to undertake any structured work or even any physical activity.

However, in most cases, the key changes of European society have been incorporated into aboriginal society and customs alongside old traditions. The gun, fishing line and power boat have become new hunting tools alongside old ways; the Toyota and aeroplane are easier forms of transport, but in their absence people still walk tens or hundreds of miles between camps and communities with minimal possessions to support them. A gathering of aboriginal people, under the trees in a shady creek bed, with a fire roasting the day's hunting, is little different from that of my childhood.

Aboriginal politics became even more heated with the Brough-Howard intervention, followed on by Kevin Rudd and other Labor's more of the same, with this legacy still pushed by the Abbot and Turnbull governments.

I hope some good has come from this massive outpouring of money and public outrage. There are glimmers of hope that some of those actively involved have a genuine understanding of the trade-offs involved, along with a goodwill towards getting aboriginal issues addressed more constructively in a way which finds a balance between responsibility of government and local people.

There is an undisputed problem of alcoholism, associated with abuse and neglect, often including children but equally adults, such as spouses, beaten in drunken rampages. The health disasters for the substance abusers themselves are crystal clear. Almost none of my childhood aboriginal friends are still alive. Most died of complications of alcohol abuse and western lifestyles.

Aborigines have no monopoly on these problems but the scale is bigger. A lost generation of children has grown up in the hollow place left by years of parental neglect and lack of education; many have far worse skills than their mission educated parents and grandparents did.

However paternalism has patently failed before. All it does is delay the need to become responsible for living in our modern society. It is hard to believe that this or any other major interventions will be more than band aids along the way, to cover some unsightly aspects of this transition. Without community wide support it will waste yet more resources and human capital and is unlikely to have any lasting legacy, as an externally imposed solution. There has to be recognition that imposing such solutions across whole communities without their agreement is another form of rights dispossession.

What is the solution; I don't really know but think it is somewhere between empowerment and responsibility, combined with acceptance that there will be many disasters along this massive social transition path. We have to try and provide compassionate help in these cases without using them as a whipping boy or an excuse to further victimise whole communities. A principle of the rule of law is that individuals are innocent until proved guilty, yet we seem to want to condemn whole communities for the deeds of some. However we do need to bring under control the outrageous behaviour of the suppliers of the substances which fuel this misery. We also must support community initiatives to keep out or make unattractive substances such as petrol and alcohol.

Europeans did not make an easy transition from feudalism to a modern post-industrial society and they had 500 years along the way, so why we should expect a clean and neat 100 year transition for aboriginal society. My sense is that we have to become more accepting of aboriginal society making its own new future, to accept that this transition belongs to them. It will create a variant of Australian society, similar to the way migrant cultures now incorporate both elements of the old and the new.

This does not mean that we accept abusive situations but, as well as using compliance solutions, we need to try and find ways to give both power and responsibility, without endlessly sitting in judgement at the inevitable failures.

In other words, we should find a little bit of the tolerance for those making a difficult journey. I am sure that aboriginal society 100 years hence will be both vibrant and different from today, keeping elements of their original traditions and bringing in elements of other cultures that suit. The problems will still be there of course but, perhaps, another 100 years will provide a bit more perspective as the successes gradually rise to balance the problems.

We can only hope for some good outcomes from the current focus.

I see little hope for quick fixes which invoke strong emotions to justify social engineering – the children are sacred becomes the justification for all sorts of dehumanising interventions. Here I see the world differently to my father who believed, when still able, that Howard dogma was pretty right, though his life's work was also about tempering big brother with compassion.

If we could wind the clock back 50 years, and maintain a high level of control on aboriginal communities, would this have really benefited most aboriginal people? Or would it have just delayed the days of transition and extended the pain along the way. I suspect that transition is always painful, causing lots of human casualties and there is no easy way through.

To suggest that a return to a previous time bubble is the right solution seems to me to be denying the right of the aboriginal communities to build their own solutions. Already some of these solutions are evident as people move back to their own homelands and try to build new ways of living in these.

Where I do agree with the Howard and Pearson philosophy is that social welfare solutions are inherently destructive and paying social security in many cases has just become 'sit down money', removing the imperative to do necessary work which is both good for self-respect and physical health. Building employment opportunities in these communities and an expectation that those able to work should work in order to receive income seems to me to be good social policy. But it will never be easy.

One thing which Noel Pearson said, in a Four Corners interview on Arrakun, which rang so true for me, is that these communities can be the best place in the world to live. This is how it was in my childhood and it was probably the same in much of his. It continues to be the experience of people who find their own space in such places. Intimate involvement in a simple daily life, following nature's abundance and seasonal patterns, with other similar people, is profoundly satisfying. It is easy to lose sight of this when problems seem just seem to keep getting bigger.

So what, overall, was the benefit of 50 years of missions, before they transitioned to towns? Missions educated a generation of aboriginal leaders, many of whom remained active in their communities for decades, with some still continuing up to today. Missions, to some extent, sheltered aboriginal communities from the worst excesses of European colonisation and contact.

The difference between the number of aboriginal people who still live in western Arnhem Land, along with the level of retention of their culture, to that of communities on pastoral stations 100 kilometres further west is striking, one remains, the other has almost vanished. Missionaries played their part in this, along with others such as Paddy Cahill, who sought to protect local aboriginals and minimise contact with exploitative, early Europeans.

Missionaries brought their own cultural values, some of which, seen from today's perspective, seem paternalistic and wrong. Missions also brought their own petty bickering and power plays, reflecting that these were a mixture of people, with a mix of better and worse features, just like others. However, my overwhelming impression is that missionaries were good people, who tried to do their best with what little they had, and to give to people, to whom they came, something they thought was of value. They also provided a social fabric which allowed sick people to be cared for, children to learn, and built a bridge of contact to the western world that was relatively benign.

In addition missionary Christian belief was not just a harmful cultural imposition. Many aboriginal people found in this new meaning for their own lives and were motivated by it to do good in their own communities. The belief, of both missionaries and aboriginal society, in transcendent spiritual being's with a role in human affairs was a shared link across cultures for those who seek to find meaning beyond human experience.

In reality it was a two way exchange with the missionaries learning and growing alongside their aboriginal companions. People in their mid-twenties, typical of most missionaries, came to these communities with limited life experience. Their incorporation into aboriginal society involved a huge learning for most of them, as they came to understand the complex layers of aboriginal life and its surrounding world. Along with this was the simple joy of living in the present in a timeless land. They also came to see that aboriginal society was not a one-dimensional place, that each aboriginal person was as individual and distinctive as their European counterparts.

My parents were part of this missionary experience, and grew and learnt through it. In doing so they became strong advocates for their own aboriginal community. To them Oenpelli represented both their aboriginal friends and the fact that they were entrusted with a responsibility for the well-being of a whole community.

What were their important contributions? I see two which stand out. The first was the continuity they gave through 40 years of involvement in one community. At Oenpelli most white people were transient; they came, stayed a few years and went off again. Mum and Dad came, then stayed involved in the community all their working lives and on into retirement. Others have done this too but they are few compared to the many that have passed through. Time builds trust and understanding; so as the years went by they became wise elders to the community, able to give sound and honest advice. This did not stop the harm but it fixed little things along the way, helping individuals deal with different problems as they arose.

The second important contribution was their willingness to get in and do whatever the situation required; a new transport system was needed so Dad went to Sydney and bought a truck. A river crossing was needed, so he helped build it, manganese was discovered so he got a miners right over the area to create employment for local people, an aeroplane was needed so he got a pilot's license and bought his own plane. This was not self-advancement; he just saw a need and a solution and joined the dots. Mum's contribution was mostly helping and supporting Dad to join the dots, rather than doing these things herself. But she also did her part, if ten extra people turned up on the medical plane for lunch, she got them lunch, if a new family arrived she did her bit to make them feel welcome. Then, when she had free time, she went off bird observing, and contributed to the national bird atlas. She also found time to walk and talk around the community and write innumerable letters to children, grandchildren and friends, adding social glue.

As Dad matured into a senior citizen one of his final contributions was supporting the establishment of an Injalak Art Centre, where local artists prepare and sell paintings and which has contributed to the maintenance of aboriginal culture. In his years of travel and meetings with aboriginal groups he was given a collection of aboriginal cultural objects; stone axes, ceremony sticks, paintings and the like. One of his final acts was to return almost all of this material to the Arts Centre, understanding that it really belonged to the community and having a future hope for something like a living museum, capturing the community's history, being established. To the extent that this book has success I also see it contributing to this.

Mum and Dad did not fix the problems at Oenpelli and many of the problems were worse when they left than arrived. But no one else has fixed the problems either. In reality, seeing aboriginal society as a problem misses the point. It is just a series of people and groups where some things go well and some don't, some people end up in trouble, and some succeed.

So any idea of a single solution to Aboriginal development is as ill-conceived and misleading as expecting all people in Sydney to aspire to drive the same cars or live in the same type of houses. Here are communities with the same breadth of aspirations and hopes as other communities. At the same time the broad values of humanity are the same, parents loving and wanting the best for their children, people enjoying laughter and the company of friends.

This is not to take away from the systemic problems and failures which have accompanied aboriginal history; the alcoholism, educational failure, and the catastrophic health situation which many people experience. But big brother can't fix them, whereas lots of individuals can, all making their own individual contributions to improve things. Government is best when it is supportive, not overly interfering, but also requires community and individual contributions to match resources from outside. With individual contribution comes self-sufficiency and self-esteem, not a victim mentality.

Government must certainly take a large share of the blame with its endless policy changes and imposed solutions, decided by others from long distance. But Government, like the Missionaries was mostly composed of well-intentioned people, working within the constraints and attitudes of their day. Blame of government should not be used to absolve others from their responsibility for what they did, or did not do, in their own communities.

So Oenpelli must make its own place in the world for its own people. It must create its own path to the future, both similar and distinctive from that of all the other little similar communities. Sometimes this will go well and sometimes not. Perhaps the best we can do, here and elsewhere, is to try and touch and improve lives of those who intersect with us, across their spectrum of cultures and colours, allowing others to give as well as receive, and all the while seeking to enjoy our own journey.

This book is my memory of part of this journey. Not all of it will be right or even remembered correctly. However it is my personal trip through this landscape, captured as best I can.

GRAHAM WILSON

APPENDIX 1 – NT AND OENPELLI BACKGROUND

For this next section I have substantially used information from Cole's book '*A History of Oenpelli*' supplemented by extracts from Nell Harris's book, '*The Field has its Flowers*', and from other sources.

Aboriginal people lived in the places we call Kakadu and Western Arnhem Land since time immemorial, building a society which endured and prospered across generations far too many to count.

Josephine Flood recounts:

"Amongst the Kakadu people of the Alligator Rivers region the great ancestress was called Imberombera . She came from across the sea and arrived on the coast of Arnhem Land. Her womb was filled with children and from her head were suspended woven dilly bags in which she carried yams, bulbs and tubers. She travelled far and wide, she formed hills creeks, plants and animals and left behind her many spirit children, giving a different language to each group.

The Gunwinggu people of Arnhem Land tell a similar story about the mother, Waramurungundji, who came across the sea from the north west, the direction of Indonesia, to land on the north Australian coast at the beginning of Creation. Not only did these dream time ancestors come from across the sea but they also came by canoe.

Some Aborigines have always believed that their ancestors came from across the seas in canoes in the Dreamtime. Now scientists have come to the same conclusion from archaeological and other evidence."

It is clear that this happened tens of thousands of years ago. Dr Carmel White, investigating rock shelters near Oenpelli in the mid 1960's found 'edge ground stone axes' carbon dated to 30,000 years ago. This was evidence of sophisticated stone tool technology in a group of people that, at that time, the academic world regarded as one of the most primitive in the world. Subsequent research has since pushed dates back much further, perhaps to 60000 years ago.

Over this time there were periods such as the last great glaciation, which extended until about 10,000 years ago, when sea levels were much lower, by up to about 150 metres. With this Australian land extended several hundred kilometres north from the existing coastline, in close proximity to the islands of Indonesia. Subsequently, at times of peak inter-glacial ocean melting a few thousand years ago sea levels were up to 20 metres higher than today and coastal floodplains we see today of the great rivers of the Top End would have disappeared into shallow coastal estuaries and deltas, fringed by the sandstones outliers and escarpments of the Arnhem Land Plateau. It is likely that some of the great wet season waterfalls of the Top End, rather than crashing into their crystal clear rock pools, instead, fell directly into the oceans of the Timor and Arafura Sea. The aboriginal people must have accommodated to these changes, at peak sea levels being driven back to the edge of the hills from which they could have surveyed the vast expanse of ocean to the north. Seashells found in middens on the top of Oenpelli hills are likely evidence of the sea just below. At other times the Arnhem Land Plateau would have been hundreds of kilometres inland, and more arid, with its watercourses meandering across vast flat plains to a very distant ocean. Aboriginal people would have moved back and forwards with these changes to exploit nature's resources. Did they wonder what vast events were shaping human history in other parts of the globe, causing their world to change so much? The timeless land we see now is no more enduring than those apparently stable worlds were.

Prior to English settlement, aboriginal people on the coast of the Top End had regular contact with Indonesian fisherman from the island of Macassar. These made annual visits to Maregge (Southland = Australia) to collect trepang, which they boiled, smoked and dried for on-selling to China, coming in fleets of 30 to 60 praus (open sail boats) on the north westerly monsoons and returning in the dry season with the south easterly winds. They made camps along the coast and appear to have been assisted by local aborigines, with whom they bartered a range of goods, although at times conflicts arose.

Captain Phillip King was the first European to explore the coast of Arnhem Land. In 1818 he explored the Alligator Rivers, named on account of the large number of crocodiles sighted. His description of the East Alligator River follows.

The banks of either side were very low: they were composed of a soft mud and so thickly lined with mangroves as to prevent our landing, until we pulled up for seven or eight miles...The banks where we landed were about 200 yards apart, but were so low, and without a hillock to ascend or a tree to climb, to enable us to obtain a view of the country, that we could form but a very slight view of the place... No inhabitants were seen, but the fires that were burning in all directions, proved that they could not be far off.

The first NT British settlement was in 1824 at Fort Dundas, Melville Island. In 1827 a second settlement was made at Fort Wellington, Raffles Bay, on Coburg Peninsula. The intent was to establish trade links with South-east Asian colonies. Both settlements had problems, including conflict with aboriginal groups, and were abandoned in 1829. A new colony, 'Victoria' at Port Essington on Coburg Peninsula was established in 1838. It too struggled but lasted more than a decade before abandonment in 1849, ending a quarter century epoch of failure.

Thus the earliest European contact with aboriginal people in the NT was with the people of the Tiwi Islands and Western Arnhem Land, including the peoples of Coburg, Murganella, Oenpelli and nearby areas.

These settlements introduced a range of domestic animals which ultimately became characteristic animals of the Top End with their escape and the abandonment of settlements. Most famous is the buffalo. Others include domestic cattle, Banteng or Bali Cattle, Timor ponies, Rusa deer and pigs. These animals are still on Coburg Peninsula with the deer and Bali cattle largely confined to the Peninsula. Timor Ponies have spread to the northern floodplains of the East Alligator drainage system. Pigs are widespread across the Top End but the extent to which their source was these settlements is unclear. Buffalo rapidly moved on to the lush floodplains of the East Alligator and expanded across the sub-coastal plains of rivers towards Darwin. Within half a century the population supported a buffalo hide industry in the Alligator rivers region. This industry led to ongoing dealings between aborigines and the white population.

These abandoned settlements began the hardship legend of the NT. In part this reflected climate and tropical diseases, as much it reflected the lack of understanding of this land, including poor site selection at Coburg, cut off from the rest of mainland Australia, with poor soils and water supply and with crops and people unsuited to the tropics. If these people moved 50 miles south to the fertile plains of the East Alligator, near Oenpelli, their experience may have been different. Buffalo certainly found this East Alligator land more to their liking.

Victoria settlement was also the endpoint of one of most significant explorations of Australia, by Ludwig Leichhardt. In 1844 he left Moreton Bay. After crossing the Gulf area of Queensland he crossed the Arnhem Land Plateau. I include extracts of his journal of this part in Appendix 2. He said the aborigines of the Alligator Rivers' region "were remarkably kind and attentive." He tells of his passage in December on the Oenpelli side of the East Alligator River as follows:

"We now travelled again to the northward following the outline of the rocky edges at the right side of the creek, having entered the plains we camped at a very broad shallow sedgy boggy lagoon, surrounded with Typhas and crowded with ducks and geese. It was about four miles east of yesterday's camp".

This is a billabong on the floodplains in what we know as the Red Lily area. Such a sight could well be found in early December to this day.

Following Leichhardt, Gregory made explorations of the NT in 1855-56 and Stuart made the first north-south overland crossing in 1862. Both praised the pastoral potential of the Territory. This led to annexation of the NT by South Australia in 1863, with a new settlement at Escape Cliffs at the eastern mouth of the Adelaide River in 1864. This was another poor site and also ended in failure. Surveys by McKinlay and Cadell for a more suitable site were also unsuccessful, becoming epic sagas of survival as they struggled to travel across the wet season Top End. During this time large tracts of imaginary land in the NT were sold off in Adelaide and London.

With the failure of Escape Cliffs the South Australian Government, desperate for a settlement to meet its obligations for the land sales, dispatched Surveyor General Goyder from Adelaide who selected Port Darwin for his new town and rapidly surveyed large areas for subdivision. A few months later, two ships set out to establish the new town of Palmerston, later renamed Darwin, arriving on the 24th June 1870.

In 1872 the Overland Telegraph was completed between Adelaide and Darwin, giving Australia rapid communication with the rest of the world, and making Darwin a pivotal communication hub. Around this time gold was found in Pine Creek leading to a huge speculative land boom, which collapsed in 1875.

These gold mines brought Chinese to the workings. Many stayed as labourers, gardeners and in other occupations, progressively establishing businesses. The release of land for pastoral purposes occurred slowly and was unable to keep pace with demand, leading to a second pastoral boom occurred between 1880 and 1882, when almost the whole of the NT, including all of Arnhem Land, was leased, much by speculators who never occupied their leases.

In 1886 a railway contract was signed for the first stage of a line from Darwin to Adelaide, bringing far more Chinese migrants. Protests from other settlers about 'yellow peril' led to laws banning Chinese migration as, by now, their population far exceeded others, with over 4000 Chinese to a total European population of 1009 in 1889. With new settlers came diseases such as smallpox and leprosy, along with Chinese opium dens and brothels in Darwin. These diseases spread into the aboriginal population, decimating it in the many areas near Darwin. New settlers expropriated aboriginal land, food, water and other resources, leaving many in pitiful conditions at the edge of settlements. There was also intermarrying between aboriginal and Chinese families leading to many of the NT's well known families of today such as the Ah Kits and Longs.

The growing number of buffalo in the late 1800's, in the Alligator Rivers region, drew white hunters. Semi-mobile camps sprang up consisting of a few whites and a varying number of aboriginal assistants and their families. One such was led by Paddy Cahill, who commenced shooting buffaloes in the 1890's in the Alligator Rivers area. Prior shooting occurred mostly from the ground but Paddy had a technique or riding alongside a buffalo, shooting it in the spine from close range, immobilising the animal for aboriginal helpers to finish. This allowed him to rapidly get many animals in a mob. In one session he was credited with dispatching 43 buffalo with only 52 bullets. His most famous horse, St Lawrence, was 'particularly sure footed and manoeuvrable over grass covered plains pitted with buffalo footprints and other potholes'. It was recorded of his absence from the 1894 Palmerston Cup, because of buffalo hunting:

"…. we are told that to witness Paddy Cahill on St Lawrence after buffalo is far more inspiring than any horse act gammon in a Wild West Show…. It requires no bridle rein to guide him near the beast…. he runs alongside a few feet off until the rifle is discharged and the buffalo drops. Then, if others are near he heads for one without the slightest hesitation; and so the game goes on…."

Cahill became familiar with aboriginal people of Oenpelli, many working in his buffalo hunting camps. He soon developed a desire to establish a farming enterprise at Oenpelli, which he described as "a nice bit of fertile country" In the early 1900s Paddy failed to gain approval for an agricultural pursuit at Oenpelli.

However, in 1908, the South Australian Government advertised the release of land for pastoral purposes east of the East Alligator River, allowing selection of up to 640 acres. Paddy applied and was granted 320 acres of land, for Agricultural Lease 45 at Oenpelli in 1909. In February 1910, with his wife and one child, he moved there. He soon established a range of crops, built houses, stockyards and other facilities, with help from the local aborigines.

In 1911 the NT administration was passed to the Commonwealth from South Australia. Its first Administrator was Dr J. A. Gilruth, Professor of Veterinary Science at Melbourne University. He established a diary at Fannie Bay in 1913, the success of which led him to establish other experimental dairies.

In 1912 Professor W Baldwin Spencer, on behalf of the Commonwealth, undertook a survey of the NT Aborigines as part of the newly established Commonwealth policy 'to safeguard the interests of the Aboriginal population.' Spencer formed a close friendship with Paddy Cahill and used Oenpelli as his base for much of this survey. Baldwin Spencer wrote:

'It is only possible to study the latter (Aborigines) when camped amongst them quietly for some time. I was able to do this with the Kakadu tribe, with which my most interesting results were obtained. I secured this only in consequence of the whole-hearted cooperation of Mr P Cahill in my work, during the time I spent as the guest of himself and Mrs Cahill on their delightful home at Oenpelli, far out in the wilds of the East Alligator River. Mr Cahill has had long experience of the Kakadu and other tribes, talks their language and has won their complete confidence. He most generously placed his time and knowledge at my disposal and thanks to him I was able to gain considerable insight into the sacred belief of the Kakadu people.'

Balwin Spencer's name was given to the Arnhem Land escarpment visible south east of Oenpelli which to this day is known as the Spencer Range.

In 1915 Dr Gilruth sought to develop further dairies at Oenpelli and the Daly River, sending additional cattle he acquired to both places. Unfortunately, in the case of Oenpelli, these 'superior' dairy cattle from Victoria were infected with tuberculosis and soon this spread through the herd and was transmitted to the buffalo in the area. From here it spread widely across the sub-coastal plains, as the high densities in which the buffaloes congregated provided ideal opportunities for transmission.

The Oenpelli dairy prospered and in 1916 the government purchased it from the Cahills, so as to produce butter, sending out refrigeration machinery.

Gilruth also arranged for Vesty to build a meatworks in Darwin which was an initial success. However World War 1 caused great difficulties with shipping and high prices and, by 1918, there was serious industrial unrest. The Australian

Workers Union then demanded that Gilruth go to Melbourne to express workers grievances. Gilruth refused, was forced to resign and the meatworks halted.

Without this enterprise Darwin's prosperity fell. Production stopped, industry ceased, shipping disappeared, no capital came into the Territory for investment, and unemployment became an ugly problem. The extremists had closed the northern gateway. The prospects for Darwin were shattered. It was reported, 'All was at peace – the peace of death.'

The fortunes of the Oenpelli dairy followed the demise of Gilruth.

Carl Warburton, who visited Oenpelli soon after World War 1, wrote:

"... the Gilruth administration decided to run a butter factory with Paddy Cahill at Oenpelli, which I claim as the finest dairy country in the world. So wonderful was it that the cows were grazing up to the bails. Butter was produced equal to the best and I took it to Darwin. There the unions refused to take delivery on the wharves because they said it had been made with black labour. When they did decide to handle it, it was so much grease since there was no refrigeration on the boat."

Warburton then describes how, as he passed through the gate at Oenpelli, *"there was a touch of civilisation about this"* and he saw *"black boys breaking a colt"* The homestead *"was a large rambling place covered with bright flowering creepers and surrounded by mango and other tropical fruit trees."*

He described the butter factory as a *"splendid structure with cement floors and, even though in disuse, it had been kept spotlessly clean. Naturally he told me the story of its failure...."* He described Paddy Cahill as *"a man of about sixty, short robust... which told of great strength."* He continued: *"Cahill was one of the earliest and greatest pioneers of the north. He went there about the time of Giles, the explorer and, after working his way through Central Australia, finally took up his wonderful holding at Oenpelli. He sold it in 1924 and took his wife and son Tommy south for well earned rest."*

Of Mrs Cahill he wrote: *"If her life was lonely – and it surely was since she saw other white women about once in twelve months – she did not show it. Indeed she looked completely happy and contented."*

Paddy Cahill was remembered with great affection by aboriginals of Oenpelli in my childhood. His role was both authoritarian and friendly. There was a reported attempt to poison him and his family, but this was said to be the work of a couple of disaffected men who resented his interference with their right to beat their wives. It appears Paddy Cahill and his wife, living at Oenpelli for two decades, were hugely important in building a good relationship between the aboriginal community and the outside world, providing protection against harm that devastated other aboriginal communities coming into first contact with the modern world. It gave a strong basis for the long, happy relationship which my parents had with the same people about a quarter century later. The Cahills' relationship was further enhanced by mostly positive relationships with the missionaries who followed.

With the departure of the Cahills' the government found itself in possession of a pastoral lease without any plans for the future. An approach was made by the Chief Medical Officer to purchase the lease, out of interest in its aboriginal history and to experiment in cattle breeding and tropical agriculture.

At the same time the government approached missionary organisations to determine their willingness to take Oenpelli over as a Mission. The Catholics and Methodists declined but the Anglican 'Church Missionary Society' decided to accept. It had already established Missions at Roper River and Groote Eylandt. Mr Alf Dyer and his wife, at Roper River, were appointed to this posting. The Mission was given an area of 200 square miles, with another 200 square miles retained as an aboriginal reserve along with a subsidy of 250 pounds per year.

The Dyer's reached Oenpelli by boat on 4th September 1925, after being stuck on the soft mud of the East Alligator River, en route, and arriving at the landing at 11 pm. Next morning Alf Dyer, leaving his wife to 'guard' the stores', walked across the plains into Oenpelli, a distance of eight miles. Meanwhile Mrs Dyer met her first Oenpelli aboriginal, clad only in a hair belt and knife. He swam across the river to meet her and, on arrival, asked "Which way boss?" He had been sent out to await their arrival but had fallen asleep. In due course Mr Dyer and Mr Campbell, the caretaker, returned with a buckboard and an aboriginal team to collect Mrs Dyer and the stores.

Dyer and Campbell soon mustered and branded 500 cattle from the surrounding bush, including some quiet dairy cattle. They also inherited 700 goats. Dyer reported that, amongst the aborigines camped at Oenpelli there were a number of excellent buffalo hunters, who had been paid for their stock work with the head stockman paid 30/- per week and the others 10/- per week.

Dyer had no money for wages so he said he could not pay them and they were free to leave, but if they stayed he would try to provide a home for them and their families and build up a community at the station. He also said that he and his wife would care for the old people and the sick and teach them and their children. Most stayed on. Dyer made a temporary chapel on the front verandah where he held church services. For their first Christmas he recorded 100 people were present at both the morning and evening services.

The following year Mrs Dyer wrote: *"I had started school some time before with 15 scholars. One result of Christmas was that eight more came along when we started in January. We both felt we would rather let other things go than school, and we had been letting them come in each day to dinner and stay for afternoon school. It was not very satisfactory, and some of the bush ones want to leave their children for "dura", their word for anything in the nature of writing on paper. Mr Dyer fixed up what had been the dairy…. into a boys dormitory. The place where they sleep is mosquito proof, and they have a very nice place. There are not so many girls, but they are anxious to come so he fixed up the old gaol with a mosquito proof door and window for them. They are very proud."*

Leprosy was a major disease in the area and Bishop Davies wrote to Dyer asking him to care for leprosy patients as best he could until the Government provided something better in Darwin. Dyer tried to isolate these people from the rest of the population but it was difficult. He told the story of Charlie, a boy with leprosy, who had been sent to Channel Island near Darwin for treatment.

'Charlie escaped, but was caught and sent back again. Again he escaped, swam to the beach and made his way to the railway which he followed south before heading east across the country until he reached Oenpelli, a distance of about 200 miles. He had no fingers or toes, was largely crippled, and how he managed to make the journey I never knew. When I asked him why he had come Charlie said "I heard that you have a good story". So I told him about God and Jesus, and how Jesus healed people with leprosy.'

Dyer found that, instead of the 500 gifted cattle, there were 1500 head, as the government drovers had been unable to remove the entire surplus herd. The extra cattle were bought for 1000 pounds. It was hoped the sale of cattle would eventually help to make the mission self-supporting.

Cattle spearing was a problem, particularly in the wet season when other food was scarce. Once, when a report came in of cattle killing nearby, Dyer went to investigate. He found some aborigines sitting, eating the killed animal, and they rushed for their spears. Despite angry looks, he walked up to them and collected their spears. He commanded the culprits to follow him, which they did, to his surprise, as they could have easy run off into the bush.

On arrival back at Oenpelli, where the previous gaol had been turned into a girls dormitory, Dyer did not want to chain up the cattle killers until the police arrived, as was the custom. So as cattle killing was an offence committed against all the people of Oenpelli, he asked other aborigines what should be done. Their reply was, 'give them the strap'. He then asked for volunteers to do the job, but all were afraid saying, 'If we do they will spear us'. So Dyer had to administer this punishment himself. After it was done he asked the culprits to stay and help with the cattle work, which they did.

In 1928 it was reported of Oenpelli: *"The native population is about 190, of which 90 are permanent residents, including school children and working natives…. Ten acres of ground, on the shore of a beautiful lagoon, are under cultivation with maize, potatoes, cassava, pumpkins and other tropical fruits and foods, all for home consumption. Native game and fish are fairly plentiful…. The country…. offers good possibilities for successful industrial development of the mission by cattle raising and agriculture. The stock number 1800 cattle, 80 horses and 200 goats …. this station, with its central position and natural resources, offers every promise of playing an important part in the work of the betterment of the natives in this part of the Territory."*

In 1932, Dyer, reviewing his work at the mission after seven years wrote:

"When we landed at Darwin in 1925 to go to Oenpelli we were told that there were very few blacks there. A missionary said. 'You will not do any good there.' We went to see. While few of the Oenpelli and nearby tribes remain, others soon started to come in and we had over 100 for our first Christmas. In 1930 we had 200 and last Christmas we had some 300 people…. the sick, the old, the blind and the leper have come to us for treatment and we do our best. Hundreds have been treated, many cured and not a few lives saved. Some have passed away but all have been told the 'Good Story' as they call the Gospel…. 70 children have been taught in our school…. They are taught the three R'.

By 1934 Mr Dyer was exhausted and Mrs Dyer was suffering from an incurable disease, so they left Oenpelli. Their role was taken over by Dick Harris and his wife, Nell. She tells of this time:

"After about ten days in Darwin we boarded the Catholic Mission boat, the St Francis.... The trip took one and a half days.... We arrived at Oenpelli in May 1933. It was good to be on land again. There was no special landing structure on the river bank. After the landing fires were lit to tell the folk at the Mission, seven miles away that the boat had arrived. A buckboard, drawn by some mules, came and some stockmen with horses. Natives unloaded the boat and the buckboard began taking stores to Oenpelli.... When Dick and I arrived at the mission gate for the first time, many boys and girls were there to greet us. A girl named Gadjibumba, later called Hannah seemed to be the oldest and most talkative. She was about twelve. She presented me with an embroidered apron.... Later all the girls came to see me as they were curious about me. I was the youngest white woman they had seen.... I arrived at Oenpelli on a Friday. All the natives went walk-about on Saturday.... We were given a bark hut in which to sleep.... I had brought a huge mosquito net which covered our bed.... There was only one toilet on the place and, to go to it, you had to walk a long distance.... There was a big kitchen for the natives and a store with well-constructed shelves at one end. There was a big passageway and we lived on the other side of the passageway. It had an ant-bed floor....

"Mosquitoes were very troublesome.... so we were under our nets before dark. The evening meal, mostly soup and bread, was served early so the house-girls could wash the dishes and go to their camp.... Oenpelli has a huge billabong teeming with fish and water lilies, both of which provided the natives with food. Hundreds of naked natives came from long distances when food was scarce in the bush.... These visitors made their camps across the billabong.... some of these people gradually stayed on and settled at the mission....

"We had no refrigerator at Oenpelli until 1940. So we had no butter. I made a cake every Saturday using bullock marrow fat or dripping. We lived as cheaply as we could. Bread was made five days a week... For breakfast we had rolled oats from sealed tins and, later, ground wheat. Sunday morning we had a tin of herrings and tomato sauce. We used one tin of jam and one tin of fruit weekly. The evening meal started with oxtail soup and bread and oxtail tail stew on toast for breakfast following the cereal and a cup of coffee at breakfast only. Sunday

evenings the people got bread and jam.... Fortunately we had meat daily. A bullock was killed weekly. We had a fresh roast once a week and every day the roasts were baked again and remained fresh. We had barramundi from the billabong and ducks and lots of goose eggs in their season. I made sponge cakes galore with those eggs.

"Our stores came twice yearly. Weevils were awful.... Bread was made communally as it was cheaper than issuing flour individually, much of which would be wasted in the damper making process.

"Outside the kitchen was a bathroom. Mr Dyer had placed a huge drum of water between the kitchen stove and the bathroom. The water became hot so we could have a hot bath.

"The natives went walkabout on Saturday and hunted. It was easy for them to get food – fish and water lilies in the billabong, land turtles on the plains.

"Mr Clymo fixed a small open boat with an engine.... so we got in the boat and went down to Field Island... (about fifty miles) , Dick used to get very seasick. This time, when we got out of the boat at Field Island, he was very sick and lay down on the beach. There were eleven or twelve big fat crocodiles basking on the beach. The boat began to drift from the anchor. Nalim, a very fine man, (Elizabeth's brother) swam out in the crocodile infested water and got into the boat. He had watched Dick start the motor and got it going and got the boat back. I don't know what we would have done if the boat had drifted off. On Field Island there is no water and we had no link with the mission and no one would have known what had happened to us.

"I gave birth to my first baby David... on 9th September 1934. When I told Mrs Dyer I was expecting a baby she was delighted. She said, 'The people here have never seen a white child'.... when we were trying to decide how and where I was to have my baby, my husband and I went up to the mission house for breakfast. Mrs Dyer said, 'We have decided that you should go to Darwin.... and Mr Harris should go with you....' There was an uproar in Darwin- everyone hated the blacks – they wanted them all wiped out – you never heard such talk.... next door was a tennis court. Most of the women who played were policemen's wives – they hated blacks. You'd go up the street and hear people talking in the shops saying, 'It would be good if they were all wiped out.'

"The heat in the Wet was very oppressive. Our unlined iron house was very hot. My husband later made two cots for David (oldest son) and for Jim, my second boy…. The cots were hot because they had two layers of gauze to keep the children safe from mosquito bites. Later Dick made a shelter outside with lots of leaves for a roof which he would water down and we could get a cool rest there. I was always thankful when the rain came for the air was cooler and the children slept…. There were two dormitories, one for girls and one for boys. They were rough buildings but could be locked at night. No child was forced to stay in the dormitories. I think they felt safer there. All girls were promised to men, most of whom had other wives."

In 1937 Reverend Long, General Secretary of CMS, Victoria, visited Oenpelli. His observations and comments, as recorded by Cole, provide an insight into the operation of Oenpelli and some of its problems at that time. He stated:

From the Mission site, however, as far as the eye can see, there are lush green meadows, set around fresh water billabongs teeming with wildfowl, whereon cattle can be fattened at any time, when other parts of the Territory are almost drought stricken. The sandstone ranges striking across the country are veritable walls, and the large area attached to the Mission insures adequate pasture, not only for a large herd of cattle (1600 at present), but also for many buffalo. The Station is the largest and most advanced of the three (CMS Missions in North Australia). Well equipped with machinery and some fine old buildings – notably the mission house and workshop – it is the focal point of much activity. A centrifugal pump lifts water from the nearby billabong to a well-constructed fluming, from which it is led off to irrigate a considerable area of good soil where fruit and vegetables are grown.

Provisioning Oenpelli was a major problem. A report of 1940 stated that the present method of chartering luggers was *'difficult and expensive'*. Mr Harris reported that the method of sending stores to Pine Creek by rail and then by Mission lorry to Oenpelli was also difficult, with the need to investigate a road train option, but the preferred method was carriage by luggers to the deep water berth at Smiths Landing on the River, where a storage facility was needed and transport then to the mission via a utility truck. Such a utility was urgently needed, as the only vehicle then available on the mission was a worn out Ford.

The Mission struggled on until the Japanese bombing of Darwin in 1942, though Dick Harris moved to Groote Eylandt in 1941, being replaced by his brother Jim.

With the war all the women were evacuated to southern Australia leaving Jim, Dick and a handful of other missionaries to carry on their work alone. For the first year each Mission had only one staff member and this was increased to two in 1943. It was not until 1944 that the first of these missionary wives were to return. This caused a major disruption to mission activities with education of children virtually ceased over this time.

For the aborigines the war brought an increase in contact with the outside world. Many assisted the military in both paid and unpaid roles. It was reported:

"Into this difficult work…. came the severe dislocation of the war and Aborigines were at once projected into a place of importance if not prominence, in the Australian war effort. Their country, Arnhem Land became an important base for the defence of Australia. The aboriginal became a hewer of wood and a drawer of water for the defence forces in the Northern Territory. His skill in bushcraft and his innate consideration enabled him to play an important part in the discovery and succour of Australian and Allied airmen who made forced landings in the Northern Territory…. it made Australia 'Northern Territory conscious', so these people now have been suddenly and in some sense, prematurely, projected into the life of Australia."

In the immediate post war years Oenpelli continued on but struggled due to lack of staff, other resources and transport of stores, trying a range of boating and trucking options with limited success and many catastrophes. It was largely isolated from the outside world. At one stage CMS purchased a 40 foot boat, 'Victory'. After a few successful trips it capsized at night in the lower reaches of the river after being caught on a mud-bank. When re-floated by a salvage company, it became the company's property, no longer available to the Mission.

In 1975, Ralph Barton, Mission Superintendent in the late 1940's reflected.

"The obvious solution to the problem appeared to be the purchase of heavy transport vehicles capable of bringing through, in the dry season, big loads of stores. Not only foodstuffs, but building materials, fuel, agricultural machinery, etc. A suitable crossing would have to be constructed up in the headwaters of the East Alligator River, so that trucks could be taken right through to the Mission Station. An aeroplane owned and operated by CMS would be a wonderful thing."

These were dreams in the 1940's, but much water was to continue to flow up and down the river before the dreams became realities.

APPENDIX 2 -EARLIEST RECORD : LEICHHARDT'S JOURNAL

In researching this book I first read about Ludwig Leichhardt passing through the Oenpelli area in other sources which quoted from his journal. It rang true of the Oenpelli I know and caught my interest. So I went to Sydney's Mitchell library, where they hold his original journal and was able to view a handwritten copy, over 170 years old. His notations, crossings out and insertions gave instant immediacy and conveyed his difficulties far better than another's transcriptions.

The more I read the more awed I was by this remarkable man and his trip over Arnhem Land, at a time when it was totally unknown, with only a limited map of the coastline and no concept of the interior. He traversed some of the most rugged country imaginable, in a trip which had already spanned more than a year, with a handful of exhausted companions, faltering livestock, and almost no stores left. The help of aborigines was critical to their survival. Their friendly demeanour was his main experience, as for later Europeans. Of course there were difficulties with aboriginal contacts and Leichhardt well understood the risks posed by hostile groups, having seen his companion, Gilbert, fatally speared in north Queensland. Discoveries included the Roper and Wilton Rivers, Hodgson and Snowdrop Creeks, all which still bear the names he bestowed.

Working in the remote parts of the Arnhem Plateau was a thing I did in the tuberculosis eradication campaign. Teams of us shot and did post mortems on buffalo in places of fractured sandstone gorges, swamps and waterless forest flats. We worked from helicopters and vehicles with two way radios, GPS, detailed maps, fresh supplies of food and water and comprehensive backup. We found this tested our limits. Being out on a November day on an exposed plateau, with the temperature at around 40 degrees with drenching humidity, was a formula for heat exhaustion and sunstroke.

To conceive a small party of exhausted explorers with a couple of bullocks and a few worn out horses finding their way through here at this time of year defies imagination. Credit must go to the two aboriginal members of their party, Charley and Brown. They supplied food, picked routes and found water holes, although the contribution and stamina of all party members was great. Their non-aggressive approach to aboriginal encounters and their willingness to follow aboriginal dietary practices and sample bush foods for edibility was also key. Perhaps the most remarkable part of the trip, which Leichhardt simply says they accomplished with much difficulty was on 20th November, 1845, when they descended off the Arnhem Land escarpment, starting at an altitude of about 1000 feet, coming down into the valley of the South Alligator River drainage system, into what is now the Kakadu woodlands below. For those who have been to Kakadu, visited places such as Nourlangie Rock and Jim Jim Falls and looked out across to this massive cliff line, it is hard to visualise a small party of explorers leading their last two bullocks and half a dozen horses down through one of the gorges and scree slopes which dissect this landscape.

To give an appreciation of this story I have included excerpts of Leichhardt's journal which relate to the final period of about two months of his passage through Arnhem Land, from first coming to the Roper River on 19th October 1845, until his party reached Victoria Settlement on Coburg Peninsula on December 17th in the same year. It is the earliest written record existing of the interior of this area. In various places I have inserted my comments as author's notes to help explain the locations and the significance of what happened.

Leichhardt's Journal Extracts

Oct. 19.—We travelled.... to the lagoon which my companions had discovered.

Authors Note : Appears to be Wadamunga Lagoon east of St Vidgeons Station

They had not exaggerated their account, neither of the beauty of the country, nor of the size of the lagoon, nor of the exuberance of animal life on it. It was indeed quite a novel spectacle to us to see such myriads of ducks and geese rise and fly up and down the lagoon, as we travelled along ... When we came to the end of the lagoon.... I observed a green belt of trees scarcely 300 yards to the northward; and on riding towards it, I found myself on the banks of a large fresh water river from 500 to 800 yards broad, with not very high banks.... The water was slightly muddy, as if a fresh had come down the river; and the tide rose full three feet. It was the river Mr. Roper had seen two days before and I named it after him, as I had promised to do. The country along its left bank was well–grassed and openly timbered with box; hills were on the opposite side. Its course was from north–west to south–east.... Natives seemed to be numerous; for their foot–path along the lagoon was well beaten; we passed several of their fisheries, and observed long fish traps made of Flagellaria (rattan). All the cuts on various trees were made with an iron tomahawk. Natives, crows, and kites were always the indications of a good country. Charley, Brown, and John, who had been left at the lagoon to shoot waterfowl, returned with twenty ducks for luncheon, and went out again during the afternoon to procure more for dinner and breakfast.

Oct. 20.—We travelled about ten miles N. 60 degrees W. up the river; and I was fortunate enough to determine my latitude by an observation of Alpheratz, which cloudy nights had prevented me from obtaining since the 15th October: it was 14 degrees 47 minutes; my longitude, according to reckoning, was 135 degrees 10 minutes.

Authors Note: Appears their camp site was 3-4 miles east of where Ngukkur (Roper Mission) was later established on the north bank. This is based on what appear to be accurate measures of latitude, whereas longitude cited is about 25 minutes or 45 kilometres further west than Leichhardt's calculations.

We followed a broad foot–path of the natives, which cut the angles of the river, and passed along several large lagoons at the foot of some low sandstone ridges.... Brown pursued two emus, and caught one of them. Wallabies were numerous; two bustards and even a crocodile were seen.

Oct. 21.—After waiting a very long time for our horses, Charley brought the dismal tidings that three of the most vigorous of them were drowned at the junction of the creek with the river. Although the banks of the Roper were steep and muddy, the large creek we had passed was scarcely two miles distant and offered an easy approach to the water on a rocky bed. It remained inexplicable to us how the accident could have happened.

Authors Note: Appears to be Mountain Creek, the largest Creek flowing into the Roper from the south between the Hodgson River and St Vidgeons.

This disastrous event staggered me, and for a moment I turned almost giddy; but there was no help. Unable to increase the load of my bullocks, I was obliged to leave that part of my botanical collection which had been carried by one of the horses. The fruit of many a day's work was consigned to the fire; and tears were in my eyes when I saw one of the most interesting results of my expedition vanish into smoke.

Oct. 22.— .... Last night we heard the calls of natives at the opposite side of the river. As soon as they saw us, they crossed the river, and came pretty close to us: the discharge of our guns, however, kept them at a distance. Several of our party, during their watches saw them moving with fire sticks on the other side of the river. In the morning, three of them came boldly up; so I went to them with some presents, and they became very friendly indeed. Presents were exchanged; and they invited us in the most pressing manner to accompany them to their camp; and were evidently disappointed in finding that we could not swim. I gave them horse–nails, and they asked me to bend them into fish–hooks. They had doubtless seen or heard of white people before; but of our horses and bullocks they were much afraid, and asked me whether they could bite: they accompanied me, however, pretty near to the camp; but kept their arms round my waist, to be sure of not being bitten. As we proceeded on our journey, they followed us for a long distance, and offered Charley and Brown a gin, if we would go to their camp. They were circumcised, and two front teeth had been knocked out; they had horizontal scars on their chests. A great number of flying–foxes (Pteropus) were in the river brush, and Brown shot three of them.

Authors Note: The site of this meeting is very close to the current site of Ngukkur so these aborigines are likely to be ones whose descendants had contact with the missionaries here from the 1920s on. It would be interesting to see if names Leichhardt records are current names within the Roper aboriginal community.

Oct. 23.—This morning, our sable friends came again to our camp; they made their approach known by a slight whistling. We invited them to come nearer, and many new faces were introduced to us. Of three young people, one was called 'Gnangball,' the other 'Odall,' and a boy 'Nmamball.' These three names were given to many others, and probably distinguished three different tribes or families…. When we started on our journey they followed us with many remarks for a very long way…. Ranges and high rocky ridges were seen in every direction. From one of them a pillar of smoke was rising, like a signal fire. The extensive burnings…. showed that the country was well inhabited. About four or five miles from the last creek,—which I shall call "Hodgson's Creek….

Authors Note: This is now named Hodgson River, continuing Leichhardt's name

—the river divided into two almost equal branches, one coming from the northward…. I named the river from the northward the "Wilton …

Authors Note: the name of the Wilton River survives to this day…. If Leichhardt followed this river north to its headwaters on the eastern side of the Arnhem Plateau, rather than continuing along the Roper, he could have passed around the eastern edge of the plateau, an easier route than crossing over its centre, though crossing northern flowing rivers such as the Cadell, Mann and Liverpool Rivers' to get to Coburg could have presented its own challenges.

About three miles above the junction of the Wilton with the Roper, we again encamped on the steep banks of the latter, at a spot which I thought would allow our horses and cattle to approach in safety. One unfortunate animal, however, slipped into the water, and every effort to get him out was made in vain. Its constant attempts to scramble up the boggy banks only tired it and, as night advanced, we had to wait until the tide rose again. I watched by him the whole night, and at high water we succeeded in getting him out of the water; but he began to plunge again, and unfortunately broke the tether which had kept his forequarters up, and fell back into the river. At last I found a tolerable landing place about fifty yards higher up; but, as I was swimming with him up to it, and trying to lead him clear of the stumps of trees, he became entangled in the tether rope by which I guided him, rolled over, and was immediately drowned. This reduced our number of horses to nine.

I started late on the 24th Oct. and travelled over a country similar to that of our late stages. About a mile up the river, a ledge of rocks crossed the bed, over which a considerable stream formed a small fall and rapids; above this was a fine sheet of water.... which made this crossing place extremely lovely.

Authors Note: appears to be Roper Bar, the main road crossing over the Roper River into southern Arnhem Land.

My grief at having lost an excellent horse I had ridden for the greatest part of the journey, was increased by now knowing that one mile more travelling would have saved him.... a bustard was shot by Charley: large fish were splashing in the water. I gathered the large vine–bean, with green blossoms, which had thick pods containing from one to five seeds. Its hard covering, by roasting, became very brittle; and I pounded the cotyledons, and boiled them for several hours. This softened them, and made a sort of porridge, which, at all events, was very satisfying. Judging by....large stones which were frequently found, in the camps of the natives, still covered with the mealy particles of some seed which had been pounded upon them, it would seem that the natives used the same bean;

Oct. 25.—We travelled about seven miles.... following the river in its various windings over more than twelve miles....

Oct. 26.—.... We accomplished about eight miles in a straight line to the westward, but went over a much greater extent of ground; as I mistook a large dry creek for the river....

As we were slowly winding our way among the loose rocks, Brown's horse got knocked up, and we were compelled to encamp.... with the failing strength of our poor brutes; and knowing only too well the state of exhaustion in which they were.... rendered me extremely nervous and restless. The death of our spare horses did not allow us any more to relieve the others by alternate rests, and we became soon aware of their increasing weakness. This was considerably aggravated by the necessity under which we were of keeping two horses tethered near the camp, not only to facilitate the finding of the others in the morning, but to form a defence against a possible attack of the natives.

Oct. 27.—We travelled about seven miles up the river.... Fine, well grassed plains of moderate size extended along the river, and between its numerous anabranches: for the river divided into several Pandanus channels....

Authors Note: Appears that at this stage Leichhardt left the Roper River and travelled up Maiwok Creek as this multichannel description better fits it and it is going in a WNW direction whereas the Roper here heads almost due south.

....Mr. Roper met and spoke with three natives, who did not appear to be afraid of him. Another of our horses became knocked up, and compelled us to encamp very early in the day, and, as they were all much exhausted, I allowed them to feed at large, without taking the usual precaution of keeping two tethered, in the event of being surprised by the natives. That this was intentionally taken advantage of seemed probable; for, after night-fall, at the commencement of Charley's watch, four natives sneaked up to the camp, and were preparing to throw their spears, when they were seen by Charley, who immediately gave the alarm. We got up instantly, but they had disappeared, and no one but Charley saw anything of them. I should have been inclined to consider it a hoax, had I not heard their distant cooees as late as 9 o'clock, when I silenced them by the discharge of a gun.

Oct. 28.—We travelled ten miles in a north–west direction.... Charley ... reported he had discovered water bubbling out of the ground at the foot of a slight rise....

At this time, I was suffering from a great irritability of the skin, and was covered all over with a prickly heat; the slightest pressure or rubbing produced inflammation and boils

Oct. 29.—We.... followed the creek about four miles, to allow our cattle and horses to drink freely at the water–hole discovered by Charley the day before.... After seven miles travelling, we came to an immense flat, lightly timbered with box and broad–leaved tea-tree, and surrounded on every side, except the S.S.E., by high ranges, protruding like headlands into the plain.... In a wider part of the valley, I observed wells of the natives dug in the creek, which we enlarged in the hope of their yielding a sufficient supply of water; but in this we were mistaken, as barely enough was obtained to quench our own thirst. Charley, however.... found a small pond and a spring in a narrow mountain gorge, to which he had been guided by a beaten track of Wallaroos.

Mr. Phillips (who was always desirous of discovering substitutes for coffee).... collected these seeds, and pounded and boiled them, and gave me the fluid to taste, which I found so peculiarly bitter that I cautioned him against drinking it; his natural desire, however, for warm beverage, which had been increased by a whole day's travelling, induced him to swallow about a pint of it, which made him very sick, and produced violent vomiting and purging during the whole afternoon and night. The little I had tasted acted on me as a lenient purgative, but Mr. Calvert, who had taken rather more than I did, felt very sick.

Oct. 30.—We travelled about four miles.... along the summit of rocky ranges, when a large valley bounded by high ranges to the north and north–west, burst upon us....

Authors Note: probably the valley of the Waterhouse River

We descended into it by a steep and rocky basaltic slope, and followed a creek which held a very tortuous course to the south–west; we had travelled along it about seven miles, when Charley was attracted by a green belt of trees, and by the late burnings of the natives, and discovered a running rivulet, coming from the.... During the night, a great number of flying–foxes came to revel in the honey of the blossoms of the gum trees. Charley shot three, and we made a late but welcome supper of them. They were not so fat as those we had eaten before, and tasted a little strong

Oct. 31.—When we were going to start, Brown's old horse was absent, and after much searching, the poor brute was found lying at the opposite side of the creek, with its back down the slope, and unable to move. We succeeded in turning him, and helping him to rise, but he was so weak, as to be scarcely able to stand: indeed all our cattle were tired and foot–sore, in consequence of several days travelling over rocky ranges, and required rest. I therefore determined on remaining here a day....The grass was young and various, the water delightfully cool, and the scattered trees were large and shady.... Charley and Brown went to shoot flying–foxes, and returned at luncheon with twelve; during the afternoon, they went again and brought in thirty more

Nov. 1.— .... A range composed of baked sandstone, approached so close to the banks of "Flying–Fox Creek," that we were obliged to cross the range.... The frequent smoke which rose from every part of the valley, showed that it was well inhabited. Brown met two natives, with their gins and children, but they ran away as soon as they saw him. At sunset, a great number of them had collected near our camp, and set fire to the grass, which illumined the sky, as it spread in every direction. They tried to frighten us, by imitating a howling chorus of native dogs; but withdrew, when they saw it was of no avail;.

Nov. 2.— .... The creek wound between baked sandstone hills, and was alternately enlarging into Nymphaea ponds, and running in a small stream over a pebbly or sandy bed.... A flight of wild geese came down the creek, at about 2 o'clock in the morning....

Nov. 3.—We continued our course up the creek, for nine or ten miles

Authors Note: still probably the Waterhouse River. It is possible they had come further east into Flying Fox Creek which runs close by in a similar direction

As we were travelling along, a native suddenly emerged from the banks of the creek, and, crossing our line of march, walked down to a Nymphaea pond, where he seemed inclined to hide himself until we had passed. I cooeed to him; at which he looked up, but seemed to be at a loss what to do or say. I then dismounted, and made signs to show my friendly disposition: then he began to call out, but, seeing that I motioned away my companions with the horses and bullocks, as I moved towards him, and that I held out presents to him, he became more assured of his safety, and allowed me to come near.

Nov. 4.—We travelled about seven miles, north–west by north, to lat. 13 degrees 56 minutes 46 seconds. After following the creek about a mile, it turned so far to the westward that I left it, and with much difficulty ascended the ranges to the northward: from their highest elevation, I saw that a high range, trending from south–east to north–west, bounded the valley of the creek I had left; another fine range was seen to the eastward.

Authors Note: They may have crossed now to the Flying Fox Creek headwaters

Following a gully, we descended into the valley of a creek flowing to the southward.... Our bullocks had become so foot–sore, and so oppressed by the excessive heat, that it was with the greatest difficulty we could prevent them from rushing into the water with their loads. One— which carried the remainder of my botanical collection—watched his opportunity, and plunged into a deep pond.... quietly swimming about and enjoying himself, whilst I was almost crying with vexation at seeing all my plants thoroughly soaked.

Nov. 5.—We travelled in all about eleven miles.... After following the creek, on which we had encamped, to its head, we passed over a scrubby stringy–bark forest; and came to watercourses going to the eastward.... we turned to the north–west and westward. We passed several sandstone hills and ridges rising out of this sandy table land, and attempted to cross one of them, but our path was intercepted by precipices and chasms, forming an insurmountable barrier to our cattle. We, therefore, followed a watercourse to the southward, winding between two ranges to the westward and southward, and continued again to the north–west, which brought us to a tributary of the creek we had just left...The remains of fresh–water turtles were frequently noticed in the camps of the natives; and Mr. Calvert had seen one depicted with red ochre on the rocks. It is probable that this animal forms a considerable part of the food of the natives. John Murphy reported that he had seen a hut of the natives constructed of sheets of stringy–bark, and spacious enough to receive our whole party; the huts which I had observed were also very spacious, but covered with tea–tree bark. Smoke from the natives' fires was seen from the range in every direction, and their burnings invariably led us to creeks.

Nov. 6. — We travelled fourteen miles.... and encamped in a little creek, at the head of which was a grassy drooping tea–tree swamp. We left all the eastern water–courses to the right, and followed several which went down to the southward, up to their heads....

Authors Note: This appears to be around the boundary between Flying Fox Creek and Snowdrop Creek which runs WSW into the Katherine River.

We had passed a large but dry swamp, having no outlet, and surrounded with Pandanus, when Brown called my attention to an opening in the forest, and to a certain dim appearance of the atmosphere peculiar to extensive plains and valleys.... we soon found ourselves at the margin of the sandy table–land, from which we overlooked a large valley bounded by high ranges to the westward. We then followed a very rocky creek, in its various windings, in search of water.... about five miles farther, we found a small pool, at which natives had very recently encamped.... Our bullocks and horses were very foot-sore, and could scarcely move over the rocky ground.

I believe that all the creeks which we passed since leaving the Roper, still belonged to that river; and that the western creek and all the western waters we met, until reaching the South Alligator River, belonged to the system of the latter. The division of the eastern and western waters was, according to my reckoning, in longitude 133 degrees 35 minutes.

Authors Note: near to 133 degrees 25 minutes, a discrepancy of 10 minutes which is where the catchment of Snowdrop Creek divides from Flying Fox Creek.

Nov. 7.— We followed the creek for about four or five miles, and halted at a well–grassed spot with good water–holes, in order to kill one of our bullocks, and allow the other two and the horses to recover. The poor brute was fairly knocked up and incapable of going any farther, even without a load... the climate in which we travelled, and the excessive heat.... The rocky nature of the ground contributed no less to their foot–weariness and exhaustion. If I could have rested two or three days out of seven, the animals would have had time to recover, and would have done comparatively well.

We were occupied during the 8th Nov. in drying our meat, mending and washing our things, and arranging the few loads which were left.

Nov. 9.— We travelled down the creek in a south–west course, for about nine miles. The banks of the creek, which I called "Snowdrop's Creek," after the bullock we had killed, were grassy and open; it was well provided with water.

Nov. 10.— We travelled about six miles and a half NNW. The creek turned so far to the westward and southward, that I left it, and crossed some ridges, beyond which a very rocky creek going down to Snowdrop's Creek, intercepted our course. Having crossed it with great difficulty, we travelled through a scrubby forest, and came to the heads of the same creek, several of which were formed by swamps.... surrounded the deep pools of spring water. These spots, which bore the marks of being much visited by the natives, were like oases in the dry, dull, sandy forest, and formed delightful shady groves, pleasing to every sense. Kangaroos and various birds, particularly the white cockatoo, were numerous; and the little bees came like flies on our hands, on my paper, and on our soup plates, and indicated abundance of honey; a small species of Cicada had risen from its slumbers, and was singing most cheerfully. One of our horses was seriously staked in the belly, by some unaccountable accident; I drew a seton through the large swelling, although, considering its exhausted state, I entertained but a slight hope of its recovery.

Nov. 11.— We accomplished about ten miles in a direct line, but on a long and fatiguing circuitous course. Starting in a northerly direction, we passed over some rocky ground, but soon entered into a sandy level, covered with scrubby, stringy–bark forest. From one of the hills which bounded its narrow valley, I had a most disheartening, sickening view over a tremendously rocky country. A high land, composed of horizontal strata of sandstone, seemed to be literally hashed, leaving the remaining blocks in fantastic figures of every shape; and a green vegetation, crowding deceitfully within their fissures and gullies, and covering half of the difficulties which awaited us on our attempt to travel over it. The creek, in and along the bed of which we wound slowly down, was frequently covered with large loose boulders, between which our horses and cattle often slipped. A precipice, and perpendicular rocks on both sides, compelled us to leave it; and following one of its tributary creeks to its head, to the northward, we came to another, which led us down to a river running to the west by south. With the greatest difficulty we went down its steep slopes, and established our camp at a large water–hole in its bed.

Authors Note: This appears to be the Katherine River which traverses the Arnhem Land Plateau heading south at this point, before meeting Snowdrop Creek and swinging to the southwest.

Nov. 12.— We had been compelled to leave the injured horse behind, and upon going this morning with Charley to fetch it to the camp, we found the poor brute dead.... Myriads of flying–foxes were here suspended in thick clusters on the highest trees in the most shady and rather moist parts of the valley. They started as we passed, and the flapping of their large membranous wings produced a sound like that of a hail–storm.

Nov. 13.— The two horses ridden by Charley and myself yesterday, had suffered so severely, that I had to allow them a day of rest to recover. In the meantime, I went with Charley and Brown to the spot where we had seen the greatest number of flying–foxes, and, whilst I was examining the neighbouring trees, my companions shot sixty–seven, of which fifty–five were brought to our camp; which served for dinner, breakfast, and luncheon, each individual receiving eight.... During the night, we heard the first grumbling of thunder since many months.

Nov. 14.— We travelled about twelve miles north by west. After crossing the river, we followed a rocky creek to its head, and passed over ten miles of level sandy country of stringy–bark forest, with Melaleuca gum and Banksia, interrupted only by a small Pandanus creek.... During the night, thunder clouds and lightning were seen in every direction; and the whole atmosphere appeared to be in a state of fermentation. Heavy showers poured down upon us; and our tarpaulins, which had been torn to pieces in travelling through the scrub, were scarcely sufficient to keep ourselves and our things dry. But in the morning of the 15th, all nature seemed refreshed; and my depressed spirits rose quickly, under the influence of that sweet breath of vegetation, which is so remarkably experienced in Australia,

Authors Note: about this point they cross from the headwaters of creeks flowing into the Katherine River into the drainage of the South Alligator River. It is only a few miles from tributaries of the Katherine to the headwaters of Jim Jim Creek, the likely creek they followed to the edge of the Arnhem Escarpment.

Our course.... for three miles to the northward, over a sandy level forest, intercepted by several rocky creeks. The third which we came to, I followed down to the westward, and came to a large creek, which soon joined a still larger one from the eastward

Authors Note: Fits with Jim Jim catchment, perhaps the headwaters of Twin Falls Creek about 20 kilometres south of Jim Jim Falls.

Both were well provided with water; and we encamped at a very large hole under a ledge of rock across the bed of the creek; and which probably formed a fine waterfall during the rainy season. Thunder–storms formed to the southward and northward....

Nov. 16.—We travelled nine miles north–west by north; crossed numerous rocky creeks, and some undulating country; and had a most distressing passage over exceedingly rocky ranges. At the end of the stage, we came to a large Pandanus creek, which we followed until we found some fine pools of water in its bed....

Nov. 17.—We travelled four or five miles.... crossed several rocky creeks; and followed down the largest of them; which in its whole extent was exceedingly rocky. The rock was generally in horizontal layers. There were many high falls in the bed, which compelled me to leave the creek, and proceed on the rising ground along its banks, when suddenly the extensive view of a magnificent valley opened before us.

Authors Note: Likely to be the valley where Jim Jim and Twin Falls come over the escarpment. The location appears to be south of Jim Jim Falls as this would provide a view of ranges to the east as well as the west and north and a more open view to the north west. Leichhardt thought the river in the valley below was the South Alligator whereas it was Jim Jim Creek. From Leichhardt's later positions and length of travel it appears that he meets the South Alligator around the location of Yellow Waters. At the stage he comes off the Arnhem Land plateau he is about 50 kilometres east of the main South Alligator drainage channel but within the drainage system of one of its major tributaries.

We stood with our whole train on the brink of a deep precipice, of perhaps 1800 feet descent, which seemed to extend far to the eastward. A large river, joined by many tributary creeks coming from east, south–east, south–west and west, meandered through the valley; which was bounded by high, though less precipitous ranges to the westward and south–west from our position; and other ranges rose to the northward. I went on foot to the mouth of the creek; but the precipice prevented my moving any farther; another small creek was examined, but with the same result. We were compelled to move back, and thence to reconnoitre for a favourable descent. Fortunately the late thunder–storms had filled a great number of small rocky basins in the bed of the creek; and, although there was only a scanty supply of a stiff grass, our cattle had filled themselves sufficiently the previous night to bear a day's privation. In the afternoon, Charley accompanied me on foot in a northerly direction (for no horse could move between the large loose sandstone blocks), and we examined several gullies and watercourses, all of a wild and rocky character, and found it impossible to descend, in that direction, into the valley. Charley shot a Wallaroo just as it was leaping, frightened by our footsteps, out of its shady retreat to a pointed rock. Whilst on this expedition, we observed a great number of grasshoppers, of a bright brick colour dotted with blue: the posterior part of the corselet, and the wings were blue; it was two inches long, and its antennae three quarters of an inch.

Nov. 18.—We returned to the creek in which we had encamped on the 16th, and pitched our tents a little lower down, where some rich feed promised our cattle a good treat. Immediately after luncheon, I started again with Charley down the creek, myself on horseback, but my companion on foot. It soon became very rocky, with gullies joining it from both sides; but, after two miles, it opened again into fine well–grassed lightly timbered flats, and terminated in a precipice, as the others had done. A great number of tributary creeks joined it in its course, but all formed gullies and precipices. Many of these gullies were gently sloping hollows, filled with a rich black soil, and covered with an open brush vegetation at their upper part; but, lower down, large rocks protruded, until the narrow gully, with perpendicular walls, sunk rapidly into the deep chasm, down which the boldest chamois hunter would not have dared to descend. I now determined to examine the country to the southward; and, as it was late and my horse very foot–sore, I remained for the night at the next grassy flat, and sent Charley back to order my companions to remove the camp next morning as far down the creek as possible, in order to facilitate the examination, which, on foot, in this climate, was exceedingly exhausting.

Nov. 19.—I appeased my craving hunger, which had been well tried for twenty hours, on the small fruit of a species of Acmena which grew near the rocks that bounded the sandy flats, until my companions brought my share of stewed green hide. We went about three miles farther down the creek, and encamped in the dense shade of a wide spreading Rock box, a tree which I mentioned a few days since. From this place I started with Brown in one direction, and Charley in another, to find a passage through the labyrinth of rocks. After a most fatiguing scramble up and down rocky gullies, we again found ourselves at the brink of that beautiful valley, which lay before us like a promised land. We had now a more extensive view of its eastern outline, and saw extending far to our right a perpendicular wall, cut by many narrow fissures, the outlet of as many gullies; the same wall continued to the left, but interrupted by a steep slope; to which we directed our steps, and after many windings succeeded in finding it. It was indeed very steep. Its higher part was composed of sandstone and conglomerate; but a coarse–grained granite, with much quartz and feldspar, but little mica and accidental hornblende, was below. The size of its elements had rendered it more liable to decomposition, and had probably been the cause of the formation of the slope. In the valley, the creek murmured over a pebbly bed, and enlarged from time to time, into fine sheets of water. We rested ourselves in the shade of its drooping tea–trees; and, observing another slope about two miles farther, went to examine it, but finding that its sandstone crest was too steep for our purpose, we returned to mark a line of road from the first slope to our camp. For this purpose I had taken a tomahawk with me, well knowing how little I could rely on Brown for finding his old tracks; but, with the tomahawk, he succeeded very well; for his quick eye discovered, from afar, the practicability of the road. We succeeded at last, and, after many windings, reached our camp, even quicker than we had anticipated. Charley returned next morning, and reported that he had found a descent, but very far off. This 'very far off' of Charley was full of meaning which I well understood.

During the night we had a very heavy thunder–storm which filled our creek and made its numerous waterfalls roar.

Nov. 20.— We proceeded on our tree–marked line to the slope, and descending, arrived, after some difficulty, safe and sound in the valley

Authors Note: there is a rocky scree slope 3-4 kilometres south of Jim Jim Falls where a spur of the ranges extends out into the valley below. This appears the most likely site for their descent.

Our horses and cattle were, however, in a distressing condition. The passage along rocky creeks, between the loose blocks of which their feet were constantly slipping, had rendered them very foot–sore, and had covered their legs with sores. The feed had latterly consisted either of coarse grasses, or a small sedge, which they did not like. But, in the valley, all the tender grasses reappeared in the utmost profusion, on which horses and bullocks fed most greedily during the short rest I allowed them after reaching the foot of the slope. The creek formed a fine waterfall of very great height, like a silver belt between rich green vegetation, behind which the bare mountain walls alone were visible.

Authors Note: A visitor to Jim Jim Falls today would give a similar description. It is only visible south of the creek due to the angle of the fissure into which it falls. It is on this side of the fall the scree slope is located, which it is likely Leichhardt descended. Jim Jim Falls does not flow throughout the dry but flow begins after early storms, as described by Leichhardt. A flow of about the amount he describes (a silver belt) is typical at this time of year. The description of following this creek for about three miles and coming to a confluence with a larger watercourse fits well with the junction of Twin Falls Creek which, due to its permanent year round flow is the larger creek in the late dry-early wet season.

I proceeded down the creek about three miles to the north–west, when it joined a larger creek from the south–west. Here one of our two remaining bullocks refused to go any further; and as our meat bags were empty, I decided upon stopping in this favourable spot to kill the bullock. But the late thunder–storm had rendered the ground very damp, and that, with the mawkish smell of our drying meat, soon made our camp very disagreeable. The bullock was killed in the afternoon of the 20th, and on the 21st the meat was cut up and put out to dry; the afternoon was very favourable for this purpose; but, at night rain set in, and with the sultry weather rendered the meat very bad. The mornings were generally sultry and cloudy; during the afternoon the clouds cleared off with the sea–breeze: and towards sunset thunder–storms rose, and the nights were rainy, which prevented me from making observations to ascertain my latitude. The longitude of the descent, was, according to reckoning, 132 degrees 50 minutes

Authors Note: Very close (within 2-3 minutes or 5 kilometres) of the longitude of Jim Jim Falls. Leichhardt's longitudes are more accurate as he approaches the north coast of the NT, perhaps because landscape features e.g. the position of the mouths of the South and East Alligator Rivers, allowed him to retrospectively correct estimates which in the remote southern Arnhem Land would have been difficult to do with a tendency to become incorrect due to the inaccuracies in time measurement devices used over long periods without re-calibration.

A little before sunset of the 21st four natives came to our camp; they made us presents of red ochre, which they seemed to value highly, of a spear and a spear's head made of baked sandstone.... I gave them a few nails and, as I was under the necessity of parting with everything heavy which was not of immediate use for our support, I also gave them my geological hammer. One of the natives was a tall, but slim man; the others were of smaller size, but all had a mild and pleasing expression of countenance.

Large fish betrayed their presence in the deep water by splashing during the night: and Charley asserted that he had seen the tracks of a crocodile. Swarms of whistling ducks occupied the large ponds in the creek: but our shot was all used, and the small iron–pebbles which were used as a substitute, were not heavy enough to kill even a duck. Some balls, however, were still left, but these we kept for occasions of urgent necessity.

Nov. 22.— As our meat was not sufficiently dry for packing we remained here the whole of this day; but, at night, the heaviest thunder–storm we perhaps had ever experienced, poured down and again wetted it; we succeeded, however, notwithstanding this interruption, in drying it without much taint; but its soft state enabled the maggots to nestle in it; and the rain to which it had been exposed, rendered it very insipid.

Poor Redmond, the last of our bullocks, came frequently to the spot where his late companion had been killed; but finding that he was gone, he returned to his abundant feed, and when I loaded him to continue our journey down the river he was full and sleek. It was interesting to observe how the bullocks on all previous occasions, almost invariably took cognizance of the place where one of their number had been killed. They would visit it either during the night or the next day, walk round the spot, lift their tails, snuff the air with an occasional shake of their horns, and sometimes, set off in a gallop.

Nov. 23.— We travelled about eight miles north–west over an equally fine country. A high range of Pegmatite descended from the table land far into the valley, from east to west; and an isolated peak was seen to the west of it at the left bank of the river.

Authors Note: Appears to the bluff at the northern edge of the Jim Jim Falls valley

A thunder–storm from the north–east, compelled us to hasten into camp; and we had scarcely housed our luggage, when heavy rain set in and continued to fall....

Nov. 24.—We travelled about nine miles.... We were.... at the South Alligator River, about sixty miles from its mouth, and about one hundred and forty miles from Port Essington.

Authors Note: Still on Jim Jim Creek not the South Alligator River

The river gradually increased in size, and its bed became densely fringed with Pandanus; the hollows and flats were covered with groves of drooping tea–trees. Ridges of sandstone and conglomerate approached the river in several places, and at their base were seen some fine reedy and rushy lagoons, teeming with water–fowl.... natives cooeed from the other side of the river, probably to ascertain whether we were friendly or hostile; but did not show themselves any farther.... John and Charley saw a native in the bed of the river, busily employed in beating a species of bark, very probably to use its fibres to strain honey. He did not interrupt his work, and either did not see them, or wished to ignore their presence. The horse flies began to be very troublesome, but the mosquitoes fortunately did not annoy us, notwithstanding the neighbourhood of the river, and the late rains. Charley and Brown shot five geese, which gave us a good breakfast and luncheon.

Nov. 25.—We travelled about seven miles and a half N.W. by W

Authors Note: this places their position about three kilometres south of Patonga where the Jim Creek begins to extend in major floodplains, lagoons and swamps

I intended to follow the sandy bergue of the river, but a dense Pandanus brush soon compelled us to return, and to head several grassy and sedgy swamps like those we passed on the last stage. Chains of small water–holes, and Nymphaea ponds, ran parallel to the river; and very extensive swamps filled the intervals between rather densely wooded ironstone ridges, which seemed to be spurs of a more hilly country, protruding into the valley of the river. Some of these swamps were dry, and had a sound bottom, allowing our cattle to pass without difficulty. Others, however, were exceedingly boggy, and dangerous for both horse and man; for Charley was almost suffocated in the mud, in attempting to procure a goose he had shot. The swamps narrowed towards the river, and formed large and frequently rocky water–holes, in a well defined channel, which, however, became broad and deep where it communicated with the river, and which in many places rivalled it in size. A belt of drooping tea–trees surrounded the swamps, whilst their outlets were densely fringed with Pandanus. ... The whole country was most magnificently grassed.

Nov. 26.—We travelled about nine miles and a half N.N.W.... After having once more seen the river, where it was joined by the broad outlet of a swamp,

Authors Note: Appears to be just north of Cooinda/Yellow Waters billabong, close to where the Jim Jim Creek joins the South Alligator River.

....About six miles from our last camp, an immense plain opened before us, at the west side of which we recognized the green line of the river. We crossed the plain to find water, but the approaches of the river were formed by tea–tree hollows, and by thick vine brush.... In skirting the brush, we came to a salt–water creek (the first seen by us on the north–west coast), when we immediately returned to the ridges, where we met with a well-beaten foot–path of the natives, which led us along brush, teeming with wallabies, and through undulating scrubby forest ground to another large plain. Here the noise of clouds of water–fowl, probably rising at the approach of some natives, betrayed to us the presence of water. We encamped at the outskirts of the forest, at a great distance from the large but shallow pools, which had been formed by the late thunder–showers.... The boggy nature of the ground prevented our horses and the bullock from approaching it; and they consequently strayed very far in search of water.... At sunset, Charley returned to the camp, accompanied by a whole tribe of natives. They were armed with small goose spears, and with flat wommalas; but, although they were extremely noisy, they did not show the slightest hostile intention. One of them had a shawl and neckerchief of English manufacture: and another carried an iron tomahawk, which he said he got from north-west by north. They knew Pichenelumbo (Van Diemen's Gulf), and pointed to the north-west by north, when we asked for it. I made them various presents... They were inclined to theft, and I had to mount Brown on horseback to keep them out of our camp.

Nov. 27.— The natives returned very early to our camp, and took the greatest notice of what we were eating, but would not taste anything we offered them. When Brown returned with our bullock, the beast rushed at them, and pursued them....

Authors Note: For these aboriginal groups of Kakadu- it would be interesting to know if any oral stories survive of Leichhardt's meeting with this tribe.

We travelled about three miles and a half north–east, but had to go fairly over ten miles of ground. We followed the foot–path of the natives for about two miles, passing over some scrubby ridges into a series of plains, which seemed to be boundless to the N.W. and N.N.W. A broad deep channel of fresh water covered with Nymphaeas and fringed with Pandanus, intercepted our course; and I soon found that it formed the outlet of one of those remarkable swamps which I have described on the preceding stages.

Authors Note: Description accords with confluence of Jim Jim Creek and the South Alligator River north of Cooinda.

We turned to the E. and E.S.E. following its outline, in order either to find a crossing place, or to head it. The natives were very numerous, and employing themselves either in fishing or burning the grass on the plains, or digging for roots. I saw here a noble fig–tree, under the shade of which seemed to have been the camping place of the natives for the last century. It was growing at the place where we first came to the broad outlet of the swamp. About two miles to the eastward, this swamp extended beyond the reach of sight, and seemed to form the whole country, of the remarkable and picturesque character of which it will be difficult to convey a correct idea to the reader. Its level bed was composed of a stiff bluish clay, without vegetation, mostly dry, and cracked by the heat of the sun; but its depressions were still moist, and treacherously boggy; in many parts of this extensive level, rose isolated patches, or larger island–like groves of Pandanus intermixed with drooping tea–trees, and interwoven with Ipomaeas, or long belts of drooping tea–trees, in the shade of which reaches of shallow water, surrounded by a rich sward of grasses of the most delicate verdure, had remained. Thousands of ducks and geese occupied these pools, and the latter fed as they waded through the grass. We travelled for a long time through groves of drooping tea–trees, which grew along the outline of the swamps, but using great caution in consequence of its boggy nature. Several times I wished to communicate with the natives who followed us, but, every time I turned my horse's head, they ran away; however, finding my difficulties increased, whilst attempting to cross the swamp, I dismounted and walked up to one of them, and taking his hand, gave him a sheet of paper, on which I wrote some words, giving him to understand, as well as I could, that he had nothing to fear as long as he carried the paper. By this means I induced him to walk with me, but considerably in advance of my train, and especially of the bullock; he kept manfully near me, and pointed out the sounder parts of the swamp, until we came to a large pool, on which were a great number of geese, when he gave me to understand that he wished Brown to go and shoot them; for these natives, as well as those who visited us last night, were well acquainted with the effects of fire arms.

We encamped at this pool, and the natives flocked round us from every direction. Boys of every age, lads, young men and old men too, came, every one armed with his bundle of goose spears, and his throwing stick. They observed, with curious eye, everything we did, and made long explanations to each other of the various objects presented to their gaze. Our eating, drinking, dress, skin, combing, boiling, our blankets, straps, horses, everything, in short, was new to them, and was earnestly discussed, particularly by one of the old men, who amused us with his drollery and good humour in trying to persuade each of us to give him something. They continually used the words "Perikot, Nokot, Mankiterre, LumboLumbo, Nana NanaNana," all of which we did not understand till after our arrival at Port Essington, where we learned that they meant "Very good, no good, Malays very far." Their intonation was extremely melodious....

Nov. 28.—Our good friends, the natives, were with us again very early in the morning; they approached us in long file, incessantly repeating the words above mentioned, Perikot, Nokot, &c. which they seemed to consider a kind of introduction. After having guided us over the remaining part of the swamp to the firm land, during which they gave us the most evident proofs of their skill in spearing geese—they took their leave of us and returned; when I again resumed my course to the northward. I understood from the natives that a large lake, or deep water, existed at the head of the swamp, far to the east and north-east. We travelled about nine miles north by east.

Authors Note: This is to the east of the Nourlangie Floodplains about ten kilometres south east of modern day Jabiru.

A foot-path of the natives led us through an intricate tea-tree swamp, in which the rush of waters had uprooted the trees, and left them strewed in every direction, which rendered the passage exceedingly difficult. In the middle of the swamp we saw a fine camp of oven like huts, covered with tea-tree bark.

The weather had been very favourable since we left the upper South Alligator River. It was evident from the appearance of the creek and the swamps, that the rains had been less abundant here. Cumuli formed here regularly during the afternoon, with the setting in of the north-west sea breeze, but dispersed at sunset, and during the first part of the night. Thunder clouds were seen in the distance, but none reached us. The clear nights were generally dewy.

The country was most beautifully grassed: .... Since the 23rd of November, not a night had passed without long files and phalanxes of geese taking their flight up and down the river, and they often passed so low, that the heavy flapping of their wings was distinctly heard. Whistling ducks, in close flocks, flew generally much higher, and with great rapidity. No part of the country we had passed, was so well provided with game as this; and of which we could have easily obtained an abundance, had not our shot been all expended. The cackling of geese, the quacking of ducks, the sonorous note of the native companion, and the noises of black and white cockatoos, and a great variety of other birds, gave to the country, both night and day, an extraordinary appearance of animation. We started two large native dogs, from the small pool at which we encamped; a flock of kites indicated to me the presence of a larger pool which I chose for our use; and here we should have been tolerably comfortable, but for a large green–eyed horse–fly, which was extremely troublesome to us, and which scarcely allowed our poor animals to feed.

We had a heavy thunder–storm from the north–east, which soon passed off.

Nov. 29.— We travelled about twelve miles to the northward over ironstone and baked sandstone ridges, densely wooded and often scrubby. The first part of the stage was more hilly, and intersected by a greater number of creeks, going down to west and north–west, than the latter part, which was a sandy, level forest of stringy–bark and Melaleuca gum....

Authors Note: Camp location appears 3-5 kilometres west of the Magela plain, on a creek, which flows north across this woodland area).

Nov. 30.— The lower part of the creek on which we were encamped was covered with a thicket of Pandanus; but its upper part was surrounded by groves of the Livistona palm. As our horses had been driven far from the camp by the grey horse–fly and by a large brown fly with green eyes, which annoyed us particularly before sunset, and shortly after sunrise, we had to wait a long time for them, and employed ourselves, in the meanwhile, with cutting and eating the tops of Livistona. Many were in blossom, others were in fruit; the latter is an oblong little stone fruit of very bitter taste. Only the lowest part of the young shoots is eatable.... We made a short Sunday stage.... we followed a large creek with a good supply of rainwater, until it turned too much to the westward, when we encamped. The clear night enabled me to make my latitude, by an observation of Castor, to be 12 degrees 21 minutes 49 seconds. We had accomplished about five miles to the northward.

Authors Note: Camp appears to be near Ramil Waterhole slightly north of.... the start of the floodplain extensions of the East Alligator

We saw two emus, and Charley was fortunate enough to shoot one of them; it was the fattest we had met with round the gulf....

Dec. 1.—We travelled about eleven or twelve miles to the northward, for the greater part through forest land, large tracts of which were occupied solely by Livistona. A species of

Acacia and stringy–bark saplings formed a thick underwood. The open lawns were adorned by various plants....We crossed two small creeks, and, at the end of three miles, we came to a Pandanus brook, the murmuring of whose waters over a rocky pebbly bed was heard by us at a considerable distance. A broad foot–path of the natives led along its banks. probably to large lagoons, of which it might be the outlet. The country became flatter, more densely wooded, and gently sloping to the northward, when we entered a tea–tree hollow, through which the mirage indicated the presence of an immense plain, which we all mistook for the Ocean. We crossed over it to a belt of trees, which I thought to be its northern boundary. The part of the plain next to the forest–land was composed of a loose black soil, with excellent grass; farther on it was a cold clay, either covered with a stiff, dry grass, apparently laid down by the rush of water, or forming flats bare of vegetation, which seemed to have been occasionally washed by the tide. Finding that the belt of trees was a thicket of mangroves along a salt–water creek, I returned to some shallow lagoons near the forest, the water of which was drinkable, though brackish.... To the westward of the plains, we saw no other limit than two very distant hills....

Authors Note: Description and latitude indicates this is Cairncurry Plain, the coastal margin between the South and East Alligator Systems midway between the two rivers. The two hills sighted would be Mt Hooper on the western side of the mouth of the South Alligator. It is likely they came to saline coastal flats between Field Island and Point Farewell. From this point they had to backtrack about 40 miles south to cross the East Alligator River.

Dec. 2.—Whilst we were waiting for our bullock, which had returned to the running brook, a fine native stepped out of the forest with the ease and grace of an Apollo, with a smiling countenance, and with the confidence of a man to whom the white face was perfectly familiar. He was unarmed, but a great number of his companions were keeping back to watch the reception he should meet with. We received him, of course, most cordially; and upon being joined by another good–looking little man, we heard him utter distinctly the words, "Commandant!" "come here!!" "very good!!!" "what's your name? !!!!" If my readers have at all identified themselves with my feelings throughout this trying journey; if they have only imagined a tithe of the difficulties we have encountered, they will readily imagine the startling effect which these, as it were, magic words produced—we were electrified—our joy knew no limits, and I was ready to embrace the fellows, who, seeing the happiness with which they inspired us, joined, with a most merry grin, in the loud expression of our feelings. We gave them various presents, particularly leather belts, and received in return a great number of bunches of goose feathers, which the natives use to brush away the flies. They knew the white people of Victoria, and called them Balanda, which is nothing more than "Hollanders;" a name used by the Malays, from whom they received it. We had most fortunately a small collection of words, made by Mr. Gilbert when at Port Essington; so that we were enabled to ask for water (obert); for the road (allun); for Limbo cardja, which was the name of the Harbour. I wished very much to induce them to become our guides; and the two principal men, Eooanberry and Minorelli, promised to accompany us, but they afterwards changed their minds.

My first object was to find good water, and our sable friends guided us with the greatest care, pointing out to us the most shady road, to some wells surrounded with ferns, which were situated in some tea–tree hollows at the confines of the plains and the forest. These wells, however, were so small that our horses could not approach to drink, so that we had to go to another set of wells; where I was obliged to stop, as one of our horses refused to go any farther. This place was about four miles E.N.E. from our last camp.

Authors Note: Site in Cairncurry Plain area closer to margin of floodplains bordering the mouth of the East Alligator River. It would be interesting to find out from local aboriginal groups whether these wells still exist and are in use.

The wells were about six or eight feet deep, and dug through a sandy clay to a stiff bed of clay, on which the water collected. It appeared that the stiff clay of the plains had been covered by the sandy detritus of the ridges, from which the water slowly drained to the wells. It was evident, from the pains which the natives had taken in digging them, that the supply of fresh water was very precarious. In many instances, however, I observed that they had been induced to do so, simply by the want of surface water in the immediate neighbourhood of places where they obtained their principal supply of food. This was particularly the case near the sea–coast, where no surface water is found; whilst the various fish, and even vegetable productions, attract the natives.... We had to water our horses and the bullock with the stew pot; and had to hobble the latter, to prevent his straying, and attacking the natives.

The natives were remarkably kind and attentive, and offered us the rind of the rose–coloured Eugenia apple, the cabbage of the Seaforthia palm, a fruit which I did not know, and the nut–like swelling of the rhizoma of either a grass or a sedge. The last had a sweet taste, was very mealy and nourishing, and was the best article of the food of the natives we had yet tasted. They called it 'Allamurr', and were extremely fond of it. The plant grew in depressions of the plains, where the boys and young men were occupied the whole day in digging for it. The women went in search of other food; either to the sea–coast to collect shell–fish,—and many were the broad paths which led across the plains from the forest land to the salt–water—or to the brushes to gather the fruits of the season, and the cabbage of the palms. The men armed with a wommala, and with a bundle of goose spears, made of a strong reed or bamboo gave up their time to hunting. It seemed that they speared the geese only when flying; and would crouch down whenever they saw a flight of them approaching: the geese, however, knew their enemies so well, that they immediately turned upon seeing a native rise to put his spear into the throwing stick. Some of my companions asserted that they had seen them hit their object at the almost incredible distance of 200 yards: but, making all due allowance for the guess, I could not help thinking how formidable they would have been had they been enemies instead of friends. They remained with us the whole afternoon; all the tribe and many visitors, in all about seventy persons, squatting down with crossed legs in the narrow shades of the trunks of trees, and shifting their position as the sun advanced. Their wives were out in search of food; but many of their children were with them, which they duly introduced to us. They were fine, stout, well made men, with pleasing and intelligent countenances. One or two attempts were made to rob us of some trifles; but I was careful; and we avoided the unpleasant necessity of showing any discontent on that head. As it grew late, and they became hungry, they rose, and explained that they were under the necessity of leaving us, to go and satisfy their hunger; but that they would shortly return, and admire, and talk again. They went to the digging ground, about half a mile in the plain, where the boys were collecting Allamurr, and brought us a good supply of it; in return for which various presents were made to them. We became very fond of this little tuber: and I dare say the feast of Allamurr with Eooanberry and Minorelli's tribe will long remain in the recollection of my companions. They brought us also a thin grey snake, about four feet long, which they put on the coals and roasted. It was poisonous, and was called "Yullo." At nightfall, after filling their koolimans with water, there being none at their camp, they took their leave, and retired to their camping place on the opposite hill where a plentiful dinner awaited them. They were very urgent in inviting us to accompany them, and by way of inducement, most unequivocally offered us their sable partners. We had to take great care of our bullock, as the beast invariably charged the natives whenever he obtained a sight of them, and he would alone have prevented their attacking us; for the whole tribe were so much afraid of him, that, upon our calling out 'the bullock', they were immediately ready to bolt; with the exception of Eooanberry and Minorelli, who looked to us for protection. I had not, however, the slightest fear and apprehension of any treachery on the part of the natives; for my frequent intercourse with the natives of Australia had taught me to distinguish easily between the smooth tongue of deceit, with which they try to ensnare their victim, and the open expression of kind and friendly feelings....

Dec. 3.— The natives visited us very early in the morning, with their wives and children, whom they introduced to us. There could not have been less than 200 of them present; they were all well-made, active, generally well–looking, with an intelligent countenance: they had in fact all the characters of the coast blacks of a good country; but without their treacherous dispositions. I started in a north–east direction; and as we were accompanied by the natives, I led our bullock, by the nose rope, behind my horse. After crossing a plain, we were stopped by a large sheet of salt–water, about three or four miles broad, at the opposite side of which a low range was visible; when Eooanberry explained that we had to go far to the south–east and south, before we could cross the river, and that we had to follow it down again at the other side. He expressed his great attachment to his wife and child, and obtained leave of us to return to his tribe, which had already retired before him. Seeing the necessity of heading the river…. the East Alligator; the longitude of which was, where we first came to it, 132 degrees 40 minutes according to reckoning;

Authors Note: This longitude places them 3-5 kilometres southwest of the mouth of the East Alligator River about opposite the inlet of Coopers Creek).

I returned to the forest land, and travelled along its belt of Pandanus, to obtain a better ground for our cattle, and to avoid the scorching heat of the forenoon sun. Observing singularly formed mountains rising abruptly out of the plains and many pillars of smoke behind them, I tried to get to them, but was again prevented by the broad salt water.

Authors Note: Appears to be the section of large hairpin bends in the River

We now steered for a distant smoke to the south–east by east, and had travelled fully seventeen miles on, or along extensive plains, when we perceived seven natives returning on a beaten foot–path, from the salt water to the forest. We cooeed—they ran! But when we had passed, and Charley stopped behind alone, they came up to him, and, having received some presents, they showed us some miserable wells between two tea–tree groves; after which they hastened home. Our cattle were tired and thirsty, but we could give them nothing to drink, except about six quarts of brackish water; which fell to the share of our bullock. The feed, however, was rich and young, and during the night a heavy dew was deposited. Many flocks of geese came flying low over the plains, which made us hope that water was not very distant. Whilst we were passing the head of a small Mangrove creek, four native dogs, started out of a shady hole; but we looked in vain for fresh water. The plains, which were very level, with a few melon–holes, were scattered all over with dead Limnaeas, which showed evidently, that fresh, or slightly brackish water, covered them occasionally, and for some length of time. Since we first entered upon the large plains of the Alligator Rivers, we had seen myriads of the small cockatoo…. which retired towards night, in long flights from the plains, to the shade of the drooping tea–trees near the shallow pools of water on which we encamped. We had also observed several retreats of flying–foxes in the most shady parts of the Pandanus groves, receiving frequently the first indication of them by the peculiar odour of the animal.

Cumuli formed very early in the morning, and increased during the day, sending down showers of rain all round the horizon. The sea breeze set in at 3 o'clock; and the weather cleared up at sunset, and during the first part of the night; but after 1 o'clock am became cloudy again, with inclination to rain; heavy dew fell during the clear part of the night.

Dec. 4.— The natives returned very early to our camp. I went up to them and made them some presents; in return for which they offered me bunches of goose feathers, and the roasted leg of a goose, which they were pleased to see me eat with a voracious appetite. I asked for Allamurr, and they expressed themselves sorry in not having any left, and gave us to understand that they would supply us, if we would stay a day. Neither these natives nor the tribe of Eooanberry would touch our green hide or meat: they took it, but could not overcome their repugnance, and tried to drop it without being seen by us. Poor fellows! they did not know how gladly we should have received it back! They were the stoutest and fattest men we had met.

We travelled at first to the east, in the direction from which the geese had come last night, but, arriving at ridges covered with scrubby forest, we turned to the north–east, and continued in that direction about seven miles and a half, over iron–stone ridges, when we again entered upon the plains of the river. Mountains and columns of smoke were seen all along its northern banks; but we afterwards found that most of those supposed columns of smoke were dust raised by whirlwinds. We now followed the river until a vine brush approached close to its bank, into the cool shade of which our bullock rushed and lay down, refusing to go any farther; our packhorse and most of our riding horses were also equally tired. The bed of the river had become very narrow, and the water was not quite brine, which made me hope that we should soon come to fresh water. Charley, Brown, and John, had gone into the brush to a camp of flying–foxes, and returned with twelve, which we prepared for luncheon, which allowed our bullock time to recover. They gave an almost incredible account of the enormous numbers of flying–foxes, all clustering round the branches of low trees, which drooped by the weight so near to the ground that the animals could easily be killed.... After a delay of two hours, we again started, and travelled in a due south direction towards some thick smoke rising between two steep and apparently isolated rocky hills: they were about four miles distant, and, when we arrived at their base, we enjoyed the pleasing sight of large lagoons, surrounded with mangrove myrtles, with Pandanus, and with a belt of reeds.... Man, horse, and bullock, rushed most eagerly into the fine water, determined to make up for the privation and suffering of the three last days. The lagoons were crowded with geese, and, as the close vegetation allowed a near approach, Brown made good use of the few slugs that were still left, and shot ten of them, which allowed a goose to every man; a great treat to my hungry party.

Authors Note: Location is almost certainly Canon Hill lagoon or a nearby billabong on the eastern margin of the Magela system west of the East Alligator River and close to the view from Ubirr Rock as seen in Crocodile Dundee.

Dec. 5.— I determined upon stopping for a day, to allow our cattle to recover. Everybody was anxious to procure geese or flying–foxes; and, whilst three of my companions went to the flying–fox camp which we had visited yesterday, loaded with ironstone pebbles for shot, and full of the most sanguine expectations, Brown was busy at the lagoons, and even Mr. Roper stirred to try his good luck. The two met with a party of natives, who immediately retreated at sight of Mr. Roper; but during the afternoon they came to the other side of the lagoon opposite to our camp, and offered us some fish…. which they had speared in the lagoons. I made a sign for them to come over and to receive, as presents in exchange, some small pieces of iron, tin canisters, and leather belts; which they did; but they became exceedingly noisy, and one of them, an old rogue, tried to possess himself quietly and openly of everything he saw, from my red blanket to the spade and stew–pot. I consequently sent Brown for a horse, whose appearance quickly sent them to the other side of the lagoon, where they remained until night–fall. Brown offered them half a goose, which, however, they refused; probably because it was not prepared by themselves, as they were very desirous of getting some of the geese which we had not yet cooked. Brown had shot nine geese, and our fox hunters returned with forty–four of the small species.

When the natives became hungry, they ate the lower part of the leaf–stalks of Nelumbium after stripping off the external skin. They threw a great number of them over to us….

Dec. 6.—The natives visited us again this morning…. They invited us to come to their camp; but I wished to find a crossing place, and, after having tried in vain to pass at the foot of the rocky hills, we found a passage between the lagoons, and entered into a most beautiful valley, bounded on the west, east, and south by abrupt hills, ranges, and rocks rising abruptly out of an almost treeless plain clothed with the most luxuriant verdure, and diversified by large Nymphaea lagoons, and a belt of trees along the creek….

The natives now became our guides, and pointed out to us a sound crossing place of the creek, which proved to be the head of the salt–water branch of the East Alligator River. We observed a great number of long conical fish and crab traps at the crossing place of the creek and in many of the tributary salt–water channels; they were made apparently of Flagellaria. Here I took leave of our guides: the leader of whom appeared to be 'Apirk', young and slender, but an intelligent and most active man. We now travelled again to the northward, following the outline of the rocky ridges at the right side of the creek; and, having again entered upon the plains, we encamped at a very broad, shallow, sedgy, boggy lagoon, surrounded with Typhas, and crowded with ducks and geese, of which Brown shot four. It was about four miles east of our yesterday's camp. Numerous flocks of the Harlequin pigeon (Peristerahistrionica, Gould) came to drink at this lagoon; and innumerable geese alighted towards the evening on the plain, and fed on the young grass, moistened by the rain. The number of kites was in a fair proportion to that of the geese; and dozens of them were watching us from the neighbouring trees.

Authors Note: Area forms western margin of Red Lily between floodplains of the East Alligator River and Arnhem Land Escarpment. This crossing point is about two kilometres upstream from the road crossing of the East Alligator River.

Dec. 7.—'Apirk', with seven other natives, visited us again in the morning, and it seemed that they had examined the camp we had last left. They gave us to understand that we could travel safely to the northward, without meeting any other creek. Apirk carried a little pointed stick, and a flat piece of wood with a small hole in it, for the purpose of obtaining fire. I directed my course to a distant mountain, due north from the camp, and travelled seven or eight miles over a large plain, which was composed of a rich dark soil, and clothed with a great variety of excellent grasses. We saw many columns of dust raised by whirlwinds; and again mistook them for the smoke of so many fires of the natives. But we soon observed that they moved in a certain direction, and that new columns rose as those already formed drew off; and when we came nearer, and passed between them, it seemed as if the giant spirits of the plain were holding a stately corrobori around us....

Towards the river, now to the west of our course, peaks, razor–backed hills, and tents, similar to those we had observed when travelling at the west side of the river on the 3rd December (and probably the same), reappeared. To the east of the mountain, towards which we were travelling, several bluff mountains appeared.... For the last five miles of the stage, our route lay through forest land; and we crossed two creeks going to the east, and then came to rocky sandstone hills, with horizontal stratification, at the foot of which we met with a rocky creek, in the bed of which, after following it for a few miles, we found water. The supply was small; but we enlarged it with the spade, and obtained a sufficient supply for the night. A thunder–storm formed to the northward, which drew off to the westward; but another to the north–east gave us a fine shower, and added to the contents of our water–hole. A well–beaten foot–path of the natives went down the creek.... The old camps of the natives, which we passed in the forest, were strewed with the shells of goose eggs, which showed what an important article these birds formed in the culinary department of the natives; and, whilst their meat and eggs served them for food, their feathers afforded them protection against the flies which swarmed round their bodies....

At this time we were all sadly distressed with boils, and with a prickly heat; early lancing of the former saved much pain: the cuts and sores on the hands festered quickly; but this depended much more on the want of cleanliness than anything else. A most dangerous enemy grew up amongst us in the irresistible impatience to come to the end of our journey; and I cannot help considering it a great blessing that we did not meet with natives who knew the settlement of Port Essington at an earlier part of our journey, or I am afraid we should have been exposed to the greatest misery by desire of …. pushing onward.

Dec. 8.—I went to the westward, to avoid the rocky ground, and if possible to come into the valley of the East Alligator River, if the country should not open and allow me a passage to the northward, which direction I took whenever the nature of the country permitted. After crossing the heads of several easterly creeks, we came upon a large foot-path of the natives, which I determined to follow. It was, in all probability, the same which went down the creek on which we had encamped last night: it descended through a narrow rocky gully, down which I found great difficulty in bringing the horses; and afterwards wound through a fine forest land, avoiding the rocky hills, and touching the heads of westerly creeks, which were well supplied with rocky basins of water. I then followed a creek down into swampy lagoons, which joined the broad irregular sandy bed of a river containing large pools and reaches of water, lined with Pandanus and drooping tea-trees. This river came from the eastward, and was probably the principal branch of the East Alligator River, which joined the salt-water branch

Authors Note: This is the Cooper Creek with the likely crossing point being not far from Mt Borradaile, which as Leichhardt correctly surmised flows in the East Alligator River near its mouth — it is a favourite fishing and camping location described earlier in the story. The lagoon teeming with large fish could have applied equally in our time when it was the home of many large barramundi.

We met another foot-path at its northern bank, which led us between the river and ranges of rocky hills, over a country abounding with the scarlet Eugenia, of which we made a rich harvest. We encamped at a fine lagoon, occupied, as usual, with geese and ducks, and teeming with large fish, which were splashing about during the whole night.

Immediately after our arrival, Brown went to shoot some geese, and met with two natives who were cooking some roots, but they withdrew in great haste as soon as they saw him. Soon afterwards, however, a great number of them came to the opposite side of the lagoon, and requested a parley. I went down to them with some presents, and a young man came over in a canoe to meet me. I gave him a tin canister, and was agreeably surprised to find that the stock of English words increased considerably; that very few things we had were new to him, and that he himself had been at the settlement. His name was "Bilge." He called me Commandant, and presented several old men to me….

Authors Note: It would be interesting to try and identify who is Bilge in relation to more recent aboriginals from this area such as Mirndabbal.

Several natives joined us, either using the canoe, or swimming across the lagoon, and, after having been duly introduced to me, I took four of them to the camp, where they examined everything with great intelligence, without expressing the least desire of possessing it. They were the most confiding, intelligent, inquisitive natives I had ever met before. Bilge himself took me by the hand and went to the different horses, and to the bullock and asked their names and who rode them. The natives had always been very curious to know the names of our horses, and repeated 'Jim Crow,' 'Flourbag', 'Caleb', 'Irongrey', as well as they could, with the greatest merriment. Bilge frequently mentioned 'Devil devil', in referring to the bullock, and I think he alluded to the wild buffaloes, the tracks of which we soon afterwards saw.

Authors Note: This indicates a very rapid expansion in the range of buffalo This year, 1845, is less than 20 years after the establishment of the first settlement in Raffles Bay in 1827 and it's abandonment in 1829, at which time it is presumed that the buffalo were left behind. Thus, in 16 years from their release, they had reached the plains of the Coopers Creek more than 100 kilometres south of Raffles Bay in such numbers they were readily sighted and one was killed by Leichhardt's party. Assuming a doubling in the original buffalo population every four years, there can have been no more than a few hundred animals at this time, for which there would have been adequate food resources remaining on Coburg Peninsula. It indicates both the buffaloes' mobility and their preference for the lush floodplain grasses of the Murganella floodplains. From here it is not far to the upper Cooper floodplains at the northern margin of the East Alligator. This good location the buffalo chose contrasts to the poor locations selected for the first European settlements.

We asked him for 'Allamurr' and they expressed their readiness to bring it, as soon as the children and women…. returned to the camp. The day being far advanced, and their camp a good way off, they left us, after inviting us to accompany them: but this I declined. About 10 o'clock at night, three lads came to us with Allamurr; but they were very near suffering for their kindness and confidence, as the alarm of 'blackfellows' at night was a call to immediate and desperate defence. Suspecting, however, the true cause of this untimely visit, I walked up to them, and led them into the camp, where I divided their Allamurr between us; allowing them a place of honour on a tarpauling near me for the remainder of the night, with which attention they appeared highly pleased….

Dec. 9.— The natives came to our camp at break of day, and Bilge introduced several old warriors of a different tribe, adding always the number of piccaninnies that each of them had; they appeared very particular about the latter, and one of the gentlemen corrected Bilge very seriously when he mentioned only two instead of three. Bilge had promised to go with us to Balanda, but, having probably talked the matter over during the night, with his wife, he changed his intentions; but invited us in the most urgent manner, to stay a day at their camp. Although no place could be found more favourable for feed and water, and a day's rest would have proved very beneficial to our cattle, yet our meat bags, on which we now solely depended, were so much reduced, that every day of travelling was of the greatest importance; as the natives told us that four days would bring us to the Peninsula, and two more to Balanda. We crossed the plain to the westward, in order to avoid the low rocks and rocky walls which bounded this fine country to the north and east. After about three miles, however, we turned to the northward, and travelled with ease through an open undulating forest, interrupted by some tea–tree hollows. Just before entering the forest, Brown observed the track of a buffalo on the rich grassy inlets between the rocks. After proceeding about five miles we crossed a chain of fine Nymphaea ponds; and, at five miles farther, we came upon a path of the natives, which we followed to the eastward, along a drooping tea–tree swamp, in the outlet of which we found good water. .... Tracks of buffaloes were again observed by Charley.

Authors Note: woodland belt separating Coopers and Murganella floodplains.

Dec. 10.—We travelled about seven miles to the northward; but kept for the first three miles in a N.N.W. direction from our camp, when we came to a small plain, with a Mangrove creek going to the westward; scarcely two miles farther, we crossed a drooping tea–tree swamp.... and, two miles farther still, a large plain opened upon us, in which we saw a great number of natives occupied in burning the grass, and digging for roots.

Authors Note: Murganella Creek Floodplain

All the country intervening between the creeks and the plain was undulating stringy–bark forest. I left my companions in the shady belt of drooping tea–trees, and rode with Charley towards the natives, in order to obtain information. They were, however, only women and children, and they withdrew at my approach, although I had dismounted and left my horse far behind with Charley. They had, however, allowed me to come near enough to make them understand my incessant calls for "obeit," water, adding occasionally "Balanda; very good; no good." When they had disappeared in the forest, Charley came with the horse, and we reconnoitred along the boundaries of the plain to find water, but not succeeding, we returned; and, when opposite to the place where I had left my companions, I cooeed for them to come over to me. My cooee was answered by natives within the forest, and, shortly afterwards four men came running out of it, and approached us most familiarly. They spoke English tolerably, knew the pipe, tobacco, bread, rice, ponies, guns, &c.; and guided us to a fine lagoon, which I named after the leading man of their tribe, 'Nyuall's Lagoon'. Two of them promised to pilot us to Balanda and to 'Rambal', which meant houses. They were very confiding, and women and children entered for the first time freely into our camp.

They examined everything, but made not the slightest attempt to rob us even of a trifle. When the women returned at night, they did not bring 'Allamurr', or, as it was here called, 'Murnatt', but plenty of 'Imberbi', the root of Convolvolus, which grows abundantly in the plain: they gave us a very seasonable supply of it, but would not taste our dried beef, which they turned, broke, smelled, and then with a feeling of pity and disgust returned to us. Nyuall gave an amusing account of our state: "You no bread, no flour, no rice, no backi— you no good! Balanda plenty bread, plenty flour, plenty rice, plenty backi! Balanda very good!"

He, Gnarrangan, and Carbaret, promised to go with us; and he first intended to take his wife with him. They imitated, with surprising accuracy, the noises of the various domesticated animals they had seen at the settlement; and it was amusing to hear the crowing of the cock, the cackling of the hens, the quacking of ducks, grunting of pigs, mewing of the cat.... A heavy thunder–storm passed over at 6 o'clock pm and the natives either crowded into my tent, or covered their backs with sheets of tea–tree bark, turning them to the storm, like a herd of horses or cattle surprised by a heavy shower in the middle of a plain. Imaru lay close to me during the night, and, in order to keep entire possession of my blanket, I had to allow him a tarpaulin.

Dec. 11.—We travelled about seven miles N.N.W. over an immense plain with forest land and rising ground to the eastward, in which direction four prominent hills were seen, one of which had the abrupt peak form of Biroa in Moreton Bay. The plain appeared to be unbounded to the westward. When we approached the forest, several tracks of buffaloes were seen; and, upon the natives conducting us along a small creek which came into the plain from the N.N.E., we found a well beaten path and several places where these animals were accustomed to camp. We encamped at a good–sized water–hole in the bed of this creek, the water of which was covered with a green scum. As the dung and tracks of the buffaloes were fresh, Charley went to track them, whilst Brown tried to shoot some Ibises, which had been at the water and were now perched on a tree about 300 yards off. At the discharge of the gun a buffalo started out of a thicket, but did not seem inclined to go far; Brown returned, loaded his gun with ball, went after the buffalo and wounded him in the shoulder. When Charley came back to the camp, he, Brown and Mr. Roper pursued the buffalo on horseback, and after a long run, and some charges, succeeded in killing it. It was a young bull, about three years old, and in most excellent condition. This was a great, a most fortunate event for us; for our meat bags were almost empty, and, as we did not wish to kill Redmond, our good companion, we had the prospect of some days of starvation before us. We could now share freely with our black friends, and they had not the slightest objection to eat the fresh meat, after baking it in their usual manner. They called the buffalo "Anaborro;" and stated that the country before us was full of them. These buffaloes are the offspring of the stock which had either strayed from the settlement at

Raffles Bay, or had been left behind when that establishment was broken up. They were originally introduced from the Malay islands. I was struck with the remarkable thickness of their skin, (almost an inch) and with the solidity of their bones, which contained little marrow; but that little was extremely savoury.

Dec. 12.—Part of the meat was cut up and dried, and part of it was roasted to take with us; a great part of it was given to the natives, who were baking and eating the whole day; and when they could eat no more meat, they went into the plains to collect Imberbi and Murnatt, to add the necessary quantum of vegetable matter to their diet. The sultry weather, however, caused a great part of the meat to become tainted and maggotty. Our friend Nyuall became ill, and complained of a violent headache, which he tried to cure by tying a string tightly round his head....The night was extremely close, and, to find some relief, I took a bath; which gave me, however, a very annoying inflammation of the eyes.

Dec. 13.—At day break, an old man, whom Nyuall introduced to us as Commandant, came with his gin, and invited us to his camp, about two miles off. We went to it with the intention of continuing our journey, and found a great number of women and children collected in very spacious huts or sheds, probably with the intention of seeing us pass. They had a domestic dog, which seemed very ferocious. A little farther on, we came to a small creek, with good water–holes, and our guides wished us to stop; but, when I told them that we were desirous of reaching Balanda as soon as possible, and added to my promise of giving them a blanket and a tomahawk, that of a pint pot, Gnarrangan and Cabaret again volunteered, and persuaded a third, of the name of Malarang, to join them. For some miles, we followed a beaten foot–path, which skirted the large plain, and then entered the forest, which was composed of rusty–gum, leguminous Ironbark.... we crossed several salt–water creeks which went down to Van Diemen's Gulf. The country near these creeks, was more undulating, the soil sandy and mixed with small ironstone pebbles; fine tea–tree flats with excellent grass, on which the buffaloes fed, were frequent. Along the plain, small clusters of brush protruded into it from the forest, or covered low mounts of sea shells, mixed with a black soil. Amongst these copses, the tracks of buffaloes were very numerous.

We travelled about ten miles north.... and encamped at a small pool of water in a creek in which the clayey ironstone cropped out. Its water was so impregnated with the astringent properties of the gum–trees that Mr. Phillips boiled and drank it like tea. Before arriving at this creek, we had a thunder–storm, with heavy rain, from the northward. After pitching our tents, our guides went out, and returned with a small Iguana and with pods.... which they roasted on the coals. I succeeded in saving a great part of our meat by smoking it.

Authors Note: probably Salt Water Creek near the neck of Coburg Peninsula

Our horses were greatly distressed by large horse–flies, and every now and then the poor brutes would come and stand in the smoke of our fires to rid themselves of their persevering tormentors. This want of rest during the night contributed very much to their increasing weakness; though most of them were severely galled besides, which was prevented only by the most careful attention, and daily washing of their backs. On this stage we again passed one of those oven–like huts of the natives, thatched with grass, which I have mentioned several times, and which Nyuall's tribe called 'Corambal'. At the place where we encamped, the ruins of a very large hut were still visible, which indicated that the natives had profited by their long intercourse with the Malays and Europeans, in the construction of their habitations.

Dec. 14.—When we started, intending to follow the foot–path, our native guides remained behind; and, when I had proceeded two or three miles, my companions came up to me and stated, that the natives had left us, but that they had given them to understand that the foot–path would conduct us safely to Balanda. They had attempted to keep the large tomahawk, but had given it up when Brown asked them for it. I was very sorry at their having left us, as the cloudy sky had prevented me for several days from taking any latitude, and determining my position. We crossed a great number of small creeks, coming from the eastward, and draining the ridges of the neck of the Peninsula.... The tracks of the buffaloes increased in number as we advanced, and formed broad paths, leading in various directions, and made me frequently mistake them for the foot–path of the natives, which I eventually lost. A course north 30 degrees west, brought us to easterly creeks, one of which I followed down, when Brown called out that he saw the sea. We, therefore, went to the sea–side, and found ourselves at the head of a large bay, with an island to the north–east, and with headlands stretching far into the ocean, which was open and boundless to the northward. It was Mount Morris Bay, with Valentia and Crocker's islands the latter, however, appeared to us to be a continuation of the main land.

We now went to the north–west and westward, until we came again on westerly waters. The country in the centre of the neck of the Peninsula, was very hilly, and some of the ridges rose, perhaps, from one hundred and fifty to two hundred feet above the level of the sea; one or two hills were still higher. They were all composed of a clayey ironstone, and clothed with patches of scrub, formed principally of Calythrix, and with a more open forest of Cypress pine, white–gum, tea–trees, bloodwood, Livistona palms, Pandanus, with shrubby Terminalias and Coniogetons. The grass was dry, but high and dense; and buffalo tracks spread in every direction, particularly down the creeks.... We followed a westerly creek in all its windings, in order to detect water in one of its rocky water–holes.... We met, however, only with salt–water.... and had consequently to continue our journey. Here we again came on the foot–path of the natives, which skirted the mangrove swamps, and I followed it for about three miles farther, crossed several dry watercourses, and at last found some pools of rain water, in a small creek....

Dec. 15.—I followed the foot–path of the natives, with the intention of continuing on it, until I came in sight of Mounts Bedwell and Roe. If I had done so, much trouble would have been saved. But, after we had travelled more than three hours, the country became very hilly and ridgy, and I supposed that we were close to those mountains, but were prevented, by the ridges, from seeing them. We went consequently to the northward, and after an hour's riding over a hilly, but openly timbered country, came to an easterly creek, which we followed down, until we found an abundance of water. The upper part of this creek was very scrubby, and with but little grass. I imagined that we had arrived at the west side of Port Essington, and that the creek on which we encamped was probably the Warvi. To ascertain this, I rode down the creek with Charley: it became more open; limited flats of sandy alluvium were clothed with the refreshing verdure of young grass, and with groves of Banksias; its hollows were fringed with large drooping tea–trees. The creek itself was a succession of shady water–holes, out of which, at our approach dashed buffaloes, three and four at a time, shaking their muddy heads, as they scrambled up the steep banks, and galloped to the neighbouring thickets. The stiff sedges of the salt–water, and the salt–water tea–trees, made their appearance about three miles from our camp; and it is probable that the sea was scarcely half a mile farther. High hills rose to the northward, openly timbered, but at their base with patches of scrub, and very stony. Here we heard the distant cooees of natives, which we answered, going in their direction, until we came to a camp, in which we found an old lame man, 'Baki Baki', and a short sturdy fellow, 'Rambo Rambo'; both of whom knew a great number of English words, and were quite familiar with the settlement, and knew the Commandant, Mr. Macarthur. They promised to guide us the next morning to Balanda, after having made many inquiries about our stock of provisions and of tobacco

Authors **Note**: This location is at the bottom of Danger Point, 20 kilometres south of where I had my crocodile encounter and close to the road camp

Dec. 16.—When we arrived with our whole train at the camp of the natives, their behaviour was quite altered, and they now showed as little inclination to guide us to the settlement, as they had been eager last night to do so. I persuaded Baki Baki, however, to go, at least part of the way; and, when we saw that he became tired, we mounted him on one of the horses, and led it by the bridle. He pointed to the W.N.W. as the direction in which the settlement lay. We travelled about five miles over stony ironstone ridges, with extensive groves of Livistona palm covering their slopes. Here Baki Baki desired to dismount; and, telling us that it was a very good road to Balanda, took his leave and returned. Soon after we came to a large creek full of water, running to the eastward, which we followed up for a long distance, before we were able to cross. Our pack–horse became bogged, and as it was so weak that it would not even make an effort to extricate itself, and as I supposed that we were near the settlement, we took off its pack–saddle and load, and left it behind. We crossed two or three more watercourses; and continued the course pointed out by the native, until it became very late, and I found myself compelled to look for water; particularly as our bullock showed evident symptoms of becoming knocked up. I therefore followed the fall of the country to the north–east; and, in a short time, came to the sea. We compared our little map of the harbour of Port Essington with the configuration of the bay.. but nothing would agree exactly, although it bore a general resemblance to Raffles Bay.

.... I followed a well beaten foot–path of the natives to the northward, crossed a creek, in the mangrove swamp of which another horse was bogged, which we extricated after great exertion; and, after two or three miles, came to a large fresh–water swamp (Marair) on which we encamped. The sun had long set, and our cattle, as well as ourselves, were miserably tired. We were here visited by a tribe of natives, who were well acquainted with the settlement; they were all friendly, and willing to assist us; and many of them spoke very tolerable English. One of them, apparently the chief of the tribe, though a hunchback, named 'Bill White', promised to guide us to the settlement. He gave us to understand that we had come too far to the northward, and that we had to go to the south–west, in order to head Port Essington, and to follow its west coast, in order to arrive at Victoria. We were, in fact, at Raffles Bay. The natives knew everybody in Victoria, and did not cease to give us all the news; to which we most willingly listened. They fetched water for us from a great distance, and gave us some Murnatt, which was extremely welcome. Perceiving the state of exhaustion and depression in which we were, they tried to cheer us with their corrobori songs, which they accompanied on the Eboro, a long tube of bamboo, by means of which they variously modulated their voices.

Authors Note: this is the lower part of Smith Point, about 10 kilometres across from Victoria settlement in a direct line, but the opposite side of Port Essington with a 20-30 kilometre trip around this inlet to reach Victoria settlement.

Dec. 17.—We started, with a willing guide, for the goal of our journey, and travelled to the south–west over a hilly country, covered with groves of the Livistona palm, which, as we proceeded became mixed with Seaforthia (the real cabbage–palm). A fine large creek, containing a chain of large water–holes went to the north–east, and disembogued probably into Bremer's Bay. We followed it for three or four miles towards its head; and, when crossing it, we had a very heavy thunder–storm; at the earliest hour we had ever witnessed one.... Our bullock refused to go any farther, and, as I then knew that the settlement was not very distant, I unloaded him. As we approached the harbour, the cabbage palm became rarer, and entirely disappeared at the head of it. We crossed several creeks running into the harbour, until we arrived at the Matunna, a dry creek, at which the foot–path from Pitchenelumbo (Van Diemen's Gulf) touched the harbour, and on which we should have come last night. We followed it now, crossed the Warvi, the Wainunmema, and the Vollir—all which enlarged into shallow lagoons or swamps, before they were lost between the mangrove thickets. At the banks of the Vollir, some constant springs exist, which induced Sir Gordon Bremer to choose that place for a settlement, and on which Victoria at present stands. All these creeks were separated from each other by a hilly forest land; but small fertile flats of sandy alluvium, clothed with young grass, and bordered by Banksias, extended along their banks.... The stringy–bark and the drooping tea–tree were the only useful timber near the settlement. The Cypress–pine (Callitris) could, however, be obtained without any great difficulty from Mount Morris Bay, or Van Diemen's Gulf. On the Vollir, we came on a cart road which wound round the foot of a high hill; and, having passed the garden, with its fine Cocoa–nut palms, the white houses, and a row of snug thatched cottages burst suddenly upon us; the house of the Commandant being to the right and separate from the rest. We were most kindly received by Captain Macarthur, the Commandant of Port Essington, and by the other officers, who, with the greatest kindness and attention, supplied us with everything we wanted. I was deeply affected in finding myself again in civilized society, and could scarcely speak, the words growing big with tears and emotion; and, even now, when considering with what small means the Almighty had enabled me to perform such a long journey, my heart thrills in grateful acknowledgement of his infinite kindness.

For those who want to read the full transcript of Leichhardt's Journal the original is held in the NSW State Library in Macquarie St, Sydney, where a copy can be viewed. In addition there are a range of sources for online transcripts including at the links below:

http://gutenberg.net.au/ebooks/e00030.html

https://ebooks.adelaide.edu.au/l/leichhardt/ludwig/l52j/

REFERENCES

The following books have been significant sources of information used in this memoir. As it is not a scientific publication they are not comprehensively referenced, however, where possible, I seek to identify places where they are the source of information I use.

Altman, J,C, 1984, Hunter Gatherers Today: an Aboriginal economy in north Australia, 251pp, Institute of Aboriginal Studies, Canberra, ISBN 0855751762

Carroll, Peter, 2000, the Development of Outstations in the Kunbarllanjnja/ Oenpelli area of the Northern Territory: an Outline History, report prepared for the Demed Association

Cole, Keith, 1975, A History of Oenpelli, 108pp, Nungalinya Publications, Darwin.

Cole, Keith, 1975, Groote Eylandt, Nungalinya Publications, Darwin,

Hill, Ernestine, 1951, The Territory [An Account of the Northern Territory of Australia], 454pp, Angus and Roberston, Sydney

Flood, Josephine, 1983, Archaeology of the Dreamtime: The Story of Prehistoric Australia and Her People, Collins Publishers, Sydney

Harris, Stephen, 1998, The Field Has Its Flowers: Nell Harris, 100pp, Historical Society of the Northern Territory, Darwin,

McMillan, Andrew,2007, An intruders guide to East Arnhem Land: 311pp, Niblock Books, Darwin

Oppenheimer, Stephen 1998, Eden in the East: The Drowned Continent of Southeast Asia, 560pp, Weidenfeld & Nicolson, London

Wilson, Alf, 2005, The Changing Scene: Auto Biography of Alf Wilson and His Work in the Northern Territory, Acacia Printing, Darwin

ABOUT THE AUTHOR

Graham Wilson lives in Sydney Australia. He has completed and published ten separate books, and also a range of combined novel box sets.

They comprise two series,

1. The Old Balmain House Series – three novels

2 The Crocodile Dreaming Series – five novels

along with this family memoir, *Arnhem's Kaleidoscope Children*

The *Old Balmain House Series* starts with the novel, *Little Lost Girl*, which was previously titled, *The Old Balmain House*. Its setting is an old weatherboard cottage, in Sydney, where the author lived for seven years. Here a photo was discovered of a small girl who lived and died about 100 years ago. The book imagines the story of her life and family, based in the real Balmain, an early inner Sydney suburb, with its locations and historical events providing part of the story background. The second novel in this series, *Lizzie's Tale*, builds on the Balmain house setting. It is the story of a working class teenage girl who lives in this same house in the 1950s and 1960s. It tells of how, when pregnant, she is determined not to surrender her baby for adoption and of her struggle to survive in this unforgiving society. The third novel in this series, *Devil's Choice*, tells of the next generation of the family in *Lizzie's Tale*. Lizzie's daughter is faced with an awful need to seek help of one of her mother's rapists' in trying to save the life of her own daughter who is inflicted with an incurable disease.

The Crocodile Dreaming Series is based in Outback Australia. It starts with *An English Visitor* which tells the story of an English backpacker, Susan, who visits the Northern Territory and becomes captivated and in great danger from a man who loves crocodiles. The second book in the series, *Crocodile Man* follows the consequences of the first book based around the discovery of this man's remains and his diary and Susan, being placed on trial for murder. The third book, *Girl in an Empty Cage*, is about Susan's struggle to retain her sanity in jail while her family and friends desperately try to find out what really happened on that fateful day before it is too late. In *Lost Girl Diary* Susan vanishes and it tells the story of the search for her and four other lost girls whose passports were found in the possession of the man she killed. The final book in the series, *Dance of Shadows* is the story of a girl who appears in a remote aboriginal community in North Queensland, without any memory except for a name. It tells how she rebuilds her life from an empty shell and how, as fragments of the past return, with them come dark shadows that threaten to overwhelm her. A series prequel, *Return of the Breaker* has just come out.

This book, *Arnhem's Kaleidoscope Children*, is a memoir of the author's life in the Northern Territory: his childhood in an aboriginal community in remote Arnhem Land, of the people, danger and beauty of this place and of its transformation over the last half century with the coming of aboriginal rights and the discovery or uranium. It also tells of his surviving an attack by a large crocodile and of his work over two decades in the outback of the NT.

Books are published as ebooks by Smashwords, Amazon, Kobo, iBooks and other publishers. Most books are available in print online.

Graham is in the early stages of planning a memoir about his family's connections with Ireland called *Memories Only Remain* and also is compiling information for a book about the early NT cattle industry, its people and its multitude of stories.

He writes for the creative pleasure it brings him and is pleased each time an unknown person chooses to download and read something he has written and write a review - good or bad, as this gives him an insight into what readers enjoy and helps him make ongoing improvements to his writing.

In his other life Graham is a veterinarian who works in wildlife conservation and for rural landholders. He lived a large part of his life in the Northern Territory and his books reflect this experience.

More information about Graham and his books and writing is available from the following sites:

Graham Wilson – Australian Author on Facebook

Graham Wilson Author Profiles on Smashwords, Amazon and Goodreads

If you want to contact Graham directly please use the email:

grahambbbooks@gmail.com

www.ingramcontent.com/pod-product-compliance
Lightning Source LLC
Chambersburg PA
CBHW021411110726
47901CB00008B/2144